INFANT-MOTHER ATTACHMENT:

The Origins and Developmental Significance
of Individual Differences in
Strange Situation Behavior

INFANT-MOTHER ATTACHMENT:

*The Origins and Developmental Significance
of Individual Differences in
Strange Situation Behavior*

MICHAEL E. LAMB
University of Utah

ROSS A. THOMPSON
University of Nebraska

WILLIAM GARDNER
University of Virginia

ERIC L. CHARNOV
University of Utah

With a contribution by
JAMES P. CONNELL
University of Rochester

LEA LAWRENCE ERLBAUM ASSOCIATES, PUBLISHERS
1985   Hillsdale, New Jersey   London

Lawrence Erlbaum Associates, Inc., Publishers
365 Broadway
Hillsdale, New Jersey 07642

Library of Congress Cataloging in Publication Data
Main entry under title:

Infant-mother attachment.

1. Attachment behavior in children. 2. Mother and
child. 3. Individuality. 4. Infant psychology.
I. Lamb, Michael E., 1953–
BF720.M68154 1985   155.4′22   85-7056
ISBN 0-89859-654-8

Printed in the United States of America
10 9 8 7 6 5 4 3 2 1

To our Attachment Figures—
Jamie and Damon; Janet and Scott;
Karleen; and Maureen.

Contents

Preface

In this book, we provide a thorough review of the literature concerning the origins, interpretation, and developmental significance of individual differences in early infant-parent attachment. The orientation we adopt borrows heavily from the ethological framework presented by Mary Ainsworth and John Bowlby. As progenitors of this powerful theoretical framework, Ainsworth and Bowlby deserve our deep gratitude, and we hope that they will view our efforts as an attempt to evaluate and build constructively upon their influential work and orientation. We hope that the thoroughness of our discussion serves our field by taking stock of the evidence currently available and providing both stimulus and orientation for future research on the formation and developmental significance of early infantile attachments.

Ainsworth's great insight led to development of the Strange Situation procedure—a laboratory paradigm designed to allow assessment of the quality or security of infant-parent attachment—that lies at the heart of all the research reviewed in this book. Behavior in the Strange Situation has been the focus of research into the antecedents of individual differences in attachment; studies concerned with the temporal stability and predictive validity of attachment status likewise employ behavior in the Strange Situation as the central predictor variable. Alan Sroufe has been a prominent contributor to the literature on all of these topics, and our collective debt to him is large. We hope that our synthesis is as heuristically valuable to the field as his research has been.

This book has been many years in the making, and it has benefitted greatly from the assistance of many colleagues. Perhaps the greatest debts are owed to David Estes, Joseph Campos, and Jack Bates. David Estes was a co-author of the early, abbreviated version of our review that was published in 1984 (*Behavioral and Brain Sciences,* 1984, *7,* 127–147). In that role, he not only helped to gather and synthesize portions of the literature, but also checked details and style in several other sections. We were disappointed when his other commitments made it impossible for him to continue. Joe Campos was present at the creation: he has nursed our growing manuscript through numerous versions and revisions — always eager to debate the issues, ever-willing to review and constructively criticize. Jack Bates first reviewed the sections of the book in which his work was discussed and later volunteered to review the complete manuscript in penultimate form. His comments, like those of Joe Campos, were extremely helpful to us, and we hope that they are as pleased as we are with the final version.

We have also received important input from a number of other individuals, each of whom reviewed and discussed at least portions of the manuscript or discussed critical issues with us. Among those we thank are Jack McArdle and Jim Connell for help with the statistical/analytical chapters, Avi Sagi, Klaus Grossmann, and Kazuo Miyake for discussions of some of the cross-cultural issues, and Rich Lerner and Steve Suomi for their encouragement and wise counsel.

Michael E. Lamb, Ross A. Thompson,
William P. Gardner, & Eric L. Charnov

BACKGROUND

1 INTRODUCTION

This book is concerned with one of the longstanding issues of developmental psychology: early experiences and their influence on child development. More specifically, it is concerned with the validity and usefulness of a particular procedure—Ainsworth's Strange Situation—designed to permit assessment of the quality or security of infant-parent attachment and its ramifications for later development (Ainsworth, Blehar, Waters, & Wall, 1978; Ainsworth & Wittig, 1969). Clearly, Ainsworth's was not the first attempt to assess the quality of infant-mother attachment and identify its impact on subsequent development. Such tasks had been undertaken earlier by psychoanalysts like Anna Freud (1965) and Melanie Klein (1957) and through the description of behavior by analytically oriented researchers like Sylvia Brody (1956), and Sibylle Escalona (Escalona & Leitch, 1953), to mention but a few. What made Ainsworth's contribution so important was that she appeared to have found a remarkably simple, brief, and systematic way of assessing the security of infant-parent attachment in a manner that was to prove valid; *that* had never been achieved before. Furthermore, the Strange Situation was designed in light of the formulations of evolutionary biology, thus providing a crucial link between evolutionary theory and empirical developmental research. That we choose to explore the impact of early experience through near-exclusive focus on research employing one experimental procedure underscores the utility and importance of this procedure, and our collective debt to Mary Ainsworth, who has pioneered research on this topic.

We focus exclusively on research involving the Strange Situation procedure because it has dominated research on the significance of early

1

experiences in social and emotional development for the last decade, and because the procedure was developed out of orientations to the study of behavioral development—those of "ethology" and "evolutionary biology"—that have become popular and influential in recent developmental theorizing. Our goal is to provide a thorough and comprehensive review of theory and empirical research pertaining to the patterning of Strange Situation behavior and the security of attachment—two constructs that, we argue, should be distinguished more clearly than they have been in the past—with the goal of presenting the results of previous research in such a way as to foster a new generation of research on individual differences in early social and emotional development.

The Strange Situation procedure was developed by Ainsworth and Wittig (1969) for the assessment of individual differences in the patterning of infant attachment behavior. Essentially, the procedure—which is described more fully in Chapter 3—involves observing how 12 to 24 month old infants organize their behavior around attachment figures (usually mothers, although attachment figures like fathers and other regular caretakers have also been studied) when they are mildly distressed by being in a strange room, encountering an unfamiliar adult, and being left briefly by the attachment figure. On the basis of the child's behavior in this context, the quality of the child's attachment is categorized using one of eight patterns of behavior described by Ainsworth and her colleagues. Four of these patterns are said to represent secure patterns of attachment, and four describe insecure attachment behavior.

In the decade and a half since Ainsworth and Wittig's (1969) report was published, many important claims have been made about the validity of the Strange Situation procedure, and it has become the central variable in a growing number of studies. Much of the enthusiasm about this procedure is attributable to claims that:

1. individual differences in the way infants behave in the Strange Situation are lawfully and interpretably related to prior patterns of parent-infant interaction;
2. infants seen more than once in the Strange Situation tend to behave in the same fashion each time (barring major disruptions in the infant's life), indicating that the procedure taps some stable dimension rather than something transitory;
3. individual differences in Strange Situation behavior predict behavioral differences in other contexts as much as several years later; and
4. from an evolutionary-adaptational perspective, one can see some patterns of Strange Situation behavior as adaptive and others as maladaptive.

Because the history of research on early socioemotional development is replete with failures to identify and measure constructs reliably and validly, to find even short-term stability in these constructs, and to identify predictable antecedents and consequences with any consistency, the apparent success of the Strange Situation has been widely acclaimed. For the first time, researchers have apparently been able to identify and measure a central developmental construct—the quality or *security* of infant-parent attachment. Furthermore, individual differences in the security of attachment as measured in the Strange Situation appear lawfully related to prior patterns of infant-parent interaction, a finding consistent with popular beliefs that the child's social relationships are shaped by its earliest social experiences (e.g., Ainsworth, 1973; Freud, 1940; Schaffer, 1971). The association between parental and infant behavior has also been deemed consistent with a theory derived from evolutionary biology (Ainsworth, 1979a; Bowlby, 1969), in which secure infant behavior is considered species-appropriate, and as the consequence of rearing by a caretaker behaving in the species-appropriate fashion. Likewise, insecure infant behavior has been viewed as maladaptive and as the result of interaction with a parent whose behavior deviated from that which is species-appropriate. In addition, individual differences in Strange Situation behavior appear to predict individual differences in various other aspects of socioemotional development—a finding confirming theoretical predictions concerning the formative centrality of the infant-caretaker relationship. All in all, the data seem to show that the observation of behavior in the Strange Situation can be interpreted in terms of prior interaction patterns and later developmental outcomes. If this is true, the Strange Situation must be viewed as the most powerful and useful procedure ever available for the study of socioemotional development in infancy, and this helps account for the popularity of the procedure.

In light of widespread assumptions regarding the usefulness and importance of Strange Situation assessments, the time is ripe for a detailed and comprehensive review of the relevant research. The goal of this book is to evaluate the empirical and theoretical basis for the claims detailed in the foregoing by conducting an exhaustive and critical evaluation of the literature.[1] We aim to appraise the extent to which the available findings paint a clear and consistent picture, the degree to which variations in Strange Situation behavior predict and are in turn predicted by theoretically relevant external variables, and the degree to which variations in Strange Situation

---

[1] We do not, however, include studies in which the Strange Situation has been used with children older than 24 months of age (as this appears inappropriate) or studies in which Ainsworth's classification system has not been employed.

behavior appear to reflect variations in attachment security, rather than other factors. In some cases, we suggest alternative ways of interpreting the available evidence, and we end with illustrations of some and suggestions of other fruitful directions that researchers would do well to pursue.

Although all of the studies reviewed here used the Strange Situation procedure, the issues raised are of broader significance to students of behavior and development. First, the review addresses the long term significance of early experience. Our conclusion is that relationships between early experiences and later outcomes have been demonstrated only when there is continuity in the circumstances that apparently produce the outcomes concerned. This suggests that early experiences per se may not be crucial determinants of the later outcomes (Brim & Kagan, 1980; Clarke & Clarke, 1976), and that future attempts to study the effects of early experiences must also consider the occurrence of intervening events that may ameliorate, accentuate, or maintain the effects of early experiences. Second, we consider attempts to explain *how* parental behavior affects child development. Although this is a topic of major concern to developmentalists, and the focus of much speculation and research, there was little conclusive evidence available before development of the Strange Situation procedure. Although research with the Strange Situation also has yet to yield conclusive and definitive evidence on this score, there is a clear pattern to the findings we review. In general, warm and sensitive parenting tends to be associated with what is considered to be the most desirable or "secure" pattern of infant behavior in the Strange Situation. Finally, we discuss the usefulness of evolutionary biology as a means of elucidating the development of individual differences in infantile or juvenile behavior. Although the principles of evolutionary biology are promising tools, we are forced to conclude that they have been of limited use thus far to proponents of the Strange Situation methodology, possibly due to a misunderstanding of how the relevant principles apply to the study of individual differences. This is somewhat disappointing because evolutionary biology has made possible major advances in the study of normative developmental processes.

OUTLINE OF THE BOOK

In the next two chapters, we step back from the Strange Situation to a review of the theory development that made possible this remarkably valuable and important line of research. Chapter 2 focuses on the development of ethological attachment theory—John Bowlby's masterful synthesis of psychoanalysis, an evolutionary biological approach to the study of behavior, cognitive developmental theory, and cybernetic control systems theory. We place ethological attachment theory in the context of prior approaches to the understanding of social and emotional development, and the major implications of Bowlby's attachment theory are then described.

Bowlby's theory was primarily concerned with normative developmental processes, although (as his later works demonstrated quite clearly—see Bowlby, 1973) it was an orientation that lent itself to consideration of individual differences. Mary Ainsworth—a one-time student/collaborator of Bowlby's—was the scholar most responsible for developing attachment theory in such a way as to elucidate the development and implications of individual differences. Inspired by Bowlby's work on institutionalization at a time when he was beginning to formulate attachment theory, Ainsworth undertook two major longitudinal studies—one in Uganda and one in Baltimore. In the second of these, Ainsworth—along with her colleague, Barbara Wittig (1969)—developed the Strange Situation procedure, the scoring and utilization of which is described in Chapter 3. Ainsworth's theoretical orientation led her to interpret the patterns of behavior seen in the Strange Situation in the context of ethological attachment theory. Her interpretations, and the subsequent interpretations of other researchers, are provided in Chapter 4, where we also provide an evaluation in the context of principles intrinsic to contemporary evolutionary biology. This chapter opens the second section of the book, which is concerned with the antecedents and explanation of Strange Situation behavior.

In Chapter 5, we switch from evaluation of theory development to a review of the empirical evidence concerning the Strange Situation. Our discussion begins with Ainsworth's pioneering study for which the procedure was initially developed. It was in the course of this research that many hypotheses concerning the origins of individual differences in Strange Situation behavior were developed. As articulated more fully in Chapter 5, Ainsworth and her colleagues (e.g., Ainsworth, Bell, & Stayton, 1971, 1974; Ainsworth, Blehar, Waters, & Wall, 1978) proposed that secure patterns of infant-parent attachment (as assessed in the Strange Situation) were the result of responsive, sensitive parenting in the preceding months of the infant's life. This broad hypothesis, and others related to it, have guided several major studies and a number of smaller-scale projects, the findings of which are summarized and synthesized in Chapter 5.

In stressing the formative importance of prior patterns of parental behavior, attachment theorists—most notably Alan Sroufe and Everett Waters (1982)—have argued that infant temperament does not play a major role in shaping Strange Situation behavior. Other theorists, by contrast, most notably Jerome Kagan (1982), Hill Goldsmith and Joseph Campos (1982), and Kazuo Miyake and his colleagues (1981–82, in press) have argued that temperament either plays a major role in shaping security of attachment, or that it influences Strange Situation behavior independent of any differences in the security of attachment. In Chapter 6, we review these theoretical formulations, as well as the relevant empirical evidence, in an attempt to determine what (if any) role temperament plays in influencing Strange Situation behavior.

In Chapter 7, we conclude the second section of the book by synthesizing the literature pertaining to the origins, interpretation, and explanation of Strange Situation behavior—a body of literature reviewed in Chapters 4, 5, and 6—and by identifying questions that deserve fuller consideration in future research.

Section 3 (Chapters 8 through 10) includes a series of chapters concerned with the temporal stability and predictive validity of Strange Situation behavior. Many have argued that if the Strange Situation really taps an important dimension of socioemotional development, then there should be a significant degree of stability over time in the manner in which infants behave in the Strange Situation (Waters, 1983). This proposition itself has since been questioned by researchers who have argued that lawful or predictable temporal instability may also constitute evidence of the procedure's validity (Thompson & Lamb, 1984b; Thompson, Lamb, & Estes, 1982; Vaughn, Egeland, Sroufe, & Waters, 1979). The empirical evidence relevant to these alternative propositions is reviewed in Chapter 8, following which (in Chapter 9) we turn to a large number of studies, all concerned with the predictive validity of Strange Situation behavior. The general goal of most of these studies is to show that individual differences in Strange Situation behavior, as assessed by the Ainsworth classifications, are associated with variations in infant/child behavior in other contexts, both contemporaneously as well as later in the child's life. Success in such endeavors obviously supports claims that the procedure taps important dimensions of psychosocial functioning. This literature is reviewed in Chapter 9, following which we summarize the implication of research on both temporal stability and predictive validity, and offer directions for future study (Chapter 10).

The popularity achieved by the Strange Situation procedure among researchers in the United States has led many investigators in other countries to employ the procedure. The results of some of these studies have already been discussed in earlier chapters, but because they have some especially important implications for the interpretation of Strange Situation behavior, their findings are discussed in a single chapter concerned exclusively with cross-national studies and their findings (Section 4, Chapter 11).

In section 5 (Chapters 12, 13, 14) we ask whether the traditional categorical classification scheme developed by Ainsworth for the Baltimore longitudinal study captures as much variation in infant behavior as we would like, or whether one might develop alternative procedures for better assessing and quantifying individual variation in Strange Situation behavior.

Two strategies are exemplified in this section of the book. In Chapter 12, we employ discriminant function and cluster analytic procedures to determine whether the classifications indeed group infants together in a systematic fashion, and whether variation on other measures of Strange Situation behavior group infants in the same way that the Ainsworth categorical system does. In Chapter 13, James Connell describes his use of factor analytic procedures, involving a variety of data sets, to identify continuous, nonorthogonal factors that allow quantitative specification of individual variation in Strange Situation behavior. In this alternative multivariate analytic approach, comparison with the current categorical technique is eschewed in favor of a "micro longitudinal" strategy in which the structure of intercorrelations among Strange Situation measures in different episodes are examined. Thus this approach lends itself both to tests of hypotheses concerning the dynamics of socioemotional behavior as well as to tests of predictive validity.

Neither of these approaches has been widely employed, and neither has yet exceeded the power or utility of Ainsworth's categorical approach. Our motive for discussing them is to encourage researchers to view the categorical system as not *the only* acceptable way of studying Strange Situation behavior, but as one possible system—a system that has proved remarkably successful in some respects, but surprisingly limited in others. In Chapter 14, which concludes the section on alternative analytic strategies, we discuss the strengths and limitations of the traditional categorical system as well as the alternative approaches described earlier in the section, and then suggest other strategies, as yet unexplored, for fruitful theory-driven research to maximize the informativeness of research using the Strange Situation as a data-gathering procedure.

Chapter 14, therefore, is replete with suggestions for future research, and it is with future direction that section 6 (Chapter 15) is concerned, as well. Here our interest is in broader issues than those discussed in Chapter 14, for we ask how evolutionary biology and our knowledge of developmental processes could and should shape the design of studies concerned with understanding individual differences in socioemotional development. The conclusion of all previous sections are brought to bear here, as we suggest alternative theoretical conceptions, new analytic techniques, and the utilization of procedures other than the Strange Situation to develop a broader understanding of socioemotional development.

2 THE DEVELOPMENT OF ATTACHMENT THEORY

THE PSYCHOANALYTIC ERA

Ever since the late 1930s, psychiatrists and developmental psychologists have been fascinated by the role of early—that is, infantile—experiences in the development of personality. This fascination emerged as a distinct contrast to an earlier concern with the formative importance of experiences that occurred after "the age of reason," around 7–8 years of age. Even Rousseau (1962), for example, ever-concerned about the corrupting effects of society, felt that there was no need for worry about the early years during which, in his view, children were unimpressionable and immune to influence. Subsequent thinkers about child development tended to adopt a view of early experience similar to Rousseau's.

The crucial catalyst for a changed perspective in modern times was the shift in Freud's position, culminating in the publication of his last book, *An outline of psychoanalysis*, in which he made the now-famous claim that the infant-mother relationship was "unique, without parallel, established unalterably for a whole lifetime as the first and strongest love-object and as the prototype of all later love-relations—for both sexes" (Freud, 1940, p. 45).

From the turn of the century, Freud and other psychoanalytic theorists had championed the role of early experiences, but the initial emphasis was on oedipal experiences—that is, on actual events and fantasized events occurring around 3 to 5 years of age. Over time, however, Freud's interpretations of his patients' histories led him to shift the focus to preoedipal events, and, in particular, to speculations about the mother's

8

role as a need-gratifying love-object. Emphasis on the importance of infancy and toddlerhood was preserved by the two major strands of psychoanalytic thought spawned by Freud—the objects relations school led by Melanie Klein (1923/1948, 1957) and the ego psychologists, championed by Heinz Hartmann (1939/1958) and Anna Freud (1949, 1965). Within psychoanalysis, as a result, no one has seriously questioned the crucial formative importance of infancy since the 1930s.

Other schools of thought—most of which developed as derivatives of or reactions to psychoanalysis—first followed Freud in placing emphasis on the formative importance of the preschool years, and later followed psychoanalysis in shifting the focus to infant development. In the ensuing decades, furthermore, professional commitment to the formative importance of infantile experiences has not waned. Indeed, a considerable proportion of current behavioral research is concerned with demonstrating at how early an age infants are both competent and sensitive to environmental input, including social stimulation (e.g., Bower, 1974, 1977; DeCaspar & Fifer, 1980; Spence & DeCaspar, 1982).

Ethological attachment theory has become the major current theoretical perspective guiding research on the role and importance of early social experience, and the purpose of this chapter is to provide an overview of attachment theory, with a focus on normative developmental issues. This provides a reference point for later discussions of the origins and importance of individual differences in attachment.

MATERNAL DEPRIVATION

The changes in psychoanalytic theory outlined above prompted the interpretation of analysands' recollections in a fashion that tended to emphasize infantile rather than oedipal experiences, but the major empirical support for Freud's hypotheses concerning the importance of early mother-infant relationships came several decades later from numerous studies on the effects of institutionalization. These reports came to be known as the maternal deprivation literature (see Bowlby, 1951; Rutter, 1972, for reviews).

The social and economic dislocations that occurred in the conduct and aftermath of the two world wars (1914–1918, 1939–1945) created a situation throughout Europe in which a large number of children were orphaned, accidentally lost by their parents, or intentionally removed from their parents in attempts to spare them the horrors and privations of war. These children were placed in orphanages designed to provide at least adequate physical care to large numbers of children. Across the Atlantic, belief in the humanitarian justification for ensuring high quality institutional care to abandoned or potentially-deprived children led Americans (who had been spared the civilian costs of a war at home) to establish orphanages for children who were abandoned, illegitimate, malparented, and/or the offspring of teenage mothers. And in the same era, isolation sanatoria were opened in Europe to place in quarantine and provide care for individuals of all ages who had contracted infectious diseases such as tuberculosis. To these sanatoria, too, many children were whisked away from their parents and familiar surroundings.

Both the sanatoria and orphanages were designed with the best of intentions, but in both cases the effects were unexpectedly tragic. Although nutritional, medical, and physical needs were assuredly met in most of these institutions, the children in them showed signs of serious psychological dysfunction. The specific effects varied depending on the ages of the children concerned, but children of all ages appeared to suffer. Furthermore, retrospective studies of children and adults who had been separated from their parents earlier in life appeared to confirm the pathogenic character of maternal deprivation. Thus Bowlby (1946) reported that maternal deprivation—actually a misnomer, as Rutter (1972) has shown, because these children were deprived of any stable, caring relationships while growing up—often produced asocial psychopathic delinquents, while others saw "maternal deprivation" as a key ingredient in the ontogenesis of schizophrenia.

Researchers reported a consistent pattern of reactions in infants and toddlers separated from their parents (e.g., Robertson & Bowlby, 1952). Infants older than 6 to 9 months initially displayed *protest*, in which they wept piteously and behaved angrily toward caretakers trying to comfort them. Thereafter, their distress was replaced by *despair*, a phase in which they appeared depressed and disinterested in social interaction. Finally, their demeanour brightened, signaling a phase labeled *detachment* because, in the interpretation of Bowlby (1958), their prior attachment bonds had been severed, and they were now able to form new attachments. Description of these three phases of response was to prove important when Ainsworth and her colleagues attempted to categorize patterns of infant-parent attachment.

Alarmed by the growing number of reports on the adverse effects of maternal deprivation and the apparent consistency in their conclusions, the World Health Organization commissioned a literature review by Bowlby. The resulting report, *Maternal care and mental health* (Bowlby, 1951), confirmed psychiatrists' and developmentalists' worst fears about the harmfulness of institutional care, and indeed, of any type of extended mother-child separation. As a result, most countries moved rapidly to terminate reliance on long-term institutional care for children, preferring whenever possible to place children in more home-like settings in which their emotional and psychosocial needs might better be met.

It is almost universally agreed today that the conclusions drawn from the maternal deprivation literature were inappropriate, with far too much emphasis placed on the pathogenic importance of mother-child separation in the early years rather than on the significance of general social deprivation (Clarke & Clarke, 1976; Rutter, 1972, 1979). In addition, the retrospective data-gathering strategy led Bowlby (and many others) to overestimate the consistency with which deprivation was associated with adverse outcomes. We do not review the evidence in support of these conclusions here, however, for regardless of the overinterpretation involved, the widespread consensus about the effects of maternal deprivation in the late 1940s and 1950s had major beneficial effects on theoretical conceptualizations of early socioemotional development. The most important of these were (1) the abandonment of the secondary drive conceptualization of infant-adult relationships and (2) the development of a new formulation in its place, ethological attachment theory. Let us consider each of these developments.

THE RISE AND FALL OF SECONDARY DRIVE THEORY

Both the ego psychological (A. Freud, 1965; Hartmann, Kris, & Lowenstein, 1949) and object relations (Isaacs, 1929; Klein, 1957) schools of thought, like their common mentor Sigmund Freud (e.g., 1940), believed that infant-adult relationships had their roots in the infant's need for and the caretaker's provision of food. As translated into learning theoretical terms by psychologists Dollard and Miller (1950) at Yale's interdisciplinary Institute for Human Relations, the formulation was as follows. The infant's need for nourishment was considered a primary drive, the gratification of which was rewarding. Through repeated association of this gratification with the caretaker's presence (an example of classical conditioning), s/he became the focus of a secondary drive, such that the infant came to manifest a desire or drive for interaction with her/him, even in the absence of food. This secondary drive constituted the basis of the relationship between infant and adult. Theoretical commitment to this formulation was strengthened by the fact that in this one area, the traditional psychoanalytic and learning theoretical antagonists could agree on the fundamental nature of certain developmental processes—notwithstanding differences in their terminology and their willingness to speculate about invisible underlying psychic processes. Consequently, no one seriously questioned the secondary drive formulation for several decades.

By the early 1950s, however, the drive theory of the Yale psychologists came under increasing attack. Much of the criticism, and many of the crucial studies, were directed by experimental psychologist and primatologist Harry Harlow at the University of Wisconsin. In perhaps the most crucial series of experiments, Harlow and Zimmermann (1959; Harlow, 1958,

1961) separated infant monkeys from their mothers and raised them with two "surrogate mothers"—one a wire manikin with a bottle in the middle of its chest through which the infant was fed exclusively and the other a terrycloth-covered surrogate that played no role in the infant's feeding. Secondary drive theory would predict a preference for the nourishing wire surrogate, but that was not the case; instead, it was the terrycloth surrogate to which infants ran when frightened and from which they organized their exploratory forays, even though they continued to feed from the wire surrogate. The results, argued Harlow, proved that "contact comfort" played a critical role in the formation of social relationships, whereas involvement in feeding was relatively unimportant.

The results of the maternal deprivation studies seemed to support this conclusion. The infants in most orphanages and hospitals certainly had their physical and nutritional needs met, yet they—like the monkeys raised in isolation—suffered from emotional deprivation. The likeliest explanations were that two critical needs were not met by institutional care—the need for adequate social stimulation and the need for continuity in multiple aspects of care, with the same person assuming responsibility for the infant's feeding, soothing, and stimulation over extended periods of time. Taken together, Harlow's experimental research and the nonexperimental studies of children in institutions led developmentalists to conclude that: (1) "contact comfort" (in addition to feeding) was important; (2) the secondary drive interpretation of early relationship formation was inadequate; and (3) the young infant needed to receive continuing care and stimulation from one or a small number of individuals if it was to thrive psychologically. It took the genius of John Bowlby (1958, 1969), a psychoanalytic psychiatrist from the object relations school, to draw these conclusions together and develop a theoretical formulation that took all three factors into account and that, 30 years later, continues to dominate our conceptualization and understanding of early social and emotional development.[1]

ATTACHMENT THEORY

Taken together, Harlow's research and the maternal deprivation literature led Bowlby (1958, 1969) to conclude that there was an innate (i.e., biologically-based) "need" for social interaction in human infants that eventually became focused on a specific figure. Harlow's findings on the importance of contact comfort suggested that this need for social interaction might best be satisfied by the attainment of physical contact with an adult.

---

[1]See Bowlby (1982) for his account of the development of attachment theory.

In attempting to explain the dynamics of this process, Bowlby then took his most courageous step. Recognizing the deficiencies of Freud's outdated hydraulic model of intrapsychic functioning, Bowlby replaced it with a model more consistent with the evolutionary biological model then gaining favor. The evolutionary model emphasized the importance of natural selection in shaping the behavioral repertoire of any species—eliminating behavioral patterns that did not promote species' survival and spreading through the population behaviors that enhanced the species' success. Bowlby suggested that in the savannah grasslands in which humans probably evolved and for which, therefore, their behavior is adapted, it would have been of survival value for defenseless and helpless human infants to seek the protective proximity of conspecific adults. As a result, they should be equipped with a repertoire of behaviors that are useful in attaining such proximity. In precocial species, proximity to adults is often obtained through the infants' own locomotor efforts, but in altricial species like humans, signals assume immense importance. Thus, active proximity-promoting and -maintaining behaviors like locomotion, grasping, and clinging are present in human newborns only in vestigial form, without the strength or elaboration needed to ensure either the attainment or maintenance of proximity. The infant's cry, by contrast, serves as a remarkable elicitor of adult responses (Frodi, Lamb, Leavitt, & Donovan, 1978; Murray, 1979), typically involving an offer to pick up the infant (Bell & Ainsworth, 1972) which in turn, proves remarkably effective in terminating the infant's cry (Korner & Thoman, 1970, 1972). Similarly, the infant's smile can be effective in prolonging proximity to the adult. Because the functional efficacy of such proximity/contact promoting signals depends upon the promptness and appropriateness of the adult's response, mutual responsiveness and interaction become critical in humans and other terrestrial primate species with altricial young. Thus infants become attached to individuals who consistently and appropriately respond to the infant's proximity-promoting signals and behaviors. Furthermore, Bowlby suggested that adults are equipped with a repertoire of caretaking responses that complement the care-eliciting repertoire of the infant, and that are also the outcome of natural selection. From this perspective, both human infants and adults are considered adapted to respond in mutually complementary ways that would function to promote infant survival in the "environment of evolutionary adaptedness."

In addition to proposing (and providing a rationale, in evolutionary terms, for) an inborn desire for proximity/contact with adults, Bowlby drew upon control systems theory—then, like evolutionary biology, an important component of the new biological approach—to describe the dynamics of infant proximity-seeking behavior (Miller, Galanter, & Pribram, 1960). Although the infant was oriented toward the maintenance of proximity/

contact, Bowlby suggested that the degree of proximity/contact needed or sought by an infant—which he termed the "set goal"—would vary over time depending on both exogeneous and endogenous factors. Among the exogenous factors would be natural cues to danger, such as the novelty or familiarity of the social and physical surroundings; endogenous factors would include illness and fatigue. Further, Bowlby proposed that each infant must conduct continual appraisals, comparing the perceived need for proximity/contact (i.e., the "set goal") with the infant's actual situation relative to the parent or attachment figure. In the presence of a strange adult (a natural cue to danger), for example, the infant's need for proximity to the attachment figure would increase, and so it would initiate behaviors designed to promote closer proximity. As wariness of the stranger subsided, the felt need for proximity would decline, and the infant might thus move away from the attachment figure to play or explore. However, the infant would still maintain the same degree of "felt security" (to use Sroufe & Waters', 1977, term) as long as the actual location relative to the adult fell within the parameters of the "set goal" defining the distance within which the infant would feel adequately protected.

This control system, Bowlby suggested, would function much like a thermostat, which includes sensors that measure the current temperature and compare it with a pre-set standard. If the current temperature is lower than the set goal, the thermostat activates a heating system to bring the current status in line with the set goal; if the current temperature is too hot, steps are initiated to reduce it. Maintaining the temperature as close to the set goal as possible thus requires constant rechecking of both the set goal (which in the case of attachment behavior, is prone to being reset in the light of changing circumstances in order to ensure a constant degree of security) and the current temperature (or situation relative to the attachment figure).

Previously, researchers had focused on discrete attachment behaviors (e.g., clinging, crying), but by shifting the focus to goal states and attempts to attain them, Bowlby argued that behaviors with very different morphological characteristics might be interchangeable, since they served similar ends. This emphasis on the function of behavior, rather than on its morphology, represented a major advance in the study of behavioral development, and permitted the research on patterns of behavior that is the focus of this monograph.

Within the control system, Bowlby (1969) implied (and Bretherton & Ainsworth, 1974, more formally proposed) that at least four hypothetical systems worked together to control the infant's behavior. The first was the *attachment behavioral system*, having as its function the maintenance of a sufficient degree of proximity/contact to attachment figures. The actual degree of proximity/contact sought, Bowlby proposed, would depend on the infant's age and capacities, current endogenous and exogenous circumstances, and perhaps (as we shall see later), the infant's cognitive representation and expectations of the adult based on the history of interaction between the infant and the particular adult (see also Lamb, 1981a, 1981b). Another behavioral system, Bowlby suggested, was the *fear/wariness system*, having as its function the avoidance of or escape from potential dangers rather than the attainment of protective proximity per se. The primary (although not the only) cue to which this system responds appears to be novelty, which functions, in Bowlby's terms, as a primary clue to danger. When this system is activated, it also often activates the attachment behavioral system, such that the fearful or wary infant not only *retreats* (if possible) *from* the novel person or object but also *approaches* the protective attachment figure. Typically, at least today, novel objects and people are not dangerous, and once the infant concludes that there is no reason for fear, the *exploratory* and/or *affiliative behavioral systems* are activated, drawing the infant into play or interaction with the person or toy. Exploration promotes mastery of the environment; affiliation the acquisition of social skills with persons other than the attachment figure that obviously have value (including reproductive value) in a complex social species such as ours. Exploration and affiliation are inimical to activation of the fear/wariness and/or attachment behavioral systems so that the four hypothetical systems operate interactively. From the standpoint of natural selection, each system functions adaptively and each may be regulated by the kind of control system outlined earlier.

Although these four systems presumably function without direct awareness, the appraisal processes and control systems proposed by Bowlby clearly involve fairly sophisticated cognitive processing—processing at a level beyond the capacities of the newborn infant. It remains unclear when the processes and systems can be considered functional, and what changes they undergo as the child's capacities and competencies develop. As we shall see in the next chapter, however, the four systems seem to be functioning in an integrated fashion by the latter half of the first year of life. Once this occurs, behavioral systems provide increased flexibility and intercoordination to the infant's behavioral functioning, reaffirming the importance of viewing behaviors in functional and organizational terms, rather than more discretely (Bowlby, 1969, 1982; Sroufe & Waters, 1977). Before we proceed to a discussion of developmental stages, however, we need first to address several important conceptual issues and distinctions raised by Bowlby and his cotheorists, notably Ainsworth.

Attachment Behavior and Attachment Bonds

To this point in our discussion of Bowlby's attachment theory we have focused on the behavior of infants in interaction with their parents. As a psychoanalyst, however, Bowlby was convinced that there was more to relationships than behavior or even interaction and he attempted to distinguish between the *attachment*—which he defined as an enduring affectional tie or bond, specific in its focus—and the *attachment behaviors* that mediated the formation and maintenance of that bond. Based on his reading of the maternal deprivation literature, Bowlby believed that a specific unbroken bond to a particular person is essential for nonpathologic-al development. A further and related implication of these studies, Bowlby suggested, is that a basic test of whether an attachment has been formed lies in the assessment of the child's reaction to a major separation. When such a separation is perceived as permanent, Bowlby concluded, the infant protests the separation vociferously and extensively, resisting all attempts by substitute figures to engage in interaction (Bowlby, 1973). Such reactions do not occur when the child is separated from persons other than attachment figures.

Obviously, such a criterion of attachment is of little value for the purpose of assessment or experimentation: It is simply not ethical to engineer major separations in order to observe the infants' reactions. Some understanding has come, however, from studies of short-term separations, both in a laboratory situation (e.g., Ainsworth, Blehar, Waters, & Wall, 1978) and in the home environment (Lamb, 1979; Stayton & Ainsworth, 1973; Stayton, Ainsworth, & Main, 1973). Although these studies may provide some evidence for qualitative characteristics of mother-infant interaction, however, they do not constitute prolonged separations and hence such separation reactions may constitute unreliable criterial measures of attachment. Based on her observations in Uganda and the U.S., Ainsworth consequently developed a broader list of behaviors—called attachment behaviors—to serve as criteria of attachment. Because the studies involved repeated observations of infants over the period when attachments were being formed and included observations in a variety of interactive contexts (including brief separations), Ainsworth's studies provided important information concerning the behaviors that index developing attachment relationships.

Attachment Behaviors.   Ainsworth (1967) reported that certain of the infants she observed among the Ganda did not protest brief separations from their mothers—for example, when their mothers left the room—though she was convinced that these infants were in fact attached to their mothers. In attempting to define what led her to this conviction, Ainsworth (1964) described 13 patterns of interaction which she labeled attachment behaviors (cf. Gewirtz, 1972). These were: (1) crying; (2) smiling; (3) vocalizing; (4) visual-motor orientation; (5) crying when the attachment figure leaves; (6) following; (7) scrambling; (8) burying face in lap; (9) exploration from a secure base; (10) clinging; (11) lifting arms in greeting; (12) clapping hands in greeting; and (13) approach through locomotion.

What is distinctive about each of these behaviors is that they occur discriminatively in response to the attachment figure.

At this point, an important difference between two kinds of "attachment behaviors" should be evident. Although Bowlby (1969) had stressed the fact that attachment behaviors mediate the development of the attachment bond, Ainsworth "was interested in the *strength and quality* of the infant's attachment formed, rather than in the behavior patterns which mediated attachment. This interest led me to attempt to establish criteria of attachment" (Ainsworth, 1964, p. 52; italics added). It is conceptually important to distinguish, therefore, between the *precursor* or mediating attachment behaviors emphasized by Bowlby (1969) and the *criterial* attachment behaviors to which Ainsworth (1964) referred. The precursor attachment behaviors—crying, sucking, smiling, and grasping—appear adaptively functional in maintaining proximity, and are thus important in promoting the development of attachment. Although they later become focused on the attachment figure and help in the formation of the attachment bond, they are displayed in the period *before* the attachment has been formed (i.e., from the newborn period). By contrast, differentiality (i.e., preference) in the display of the criterial attachment behaviors is used to infer the existence of an attachment bond. Most of the criterial attachment behaviors described above demand more active, goal-corrected behavioral patterning[2] than do the precursor attachment behaviors, and thus they are behaviorally more complex. In addition, as intended by Ainsworth (1964), they reflect the nature of relationships which have already developed.

The differential focus of the criterial attachment behaviors reflects the attachment that has developed and also serves to reinforce this bond. It is important to note, however, that none of these behaviors (except burying face in mother's lap—a behavior not found in Ainsworth's American sample, [Ainsworth, 1973]) were displayed *only* in interaction with the mother; most were directed—presumably as affiliative behaviors—towards other persons (such as the observer) to whom the infant was obviously not attached. Thus the emphasis must be placed on the consistency in preferential responding over time (reflected in multiple attachment behaviors) rather than on discrete behaviors observed on single occasions (Lamb, 1974; Sroufe & Waters, 1977).

Later empirical research has indicated that the set of criterial attachment behaviors described by Ainsworth (1964) and later Bowlby (1969) might be too crude, and that the behaviors need to be redefined in less global terms, with greater emphasis placed on their qualitative and contextual aspects

---

[2]In other words, they involve the selection of specific behaviors from a repertoire depending on continual appraisal of the discrepancy between the child's current status and the set goal.

(Lamb, 1976; Tracy, Lamb, & Ainsworth, 1976). For example, it seems that, given the choice, a one-year-old in the secure context of mother's presence will look at an unfamiliar person more than at its mother (Bretherton & Ainsworth, 1974); that in the familiar home environment following is not differential to mother (Lamb, 1979; Stayton et al., 1973), although it is differential to her in an unfamiliar, and hence more stressful, situation (Ainsworth & Bell, 1970; Corter, 1973; Corter, Rheingold, & Eckerman, 1972); and that locomotor approach in the home environment is not differential to mother in many infants although it is extremely rare for an infant to approach an unfamiliar person when it wants to be picked up, or when it is distressed (Lamb, 1977a, 1977b; Tracy et al., 1977). Thus it is important not only that multiple criterial attachment behaviors be employed in any research but also that the social context be clearly defined when seeking to interpret or compare findings.

Clustering and Intercorrelation

A second point that Ainsworth and her colleagues made is that measures comprising frequency counts of criterial attachment behaviors do not appear to form consistent clusters in all attached infants. Intercorrelations among discrete attachment behavior measures are not impressive (Coates, Anderson, & Hartup, 1972; Lamb, 1976; Lewis & Ban, 1971; Maccoby & Feldman, 1972; Masters & Wellman, 1974; Waters, 1978) so that, for example, an infant may seldom cry when the attachment figure leaves, yet frequently approach him or her. The implication is that none of these criterial attachment behaviors alone is sufficient to indicate that an attachment has been formed, nor is the absence of differentiality on any one behavioral measure consistent evidence for the absence of an attachment.

From the standpoint of Bowlby's attachment theory, in fact, intercorrelation of discrete behaviors would not be anticipated. At any moment, the particular patterning of attachment behaviors is determined by contextual and situational variables independent of the quality of attachment (see Lamb, 1976; Lewis, 1972; Moss, 1967) and, over time, it may also be dependent upon social class factors (Lewis & Wilson, 1972; Messer & Lewis, 1972; Tulkin, 1973), individual interactional differences within the dyad, and developmental differences (e.g., Lamb, 1977a; Lewis, Weinraub, & Ban, 1972). Further, the very nature of attachment behaviors would demand a low positive, and, in some cases negative, intercorrelation. For example, although both crying and smiling to the caretaker are generally accepted as attachment behaviors (both serve to promote proximity), one would not—particularly during brief periods of observation—expect a high degree of intercorrelation between the two. The absence of intercorrelation between these two behaviors thus does not invalidate the notion that a number of morphologically distinct behaviors can serve the same function—promotion of infant-adult proximity. Instead of intercorrelation, therefore, evaluation of Bowlby's approach demands assessment of the ways in which an implicit goal is achieved, ways that vary depending on context and age (cf. Rosenthal, 1973). Finally, the control systems model and behavioral systems perspective both indicate that different specific behaviors may be functionally interchangeable in pursuit of a specific goal—thus undermining any expectation of high intercorrelation among these behaviors. To summarize, the fact that the interrelationships among specific attachment behaviors may vary in different interaction sequences does not imply that the concept of attachment is inadequate—simply that the specific attachment behaviors used to infer attachment should be used cautiously, and with a full understanding and appreciation of the fact that they provide only an indirect measure of attachment bonds.

Discrete behavioral measures, ratings, and organized patterns of behavior

In an important study, Waters (1978) showed that the degree of intercorrelation among measures of attachment in a standardized procedure was least for the discrete attachment behavior measures (e.g., vocalizing, smiling), somewhat better for rating scales tapping dimensions that might be reflected in alternate discrete behaviors (e.g., proximity-seeking), and remarkably high—96% over a 6 month period—for categorical classifications constituting a single global judgement concerning the quality of the attachment relationship (e.g., secure or insecure). These categorical classifications involved considering the corpus of infant behavior from an organizational perspective in which the emphasis was on the overall function of the infant's behavior, rather than on the specific behaviors employed to achieve this function (Sroufe & Waters, 1977). For example, two infants could evince similar degrees of "proximity seeking" by using very different behaviors: one by crying and reaching, and one by crawling over and pulling herself up on the adult. Such an interpretation or perspective, of course, was not possible prior to Bowlby's formulation of a control-systems approach to the organization of behavior. Importantly, Waters' findings—and the organizational perspective they supported—indicated that meaningful individual differences in the quality of infant-parent attachments *could* be identified, even without high intercorrelations among discrete criterial attachment behaviors. This goal was achieved by using a method of behavioral assessment that was appropriate to the level of organization of the attachment behavioral system—specifically, by identifying coherent constellations or patterns of infant behavior (i.e., Ainsworth's classificatory taxonomy).

The patterns of behavior studied by Waters concerned the child's behavior in the Strange Situation and the classifications concerned are the focus of this book. Suffice it to say at this point that Waters' study played a major role in eliciting interest in the concept of attachment, and in empirical research on this topic, by showing how some of the earlier methodological objections to the study of infant-parent attachment could be surmounted.

THE DEVELOPMENT OF ATTACHMENT BONDS

Bowlby (1969) proposed that there were four stages in the development of attachment bonds. In the first, *Orientation and signals without discrimination of figure* (from birth through 8–12 weeks), infants emit precursor attachment behaviors promiscuously; provided that someone satisfies their needs and respond to their signals, they appear content. The limiting factor appears to be the infants' inability to perceptually discriminate among individuals. Once they attain this capacity, they begin to direct precursor attachment behaviors preferentially to those individuals to whom they have had greatest exposure during the preceding weeks. Although it has little bearing on the theory's usefulness, research since the publication of Bowlby's book suggests that the ability to discriminate among people may develop earlier than Bowlby believed, and hence that the stage may end around 4 to 6 weeks, if not earlier.

The infant then moves into the phase of *Orientation and signals directed towards one (or more) discriminated figures* (to about 6 or 8 months of age), which is marked by increasingly clear preferences for a small number of especially familiar people, such as parents and regular caretakers. Thus infants soothe more rapidly with some adults than with others, and respond more positively to the playful social bids of the preferred adults. Until about 6 to 8 months of age, however, infants seem willing to accept the ministrations and attention of less preferred individuals as well.

Despite the evident preferences during this second stage, Bowlby argues that we cannot speak of attachment bonds until around the middle of the first year of life when, he suggests, the third stage in attachment formation (*Maintenance of proximity to a discriminated figure by means of locomotion as well as signals*) begins. This transition is marked by the emergence of separation protest when infants are separated from their attachment figures (Schaffer & Callendar, 1959; Yarrow & Goodwin, 1973). Separation protest, according to Bowlby, represents the infant's attempt to summon the absent adult back into proximity; the onset of this behavior reflects the infant's awareness that the adult continues to exist, even when s/he is not visible, audible, or palpable. According to Bowlby and Ainsworth, the transition depends on the acquisition of the cognitive capacity to understand the continuing existence of people even when they are not present ("person permanence"), and represents the onset of real emotional attachments. The latter postulate reflects Spitz' (1950) dictum that "love is not possible as long as people are interchangeable, "as well as the important interaction of social and cognitive variables. The transition also coincides with the emergence of the infant's capacity to locomote independently; henceforth, infants can achieve proximity/contact of their own accord and are not always dependent on the adults' willingness to respond to their signals. The infant thus begins to take a much more active or independent role in relation to attachment figures.

One powerful indication of a dramatic change in the nature of infant social relationships around this time is evident in the different reactions to long term separation on the part of younger and older infants. Prior to the middle of the first year, infants appear to adjust quite readily to changes in their living arrangements (as in adoption). Following a brief period of disruption while they adjust to new caretaking styles, foods, people, and practices, infants settle into relationships with the new caretakers, often forming attachments on schedule despite limited periods of time with the new parent figures (Schaffer, 1963; Yarrow & Goodwin, 1973). When the infant moves to a new living arrangement after 7–8 months of age, however, the initial reaction is one of dramatic anger and protest, followed by a phase of withdrawal or despair, followed by renewed sociability (Robertson & Bowlby, 1952; Yarrow & Goodwin, 1973). Only in this last phase does the infant begin to form attachments afresh, Bowlby argues, because in the preceding phases it is preoccupied with grief over the loss of the former attachment objects, and it is not possible to form new attachments until these bonds are psychologically severed.

Bowlby was firmly convinced that infants were initially capable of forming only one attachment bond, and he developed a new term, *monotropy*, to describe this propensity. He suggested that this primary bond, typically to the mother or mother figure, not only developed first temporally, but also served as a kind of prototype for attachments to other persons (such as father or grandparents), which developed somewhat later in this third phase of attachment formation.

According to Bowlby, a final transition occurs sometime during the third or even fourth year of life, when children acquire the capacity to recognize that others (e.g., their attachment figures) have desires and needs of their own which have to be taken into account when interacting with them (Marvin, 1977). This transition marks the onset of the fourth stage in attachment formation, which, according to Bowlby, is characterized by the *Formation of a goal-corrected partnership*. The development and characteristics of these partnerships have been little studied, and are not discussed here because the Strange Situation procedure is designed for use with younger infants.

Our focus in this book is on the organization of attachment behavior during the third stage, particularly on the development and importance of individual differences among infants during this phase. In order to elucidate these individual differences, we discuss research concerning patterns of infant-adult interaction in the preceding phases at some length, because it has frequently been argued that individual differences in these patterns of interaction may be the cause of individual differences in the child's later Strange Situation behavior. Likewise, we discuss studies of parent–child interaction and child behavior in the years after the third phase in order to test hypotheses regarding the predictive validity of the patterns of attachment behavior observed in younger infants. In the next chapter, we introduce the theoretical framework and methodological procedure that has guided research on individual differences in infant attachment, as distinct from Bowlby's conceptualization of normative developmental processes.

RECAPITULATION

To recapitulate, we have suggested that Bowlby achieved at least two important theoretical insights. First, he proposed that attachment served the fitness (here meaning survival) interests of the child. In other words, he suggested that we might understand some aspects of attachment by reference to its *biological function* in a fitness or adaptive sense. In the terminology of behavioral ecology, this question is one concerned with *ultimate factors* (e.g., Krebs & Davies, 1981; Tinbergen, 1963). He further proposed, with reference to control systems theory, a model of how the "biology" (narrowly defined) of the child would interact with the external environment (including other people) to bring about attachment behavior and its variation. Here he was concerned with *proximate mechanisms* (see Krebs & Davies, 1981). It is useful to keep questions concerning ultimate factors distinct from questions concerning proximate mechanisms, even though they are clearly related. For example, asking questions about function (i.e., ultimate factors) may suggest what the organism is designed to do, whereas asking questions about proximate mechanisms may suggest constraints on function.

ETHOLOGICAL ATTACHMENT THEORY: AN EVALUATION

Since the early 1970s when there was considerable controversy about attachment theory (e.g., Gewirtz, 1972; Maccoby & Masters, 1970; Masters & Wellman, 1974; Rajecki, Lamb, & Obmascher, 1978)—particularly about the distinction between attachment behaviors and attachment bonds and the implications of this distinction for the measurement of attachment—the focus in the field has shifted from normative developmental processes to the development and meaning of individual differences in attachment. The fact that this topic has dominated the theoretical and empirical literature almost to the exclusion of controversy about normative issues stands as testimony to the widespread acceptance of Bowlby's ethological attachment theory, at least within developmental psychology. Interestingly, Bowlby's ideas have been roundly criticized and rejected within psychoanalytic circles (e.g., Engel, 1971), largely because orthodox psychoanalysts rejected Bowlby's revision of Freud's drive model. This reaction was ironic since Bowlby, as a practising psychoanalyst, was initially most concerned about influencing psychoanalytic theorizing.

Behavioral Biology

In the years since Bowlby's ideas were formulated, of course, major advances have been made in our understanding of biology, cognition, and development. Among evolutionary biologists, it is now generally agreed that natural selection operates at the level of the individual organism—functioning to propogate its own genes so as to maximize inclusive fitness (Hamilton, 1964; Williams, 1966)—rather than at the level of the species or group as Bowlby believed. This does not substantially affect the implications of evolutionary biology for the ontogeny of infantile attachment as we have described it here, however, although the application of a contemporary biological perspective might lead us to ask a number of questions that Bowlby took for granted.

For example, Bowlby concluded that the infant needed behavioral mechanisms to help it attain or maintain proximity to adults, but he never asked about the adult's motivations: Why *should* adults respond to the infant's signals and needs? Since an attachment bond constitutes a link or relationship between two individuals, we must understand the factors affecting the behavior of *both* parties in order to explain attachment. Behavioral ecologists and sociobiologists have argued that since the infant shares some of the parent's genes, the parent's inclusive fitness is served by protecting and caring for it, but only until the anticipated benefits of caring for the particular infant exceed the costs of alternative opportunities for advancing inclusive fitness (e.g., devoting care to younger siblings).

In addition, it cannot be assumed that infantile proximity-seeking emerged in response to selection by predation (see Gubernick, 1981) although this seems likely. Konner (1977) reports that no infants are known to have been lost to predation among the Kalahari-San hunter-gatherers, whereas there is a 20% mortality rate in the first year due to infection, the spread of which may even be facilitated by proximity-seeking. Thus the function and importance of infantile proximity-seeking requires further elaboration within the evolutionary model. We return to issues such as these in Chapter 4, when we discuss the interpretation—in terms of biological principles—of individual differences in infant-adult attachment. Interestingly, while several researchers have recently expressed interest in the determinants of individual differences in parental behavior (e.g., Belsky, 1984; Belsky, Garduque, & Hrncir, 1984; Lamb & Easterbrooks, 1981) they have, with perhaps one exception (Lamb, Pleck, Charnov, & Levine, in press) not considered the potential contributions of behavioral ecology (Krebs & Davies, 1981).

Perhaps because the concept of imprinting, as described by the ethologist Konrad Lorenz (1935), was being widely discussed when Bowlby was developing attachment theory, Bowlby was impressed by the potential for critical or sensitive periods during which human infants form attachments. Notions about critical or sensitive periods also impressed those theorists concerned with the formation and development of individual differences in infant-adult attachment, and so the issue is discussed further later in this book. For the present, we need only note that we have understandably little direct evidence available concerning the existence of critical or sensitive formative periods in human development. There is reason, on both empirical and theoretical grounds, however, to doubt the usefulness of sensitive period notions regarding the formation of attachments (Reed & Leiderman, 1983; Rutter, 1979). Indeed, the question might perhaps be cast a little differently: Instead of asking whether early experiences have a crystalizing *general* effect, we might ask whether early experiences crystalize *specific* aspects of development while leaving other developmental domains unaffected. From the perspective of behavioral ecology, therefore, where should we expect to find the developmental program closed, and where would we expect to find it left open?

In addition, we need to ask in what circumstances attachment or imprinting-like phenomena might be expected to occur. For example, Lorenz' (1935) own work showed that rapid imprinting during an early sensitive period occurred in species (like ducks) with extremely precocial young who needed some immediate means of ensuring proximity to protective adults, given their capacity to wander off independently. In more altricial avian species like jackdaws, however, the same phenomenon was not evident. Indeed, among jackdaws (as among humans) recognition of the parent figure precedes preferential attachment, whereas this is not true of the precocial imprinting species like geese and ducks. Thus, it seems unlikely that an imprinting mechanism would exist among humans, who are extremely altricial and wholly dependent on adult intervention and care for an extended period of time. The imprinting model, therefore, is probably not a useful one for conceptualizing the processes of infant-adult attachment among humans (Lamb & Hwang, 1982; Reed & Leiderman, 1983). Consideration of such issues colors the discussion of early experience in this volume.

Cognitive and Developmental Sciences

Within the cognitive sciences, the information processing approach—which is ideally suited for interpretation and understanding of the appraisal process underlying the control systems model described by Bowlby—has come to dominate conceptualization and research. Unfortunately, few attempts have been made to test Bowlby's assumptions about the appraisal process, although attempts have been made to model the processes (e.g., Bischof, 1975) and to study the predicted relationships among the four putative behavioral systems (e.g., Bretherton & Ainsworth, 1974; Sroufe, Waters, & Matas, 1974). The issue remains ripe for investigation of the functioning of these appraisal processes. Even more seriously in need of elaboration and empirical test is Bowlby's proposal that appraisal plays a key role in ensuring that an emotional bond, not simply patterns of behavior, becomes consolidated in the first year of life. The development of these appraisal capacities has not been studied systematically, nor have the implications of this model been formalized into specific, testable hypotheses.

Finally, despite growing evidence that the attainment of person permanence may *not* coincide with the emergence of attachment bonds around 6–8 months (e.g., Jackson, Campos, & Fischer, 1978), researchers and theorists have yet to ask what factors might then be responsible for the emergence of attachments around this time. Why, for example, do they not emerge sooner, as they appear to do in other species in which even rudimentary degrees of person permanence are never attained? Part of the answer seems to lie in the fact that many attachment behaviors do not become functional until the emergence of locomotion, which allows the child to wander afield from the adult. In fact, human infants do appear to establish attachments at about the same time that locomotion typically emerges, and the same appears to be true in other species—both avian and mammalian. Of course, this "answer" does not explain *how* attachments form in humans and other species, it only suggests *why* they emerge when they do, based on a particular conceptualization of attachment phenomena. Since other behaviors (e.g., smiling, vocalizing) are directed preferentially to familiar adults well before the onset of locomotion, there is some uncertainty concerning why locomotion ability should have the importance it has in defining the onset of attachment. At the very least, the issue underscores the needs for careful thinking in the area and to recognize that apparently similar phenomena in different species may be (at best) analogous rather than homologous. We thus need to consider the evolutionary history and ecology of each species when seeking to understand its behavior, phylogeny, and ontogeny.

It also appears that Bowlby's notion of monotropy is incorrect. Several studies have shown that infants can, and frequently do, form attachments to more than one person, even though (consistent with Bowlby's notion) the relationship to the primary caretaker seems to remain the more important attachment to the child (see Lamb, 1981c, for a review). Some of the research exploring the formative implications of this fact is discussed in Chapter 9.

Clearly, questions about Bowlby's attachment theory remain even though, equally clearly, it is one of the most powerful integrations yet seen in the study of socioemotional development. Some of these questions are raised again below, when they are directly relevant to the central focus of this book—individually differentiated patterns in the organization of attachment behavior.

3 INDIVIDUAL DIFFERENCES IN ATTACHMENT

ISSUES OF ASSESSMENT

As pointed out in the last chapter, Bowlby's ethological-adaptational theory of attachment, first proposed in the late 1950s, has come to dominate the conceptualization of infant social development within developmental psychology. After heated debate (e.g., Gewirtz, 1972) shortly after the near-simultaneous publication of "Attachment and dependency" (Maccoby & Masters, 1970), and *Attachment* (Bowlby, 1969), therefore, even early critics of Bowlby's formulation now appear to have accepted its validity and usefulness (e.g., Maccoby, 1980).

Like most widely-accepted theories, there has been some research on the central normative issues raised by Bowlby's theory, but the main focus of controversy has shifted within the last decade from normative issues concerning the development of attachment to the study, interpretation, and implications of individual differences. This shift in focus was not displeasing to Bowlby, whose psychoanalytic background guaranteed and other writings (e.g., Bowlby, 1973) demonstrated a clear concern with the origins, development, and formative importance of individual differences in attachment. In fact, attachment theory suggested several ways in which varying experiential histories might shape individual differences in infant-adult attachment.

First, Bowlby asserted that infant behavior is adapted to complement that of a caretaker who responds contingently and appropriately to infant cues. When the caretaker's behavior departs markedly from this evolutionary norm (e.g., by responding inconsistently and/or inappropriately), much of the infant's proximity-promoting and -maintaining repertoire is rendered functionally ineffective, with adverse consequences for functioning of the attachment system. In particular, differences in the adult's responsiveness are likely to have an important effect on the appraisal processes underlying Bowlby's control-systems model. An infant who lacks confidence in the caretaker's accessibility or responsiveness may have a more narrowly-defined set-goal for proximity, for example, or may appraise situational events (e.g., a stranger's entrance) more negatively than an infant who has more confident expectations. Thus there is a crucial link between caretaker responsiveness and the functioning of the attachment system.

Second, Bowlby (1969 and especially 1973) discussed in some detail the psychological significance of caretaker responsivenss by suggesting that infants construct "working models" of their attachment figures. These working models constitute internalized representations of the adults' pertinent attributes—in particular, conceptions of the caretaker's accessibility and responsiveness—based on their history of prior interactions. Bowlby believed that, once formed, such "working models" were relatively resistant to change, and thus influenced child-caretaker relations in an ongoing fashion at later ages also. Furthermore, Bowlby (1973) suggested that infants also develop working models of themselves based on these early experiences, and that those too were likely to affect later behavior. In fact, Bowlby suggested on various occasions in his 1969 and 1973 volumes that many aspects of adult psychological dysfunction could ultimately be traced to inadequate or unsatisfying working models developed early in life.

The formative influences of early caretaking experiences on the development of differences in attachment—and the significance of these differences for later psychological functioning—is also reflected in current elaborations or extentions of attachment theory. For example, Sroufe (1979) and his colleagues (e.g., Matas, Arend, & Sroufe, 1978) have proposed that a "continuity of adaptation" exists with respect to early development, with the successful resolution of earlier "developmental issues" providing the groundwork for success with subsequent issues. Thus the development of an effective attachment relationship during the first year is believed to render the child better equipped for the later development of psychological autonomy and subsequently for the establishment of successful peer relations.

Clearly, therefore, Bowlby's formulations and those of his students provide the theoretical basis for examining individual differences in attachment.

Pioneering observational studies, such as that conducted by Ainsworth (1967) among the Ganda, and experimental research with animals (Rajecki et al. 1978) had demonstrated that most infants formed attachments to their parent figures, regardless of variations—and even frank deficiencies—in the quality of care. However, these attachments appeared to vary greatly in quality. Some infants appeared consistently clingy; some showed remarkably great and others remarkably little separation protest. Others seemed so anxious about strangers and/or the accessibility of their mothers that they were totally unable to explore effectively, even in familiar circumstances and in the caretaker's presence. The key questions for researchers thus were: (1) can we measure stable individual differences in patterns like these, (2) do they have clear and measurable origins in prior patterns of infant-adult interaction, and (3) do they have formative impact on the child's later development? The latter two questions are clear derivatives of attachment theory and have generated much of the research reviewed in this volume. It is with the first of these issues that the present chapter is concerned.

Although Bowlby (1969) had emphasized in formulating attachment theory that consistent, continuing exposure of the infant to a particular adult determined whether and to whom attachment bonds would form, his theory placed great emphasis on the importance of adult responses to infant signals as the process by which proximity/contact is achieved, and thus as the mechanism through which attachment bonds are consolidated. Different adults, however, certainly vary in their responsiveness to infant signals for a variety of reasons, not least among them the adult's experience, social situation, and personality, infant temperament, and the readability of the infant's signals (Belsky, 1984; Lamb & Easterbrooks, 1981). It is not unreasonable to propose, given the attachment mechanism suggested by Bowlby, that this variation in adult responsiveness must have some effect on the quality of the attachments formed.

How does one measure these individual differences in the quality of attachment? As mentioned in the previous chapter, this appeared for some time to be an impossible task. In a number of studies conducted in the late 1960s and early 1970s, researchers found very low intercorrelations among multiple attachment behavior measures (Coates et al., 1972; Lewis & Ban, 1971; Maccoby & Feldman, 1972; Masters & Wellman, 1974; Waters, 1978). From the trait perspective often adopted by these researchers, these results were considered devastating to attachment theory, because they showed that attachment behavioral measures constituted unreliable measures of individual differences in infant attachment (e.g., Coates et al. 1972; Masters & Wellman, 1974).

Attachment theorists, however, were not distressed by these results; they argued that they would not have predicted or expected high intercorrelations among attachment behavior measures for a number of reasons (Lamb, 1974; Waters, 1978). First, they believed that the specific attachment behaviors evident in any given period are determined by endogenous (e.g., fatigue, illness), contextual (e.g., familiarity and friendliness of others present), and situational (e.g., familiarity of the environment) factors. As mentioned earlier, activation of the attachment behavior system is also affected by the activation of the fear/wariness, exploration, and affiliative behavior systems (Bretherton & Ainsworth, 1974). Thus one would not expect high intercorrelations across time and context, because specific behaviors are multiply and complexly determined. Second, most of the studies involved very brief assessment periods, all of which are certain to yield measures of extremely poor reliability among which intercorrelations are necessarily difficult to interpret. Third, ethological attachment theorists argue that it is the *patterning* of attachment behaviors that is critical, not the absolute levels of any individual measure viewed in isolation, because many different behaviors can serve the same function, and must thus be considered functionally equivalent. That is, multiple specific behavioral indicators, viewed in the context of other ongoing events, can reflect comparable levels of behavioral functioning (e.g., proximity seeking or contact maintenance). The fallacy of the intercorrelational studies, then, was that they focused on intercorrelations among discrete measures without regard for the overall patterning, goals, and functions of behavior (Ainsworth, 1972; Waters, 1978).

The validity of the alternative organizational perspective (emphasizing the patterns and functions of behavior rather than discrete behaviors) was empirically demonstrated by Waters (1978) in an important study that we discussed earlier. Waters (1978) showed that there were nonsignificant correlations among discrete attachment behavior measures (e.g., smiling, approaching), more substantial intercorrelations among broader rating scales of higher-order constructs (such as proximity-seeking), and substantial stability, even over a 6-month period, in categorical assessments of the quality or security of attachment. These findings suggested that, although there were changes over time in the behavioral modes by which infants interacted with attachment figures, there was stability in terms of the goals subserved by these specific behaviors.

The procedure used by Waters to assess the security of attachment was the Strange Situation, a procedure developed by Ainsworth and Wittig (1969) as part of their longitudinal study of infant-mother attachment in Baltimore. Although Ainsworth and her colleagues (e.g., Ainsworth, Bell, & Stayton, 1971, 1974) had reported on the usefulness of Strange Situation classifications in organizing the results of their Baltimore study, particularly with respect to the relation between prior maternal behavior and subsequent Strange Situation behavior, Waters' findings were crucial for demonstrating to developmental psychologists that the classifications were indeed reliable. Because of this, Waters' study played a major role in drawing attention to the Strange Situation procedure, which we now describe. We describe the procedure and its special scoring conventions at some length because most research on the Strange Situation has involved an "hourglass methodology"

(Connell & Goldsmith, 1982)—that is, relating the classifications assigned on the basis of Strange Situation behavior to measures of infantile and/or maternal behavior in prior, contemporaneous, or subsequent observations. Furthermore, the availability of a standard, easily-scorable assessment procedure focused research interest on attachment theory by operationalizing constructs that had earlier proven to be frustratingly difficult to observe or measure. It is thus crucial to understand how these classifications are achieved and what characteristics distinguish the various categories. In the short history of developmental psychology, no other measure of socioemotional characteristics has ever received as much attention or popularity as have the Strange Situation classifications.

THE STRANGE SITUATION PROCEDURE

The Strange Situation was initially designed to assess the way in which infants: (1) used adults as "secure bases" from which to explore, (2) reacted to strangers, and (3) reacted to separation and reunion. According to Ainsworth, the initial emphasis was on secure base behavior because "one of the most important criteria of a healthy attachment was ability to use the mother as a secure base for exploration" (Ainsworth & Wittig, 1969, p. 112). Since the basic function of the attachment system in Bowlby's ethological model is to promote protective proximity to the adult in the face of threat or alarm, the Strange Situation was designed to create gradually escalating stress for the baby so that consequent changes in infant behavior toward the caretaker could be observed. The assumption was that variations in the security of attachment—and in the "working models" that underlie them—would be most clearly evident in such circumstances.

The Strange Situation procedure involves seven, 3-minute episodes arranged to create increasing amounts of stress for the baby so that researchers can observe how infants organize their behavior around attachment figures when distressed.[1] The procedure is usually conducted in a carpeted laboratory playroom, in which toys are provided for the baby and chairs are available for parent and stranger. The procedure is considered appropriate for use with infants between the ages of 12 and 24 months.

As indicated on Table 3.1, parent and baby are initially alone together (episode 1). They are joined by a female stranger (episode 2) who later engages the infant's attention so that the parent can leave the room (episode

---

[1]The original version of the Strange Situation developed for use in the Baltimore study differed in some ways from the version currently in use (see Ainsworth & Bell, 1970; Ainsworth & Wittig, 1969; Willemsen, Flaherty, Heaton, & Ritchey, 1974). Most notably, the two reunion episodes were variable in duration but were characteristically briefer than three minutes, providing less time for infant soothing following separation.

TABLE 3.1
The Strange Situation Procedure

Episode[a]	Persons Present	Entrances and Exits
1	Parent and Infant alone	
		Stranger enters
2	Parent, Infant, Stranger[b]	
		Parent leaves
3	Infant, Stranger	
		Parent returns, Stranger leaves
4	Parent, Infant[c]	
		Parent leaves
5	Infant alone	
		Stranger returns
6	Infant, Stranger	
		Parent returns, Stranger leaves
7	Parent, Infant[c]	

Note: All episodes are intended to be three minutes long, but some (especially the separation episodes—3, 5, 6) may be abbreviated if the child is unusually distressed, and others (especially the reunion episodes—4 and 7) can be extended if the child is slow to soothe.

[a]Ainsworth and her colleagues also describe an initial 30-second episode, during which child and parent are introduced to the room, as episode 1. Thus what we call episode 1 is labeled episode 2 by Ainsworth, etc.

[b]The Stranger is instructed to sit quietly for one minute, then to chat to the parent for one minute, and in the final minute to engage the infant in play.

[c]The parent is instructed to speak loudly before entering the room so as to attract the infant's attention. Upon entering, s/he pauses to permit the infant time to mobilize a response. The parent is instructed to make the child comfortable, and reinterest him/her in the toys.

3). When the parent returns, the stranger leaves (episode 4) and she is followed 3 minutes later by the parent who leaves the child alone for 3 minutes or less if the infant becomes markedly upset (episode 5). The infant is then joined by the stranger (episode 6) and then by the parent, whose entrance signals the departure of the stranger (episode 7). Both adults are instructed to respond to the infant's bids but to avoid initiating interaction except when the baby is distressed.

THE SCORING SYSTEM

The scoring or coding scheme conventionally applied to Strange Situation behavior is responsive to Bowlby's views regarding the goals, functions, and interchangeability of behavior. It is thus assumed that multiple specific behavioral indicators, viewed in the context of other ongoing events, can reflect comparable levels of behavioral functioning (e.g., proximity-seeking or contact maintenance). Two levels of analysis are typically employed. At the first, more molecular, level, videotaped or narrative records of the session are reviewed by trained scorers who score the infant on unidimensional seven point scales quantifying important aspects of the infant-adult interaction—proximity and contact seeking, contact maintaining, resistance to contact or interaction, avoidance, search for the parent during separation episodes, and distance interaction. Each scale includes behavioral exemplars defining each point as well as more general descriptors of the relevant construct.

> *Proximity and contact seeking*...refers to the degree of active initiative a baby shows in seeking physical contact with or proximity to another person. *Contact maintaining*....refers to the degree of active initiative a baby exerts in order to maintain physical contact with a person, once such contact is achieved....*Resistance*....is shown by pushing away from, striking out at, or squirming to get down from an adult who has offered contact, or by pushing away, throwing away, or otherwise rejecting toys through which an adult attempts to mediate interaction. The highest scores imply an obviously angry emotional tone....*Avoidance* [is scored when] babies actively avoid proximity and interaction with their mothers in the reunion episodes, in which a common response is to seek close proximity or contact....*Search*....is defined as behavior in which the baby, through means other than crying, attempts to regain proximity to his mother" (Ainsworth et al., 1978, pp. 53–54).

These rating scales are briefly described in Table 3.2; they are fully described in an Appendix to Ainsworth et al.'s volume.

TABLE 3.2
The Interactive Rating Scales

Scale	Abbreviated description of selected anchor points
Proximity and Contact Seeking	7. Very active effort and initiative in achieving physical contact (e.g., fully approaches the adult and achieves contact through its own efforts)
	5. Some active effort to achieve physical contact (e.g., approaches but is picked up without any clear bid for contact)
	3. Weak effort to achieve physical contact or moderately strong effort to gain proximity (e.g., approaches, does not request pick up, and is not held)
	1. No effort to achieve physical contact or proximity
Contact Maintaining	7. Very active and persistent effort to maintain physical contact (e.g., while held more than 2 minutes, infant at least twice actively resists release)

(Continued)

TABLE 3.2
(*Continued*)

Scale	Abbreviated description of selected anchor points
	5. Some active effort to maintain physical contact (e.g., while held for less than 1 minute, the infant actively resists release once)
	3. Some apparent desire to maintain physical contact but relatively little active effort to do so (e.g., infant initiates contact at least twice in an episode, but on each occasion the hold is brief, and its cessation is not protested)
	1. Either no physical contact or no effort to maintain it
Resistance	7. Very intense *and* persistent resistance (e.g., two or more instances of: repeatedly hitting the adult, strong squirming against hold, temper tantrum, repeated angry rejection of the adult or toys)
	5. Some resistance—either less intense or more isolated and less persistent (e.g., at least 3 instances of the above, without as great a degree of anger)
	3. Slight resistance (e.g., two rather modest instances of resistance)
	1. No resistance
Avoidance	7. Very marked and persistent avoidance (e.g., no attention to adult despite repeated attempts by her/him to attract attention)
	5. Clear-cut avoidance but less persistent (e.g., 30 seconds of ignoring in the absence of attempts by the adult to gain attention)
	3. Slight isolated avoidance behavior (e.g., brief delay in responding)
	1. No avoidance
Search[a]	7. Very active and persistent search behavior (e.g., approaches door promptly and actively bangs or attempts to open it)
	5. Some active search (e.g., approaches door after delay or fails to make active effort to open it or bang)
	3. Some apparent desire to regain the attachment figure, but the search behavior is weak (e.g., infant looks toward door for at least 30 seconds)
	1. No search
Distance Interaction	7. Very active and persistent distance interaction (e.g., reciprocal interaction for more than 45 seconds)
	5. Active distance interaction (e.g., smiles and vocalizes to parent at least 4 times)
	3. Little distance interaction (e.g., looks frequently at adult, and orients for at least 15 seconds)
	1. No distance interaction (e.g., just occasional glances)

[a]Rated only in separation episodes
Full details regarding the rating scales are provided by Ainsworth et al.
(1978) in their Appendix III.

Some researchers (e.g., Grossmann, Huber, & Wartner, 1981) rate proximity-seeking, contact-seeking, avoidance, resistance, and distance interaction only in the reunion episodes (4 and 7); some disregard the distance interaction rating scale (e.g., Main & Weston, 1981); some do not systematically employ the rating scales at all (e.g., Easterbrooks & Goldberg, 1984), and others, following Ainsworth et al. (1978), assess each dimension of behavior in each episode even though for purposes of the classifications described below, they place special emphasis on behavior directed toward the parent in the reunion episodes (e.g., Lamb, Hwang, Frodi, & Frodi, 1982; Sagi et al., in press; Thompson et al., 1982). These differences in rating practices do not appear to affect the patterns of results reported, however, as most researchers focus on correlates of the molar classifications, rather than correlates of the rating scales.

At the second, more molar level, judges, usually guided by the scores on the 7-point dimensions, classify the infant into one of 3 groups (A, B, C) and 8 subgroups (A_1, A_2, B_1, B_2, B_3, B_4, C_1, C_2) representing an overall judgement regarding the infant's behavior. Because these classifications represent the highest order, multidimensional assessment of the patterns of infant attachment behavior and thus represent an appraisal of the entire attachment behavioral system, they have been used almost exclusively as indices of individual differences in the research reviewed in this book (see also Sroufe & Waters, 1977). The classifications reflect the flexibility and appropriate functioning of the attachment system, including the infant's ability to use the parent as a "secure base" from which to play or explore, as well as the quality and tone of the baby's reunion responses after the two separation episodes.

The B group infants are considered "securely attached" on the grounds that, whether or not they are manifestly distressed by separation, they greet the parent upon reunion either by seeking proximity/contact or by distal interaction (e.g., by smiling, vocalizing, or waving). These infants also manifest clear secure base behavior, moving out from the attachment figure to explore and interact with the environment in forays punctuated by returns to the attachment figure. The presence of and proximity to the adult apparently provide these infants with the comfort and security needed to interact with the environment, even after a distressing separation. Thus the behavior of securely-attached infants accords with the proper functioning of the attachment behavioral system within Bowlby's ethological formulation: seeking proximity, under stress, but using the parent's presence as a resource that potentiates play and exploration in nonstressful circumstances. Despite these group characteristics, infants in the four B subgroups differ in the degree of proximity/contact they seek. They range from the B_1 infants, who are content with distance interaction, to the B_4 infants who are highly concerned about achieving contact and, indeed, are slow to comfort even when in contact.

The A and C group infants are considered "insecurely attached." The A group infants are called Avoidant because they tend to avoid or ignore their parents rather than seek interaction, especially upon reunion. A_1 infants are conspicuously avoidant, whereas A_2 infants mingle avoidant and proximity-seeking behavior. In addition, these infants play noninteractively during preseparation episodes, contributing to an overall picture of disinterest in or rejection of the caretaker. The C group infants are called Resistant because they mingle proximity/contact seeking behaviors with angry, rejecting behavior, especially in the reunion episodes.[2] Thus their reunion responses seem ambivalent in quality. Those in the C_2 subgroup are distinguished by the passivity of their proximity-seeking behaviors whereas C_1 infants are much more active in both proximity-seeking and resistance. For example, the C_2 infants may simply cry helplessly instead of crawling toward the adults or reaching for a pick-up, whereas the C_1 infants push away or hit the parent. In addition, C group infants are often so preoccupied with the parent during preseparation episodes that they are unable to play independently, and thus the adult seems not to function as a secure base for the child's exploration. In the case of both the avoidant and resistant patterns, therefore, infant behavior is not only markedly different from the pattern deemed securely-attached, but also deviates significantly from the functionally adaptive pattern of behavior, as defined from the standpoint of Bowlby's ethological model.

In Table 3.3, we provide brief descriptions of the 8 categories and then in Table 3.4 we indicate how scores on the interactive rating scales are related to the classification judgements. Again, fuller details were provided by Ainsworth et al. (1978).

TRAINING AND RELIABILITY

Because the primary measures of Strange Situation behavior employed in programmatic research are categorical judgements concerning the infant's behavior, the establishment of inter-scorer reliability requires substantially more training and experience than would be the case if discrete behaviors were being scored and tabulated. The situation is ameliorated somewhat by the availability (initially through private channels and since 1978 in

---

[2]Ainsworth, Bell, and Stayton (1971, p. 24) note that "from the beginning group C was considered a heterogeneous group, distinguished from the other groups only by what was loosely specified as 'maladaptive behavior.'" Later, however, Ainsworth et al. (1978, p. 58) wrote: "instead of the loose designation of 'maladaptive' it was now perceived that Group C infants shared, in addition to strong interest in proximity to and contact with the mother in the reunion episodes, a tendency to manifest angry resistance to the mother upon reunion."

TABLE 3.3
The Attachment Classification Categories

Label	Brief Description
A₁	Conspicuous avoidance of parent in reunion episodes (e.g., ignoring, pointed looking, turning or moving away). No approach in reunion, or approach is abortive. Little or no contact maintaining if picked up. Tendency to treat the stranger much as parent is treated.
A₂	Some tendency to greet and approach the parent mixed with tendency to turn, move, or look away, or to ignore. Maybe some contact maintaining, but in the context of avoidant behavior.
B₁	Greets parent on reunion with positive distance interaction rather than approach and contact seeking. Little contact-maintaining if picked up. Little separation distress, and perhaps some avoidance during reunions.
B₂	Tends to approach and greet the parent, but only low degree of contact-seeking behavior. Perhaps avoidance in episode 4. Low contact maintaining if picked up.
B₃	Actively seeks physical contact on reunions, and shows active contact maintenance. Gains comfort from attachment figure, and thus soothes after separations and is subsquently able to explore in his/her presence. Little avoidance or resistance.
B₄	Clear contact seeking, especially in reunion episodes, but the contact seeking and contact maintaining behaviors are less active and competent than those of B₃ infants. The infant does not gain sufficient security or comfort from the adult's presence to permit subsequent exploration and affiliation, particularly in the post-separation episodes. Seems anxious throughout. May also show some resistance to parent.
C₁	Strong proximity- and contact-seeking and contact-maintaining in reunion episodes, mingled with conspicuously resistant, angry behavior. High separation distress. Resistance may also be directed toward stranger.
C₂	Extreme passivity, with litle exploration even in preseparation episodes, and little active proximity/contact seeking or contact maintenance although, largely by crying, they manifest a desire to be held. Resistant behavior not as strong as in C₁ infants.

Note: Fuller details regarding classification are provided by Ainsworth et al. (1978). Only central distinguishing characteristics are selected for mention in this table.

.

TABLE 3.4
Patterns of Interactive Behavior and Crying in the Strange Situation

	Behavior to mother on reunion					Crying	Additional Characteristics
	Proximity seeking	*Contact maintaining*	*Proximity avoiding*	*Contact resisting*		*Preparation/ Separation/ Reunion*	
Avoidant							
A1	Low	Low	High	Low		Low/low or high/ low	Avoidance is the same or greater on second reunion
A2	Moderate to high	Low	High	Low to moderate		Low/low or high/ low	Avoidance is the same or greater on second reunion
Secure							
B1	Low to moderate	Low	Low	Low		Low/low/low	Positive greeting to mother on reunion and active distance interaction.
B2	Low to moderate	Low to moderate	Low to moderate	Low		Low/low to moderate/low	Avoidance decreases on second reunion. May show proximity seeking in pre-separation episodes.
B3	High	High	Low	Low		Low/moderate to high/low	Proximity seeking and contact main-

38

					taining vary directly with separation distress. Recovery from distress before 2 min and return to play is typical.
B4	High	High	Low	Low	Low/high/low to moderate	Proximity and attention to mother throughout.
Resistant						
C1	High	High	Low	High	Low to moderate/high/moderate to high	Difficult to comfort on reunion. Strong resistance of contact with stranger during separation. Often angry toward mother on reunion.
C2	Low to moderate	Low to moderate	Low	High	Low to moderate/high/moderate to high	Exploratory behavior is weak throughout. Difficult to comfort on reunion.

aScored on 7-point scales, scale points anchored to behavioral descriptions selected from typed transcripts of the behavior of 1-year-olds in the Strange Situation.
Source: Sroufe & Waters (1977). Reprinted by permission of the Society for Research in Child Development.

published form: Ainsworth et al., 1978) of detailed coding and classificatory instructions which are considered definitive by all users of the Strange Situation procedure.

Nevertheless, most users of the procedure agree that extensive training is required. Typically this involves scoring videotapes with an experienced coder so that the trainee becomes familiar with the range of behavior likely to be seen and the concrete interpretation of terms such as "persistent," "intense," and "marked," Because videotapes rather than dictated narratives are now used almost universally, it is easier to train coders, rescore unclear patterns of behavior, and ensure interlaboratory reliability by having the same videotapes employed by raters from different research groups. Most users of the procedure have many, if not all, videotapes rated by two or more independent judges, and the agreement among or between experienced judges usually exceeds 80%. This indicates that, despite the complexity of the scoring system and the occasional difficulties involved in trying to apply the closed-ended classification system, the judgements are typically made with high reliability.

PSYCHOMETRIC CONSIDERATIONS

Although several other interactional patterns could certainly be imagined, the 3-group/8-subgroup classification system seems to encompass much of the theoretically-relevant variability in infants' Strange Situation behaviors. Nevertheless, some investigators have found it necessary to consider a small proportion of infants "unclassifiable" (e.g., Grossmann, Grossmann, Huber, & Wartner, 1981; Main & Weston, 1981). In most cases, these researchers suggest that these infants would be deemed securely-attached under a forced classification procedure, although they do not seem really secure to observers. Other investigators have, on occasion, found it necessary to create new categories. For example, Egeland and Sroufe (1981b) used a Group D—comprising infants who were "anxiously attached but neither avoidant nor resistant (for example, apathetic or disorganized)" (p.84)—to classify a small proportion of the 18-month-olds from their socioeconomically disadvantaged sample. Crittendon (1983), working with maltreated infants ranging in age from 11 to 24 months, also found it necessary to add an "A/C: avoidant/ambivalent" classification category. Surprisingly, this category was used in large measure for infants who would otherwise have been deemed securely-attached in the threefold classification system. The need for new categories in these studies may suggest the need for revision of the existing taxonomy when dealing with infants older than 12 months of age, and/or infants from backgrounds much different from those of most middle-class American infants (see also Chapter 11).

In addition, several investigators (e.g., Sagi, Lamb, Lewkowicz, Shoham, Dvir, & Estes, in press; van IJzendoorn, Tavecchio, Goossens, Vergeer, & Swaan, 1983) have questioned whether infants in the B_4 subgroup should be considered securely-attached. Although infants in this subgroup show strong contact-seeking and contact-maintaining behaviors when reunited with the parent, and do not exhibit the degree of resistance characteristic of C group infants, they manifest other indications of insecurity in the Strange Situation. In particular, they do not comfort easily in the caretaker's presence and thus do not easily return to exploratory play after separation and reunion. This suggests that the parent fails to serve adequately as a secure base for the infant.

Although Tables 3.3 and 3.4 point to strong linkages between interactive scale ratings and classifications, this convergence has not been seriously assessed by attachment researchers. To be sure, Waters (1978) and Ainsworth et al. (1978) have employed multiple discriminant functions analyses, in which they found that the interactive scales and other measures satisfactorily differientiated the A, B, C classifications. (These analyses are reviewed in Chapter 12.) Since such analyses ask whether, *given the three-group classifications*, one can derive a weighted combination of (interactive) variables which accurately predicts classification to a high degree, they provide an incomplete assessment of the relationship between the interactive scores and the A, B, C classifications. Thus in Chapter 12, we describe an alternative analytical strategy (cluster analysis) in which one asks whether, *given the interactive data*, infants can be satisfactorily aggregated into clusters or groups that resemble Ainsworth's categories.

SUMMARY

Ainsworth and her colleagues (1971, 1978) developed the Strange Situation procedure in order to assess the organization of attachment behavior in infants. They have also described a multilevel coding scheme for describing infantile behavior in the Strange Situation, and some central features of their approach are summarized in this chapter. Most of the research reviewed in this book has involved the highest-level type of coding, in which categorical judgments are made about the quality of infant behavior in the Strange Situation. The three groups and eight subgroups are often replaced for purposes of analysis with a dichotomous distinction between secure and insecure attachment patterns. The categorical system has stood up well to repeated investigation, although there remains some question about the appropriateness of some designations, and the inclusiveness of the categories.

II INTERPRETING STRANGE SITUATION BEHAVIOR

4

THE BIOLOGICAL INTERPRETATION OF STRANGE SITUATION BEHAVIOR

THE ADAPTATIONIST INTERPRETATION

Although the A, B, C classification system had strictly empirical origins in Ainsworth's early research (see Chapter 3), the interpretation of these patterns has been consistent with other aspects of attachment theory. Most of these interpretations have been stated in terms of the principles of evolutionary biology. Thus several theorists (e.g., Ainsworth, 1979a; Main, 1981; Sroufe, 1979, 1983; Waters & Deane, 1982) have suggested that the patterns of behavior in the Strange Situation can be understood by reference to Bowlby's (1969) ethological perspective. From this viewpoint, the normative B pattern of behavior can be considered "secure" because it is *adaptive*, since the infant behaves in a way that would have enhanced its chances of survival in the species' "environment of evolutionary adaptedness" (Bowlby, 1969). Thus it seeks proximity, contact, or interaction when they return after an absence, maintains interaction with the attachment figure, and uses them as secure bases from which to explore. This interpretation is based on Bowlby's claim—earlier discussed in Chapter 2—that natural selection has produced infants who are predisposed to emit proximity-promoting behaviors (such as smiling and crying) to which adults are predisposed to respond. The attainment of the protective proximity that is of survival value for the infant depends on the prompt and appropriate responsiveness of the adult to the infant's signals. The A and C patterns, by contrast, are viewed as maladaptive because these infants fail to behave in the fashion that would have maximized the possibilities of survival in the environment of evolutionary adaptedness. Thus, for example, they do not use the adult as a secure base from which to explore, and do not seek protective proximity when alarmed or distressed.

One might wonder what "the environment of evolutionary adaptedness" is, and how it is relevant to the behavior of infants today. Ainsworth argues that

> It is reasonable to assume that infant attachment behavior and reciprocal maternal behavior are preadapted to each other. Thus, we suggest, one major aspect of the environment of evolutionary adaptedness for infant attachment behavior is not merely a mother figure but one who is sensitively responsive to infant behavioral cues. Bowlby suggested that to the extent that the present environment of rearing departs from the environment to which a baby's behavior is preadapted behavioral anomalies may be expected to occur (Ainsworth, 1979a, p.5).

An infant who seeks proximity (especially when distressed) is thus seen to be behaving adaptively in the context of our species' adaptive niche, which for an infant includes a sensitively responsive adult. When the adult fails to behave appropriately (i.e., fails to provide the species-appropriate niche) the child will behave maladaptively, failing to seek protective proximity and to use the adult as a secure base.

This interpretation of Strange Situation behavior raises several important questions that we address in this chapter. We begin by briefly describing the major principles of evolutionary biology, as understood by contemporary behavioral ecologists (e.g., Krebs & Davies, 1981). Then we relate these to the attempted interpretation of individual differences in Strange Situation behavior, addressing (1) the assumption that it is always adaptive for parents to behave in a sensitive fashion; (2) several frequently confused meanings of the term "adaptation"; and (3) the implication that there might be a single pattern of adaptive parental and infantile behavior.

PRINCIPLES OF EVOLUTIONARY BIOLOGY

Let us begin with some general theoretical considerations concerning the concept of adaptation, as understood by evolutionary biologists. Biologists point out that natural selection tends to favor traits which increase inclusive fitness—the reproductive success of individuals, and, in some cases, their close relatives who share many genes through common descent (Hamilton, 1964). Survival per se is not selected for: Selection is for relative success in the context of lifetime reproduction (for a review of life history evolution, see Charlesworth, 1980; Stearns, 1976, 1977) with organisms striving to maximize the representation of their genes (directly or indirectly through the reproduction of their relatives), relative to those of unrelated individuals, in future generations.

Attachment theory focuses on factors that enhance the survival of individual infants and takes for granted that adults can be expected to behave appropriately. But why (in a fitness sense) *should* adults care for infants? The answer is that they should be willing to expend resources and take risks for their own children and close relatives so as to ensure the propagation and survival of their genes. Unrelated adults should not be willing to invest resources in, or take risks for, infants unless some reciprocity exists or the adults are unable to distinguish kin from nonkin. Consequently, infants (at least when they have the choice) should direct attachment behavior only toward individuals who have shown, by their prior actions, a willingness to bear the risks and costs of childcare. There will be circumstances, however, in which it would not be in the fitness interest even of related adults to aid, give resources to, or even remain near their youngsters. Only by considering the alternative opportunities for fitness gain can the adult's actions toward a specific youngster be understood in terms of a natural selection.

A key notion in evolutionary thinking is that fitness always involves tradeoffs. In many species, for example, the expenditure of resources in reproduction involves increased risk of mortality to the reproducer (Stearns, 1976). Natural selection favors an optimal balance between parental survival and the production and care of offspring, with "optimal" defined by the balance which maximizes lifetime parental fitness (Charnov & Krebs, 1974). Moreover, since there are limits to the amount of effort, time, and resources that a parent can devote to reproduction, investment in one offspring must sometimes occur at the expense of others. This implies that parents are not necessarily selected to maximize the survival and/or development of individual offspring, but to divide parental resources among the entire brood so as to maximize parental fitness gains over the whole family (Alexander, 1974; Ghiselin, 1974; Trivers, 1974). For this reason, the interests of offspring and parents are often somewhat in conflict (Trivers, 1974), since the level of parental investment that would be optimal for an individual offspring from the offspring's point of view may exceed the level that would be optimal from the parent's point of view. In particular, if parental sensitivity to offspring signals implies that the parent must expend effort and care, then the parent's reproductive success may involve ignoring the signal and behaving insensitively. Trivers (1974) has used the example of conflict over weaning to illustrate how the desired level of parental investment in an individual offspring will, on occasion, differ significantly from the parent's and offspring's viewpoints—in accord with the fitness considerations for each. This means that natural selection fosters parental rejection on certain occasions as well as sensitivity on other occasions and thus that, in Hinde's (1983, p. 62) view, "infants are presumably adapted to cope with mothers who reject them."

Trivers also emphasized that the interests of both adult and infant change over time, as the opportunity costs for the parent of further reproduction change and the chances of infantile survival improve. Thus we might expect developmental changes in parental and infantile behavior—and their relational harmony—as a function of these. Quite clearly, it will not *always* be in the adult's interests to respond sensitively and promptly to the infant's signals and needs, as attachment theorists have assumed. Rather, the adult's behavior should vary in relation to the child's and adult's age and gender, the number and age of other offspring, the opportunities for reproduction, and the quality and characteristics of the ecology. Instead of exclusively emphasizing behavioral patterns that were of survival value in "the environment of evolutionary adaptedness," behavioral ecologists and most others concerned with the evolution of behavior conceive of organisms as flexibly deciding how to behave, depending on ecological constraints and resources, so as to maximize their inclusive fitness.

THE ADAPTATIONIST INTERPRETATION REASSESSED

Several implications of these principles bear directly on the interpretation of infant-adult attachment, and thus (to the extent that they are related) to infant behavior in the Strange Situation.

Should Adults Always Be Sensitive?

Even though adults may have been selected to protect their offspring under most circumstances, with attachment relationships mediating this protection, we cannot assume that adults will always behave accordingly. The tradeoffs between parental reproduction and parental survival (and hence, opportunities for future reproduction) are subtle, and it is critically important to assess the relative costs and benefits to both the adult and individual infant when determining the adaptive significance of attachment behavior (Parker & MacNair, 1979; Trivers, 1974). The assessment of these costs and benefits has never been attempted. In its absence, as we have noted, we should not assume that it is always adaptive for parents to behave in an appropriately sensitive fashion, and that their behavioral tendencies will be consistent over time. In particular, certain events in the infancy period (e.g., weaning: Trivers, 1974) may result in parental "insensitivity" and parent-offspring conflict which is, from the standpoint of natural selection, as adaptive as is parental sensitivity on other occasions. It is thus questionable whether it is wise to view infantile behavior as preadapted to an evolutionary niche that consists primarily of a sensitively responsive adult.

The Meanings of "Adaptation"

It is also not clear whether "adaptive" attachment behavior is believed by ethological attachment theorists to bring fitness advantages to infants in contemporary times. Ainsworth (1984a) has recently distinguished three different meanings of "adaptation" in attachment theory:

> (1) In the *phylogenetic* or evolutionary sense adaptation implies that in the course of natural selection those behaviors that yield survival advantage in the environment in which the evolutionary change is taking place become part of the repertoire characteristic of the species....This phylogenetic view is a normative view, concerned with species characteristic behavior and its function, and is not concerned with individual differences....
>
> (2) In the *ontogenetic* sense adaptation refers to the processes through which an organism adjusts to the environment in the course of development....This usage of the term "adaptation" implies that whatever the genetic foundation of structures may be, the nature of their development is influenced both by the genetic program and by the environment in which development takes place. Nonetheless, this general ontogenetic approach is not concerned with individual differences, but with the basic biological properties of developing organisms....
>
> (3) In the *developmental mental health* sense the focus is on individual differences in development, and on evaluation of how well or how poorly such development equips the individual to cope with the impact of the environment in which he lives. (Ainsworth, 1984a, ms pgs. 4 – 5; italics in original)

An example of Ainsworth's "phylogenetic" adaptation is the view originally put forward by Bowlby (1969), that "attachment failure" heightened the risk of death for the child in the environment of evolutionary adaptedness. This view is highly plausible. We do not, however, agree with Ainsworth's assertion that phylogenetic adaptations—"the behavioral repertoire characteristic of the species"—are not concerned with individual differences between organisms. As we make clear in the next section, evolution typically does not equip individuals with a single ideal pattern of behavior, but rather with a repertoire of responses that may be selectively applied in different circumstances.

Furthermore, although there is heuristic value in making assumptions concerning an "environment of evolutionary adaptedness," hypotheses deriving from such assumptions are inevitably speculative. The fitness consequences of specific social behaviors are often complex, and we know too little about the physical and social ecology of human evolution. Concerning the potential complexities of selection arguments, for example,

MacNair and Parker (1978) have developed mathematical models suggesting that the degree of conflict between parent and offspring about the level of parental investment can be affected by the degree to which parents are monogamous or promiscuous. Unfortunately, we do not know anything about monogamy and promiscuity during earlier phases of human evolution. Similarly, attachment theorists argue that since a sensitively responsive mother improves the offspring's chances for survival, selection would favor such maternal characteristics. Perhaps so, but it is also possible that there would be individual differences in maternal sensitivity among early (as well as contemporary) humans. Thus infants who developed a repertoire of behavioral strategies permitting them to deal with *both* sensitive and insensitive mothers would survive under a wider range of circumstances than would infants adapted exclusively for sensitive mothers. Why not suppose, then, that contemporary infants are as well adapted to cope with insensitive as sensitive mothers (see Hinde, 1983)? Unfortunately, both hypotheses can be of limited heuristic value in the absence of specific models for the natural selection of social behaviors and evidence concerning the range of individual differences in parental sensitivity during human evolution.

In Ainsworth's terminology, "ontogenetic" adaptations are concerned with the development and transformation of the attachment system over the life span, an important topic that has not yet received close attention in theoretical discussions. It would be unwise, however, to assume that ontogenetic processes have no consequences for either reproductive success or individual differences. Many of the activities in which young offspring engage are necessary for their future reproductive success, and there may be several different ontogenetic pathways whereby reproductive success is achieved. (See, for example, Charnov, Gotshall, & Robinson, 1978, and Gross & Charnov, 1980, for discussions of alternative life histories in Pandalid Shrimp and Bluegill Sunfish.)

Another distinction important here is that between *juvenile* and *ontogenetic* or *developmental* adaptations. Juvenile adaptations are traits that aid individuals through their youth, and attachment behavior can be viewed in this way. Once the stage is passed, these traits have little value. Fitness, however, refers not just to survival and development through the prereproductive years, but to lifetime reproductive success. Many things children do are in fact necessary for effective functioning as reproductive adults, and these are developmental adaptations. *Developmental adaptations can only be understood by considering what the "traits" mean to reproductive success when adulthood is reached*, and it is not clear whether patterns of Strange Situation behavior viewed as juvenile adaptations have any relevance to later reproductive performance.

Finally, the "developmental mental health" meaning of the term, adaptation, is concerned with the long range outcome criteria by which the success or failure of an infant's attachment can be appraised (Ainsworth, 1984a, p. 6). This usage is consistent with Sroufe's contention that

> A healthy pattern of adaptation is one which promotes a flexible, effective behavioral organization with respect to subsequent issues (in behavioral development); an unhealthy pattern is one which does not (1983, p. 46).

It is unclear whether ethological attachment theorists believe that adaptiveness in the developmental mental health sense bears any relationship to adaptiveness in the inclusive fitness sense, and there is no reason for us to assume that the two types of adaptation are related. Thus, behavioral patterns that are "adaptive" in human evolution *may* have little or no relevance to healthy psychological functioning. Confusion about these different conceptions of adaptation has contributed to considerable confusion about the psychological significance of different patterns of attachment.

From either perspective, furthermore, we question the usefulness of a general concept of adaptation defined by "flexible behavioral organization." The claim that secure attachment promotes flexible, effective behavioral organization appears to endow some infants but not others with a excessively generalized non-specific adaptation, good for any and all environmental tests. (It is also not clearly supported by the empirical evidence, as reported in Chapter 9.) It is thus misleading to reify adaptiveness into a general trait: More appropriately, adaptiveness refers to the consequences (for either inclusive fitness or particular aspects of later functioning) of specific patterns of behavior in particular stages of the life-span.

In all, it is apparent that more precise and consistent definitions of adaptation are required in considering the implications of different patterns of infantile attachment. Behaviors that were phylogenetically "adaptive" in the environment of evolutionary adaptedness may have little or no significance for psychological functioning in contemporary settings. This is especially true if alternative attachment patterns reflect equally adaptive accomodations to different rearing conditions (see below). Behaviors may also be adaptive for specified portions of the life-span (i.e., juvenile vs. ontogenetic adaptation, which means that assumptions about the general-ized, long-term benefits of secure attachment are misleading. Thus, whereas attachment behaviors may be adaptive for infants (in a fitness sense), we must be cautious about infering implications for psychological functioning or mental health.

The "Ideal Single Pattern" Model

The modern biological view of adaptation also leads us to question the belief that there is a single, normative, pattern of parental behavior forming the sole adaptive niche for human infants, and that infantile behavior must also accord with a single adaptive behavioral template.

As mentioned earlier, the assumption that adults can always be expected to respond appropriately is dubious at best. In general, they should be willing to expend resources and take risks for their own children and close relatives, and even then parental behavior toward any given infant will be a function of, among other things: the social context of child rearing; the temporal, energetic, and physical resources available to the parent; the alternative uses the parent could make of these resources; and the parent's sex, since the costs and benefits of parental investment are different for males and females (Lamb, Pleck, Charnov, & Levine, in press; Trivers, 1974). Behavioral ecologists note that stable behavioral strategies are typically both conditional (i.e., dependent on the relative costs and benefits of alternative strategies) and, more specifically, frequency dependent (Maynard Smith, 1982, 1984). In other words, the optimal strategy for any individual may vary depending on what others are doing, and in many cases it may be beneficial to adopt a strategy different from that which others adopt. (As an everyday example, when the preference of the majority for a freeway route ensures congestion, an individual may do well to choose a route via secondary roads on which there is little traffic.) Since the selection of an optimal strategy depends on such ecological factors, it seems unlikely that there is a single adaptive pattern of parental behavior and a single adaptive pattern of infantile behavior to which we can expect all potentially successful parents and infants to adhere.

In a recent article, Hinde (1982) has clearly identified the fallacy of viewing a single pattern of parental behavior as adaptive:

> the picture of an environment of evolutionary adaptedness serves well enough as a first stage in our thinking. But as we go beyond that, we must accept that individuals differ and society is complex, and that mothers and babies will be programmed not simply to form one sort of relationship but a range of possible relationships according to circumstances. So we must be concerned not with normal mothers and deviant mothers but with a *range* of styles and a capacity to select appropriately between them.
>
> At one level of approximation, there are general properties of mothering necessary whatever the circumstances. At a more precise level, the optimal mothering behavior will differ according to the sex of the infant, its ordinal position in the family, the mother's social status, caregiving contributions from other family members, the state of physical resources, and so on. *Natural selection must surely have operated to produce conditional maternal strategies, not stereotypy.* (Italics in original; p. 71)

The same applies to individual differences in infant behavior: There is no a priori reason to believe that the B pattern is necessarily "more adaptive" (in a fitness sense) than either the A or C pattern. Indeed, these patterns may represent adjustments by infants to varying styles of parental care.[1] Main (1981) has, for example, described infantile avoidance as an adaptive strategy under certain conditions. The A, B, and C patterns may thus be equally adaptive, such that in specific circumstances, the "avoidant," "secure," and "resistant" patterns represent appropriate adjustments designed to maximize the infants' chances of living to reproductive maturity, given particular circumstances. There may therefore be no differences between A, B, and C infants in adulthood because these behavioral patterns simply represent alternative pathways to maturity, given the constraints and characteristics of specific rearing environments. As we have earlier suggested, it would confer greater flexibility if infants were capable of coping in this way with a variety of niches, rather than only with one entailing sensitive parenting.

Like Hinde, we believe that natural selection is likely to produce *conditional strategies* that lead to different patterns of behavior in different environments. Thus although it is possible that genetic differences underlie individual differences in attachment (cf. Ainsworth, 1984a, ms. pp. 9-10), the alternative interpretation offered by Hinde proposes that natural selection could have equipped *each* normal human infant with a set of different behavioral strategies from which one can be selected depending on the specific physical and social environment encountered. As this interpretation implies, however, there may be more than three attachment patterns fostered by natural selection, suggesting that there are multiple pathways to A, B, and C patterns of Strange Situation behavior, and that alternative patterns of infantile behavior may emerge when different assessment procedures are employed. A similar argument applies to parental behavior: Parents may be equipped with a set of child rearing strategies (vastly augmented and elaborated by cultural transformation) that can be adopted selectively in response to the emerging characteristics of their newborns and of their ecological conditions.

Consistent with this, one could interpret cross-cultural differences in the distribution of children into A, B, and C groups to mean that the existing categories of Strange Situation behavior are not consequences of corres-pondence to or deviation from a single adaptive pattern of parenting, but rather different patterns of adaptive parental and infantile accomodation to various ecological conditions. As discussed more fully in Chapter 11, the

---

[1]Lamb (1981a, 1981b), for example, has suggested that all three patterns can be seen as behavioral manifestations of the infants' expectations regarding the likely behavior of their parents in the Strange Situation.

North German sample reported by Grossmann et al. (1981) contained a far higher proportion of A group children and many fewer B group children (49%A, 33%B, 12%C) than do most US samples, which yield approximately 20% A, 65% B, and 15% C group infants. The sample collected from several Israeli kibbutzim (Lamb et al., 1982; Sagi, Lamb, Estes, Lewkowicz, Shoham, & Dvir, 1982; Sagi, Lamb, Lewkowicz, Shoham, Dvir, & Estes, in press) produced an exceptional number of C group babies relative to American norms (35% C, 9% A, 56% B). If we believe that the B pattern is adaptive and species-typical, then these differences imply that the North German and Israeli kibbutzim cultures are maladaptive environments for child development. This conclusion seems premature, however, in the absence of much evidence regarding the convergent and predictive validity of Strange Situation classifications in these cultures. As Miyake, Chen, and Campos (in press) note,

> There has often been a subtle implication that the Ainsworth B pattern represents the one to which the human infant is phylogenetically adapted, and that the A and C classifications reflect failures of adaptation (i.e., "insecure attachment"). We believe that this facile equation of index with construct is misleading within national groups and is especially problematic in cross-national comparisons. In cognitive development, it is well- known that inferences about level or cognitive competence in a cultural group often differ depending upon the appropriateness of the materials used for the cognitive assessment. Similar contextual factors constrain inferences about level of social competence from observations of specific levels of social behavior. (Miyake et al., in press, ms. p.23)

Although this criticism concerns the appropriateness of the Strange Situation for making cross-cultural comparisons regarding attachment security (see Chapter 11), these researchers also question the extent to which parental and infantile behaviors are adaptive *in different ways* in different ecological (e.g., cultural) conditions. Judging non-American patterns in terms of American norms may thus be highly misleading.

Such a conclusion has important implications for our appraisal of individual differences in both parental and infantile behavior. From the standpoint of the parent, it is inappropriate to expect consistently sensitive responsiveness to infant cues as an evolutionary norm, both because parental insensitivity may be adaptive on certain occasions, and also because the fitness value of sensitivity varies according to the ecological circumstances. This conclusion raises interesting questions about the factors which may make parental insensitivity more adaptive in a fitness sense, and how these factors change with the child's development (Trivers, 1974). Study of such questions by developmentalists with a biological orientation will take us beyond simple models of parenting to a more sophisticated understanding of the fitness implications of variations in parental behavior.

From the infant's standpoint, it may be equally misleading to consider the B pattern of Strange Situation behavior as species-appropriate and the A and C patterns as maladaptive deviations. Rather, each pattern may represent a unique adaptation to a specific ecological niche, and there is no reason to assume that natural selection has mandated only three such alternatives. Viewed from this perspective, it therefore becomes important to specify *how* these alternative patterns may be adaptive under *what* caregiving circumstances (cf. Lamb, 1981a, 1981b; Main, 1981). Such a perspective would cast doubt on the usefulness of studies designed to confirm the association between B-type Strange Situation behavior and a variety of positive correlates or between A- and C-type behavior and negative behavioral correlates.

Efforts to relate Strange Situation behavior to a variety of contemporaneous and predictive correlates are hampered by considerable confusion concerning the meaning of the term, "adaptation." As we have concluded, adaptation has different meanings when viewed phylogenetically, ontogenetically, and in an evaluative, "developmental mental health" sense, and there is no reason to assume that different types of adaptation are related. Thus phylogenetic adaptation need not confer optimal psychological functioning on the developing organism. In addition, concepts of adaptation have been defined with excessive generality by many attachment theorists, further undermining theoretical efforts to identify *why* and *under what circumstances* patterns of attachment should have advantages for contemporary infants. Taken together, the failure to distinguish various types of adaptation and excessive generality in the definition of "adaptation" has fostered theoretical ambiguity about the immediate and long-term significance of secure or insecure attachments. This ambiguity also has important implications for research design, since it means that researchers—in the absence of more specific, theory-driven hypotheses—have tended to look for associations between B group behavior and a broad range of optimal outcomes, and links between A- or C-group behavior with more negative or maladaptive outcomes (see Chapters 5, 9, and 11).

In the end, these issues illustrate the fact that considerable work remains to be done on the applications of evolutionary biology to issues of infant-parent relationships. While the relevance of evolutionary formulations to relationship patterns are neither as clear nor as direct as they were when Bowlby (1969) developed his theory, they are nevertheless important both to developmental psychologists and to evolutionary biologists. Because of their direct links to issues of inclusive fitness, study of the dynamics of parent-offspring interaction are likely to further evolutionary thinking in useful ways. For attachment researchers, they are likely to lead to clearer conceptualizations of the meaning and significance of alternative patterns of attachment, as well as the derivation of more specific, testable hypotheses.

These points are especially important if one considers that a different set of groups might have emerged if the classification system had been developed from a non-American sample. It is worth recalling that the A, B, and C groups were not described on the basis of predictions from evolutionary biology concerning an adaptive pattern of behavior and two maladaptive patterns, but rather as an empirical summary of similarities among pairs or groups of infants. Three groups were originally devised to reflect low, moderate, and high degrees of separation distress (Ainsworth & Wittig, 1969). Only later did the focus shift to reunion behavior—"not because of preconceived theoretical convictions but because behavior in the reunion episodes contributed the most convincing evidence of clustering behaviors, in contrast to a continuous distribution along one or even two major dimensions" (Ainsworth et al., 1978, p. 59). Thus the classification system was empirical in origin, rather than theoretically motivated. This is underscored by the experience of many investigators (e.g., Main & Weston, 1981; Miyake et al., in press; Egeland & Sroufe, 1981a), who report that infants do not always fit into the available categories. It is possible that an entirely different classification system might have emerged if it was derived from an intuitive search for clusters using Grossmann et al.'s (1981) North German sample (in which the frequency of A group relationships was greater than in the U.S.), or using Sagi et al.'s (in press) sample of infants from Israeli kibbutzim (who were much more likely to fall into the C group), or Miyake's Japanese samples (in which no avoidant infants have yet been found). Because of the post hoc way in which the groups and sub-groups were initially identified, we should be cautious of describing some patterns as more evolutionarily adaptive than others.

Fortunately, it is not necessary to interpret cross-cultural differences in the distribution of children into A-B-C patterns as evidence of maladaptive parenting or maladaptive infantile behavior. Instead, one could argue, as we do more fully in Chapter 11, that the cross-cultural differences represent behavioral strategies developed in response to a particular set of environmental conditions. In that sense, the avoidant behavior of the modal North German baby may indeed be adaptive because the child is accommodating its behavior to the independence training initiated by its parents. As Hinde points out, therefore:

> We must consider the possibility that not only may the best mothering style vary with the situation,...but also the significance of the strange-situation categories, in terms of predictions for other situations, may not be absolute and biologically based but may, in fact, differ among cultures (1982, p. 73).

And, one might add, within cultures as well.

We are clearly sympathetic with Hinde's (1982, 1983) views regarding individual differences in attachment. It is probably more useful to view them as conditional strategies rather than as variations from a single normative pattern. However, the *meaning* of the differences remains uncertain, and a thorough reevaluation of the fitness consequences of individual differences in attachment is clearly in order.

SUMMARY

One conclusion emerging from this reconsideration of attachment theory is that, in light of current theory in evolutionary biology, it is not easy to designate certain behavioral patterns as adaptive or maladaptive. Although not all behavioral patterns are equally adaptive, of course, it is clear that there is no single, species-appropriate pattern or template of behavior against which all other patterns can be evaluated. More plausibly, persons are equipped with a flexible repertoire, the selection from which depends on the specific environment in which he or she lives, the behaviors of others, and the person's inherent characteristics. Thus the evaluation of adaptation—even in a phylogenetic sense—must take into account the individual's current living conditions, not just the environmental circumstances of evolutionary adaptation.

Such a conclusion has important implications for our appraisal of individual differences in both parental and infantile behavior. From the standpoint of the parent, it is inappropriate to expect consistently sensitive responsiveness to infant cues as an evolutionary norm, both because parental insensitivity may be adaptive on certain occasions, and also because the fitness value of sensitivity varies according to the ecological circumstances. This conclusion raises interesting questions about the factors which may make parental insensitivity more adaptive in a fitness sense, and how these factors change with the child's development (Trivers, 1974). Study of such questions by developmentalists with a biological orientation will take us beyond simple models of parenting to a more sophisticated understanding of the fitness implications of variations in parental behavior.

From the infant's standpoint, it may be equally misleading to consider the B pattern of Strange Situation behavior as species-appropriate and the A and C patterns as maladaptive deviations. Rather, each pattern may represent a unique adaptation to a specific ecological niche, and there is no reason to assume that natural selection has mandated only three such alternatives. Viewed from this perspective, it therefore becomes important to specify *how* these alternative patterns may be adaptive under *what* caregiving circumstances (cf. Lamb, 1981a, 1981b; Main, 1981). Such a perspective would cast doubt on the usefulness of studies designed to confirm the association between B-type Strange Situation behavior and a variety of positive correlates or between A- and C-type behavior and negative behavioral correlates.

Efforts to relate Strange Situation behavior to a variety of contemporaneous and predictive correlates are hampered by considerable confusion concerning the meaning of the term, "adaptation." As we have concluded, adaptation has different meanings when viewed phylogenetically, ontogenetically, and in an evaluative, "developmental mental health" sense, and there is no reason to assume that different types of adaptation are related. Thus phylogenetic adaptation need not confer optimal psychological functioning on the developing organism. In addition, concepts of adaptation have been defined with excessive generality by many attachment theorists, further undermining theoretical efforts to identify *why* and *under what circumstances* patterns of attachment should have advantages for contemporary infants. Taken together, the failure to distinguish various types of adaptation and excessive generality in the definition of "adaptation" has fostered theoretical ambiguity about the immediate and long-term significance of secure or insecure attachments. This ambiguity also has important implications for research design, since it means that researchers—in the absence of more specific, theory-driven hypotheses—have tended to look for associations between B group behavior and a broad range of optimal outcomes, and links between A- or C-group behavior with more negative or maladaptive outcomes (see Chapters 5, 9, and 11).

In the end, these issues illustrate the fact that considerable work remains to be done on the applications of evolutionary biology to issues of infant-parent relationships. While the relevance of evolutionary formulations to relationship patterns are neither as clear nor as direct as they were when Bowlby (1969) developed his theory, they are nevertheless important both to developmental psychologists and to evolutionary biologists. Because of their direct links to issues of inclusive fitness, study of the dynamics of parent-offspring interaction are likely to further evolutionary thinking in useful ways. For attachment researchers, they are likely to lead to clearer conceptualizations of the meaning and significance of alternative patterns of attachment, as well as the derivation of more specific, testable hypotheses.

5 PARENT–INFANT INTERACTION AND SUBSEQUENT STRANGE SITUATION BEHAVIOR

INTRODUCTION

The popularity of the Strange Situation procedure is due in large measure to the pervasiveness of claims regarding its validity and reliability. The major evidence for claims regarding its validity is drawn from two sorts of studies. One body of studies is concerned with the relationship between Strange Situation behavior and subsequent behavior in a variety of settings with different social partners and a range of task demands. These studies of predictive validity are reviewed in Chapter 9. The other body of studies is concerned with the relationship between prior parent–infant interaction or parental behavior and subsequent Strange Situation behavior. These studies constitute the main basis for claiming that the Strange Situation assesses the quality of the infant–parent relationship. Simply put, the claim here is that sensitively responsive parental behavior produces secure (i.e., B-type) Strange Situation behavior, whereas insensitive parental behavior is associated with insecure (A-type or C-type) infantile behavior in the Strange Situation.

In this chapter, we focus on studies in which attempts have been made to relate infant behavior in the Strange Situation to prior characteristics of parent–infant interaction or parental behavior in order to elucidate the origins or antecedents of individual differences in the security of attachment. The central hypothesis under consideration here is that securely-attached infants have more sensitively responsive caretakers than infants who behave insecurely in the Strange Situation and that the patterns of caretaking associated with the two insecure classifications should also differ. In certain key respects, the hypotheses of attachment theory differ from those offered by social learning theorists (see Ainsworth, 1969, and Rajecki et al., 1978, for a summary of these differences). For example, social learning theorists proposed that prompt responsiveness to infant crying would render infants more likely to cry, whereas attachment theorists predicted that it would make infants less likely to cry because adults were behaving appropriately. Appropriate parental behavior was also expected to yield "secure" Strange Situation behavior. This hypothesis was most explicitly developed in Ainsworth's pioneering longitudinal study (see Ainsworth, 1979a; Ainsworth et al., 1978; Ainsworth, Bell, & Stayton, 1974, for reviews). Only recently has this hypothesis been addressed empirically by other researchers, and thus we pay especially close attention to Ainsworth's widely-cited study in our review.

THE BALTIMORE LONGITUDINAL STUDY

Ainsworth's study involved a total of 26 infants from middle class homes in Baltimore, Maryland. Each infant–mother dyad was observed at home, usually for four hours every three weeks throughout the first year by the same one of four observers, who made notes on their interaction during the visits, and later dictated a narrative account on the basis of these notes. Time-markers were included irregularly by the observers, so the duration of activities could only be estimated very roughly. The narrative accounts included objective reports of the interaction, evaluative comments by the observer, and a summary of statements made by the mother about the baby or her own attitudes toward child care.

When the infants were 51 weeks old, they came to the University for assessment in the Strange Situation. During these sessions, two or three individuals dictated accounts of or made notes concerning the infants' (and to a lesser extent, adults') behavior. These narratives were later collated into a combined account (Ainsworth & Wittig, 1969). No conventional measures of interobserver reliability during home observations were obtained, although there were occasional joint visits with a second observer. In the laboratory (Strange Situation), interobserver agreement was calculated for some frequency behavioral measures, but not for the interactive scales relevant to the classification of Strange Situation behavior. Intercoder agreement for certain frequency measures and the interactive scales, based on scoring of the observational narratives, was satisfactory. For three infants, behavior in the Strange Situation was missing or was considered atypical (e.g., the child was sick when observed) and thus relationships between home and Strange Situation behavior were estimated based on data from only 23 infants and mothers.

The three groups and seven original subgroups were derived by seeking similarities among two or more infants, who were then defined as members of a subgroup. Subsequently, Ainsworth and her colleagues searched for similarities between subgroup clusters, and thus the three major groups or classifications were formed. In the initial attempts to identify groups and subgroups, the focus was on responses to separation, but it later shifted to reunion behavior. Of the 23 infants, 13 infants were considered secure (1 as B_1, 3 as B_2, 9 as B_3), 6 were rated as avoidant (4 as A_1, 2 as A_2) and 4 were rated resistant (2 as C_1, 2 as C_2)[1]. The classification system devised by Ainsworth and her colleagues has since become standard among researchers in this area.

Ainsworth and her colleagues (1971) then explored relationships between Strange Situation behavior and patterns of infant behavior at home. The sample was divided into five groups by assessing the quality of the baby's attachment-exploration balance at home during the fourth quarter as reflected in the transcripts. Inspection of the data suggested that the B—especially B_3—infants exhibited a better attachment-exploration balance at home, with most of the A and C group infants apparently failing to use their mothers as secure bases for exploration. However, the A, C, B_1, and B_2 groups were not well distinguished from one another on this index.

Ainsworth also focused on maternal behavior, scoring trans-contextual dimensions such as "maternal sensitivity" (Ainsworth et al., 1971, 1972, 1974) as well as behavior in specific contexts—such as separation and reunion (Stayton & Ainsworth, 1973), feeding (Ainsworth & Bell, 1969), discipline and socialization (Stayton, Hogan, & Ainsworth, 1971), crying and distress relief (Bell & Ainsworth, 1972), face-to-face interaction (Blehar, Lieberman & Ainsworth, 1977), physical contact interaction (Ainsworth et al., 1972; Ainsworth, 1979a), and the display of maternal affection (Tracy & Ainsworth, 1981). Twenty-two rating scales were constructed to assess maternal behavior during the first quarter year of life, with a mean score on each scale being based on the four to six visits from that quarter (Ainsworth et al., 1978). Since this was intended to be an hypothesis-generating study, scales were defined after examination of the narratives, rather than a priori. Only six of the 22 scales were discussed by Ainsworth and Bell (1969), and only four scales dealing with feeding were considered by Ainsworth et al. (1978). (The results obtained using the remaining scales have not been reported.) The emphasis on scales pertaining to feeding was justified by noting that

> during the earliest weeks the largest proportion of interaction between an infant and his mother has reference to feeding. Moreover, as suggested by

---

[1]The B_4 subgroup was added to the classificatory system after Bell's (1970) study.

Brody (1956), "...most things that a mother does with her infant, however unrelated in style they may be to each other, are related to her style of feeding behavior with him." (Ainsworth & Bell, 1969, pp. 134–135).

In addition to these measures of specific behavioral dimensions, four transcontextual scales were rated from the fourth quarter narratives—sensitivity, cooperation, acceptance, and accessibility—because they "seemed especially related to individual differences in the baby's response to the mother" (Ainsworth et al., 1978, p. 138). Later, two broad ratings pertaining to physical contact interaction, one related to emotional expressiveness, and one to maternal rigidity were made (Ainsworth et al., 1978). At least 10 other more quantitative measures, tapping either the proportion of opportunities mothers behaved in certain ways or the average duration of events such as "unresponsiveness to distress," were scored using narratives from each quarter year, although Ainsworth et al. (1978) only reported scores from the first and fourth quarters.

The summary of findings by Ainsworth et al. (1978) only discusses results involving the measures (many reported for only one quarter) mentioned earlier, although earlier reports describe others, including two in the Ainsworth and Bell (1969) paper concerned with feeding and nine measures of face-to-face interaction in the first quarter scored by Blehar et al. (1977). It is not clear, therefore, exactly how many different measures were scored from the narratives. Interrater reliability (based on the transcribed narratives) was usually highly satisfactory.

The results of Ainsworth's important study have been reviewed many times, most fully in Ainsworth et al.'s (1978) monograph, and most recently by Ainsworth (1983). Our own summary of the findings follows.

The analyses of maternal behavior in specific contexts generally yielded results consistent with those obtained in analyses of the broad transcontextual maternal characteristics. In each case, the principal dimension underlying individual differences in infant–mother interaction was one that had to do with the mother's sensitivity and "appropriate" responsiveness to infant cues. For example, of 14 fourth quarter measures of maternal behavior discussed by Ainsworth et al. (1978), eight showed significant differences between the B and A groups, and eight showed differences between the B and C groups. The largest differences were on the four transcontextual dimensions, with the B group mothers being much more sensitive, accessible, cooperative, and accepting than the mothers of A and C group infants. All but three of the 17 first quarter and whole year measures reported by Ainsworth et al. (1978) yielded differences between the B and non-B group mothers, including differences on measures of behavior during episodes of feeding and close contact with the baby. Eight of the 12 measures of maternal or dyadic behavior during face-to-face interaction in the first quarter revealed differences between the mothers of B_3 infants and the mothers of C and A infants (Blehar et al. 1977). In every case, analyses indicated that the B_3 mothers engaged in better-paced, more satisfying, and better-rounded interaction than did the mothers of other infants. In these analyses, the B_1 and B_2 infants and mothers were excluded "out of a desire to obtain the clearest possible contrast between infants who had developed the most [B_3] and least [A, C] secure attachments" (Blehar et al., 1977, p. 186), although their means differed significantly from those of the B_3 dyads on only one of 12 measures.[2] Individual differences on some of these measures were fairly stable over the first year (e.g., Bell & Ainsworth, 1972).

The transcripts from Ainsworth's study were later analyzed by Main and Stadtman (1981), who coded maternal aversion to physical contact from the first quarter narratives. They reported fairly high stability over the first year (r's = .51, .67, .72) and moderate to high correlation with fourth-quarter ratings of the infants' overt aggression to mother ($r = .44$) and of the extent to which anger dominated the infants' mood ($r = .65$). Data from other samples suggested moderate correlations between contemporaneous assessments of maternal aversion to contact and infant conflict behavior.

It is important to note that infant behavior also differed by group in these early home observations. For example, infants later deemed insecurely-attached cried more and showed fewer positive responses to being held than did securely-attached infants in both the first- and fourth-quarters (Ainsworth et al., 1978; see also Blehar, Lieberman, & Ainsworth, 1977). Since both maternal and infant behaviors were rated from the same obervational narratives, however, interpretation of these findings is difficult (e.g., did persistent infant crying cause or result from maternal unresponsiveness).

Overall, the findings obtained in Ainsworth's longitudinal study are less compelling than they appear at first glance. First, although it is often suggested that the overall pattern of findings from Ainsworth's study provides compelling support for hypotheses concerning the effects of parental behavior on infantile behavior in the Strange Situation, this conclusion is not warranted in view of the confounding of maternal and infant influences during the home observations. Furthermore, the measures were not mutually exclusive; indeed, intercorrelations among them—especially the transcontextual dimensions—were extremely high. For

[2]Note that in various analyses, Ainsworth and her colleagues sometimes chose to compare B with non-B group infants, sometimes B_3 with insecure (A and C) infants, and sometimes all three of the groups. Such inconsistency is understandable in an hypothesis-generating study, but it does of course capitalize on chance and thus leads to overstatements and overgeneralizations.

example, Ainsworth and Bell (1969, p. 159) reported intercorrelations among six maternal rating scales; *all* inter-correlations were above .80 and nearly half were at or above .90! Despite the proliferation of measures, therefore, the evidence suggests—as Ainsworth et al. (1978) acknowledged—that there is really one primary dimension tapped by all the measures used in this study: the harmony of mother–infant interaction. Furthermore, all measures for each observational context were scored from the same narratives and often involved examination of the same behavior sequences. Since the measures were non-independent, the reliability of the results cannot be assessed by determining what proportion of the measures show significant group differences. Moreover, the extraordinarily low ratio of subjects to variables and the conceptual and statistical interrelations among the variables ensure that individual significance tests provide no real protection against capitalization on chance. There are simply not enough independent measures to reveal a pattern of findings.

Second, although a general theoretical orientation clearly guided the selection of dependent measures, the specific measures themselves were not derived on a priori theoretical grounds; instead they were developed after an examination of the narratives. Thus, all results must be replicated in independent samples before they can be considered reliable. The use of naive raters provides very little protection against capitalization on differences detected during the measurement construction phase, because these measures were all derived by individuals who were familiar with the classification status of the infants and with the general theoretical framework. The fact that group differences later "emerged" on measures chosen in this fashion is neither surprising nor informative. Independent replication would help assure the reliability and generalizability of the findings.

Third, despite striking differences in infant behavior in the Strange Situation, the mothers of babies in groups A and C differed from each other less than they did from the mothers of babies in group B. This is a problem if one wishes to view individual differences in infantile Strange Situation behavior as the consequence of variations in parental behavior. Among the few reported differences between A and C mothers are differences in ratings of compulsiveness and rigidity, with the six mothers of avoidant infants being rated more compulsive and rigid than the four mothers of C group infants (Ainsworth, 1979a). Whatever the reason for the more frequent similarities than differences between A and C group means, the absence of clear differences between mothers of infants in these groups precludes a conclusion that behavior in the Strange Situation is lawfully determined by prior patterns of infant–mother interaction.

Just as the absence of clear differences between the A and C mothers is problematic, subgroup differences preclude simple statements about the groups as well. On the sensitivity ratings for the fourth quarter, the groups were ranked $B_3 > B_{1,2} > A_2 C_1 A_1 C_2$; on acceptance–rejection, $B_3 > B_{1,2} > C_{1,2} > A_2 A_1$; on cooperation–interference, $B_3 > B_{1,2} A_2 > C_{2,1} A_1$; and on accessibility–ignoring, $B_3 > B_{1,2} > C_1 A_1 > C_2 A_2$ (Ainsworth et al., 1971). No statistical tests of these rankings were provided, but there appear to have been important differences across measures in the rankings of the C and A subgroups, despite high intercorrelations among measures.

Fourth, observer reliability was never assessed in the homes and was inadequately assessed in the Strange Situation, providing an opportunity for contamination of data that should, for analytic purposes, have been independent. Some of the individuals observing behavior in the Strange Situation were aware of the infants' prior behavior at home, even if they were unaware of the specific measures that would be derived later. Thus the two data sets were not independent of one another. Furthermore, the fact that the same individuals observed each family at home throughout the year without quantitative checks on reliability means that there was extensive opportunity for bias to color all data concerning a given family—especially since the observers included subjective evaluations in their narratives, which may have had an impact on the ratings or codings. Unfortunately, scores on the more quantitative measures are also questionable because details were often recorded imprecisely, and all the duration measures had to be estimated years later by an assistant who reviewed the narratives and guessed at the duration of the activities reported. All in all, even with high agreement between independent raters who were naive regarding hypotheses and Strange Situation classifications, the unknown reliability of the raw data is critical.

Fifth, it is important not to over-interpret and over-generalize small differences between small groups or subgroups. For example, a group difference in maternal unresponsiveness to crying in the first quarter led to the conclusion that "Mothers who are promptly responsive to crying signals in the early months have babies who later become securely attached" (Ainsworth et al., 1978, p. 150). In fact, when the measure is expressed as a proportion (Maternal unresponsiveness per hour/Infant crying per hour), mothers of A and B infants are equivalent, and the deviant group (C) contains only four dyads. Similarly, on the basis of a net difference between A and B infants of .7 physical interventions per four-hour visit, it was concluded that "Mothers of A babies . . .more frequently use forcible physical interventions" (Ainsworth et al., 1978, p. 147), even though the finding does not reach conventional levels of significance. A sample of 23 mothers and infants is simply too small to reveal reliable and generalizable differences between three groups.

For all these reasons, this initial longitudinal study must be viewed as an hypothesis-generating pilot study—not an hypothesis-testing investigation.

It remains for future researchers to explore the hypotheses raised by Ainsworth through studies that attempt to control for bias, to estimate observer reliability, to state hypotheses a priori, and which employ adequately large samples to permit identification and explanation of differences between infants and mothers in all three groups. Indeed, the interpretational cautions we have mentioned would not be as important if developmentalists were more careful to describe Ainsworth's data as the source, rather than the confirmation of, hypotheses concerning the antecedents of Strange Situation behavior. Clearly, some of the problems we have identified would not be shortcomings in an hypothesis-generating study, but the findings can obtain generalizability only when replicated in independent studies. In fact, Ainsworth's hypotheses have stimulated a number of longitudinal studies, and it is to their results that we now turn.

THE MINNEAPOLIS STUDY OF DISADVANTAGED FAMILIES

The largest attempted replication (Egeland & Farber, 1982, 1984[3]) began with 267 primiparae and their infants, 212 of whom were observed in the Strange Situation at 12 months and 197 of whom were assessed again at 18 months (189 at both ages). Many of the mothers were poor and the majority (62%) were single; 55% of the infants were boys.

A large number of measures were obtained on the dyads in this sample. Both prenatally and 3-months postnatally, the mothers completed a battery of psychological tests tapping aspects of their personality, attitudes, and life stresses.[4] These tests yielded at least 17 scores each time. Maternal reports of life stresses were obtained at 12 and 18 months, and an inventory of living arrangements was completed at 6, 12, 18, and 24 months; a variety of measures were constructed from this. Nurses' ratings of the newborns and their mothers were factor analyzed to yield four factor scores tapping infant and maternal characteristics. Infant characteristics were also measured by the Brazelton Neonatal Behavioral Assessment Scale (six scores derived from each of two administrations, see Vaughn, Crichton, & Egeland, 1982), maternal reports of infant temperament at 6 months using Carey's (1970)

---

[3]Portions of the data reported by Egeland and Farber (1982) and Farber (1981) in unpublished reports were later published by Egeland and Farber (1984). In our summary of their findings we have relied upon the more inclusive unpublished reports, although we have turned to the published report for clarification when it provides information not contained in the unpublished papers.

[4]In several instances, fuller details about the number of measures and the manner in which they were derived are contained in other reports from the study, rather than in the Egeland and Farber (1984) report.

Infant Temperament Questionnaire (yielding 10 scores) and Bayley mental and motor scale scores at nine months. Mother–infant interaction was assessed by observations of feeding at 3 months (once) and 6 months (twice) and of infant–mother play at 6 months (once). At least 20 measures were obtained from the feeding observations at each age (measures were averaged across the two six-month observations), and 12 were obtained from the 6-month play observation. Inter-rater agreement for these measures was only moderate. In addition, maternal sensitivity and cooperation were rated during the feeding sessions at 6 months using Ainsworth's scales.

Multivariate analyses of variance (MANOVAs), one way ANOVAs, and subsequent Newman–Keuls tests were used to compare A, B, and C group infants using both the 12- and 18-month Strange Situation classifications. The sample was also divided into two subsamples on the basis of infant sex and the same statistical tests were performed.

With respect to maternal characteristics, an attachment group by sex MANOVA (using 12-month classifications) yielded no significant effects for either factor for either the prenatal or 3-month variables, although there was a significant interaction in analysis of the 3-month variables. Egeland and Farber (1984) did not report the results of MANOVAs using the 18-month attachment classifications. In the 1982 report, however, 11 of the more than 60 tests relating maternal characteristics (prenatal or postnatal) to Strange Situation classifications at either age yielded significant group differences. However, in no case were the same measures significantly related to both 12- and 18-month classifications. On nine measures, the B group means were significantly distinguished from those of only one of the insecure groups; the one exception was that the 18-month B group mothers were less aggressive than both the A and C group mothers, both prenatally and postnatally. Further, both pre- and postnatal maternal scores on only two measures were related to either one of the classifications (i.e., aggression and feelings of competence). Among boys, only five of the 60 tests revealed significant relationships between Strange Situation classifications and maternal characteristics (and in only three cases were post hoc contrasts between B and non B group infants significant), while among girls, nine tests (six contrasts) were significant. In the tests involving the subsamples of boys and girls, only five of the significant effects were comparable to those obtained for the full sample, and none of these was significant for both boys and girls. These results, taken together, reveal few relationships between maternal characteristics and the Strange Situation behavior that were reliable or consistent. Further, most of the variables on which group differences might be predicted (e.g., certain measures of maternal personality) failed to demonstrate any.

No overall MANOVA for infant variables using 12-month attachment classification and sex as factors was reported, although MANOVAs were conducted using specific subsets of these variables (Egeland & Farber, 1984). These revealed: (1) a significant main effect for attachment group on the nurses' neonatal ratings, but no effects for sex and no interaction; (2) no attachment or attachment by sex interaction on the Brazelton scores, although there was a main effect for sex; and (3) no effects at all on the Carey temperament scores. Again, the results of similar MANOVAs using the 18-month classifications as an independent variable were not reported. In the 1982 report, however, six measures of infant characteristics showed significant group differences (using either 12- or 18-month classifications), although only three revealed significant post hoc contrasts distinguishing B group infants from the others. There were more relationships between infant characteristics and 12-month than with 18-month classifications (four vs. one), but in no case was the same factor related to both 12- and 18-month assessments. Separate comparisons involving the male and female sub-groups revealed three significant ANOVAs for boys and five for girls, with only three of the eight yielding a pattern of group differences similar to that for the sample as a whole. Once again, none of the differences characterized both subsamples and the total sample. There was thus no clear and consistent pattern of relationships between infant characteristics and the pattern of Strange Situation behavior.[5]

With respect to the feeding and play observations, separate MANOVAs were conducted for each group of variables using 12-month attachment classifications and infant gender as factors (Egeland & Farber, 1984). These revealed: (1) only a significant effect for attachment group on the 3-month feeding scores; (2) only an attachment group by sex interaction on the 6-month feeding scores; and (3) only a significant attachment group effect on the 6-month play session variables. Again, the results of MANOVAs using the 18-month classifications were not reported. In the 1982 manuscript, however, Egeland and Farber reported that out of more than 100 tests, six of the 3-month feeding variables, six of the 6-month feeding variables, and three of the 6-month play variables were significantly related to the 12-month classifications, whereas only one, three, and one of the respective variable sets were related to the 18-month assessments. Of these 20 variables, 12 yielded significant B vs. non-B group contrasts. In no instance was the same variable related to both assessments of attachment security. On only one feeding variable—"determination of beginning of feeding"— scores from both 3-month and 6-month feedings were related similarly to 12-month attachment status, and this variable was unrelated to 18-month classification. Of the 19 significant overall relationships for boys and six for

---

[5]In a previous report involving 100 of these subjects and only the 12-month classifications, Waters, Vaughn, and Egeland (1980) analyzed data from the Brazelton scale assessments rather differently and reported somewhat different results. See Chapter 6 for further details.

girls, eight of those for boys and three of those for girls matched those for the total sample, but there were only two cases in which the same measures yielded significant effects for boys, girls, and the whole sample (i.e., frequency of maternal verbalization during the 3-month feeding and "facility in caretaking" in the 6-month feeding). In almost every case, pairwise contrasts revealed different effects among boys, girls, and the total sample.

Direct tests of predictions derived from Ainsworth's longitudinal study were few. Only two of the rating scales (cooperation and sensitivity) developed and used by Ainsworth were employed by Egeland and Farber (1982, 1984) and then only for the 6-month play and feeding sessions. On these measures, significant group differences consistent with Ainsworth's were apparent for the sample as a whole and for boys only. Unfortunately, however, these scales were related to the 12-month but not to the 18-month Strange Situation classifications. As indicated earlier, the measures providing less direct tests of Ainsworth's hypotheses yielded even more disappointing results.

Overall, this study provided modest insight into the antecedents of Strange Situation behavior and some support for hypotheses generated by Ainsworth's investigation. Notably, there were effects at 12 months on two Ainsworth scales comparable to those obtained in Ainsworth's longitudinal study, thus supporting Ainsworth's hypotheses. In addition, almost all of the significant group differences were in the predicted direction, with B group mothers being more perceptive, sensitive, and empathic. On the other hand, there were, on the whole, relatively few significant group differences, and there were also unpredicted sex differences, further suggesting that the few significant findings were unreliable. This impression is reinforced by the fact that the variables that did and did not distinguish the groups do not fit into an overall pattern that is theoretically interpretable. Furthermore, although one would expect fewer significant relationships between the independent variables and 18-month classifications than between these measures and the 12-month assessments simply because of attenuation due to the impact of intervening events, there is no a priori reason to expect *different* patterns of association with the two Strange Situation assessments, and none was predicted. Clearer insight might have been obtained if maternal characteristics were reassessed closer in time to each Strange Situation assessment, particularly between the two Strange Situation assessments.

Subanalyses of Data from The Minneapolis Study of Disadvantaged Families

Analyzing the data from a subsample ($N = 104$) of this study, Vaughn, Gove, and Egeland (1980) compared the attachment status at 12 and 18 months of infants whose mothers had returned to work by 12 months ("Early

Work," $N = 34$), between 12 and 18 months ("Late Work," $N = 18$), or not at all ("No Work," $N = 52$). The proportion of non-B group attachments was not significantly different across the three groups, but there were disproportionate numbers of avoidant infants in the Early Work (but not Late Work) group at both 12-month and 18-month assessments.

These results suggested that early maternal employment biases toward "insecure" relationships that are avoidant, but they did not indicate why these relationships tended to be insecure in the first place, since employment was not associated with an increase in the total number of insecure (i.e., A plus C) attachment classifications. Interpretation of these findings is complicated by the fact that family intactness (i.e., whether mother was a single parent or not) was confounded with maternal employment, and inspection of the data reveals that the heightened frequency of avoidant attachments in the Early Work group occurred primarily in single-parent families. Thus maternal employment per se may not affect attachment status; instead it may interact with other family characteristics.

Joffe (1981) drew data from another subsample involving 112 of those infants seen in the Strange Situation at 12 months and 69 of those seen at 18 months. Strange Situation classifications were related to 17 measures of maternal behavior and four measures of infant behavior in "Prohibition Situations" also occurring at 12 and 18 months. On the 12-month data, there were significant B vs. non-B group differences on one of the infant measures and one of the maternal measures, and significant A vs C group differences on two infant and four maternal behavior measures. On the 18-month data, there were significant B vs non-B group differences on one infant and nine maternal measures, but no significant A vs C group differences. Only one difference was found in both the 12- and 18-month data: B group infants were consistently more compliant than non-B group infants.

It is noteworthy that the one reliable difference reported was theoretically interpretable and was predicted a priori. However, the absence of other consistent differences on related measures on which differences should also have been found raises questions about the magnitude of group differences. In addition, there were no consistent differences in maternal behavior. We should finally note that this investigation was, of course, a study of contemporaneous rather than antecedent correlates of Strange Situation behavior.

Analyzing data from the whole sample, Pastor, Vaughn, Dodds, and Egeland (1981) found no overall relationship between maternal living arrangements and Strange Situation behavior at 12 months, although B group attachments were more common at 18 months when mothers were living with husbands or boyfriends than when they either had no such relationships or lived separately from the men. (See earlier discussion of Vaughn, Gove, & Egeland, 1980, for similar results.)

As with Egeland and Farber's (1982) and Joffe's (1981) results, these findings are difficult to evaluate because of differences in the correlates of 12 and 18 month Strange Situation classifications.[6]

Summary

Overall, therefore, these subanalyses of the Minneapolis Study of Disadvantaged Families do not reveal much about the antecedents of Strange Situation behavior. Vaughn et al. (1980) showed that maternal employment did not affect the overall incidence of "insecure" attachment, although it was associated with a preponderance of avoidance among insecure relationships when it was combined with single parenting. Joffe (1981) found different correlates of 12- and 18-month Strange Situation behavior, as did Pastor et al. (1981). In many of these studies, many measures were used but emphasis was placed only on those yielding significant attachment group differences. The interpretability of significant findings is limited by the absence of a priori predictions and the failure of the findings, taken as a whole, to provide a theoretically coherent picture.

THE GERMAN STUDIES: BIELEFELD AND REGENSBURG

Bielefeld

The second attempted replication of Ainsworth's findings was conducted in Bielefeld, Northern Germany, by Karin and Klaus Grossmann (1982). These researchers followed 49 mothers and infants from birth in an attempt to replicate Ainsworth's study as closely as they could. Two-hour home observations were conducted by the authors when the infants were 2-, 6-, and 10-months-old. Narratives based on the notes made by both observers constituted the data base. No measures of interobserver reliability were reported. Later, two assistants coded from the 10-month narratives: Infant crying and maternal responsiveness, behaviors relative to close bodily contact, the infant's reactions to the mother's comings and goings, maternal sensitivity, and maternal cooperation, in each case using Ainsworth's rating or coding conventions. The 2 and 6 month visits were also rated for maternal sensitivity whereas maternal acceptance/rejection was rated from inter-

---

[6]In a study of potential interest, Ward, Malone, and DeAngelo (1983) compared the Strange Situation classifications of firstborn and secondborn infants of the same families from the Minneapolis Study of Disadvantaged Families. Firstborn infants were observed at 12 and 18 months in the Strange Situation, secondborn infants at 12 months only. Although Ward et al. found that 54% of the families had offspring sharing the same attachment classification (A, B, or C), this finding is significantly qualified by the fact that for firstborns, attachment classifications for *both* 12- and 18-month assessments were taken into account, with children considered secure *only* if they exhibited B-type behavior on both occasions.

views. Infants were observed and videotaped in the Strange Situation at 12 months with their mothers and at 18 months with their fathers. Patterns of Strange Situation behavior were rated from the videotapes and all inter-rater reliability coefficients were satisfactory.

At 10 months, the majority of the 11 maternal measures were significantly correlated with the overall rating of sensitivity, as in Ainsworth's sample. The German mothers were, on average, rated as less affectionate, less inept, more interfering, less tender, and they acknowledged the baby more when entering or leaving the room than did Ainsworth's subjects. There were also differences in infant behavior, with the German infants making fewer communicative initiatives (e.g., crying, greeting, protest) than the Baltimore babies. As in Baltimore, the infants of sensitive mothers cried less than infants of insensitive mothers, they sought close bodily contact more often, responded more positively to being picked-up, and protested less when put down again.

When the maternal variables were related to Strange Situation classifications, however, Grossmann and Grossmann (1982) found that the mothers of B-group infants were significantly more sensitive than those of C group, but not A group, infants at 2 months; significantly more sensitive than both at 6 months; and equivalently sensitive at 10 months. The magnitude of the differences between group means was substantially greater in Baltimore (about four points on an eight-point scale) than in Bielefeld (a maximum of two points on the same scale). Interestingly, Grossmann and Grossmann (1982) found that the mothers of B_3 and A group infants were equivalently insensitive at 10 months, although the B_3 mothers had been the most sensitive mothers at 2 and 6 months and were consistently the most sensitive in Ainsworth's sample. One wonders, therefore, why these infants behaved in the B_3 pattern despite maternal insensitivity in the period immediately preceding observation in the Strange Situation.

Grossmann and Grossmann noted that German mothers are more concerned than American mothers about making their babies independent, and that independence training could be considered insensitive on Ainsworth's measure. This could explain the large number of A group infants in their sample (49% A, 33% B, and 12% C group assignments), the unusually low correlations between maternal acceptance and sensitivity (Grossmann, Grossmann, Huber, & Wartner, 1981), and the puzzling absence of a relationship between sensitivity at 10 months—when independence training was proceeding in earnest—and Strange Situation behavior. It would also explain why the variability in maternal sensitivity ratings was markedly diminished at the 10-month observations, compared to the earlier observations, and thus why sensitivity at this age did not predict Strange Situation behavior at 12 months. Even so, mean scores for sensitivity and acceptance at 10 months were not significantly different for

German mothers than they were for the Baltimore mothers in the fourth quarter.

These findings raise questions about the appropriateness of value-laden terms like "insensitivity" when we may be observing cultural variations in the goals and practices of parents. As discussed in Chapter 11, we know little about the implications of cross-cultural differences in the patterns of Strange Situation behavior.

Overall, Grossmann and Grossmann's findings appear consistent with the general tenor of Ainsworth's results even though they do not replicate specific results. Indeed, this study provides some interesting evidence concerning the relationship between early maternal behavior and later Strange Situation classifications. Like the Ainsworth and Egeland studies, however, the findings do not identify the *specific* dimensions of maternal behavior that were of formative significance. It also raised many questions about cross-cultural comparisons that are taken up more fully in Chapter 11.

Regensburg

Subsequently, the Grossmanns initiated another study in Regensburg, a medieval city in the South German Bavaria (Grossmann & Grossmann, 1982, 1983). In this study, however, no attempt was made to assess mother–infant interaction in the home. Grossmann and Grossmann (1982) reported a distribution somewhat more similar to the pattern typically found in U.S. samples than to the proportions found earlier in Bielefeld, although one still finds substantially more A-type and fewer B- and C-type attachments (43% A, 52% B, 4% C: Grossmann, personal communication). The Grossmanns suggested that the difference between the Bielefeld and Regensburg findings is attributable to subcultural differences between Bavaria and the industrial north in maternal behavior and parental goals. This suggestion is, of course, only speculative in the absence of empirical support, and must also be viewed in the context of the greater tendency toward avoidant attachments observed in *both* German samples than in American samples. Indeed, the German samples appear more similar to one another than to the typical American distribution.

THE PENNSYLVANIA INFANT AND FAMILY
DEVELOPMENT PROJECT

In a recent longitudinal study of 60 middle-class mothers and their infants, Belsky, Rovine, and Taylor (1984a) related characteristics of interaction at 1, 3, and 9 months to Strange Situation behavior at 12 or 13 months. Belsky et al. tested four hypotheses:

(a) securely attached (B) infants should experience intermediate levels of stimulation (i.e., infant-directed maternal behavior), with avoidant (A) infants being over-stimulated and resistant (C) infants being understimulated;
(b) resistant infants should have the least responsive mothers;
(c) avoidant infants should have the least physical contact with their mothers; and
(d) resistant and avoidant infants should be more irritable than secure (B) infants during the first months of life.

The first two hypotheses do not flow directly from those generated in Ainsworth's initial longitudinal study. Amount of stimulation had not previously been emphasized, but Belsky and his colleagues saw the amount of stimulation as one aspect of sensitive parenting, and formulated the relationship between parental behavior and Strange Situation behavior in a way that permitted differentiation of the origins of avoidant and resistant patterns of insecure Strange situation behavior (hypotheses a). Hypothesis (b) implied, in addition, that only the C group dyads would be distinguished by maternal unresponsiveness, which is often seen as the key component of insensitivity, and thus is viewed as an antecedent of both A and C group behavior. Hypothesis (c) was suggested to Belsky et al. (1984a) by Ainsworth's (Ainsworth et al., 1978; Tracy & Ainsworth, 1981) comment that the mothers of A infants found physical contact aversive, and that their bouts of physical contact were abrupt and infrequent, often frustrating the child's proximity/contact seeking (Main & Stadtman, 1981). Finally, hypothesis (d) was designed to explore the effects of infant characteristics on Strange Situation behavior.

Belsky et al. (1984a) recorded instances of 13 behaviors during 45-minute home observation sessions in which only mothers, children, and observers were present. Most of the behavior categories were recorded with high reliability. Subsequently, scores on nine of the 13 behavior categories were summed, following an a priori theory-guided approach developed by Belsky, Taylor, and Rovine (1984b) to yield a summary measure of reciprocal interaction.[7] This measure had proved to be highly internally consistent in prior analyses of these data (Belsky et al., 1984b). Linear trend analysis revealed that, at 9 months, the avoidant children experienced the most and resistant children the least reciprocal interaction, with B group infants in between. No significant effect was evident at either 1 or 3 months,

---

[7] The 9 behaviors summed were: maternal vocalization, infant vocalization, maternal response to infant vocalization, maternal stimulation/arousal, infant response to stimulation, maternal positive affect, infant look at mother, maternal individual attention, and three-step contingent exchange.

although the means ranked similarly at all three ages. Contrasts or planned comparisons between the means for the A group and B group, or the C group and B group, were not reported. Further analyses, in which the maternal and infantile components of the summary behavior measure were distinguished, revealed similar trends (i.e., A > B > C) on a summary measure of maternal behavior (significant only at 9 months) but no effects on a summary measure of infantile behavior.

These analyses thus yielded findings consonant with the researchers' first hypothesis, although it is not clear why the associations were not found at either 1 or 3 months of age. One possible implication is that as patterns of infant–parent interaction became consolidated over the course of the first year, they had greater formative significance for Strange Situation behavior at one year. Recall, however, that Grossmann and Grossmann (1982) reported a different pattern of results.

Belsky et al.'s analyses partially supported their second hypothesis. The mothers of resistant infants were significantly less responsive to infant distress signals at 3 and 9 (but not 1) months of age, and these mothers were significantly less responsive to positive vocalizations at 9 (but not 1 or 3) months, than the mothers of B group infants. However, the rates of responsiveness to distress vocalizations were very similar for A and C group infants at both 3 and 9 months, suggesting that the maternal unresponsiveness characterized mothers of infants in *both* "insecure" groups, not just those in the resistant (C) group. No comparison of maternal responsiveness to A and B group infants, nor of B vs. non-B group, were conducted. In the case of responsiveness to positive vocalizations at 9 months, the responsiveness of A group mothers was midway between the responsiveness of C group and B group mothers.

No significant differences were observed between A and B group infants in the frequency of close bodily contact, contrary to Belsky et al.'s (1984a) third hypothesis. Belsky et al. suggested that this may have been because the measure (total duration of holding minus total duration of feeding) was inappropriate because it did not adequately represent variations in the quality of physical contact. Finally, consistent with the fourth hypothesis, A and C group infants (combined) expressed more distress than B group infants at both 3 and 9 months, although the A infants' distress was higher at 3 months and the C group infants' higher at 9 months. Interestingly, other analyses indicated that infant fussing was significantly correlated with an index of maternal involvement during the *preceding* observation at home, but was uncorrelated with involvement during the *same* home observation. This finding, along with others concerning the influence of temperament on Strange Situation behavior, are discussed more fully in the next chapter.

Overall, Belsky et al. obtained at least some empirical support for three of their four hypotheses. In focusing on the amount of stimulation (viewed as a novel index of maternal sensitivity) as a determinant of Strange Situation behavior, Belsky et al. (1984a) provide an interesting perspective on the antecedents of Strange Situation behavior. The findings must be viewed cautiously until replicated, however, because they were not reliable (although consistent) across observations at each age. More importantly, although there is no a priori reason why maternal behavior in father's presence should be less significant than maternal behavior in dyadic contexts, Belsky (personal communication) reports that comparable analyses—involving data from the same subjects observed in a triadic (mother–father–infant) rather than dyadic (mother–infant) context—revealed no consistent relationships between either maternal or paternal behavior and subsequent Strange Situation behavior. In addition, it is not clear that *amount* of stimulation constitutes a generalizable index of sensitivity, particularly as levels of stimulation vary widely depending on parity, cultural norms, and the like. The quantity of stimulation only seems to tap part of the "maternal sensitivity" construct defined by Ainsworth; other aspects pertain to the quality of stimulation, which was not studied by Belsky et al. On the other hand, Belsky et al. did find the mothers of B group infants to be more responsive, as Ainsworth et al. (1978) predicted. Like Grossmann et al., therefore, Belsky et al. obtained some general support for Ainsworth's hypotheses.

THE BLOOMINGTON LONGITUDINAL STUDY

Bates and his colleagues (Bates, Maslin, & Frankel, in press) have also undertaken a major longitudinal study designed to explore both the antecedents and consequences of individual differences in Strange Situation behavior. The study involved a predominantly middle class sample of 168 mother–infant dyads followed from the time the infants were 6 months old until they were 3 years of age. One hundred and twenty infants completed the study. The results of this study are reported, as relevant, in this chapter and the next, as well as in Chapter 9.

Mother–child interaction was observed at home when the infants were 6 months old during two 3-hour observations. Observers used event recorders for molecular coding, four of Caldwell's (1970) HOME scales for more molar ratings, and the age-appropriate Infant Characteristics Questionnaire (ICQ: Bates, Freeland, & Lounsbury, 1979) scales for impressions of the child's characteristics. The 27 scores generated by the molecular coding were then subjected to factor analyses, and the resulting five maternal and four baby behavior factor scores were employed in subsequent analyses (Bates, Olson, Pettit, & Bayles, 1982). The subjects also visited the laboratory where the Bayley scales were administered, the mothers were interviewed about family adjustments since the baby's birth to allow computation of a composite social support score (Bates et al., 1982), and the dyads were observed in three 3- minute face-to-face play segments—mother responsive, mother unresponsive, mother responsive—during which "qualities of interaction were scored on dimensions theoretically relevant to the development of attachment, e.g., maternal responsiveness to infant cues" (Bates et al., in press, ms. page 7) to yield a total of 30 scores (Kiser, Bates, Maslin, & Bayles, 1982). The first of the face-to-face segments was viewed as the ideal context for assessing general communication styles, the second as analogous to a separation in the Strange Situation, and the third as analogous to a reunion (Kiser et al., 1982). Although a great deal of effort was invested in time series spectral analyses of microbehavioral codes based on the face-to-face interaction (Bates, Bayles, & Kiser, 1981), Bates and his colleagues relied upon molar rating scales rather than microbehavioral codes in the research reported here, because they believe that the microbehavioral codes yielded data with low external validity. All mothers also completed the ICQ and either Rothbart's (1981) Infant Behavior Questionnaire (IBQ) or Carey and McDevitt's (1977) Revised Infant Temperament Questionnaire (RITQ), as well as the Jackson (1974) Personality Research Form from which a measure of social desirability in responding was obtained.

When the infants were 13 months old, one 3-hour home visit like that at 6 months yielded scores on 31 measures which were reduced to scores on 8 factors: 4 for mother and 4 for baby and scores on the four HOME scales (Bates et al., in press; Pettit & Bates, 1984). Although the factors were different, however, there was sufficient similarity to indicate some modest continuity in specific maternal behavior and substantially less continuity in infant behavior between the 6- and 13-month observations. Canonical correlation analysis suggested three significant canonical variates revealing more impressive continuity: (1) Affectionate, intellectually-stimulating mothering; (2) infant temperamental difficulty, and (3) intense involvement (positive and negative) that may be pathognomonic (see Pettit & Bates, 1984). Mothers also completed two questionnaires—a 13-month version of the ICQ and the Maternal Perceptions Questionnaire (Olson, Bates, & Bayles, 1982). All infants were again assessed using the Bayley scales, and approximately half ($N = 74$) of the subjects were then seen in the Strange Situation. Sixty-eight were classified confidently, to yield 66% (45) B, 13% (9) A, 16% (11) C type, and 5% (3) mixed A–C classifications. For some analytic purposes, a 3-point attachment security scale was computed by assigning 1 point to infants classified in the A, C, and A/C categories, 2 to those in the B_1, B_2 and B_4 subgroups, and 3 to those in the "optimal" B_3 group. The use of an interval-type measure of this type presumes, of course, that differences within the secure classification (e.g., B_2 vs. B_3) are equivalent to secure–insecure differences (e.g., A vs. B_2). In other cases, group comparisons were made between A, B, and C group infants and/or dyads.

Analyses concerning the origins of Strange Situation behavior were presented in three papers (Frankel & Bates, 1983; Kiser et al., 1982; Maslin & Bates, 1983) and were summarized by Bates et al. (in press). Correlations between the five maternal factor scores obtained from the 6-month home observations and the 3-point attachment security index yielded only one significant correlation ($r = .24$, $p = .03$, one tailed). However, this was for the only factor, Mother affectionate contact, for which a priori predictions were made. In addition, scores on three of the 6 HOME scales (Organization of the environment, $r = .32$, $p = .01$; Emotional and verbal responsivity $r = .18$, $p = .07$; Involvement, $r = .18$, $p = .07$: all tests one-tailed) were associated in the predicted direction with the attachment security index. That is, mothers of infants later deemed securely-attached showed more involvement and responsivity and organized the home environment better. The authors found no significant relationships between attachment security and the four baby behavior factors. As Bates et al. (in press) conclude:

> While these correlations support Ainsworth et al., 1978, their smallness may indicate either that generalizability of the link between [Strange Situation behavior and] early maternal warmth and responsiveness is limited, or that our measures are not equivalent to Ainsworth's sensitivity ratings. (ms p. 10)

As far as the face-to-face play results were concerned (Kiser et al., 1982), discriminant function analyses involving 14 independent variables (10 composite scores derived following principal components analyses and 4 others) and the A–B–C classifications of 63 infants as dependent variables produced one statistically significant and one nonsignificant ($p < .07$) function. The first function, which distinguished the B group from the C group ($N = 9$), weighted the number of interactive bouts initiated by mother, and the amounts of distress in segments 2 and 3 of the face-to-face play sequence. The second (nonsignificant) function distinguished B group from A group infants on the basis of positive mutuality in segment 1, the number of short bouts in segment 1, and the degree of upset in segment 3. In all cases but one (the B infants were fussier in segment 3 on the first factor), the group differences were in the expected direction. The discriminant functions correctly classified 82.5% of the sample[8] although largely because so many of the subjects fell into the B group. Overall, 94% of the B's, but

---

[8]Kiser et al. (1983) report that similar results were reported by Ricks (1982), but unfortunately we have not been able to obtain copies of this report.

only 50% of the A's and 56% of the C's, were correctly classified. Evidently, discrimination of the A's and C's from each other and from the B's was not very well achieved, but in other respects the pattern of results was predicted.

Three of eight factor scores generated from the 13-month home observations were significantly correlated with the attachment security scale: mother teaching, infant object communication, and mother affection and caregiving. T-tests comparing the B and non-B groups revealed significant effects on these three variables as well, and all differences were in the predicted direction, with B group mothers teaching better and being more affectionate. Analyses of variance revealed significant effects across the three groups on only one factor (infant persists) and a trend ($p = .08$) on another (mother affection and caregiving). Scores on none of the other factors nor the four HOME scales scored at this age were significantly correlated with attachment security, even though Ainsworth's hypotheses would lead one to expect significant correlations with at least three of the HOME Scales (Emotional and verbal responsivity, Avoidance of restriction, Maternal involvement) as well as both of the other maternal behavior factors (Management and response to speech).

As Bates et al. (in press) summarize their findings concerning the interactional antecedents of Strange Situation behavior:

> the data give a limited validation of prior interpretations of attachment security....However, in our study the degree of overlap between attachment security and the other relevant measures was consistently small. Some proportion of this non-overlap must be due to measurement error [but this]...could not be the major explanation because the generalizability of observational variables was good. Likewise idiosyncracies of our sample should not be too important, because the sample was a typical demographic cross-section. The remaining explanation is that observation measures of the Ainsworth tradition tap different aspects of mother–child relations than those of the behavior coding tradition from which our measures derived. (p. 25)

This discussion presumes, of course, that "measures of the Ainsworth tradition" have proved better in predicting Strange Situation behavior; as the review provided in this chapter suggests, however, such measures have not been able to explain much more of the variance or to specify which particular aspects of maternal behavior (within a general class of positive maternal care) are of formative significance.

THE ANN ARBOR STUDY

Goldberg and Easterbrooks (1984) observed 75 toddlers (averaging 20 months of age) in the Strange Situation on two occasions about a month apart. One session was with mother and one with father, with the order counterbalanced. All toddlers came from middle to upper-middle class family backgrounds. Parental supportiveness, quality of parental assistance, child task orientation, and task affect were rated in a 5-minute parent-assisted problem solving task. After the father–infant observations, marital harmony was rated from observations of husband–wife interaction in a conflict resolution task. In addition, both parents completed questionnaires assessing their perceptions of the child's interference in their lives (two subscales of the Bother Scale: Wente & Crockenberg, 1976), an index of marital adjustment, Spanier's (1976) Dyadic Adjustment Scale (DAS), and a newly developed Parent Attitudes Toward Childrearing question-naire, yielding four independent scores.

Using log-linear multidimensional contingency table analysis, Goldberg and Easterbrooks (1984) found that "there were more *insecure* child–parent attachments (and fewer secure attachments) in the *low*-marital adjustment-...group than expected by chance and more *secure* and fewer insecure attachments than expected in the *high* marital adjustment group (p. 509; italics in original)." The observational measure of marital harmony, however, was significantly related to Strange Situation behavior only for father–daughter attachment. Variations in marital adjustment, as assessed by DAS scores, were not significantly related to measures of toddler behavior in the problem-solving task, but the behavioral measure of marital harmony was related to both measures of toddler behavior in the father–child, but not mother–child, situation.

Because the measures of marital adjustment and marital harmony were generally associated in the predicted direction with reported parental attitudes to childrearing (5 of 16 correlations significant), and measures of the degree of bother (4 of 8 correlations significant), the results seem to suggest that marital quality potentiated sensitive or high quality parenting which in turn potentiated secure infant–parent attachment. Unfortunately, however, the observed measures of parental sensitivity in the problem solving task (the putative mediating variable) were not related to marital adjustment scores for fathers, and were correlated in the *un*expected direction (i.e., the better the marital adjustment, the lower the scores for sensitivity) for mothers. In addition, as the authors acknowledged, since all assessments were conducted contemporaneously, causal relationships could not be discerned (e.g., secure infant–parent attachments could have fostered good parenting and improved marital quality). Thus the study provided some general support for the hypothesis that desirable family circumstances were associated with measures of desirable child behavior (including secure Strange Situation behavior), but there was little clear evidence regarding the specific antecedents of Strange Situation behavior.

In further analyses of these and additional data on this sample, Easterbrooks and Goldberg (1984) examined the associations between various indices of the father–child relationship, Strange Situation behavior with mothers and fathers, and measures of the child's behavior in the problem-solving task. The additional independent variables were three quantitative measures of father involvement (combined into a composite), and a composite measure of "behavioral sensitivity" created by summing the observed paternal behaviors—quality of assistance and emotional supportiveness—in the problem solving task. Multiple regression procedures were employed to assess the relationships between parent-related predictor and child-related dependent variables, with the set of predictor variables reduced by selecting variables that demonstrated adequate variance and still involved measures within each of the major domains. Different sets of predictors were included in analyses for each of the three child outcome measures. Easterbrooks and Goldberg (1984) summarize their findings:

> In general, our hypotheses relating optimal child development—secure attachment, positive task affect and task orientation—to high father involvement and positive parenting characteristics were supported. For all child outcomes, the equations including both father involvement and qualitative parenting characteristics simultaneously account for a larger portion of the variance than either set of characteristics alone. Thus, both are linked with child development. However, it can be seen that in general, qualitative parenting characteristics are more strongly associated with child development than is the quantitative measure of father involvement (p. 746).

In regression analyses, the qualitative composite measures of parenting characteristics accounted for 15% (ns) of the variance in girls' and 30% (ns) of the variance in boys' Strange Situation behavior with fathers, compared to 50% ($p < .01$) and 22% (ns; $p < .10$) of the variance in girls and boy's Strange Situation behavior with mothers. The quantitative measures of father involvement never accounted for a significant proportion of the variance in the regression analyses involving Strange Situation behavior, although the equations combining *both* father involvement and qualitative measures of parental characteristics were significant for all but one of the subgroups (i.e., girls with fathers). Interestingly, other analyses indicated that whereas maternal caretaking characteristics were more exclusively related to the security of child–mother attachment, paternal caretaking characteristics were associated with child attachments to both parents. Two of 22 or more paternal measures were significantly correlated with boys' Strange Situation behavior with their fathers, but none of them was correlated with the father–daughter Strange Situation assessments. None of the 23 or more maternal measures was associated with mother–son Strange Situation behavior (although three approached significance) and two were associated with mother–daughter attachment.

Again, therefore, these results provide some support for the general hypothesis that more desirable parental characteristics tend to be associated with secure Strange Situation behavior, but they do not specify those aspects of parental behavior that are important.

THE JAPANESE STUDIES

In another recent (and currently ongoing) study, Miyake and his colleagues studied 29 first-born, middle-class Japanese infants and their mothers (Miyake, Chen, Ujiie, Tajima, Satoh, & Takahashi, 1981–82; Miyake, Chen, & Campos, in press). Observations on a second sample of infants are currently being analyzed. In an early report of their findings concerning the first cohort, Miyake et al. (1981–82) reported that when observed in the Strange Situation at 12 months, 19 were classified as B group and 10 as C group—a remarkably high proportion (34%) of C group infants (no infants were deemed avoidant). In more recent reports, however, Miyake et al. (in press) have relabeled some of the latter as "pseudo-C" infants, whose behavioral profile appeared to fall somewhere between the profiles of B and C group infants. Whatever their group designations, it appears that the Strange Situation procedure aroused more distress among Japanese infants than among comparable groups of U.S.-raised infants—suggesting that the Strange Situation may not have psychologically similar meaning to infants in different cultures. This issue is pursued further in Chapter 11, in which we focus on cross-cultural uses of the Strange Situation.

In examining the antecedents of Strange Situation behavior, Miyake et al. (in press) coded six discrete measures of maternal behavior during infant awake and fussy states during home observations at 1- and 3-months of age. Of the 12 comparisons conducted using data for each age, there were no significant differences between mothers of future B and C group infants at 1 month, and only one significant difference at 3 months. Miyake et al. (1981–82) also reported that during an observation of mother–infant interaction at 7.5 months, mothers interrupted the free play of future C group (i.e., C plus pseudo-C) infants more than did the mothers of future B's, who were more responsive to their babies. There were no group differences in level of stimulation or in levels of "effective stimulation" at 7.5 months—findings that appear at variance with Belsky et al.'s (1984a) results. However, as there were differences in age (7 vs. 9 months), context (laboratory vs. home), and culture (Japan vs. US), the failure to replicate could have multiple explanations.

Overall, there were few clear group differences in maternal antecedents of Strange Situation behavior. We will have more to say about Miyake et al.'s study in the next chapter, however, in which we discuss the temperamental factors that have been emphasized by Miyake in interpretations of his findings, as well as in Chapter 11, where we discuss cross-cultural studies using the Strange Situation.

THE ISRAELI KIBBUTZ STUDY

Yet another of the recent studies whose findings cast some light on the antecedents of Strange Situation behavior was conducted outside the United States. Sagi, Lamb, Lewkowicz, Shoham, Dvir, and Estes (in press) observed 86 infants from Israeli kibbutzim in the Strange Situation with their mothers, fathers and metaplot (i.e., caretakers). The sessions with each of the adults were scheduled 6 weeks apart, and the order in which the three adults were involved was systematically counterbalanced in order to control for order effects. All the families lived on kibbutzim in which infants were housed together in centralized "infant homes" where they were cared for by metaplot except between 4 and 7pm when they visited their parents' living quarters.

Sagi et al. reported that these infants were much more likely to form insecure C group relationships to mothers, fathers, and metaplot than infants raised in more traditional nuclear family settings, although only the distributions for mothers and metaplot deviated significantly from the "norms" reported in studies of infant–adult attachment in the United States.[9] With mothers, 8% of the kibbutz infants were classified in the A group, 48% $B_{1,2,3}$ groups, 8% B_4, and 33% C group. For metaplot, the distribution was 15%, 45%, 7%, and 32% respectively, while for fathers it was 21%, 63%, 4%, and 11%. (In the U.S., the distribution reported by Ainsworth et al., 1978, was 21%, 63%, 4%, and 12%.) Assessments of a small ($N = 36$) number of Israeli city dwelling mothers and infants produced a distribution midway between the kibbutz and U.S. distributions (i.e., 3%, 75%, 6%, and 16%).

Sagi et al. suggested that since the kibbutz arrangement prevents infants from learning to count on specific people to be available around the clock, and because it ensures that responses to the infants' cries may go unanswered for long periods of time (especially at night), the large number of C group infants could be consistent with predictions that insecure relationships should predominate when infant care deviates from the normal range. However, there are as yet no data concerning the external correlates or validity of Strange Situation assessments in this cultural context and, as

---

[9]Many Strange Situation assessments had to be prematurely terminated because of infant distress, and most of these infants were classified in the C or B_4 categories.

discussed in Chapter 11, there are reasons to believe that some factors other than security of attachment affect Strange Situation behavior. Furthermore, it is puzzling that there was no significant increase in the proportion of insecure (A and C group) infants, only an apparent change in the relative proportions of C and A group infants. One would predict heightened insecurity in general, if the inferences drawn by Sagi et al. concerning the caretaking circumstances are accurate.

One other finding reported by Sagi et al. (in press), however, does suggest that patterns of childcare experience affected Strange Situation behavior. Sixteen of the metaplot in the study were observed with more than one of the infants in their care (a total of 39 infants were involved). In seven cases, all of the attachments with a given metaplot were of the same general type (B group or non-B group) and in an additional five cases, the majority of the three or four attachments with a given metaplot were of the same type. In only four cases did the number of dissimilar classifications exceed or equal the number of similar classifications. According to Sagi et al.,

> this finding is important because it strongly suggests that the security of infant–metapelet attachment as assessed in the Strange Situation is determined by the characteristics and quality of their prior interaction. Some metaplot apparently have characteristics that potentiate insecure attachments whereas others have characteristics that potentiate secure attachments. These findings thus support Ainsworth's contention that adult characteristics are more influential than infant characteristics in shaping the security of attachment (ms pp. 17–18).

This conclusion must be qualified in several ways, however. First, in studying the consistency of attachments to metaplot, classifications were considered similar even when one was A-type and one was C-type (i.e., both were considered insecure) even though these two patterns presumably have different determinants. Second, the reliability of the findings was not tested statistically. Third, systematic tests of the association between several questionnaire items concerning factors that might affect Strange Situation behavior (e.g., lengthy separations) all yielded nonsignificant results— perhaps, as the authors suggested, because the reliability and relevance of the items were low. Fourth, there were no independent assessments of caretaking behaviors to lend credence to Sagi et al.'s conjecture regarding the experiential origins of Strange Situation behavior. Finally, Strange Situation assessments were always preceded by two brief (3–5 minute) assessments of stranger sociability. These may have influenced the amount of distress subsequently exhibited by infants in the Strange Situation, complicating interpretation of findings concerning both the distribution across attachment categories and the origins of similarities among infants with the same metapelet.

EFFECTS OF CHILD MALTREATMENT

Further evidence concerning the association between undesirable maternal characteristics and the insecurity of later infant–mother attachment comes from a series of studies in which grosser variations in maternal characteristics were assessed and related to Strange Situation behavior. The implicit logic of these studies is that if the quality of prior parental care affects Strange Situation behavior, then the extreme degree of poor quality care represented by maltreatment must surely affect Strange Situation behavior, increasing the proportions of insecurely attached (A and C group) infants. Following a line of reasoning similar to that outlined by Belsky et al. (1984a), one might expect chronic abuse to potentiate A-type behavior and neglect to potentiate C-type behavior in those cases where the two types of maltreatment can really be distinguished, as the former group are in many respects overstimulated while the latter experience understimulating and unresponsive care.

Using data from the Minneapolis Study of Disadvantaged Families, Egeland and Sroufe (1981a) reported that when maternal care was extremely poor—bordering on abusive or neglectful—infants were more likely to be insecurely attached. The pattern of effects was different for the 12 and 18 month attachment assessments, however: C-type relationships were associated with abuse/neglect at 12 months, whereas A-type relationships were most common among the maltreated infants at 18 months.

Somewhat similar results were reported by Lamb, Gaensbauer, Malkin, and Shultz (1985), who collected data from a sample of 62 infants, 23 of whom had been abused and/or neglected by their mothers. Seventy percent of the abused subjects were rated avoidant when assessed in a modified Strange Situation at an average of 18 months of age, compared with a minority (22%) of the children in a matched comparison group. Lyons–Ruth, Connell, Grunebaum, Botein, and Zoll (1983) used Connell's (1976) modification of Ainsworth's classification system (see Chapter 8) to study the Strange Situation behavior of 26 "at risk" 12-month-olds from "multiproblem families." As in the foregoing studies, they found that 46% of the 11 infants in the group whose mothers had been referred to protective services had A-type attachments (with 36% B- and 18% C-type), compared to 27% of the remaining 15 infants (60% B- and 7% C-type). By contrast, there was a more typical distribution across categories (30% A, 70% B, 0% C) in a low-income control group, although there were still more A- and fewer C-type attachments than one would expect.

Schneider–Rosen and Cicchetti's (1984) study involved 37 children of around 19 months of age, of whom 18 had been abused or neglected. They too reported a heightened incidence of A and C group attachment behavior among maltreated children (67%) compared to matched, non-maltreated peers, although there were almost as many C group (28%) as A group (39%) toddlers in the maltreatment group. Subsequently, Schneider–Rosen, Braunwald, Carlson, and Cicchetti (in press) reported data on the Strange Situation behavior of maltreated infants and toddlers seen at both 12 and 24 months of age. At 12 months, 7 (42%) of the 17 maltreated infants were classified as C-type, 5 (29%) as A-type, and 5 (29%) as B-type, compared with 17% (3), 11% (2), and 72% (13) respectively in the comparison group of 18. The group differences across the three categories was statistically significant. At 24 months the maltreatment group ($N = 25$) contained 12 (48%) A-type, 6 (24%) C-type, and 7 (28%) B-type patterns of behavior, a distribution that differed significantly from the 3 (12%), 4 (16%), and 18 (72%) (respectively) distribution across the 3 groups in the nonmaltreatment comparison group ($N = 25$). There was no significant relationship between type of maltreatment and Strange Situation behavior, probably (as the authors suggest) because there was such heterogeneity within the maltreatment group, and many of the maltreated infants experienced more than one type of maltreatment.

Finally, Crittenden (1983) observed 46 mother–infant dyads who had been referred on suspicion of child maltreatment; infants ranged in age from 11 to 24 months. The majority (29 of 37, or 78%) of dyads for which maltreatment was documented were deemed insecurely attached (i.e., A, C, or "A/C" classification). By contrast, of the nine dyads who were assumed to be functioning adequately (i.e., without maltreatment), eight (89%) were classified in the B group.

Overall, therefore, it seems that maltreatment often—though not always—is associated with insecure patterns of attachment behavior, but that both A-group and C-group patterns are found. These studies thus confirm that very poor quality maternal care *is* associated with insecure patterns of attachment behavior in the Strange Situation, although these studies do not help us to understand the differential origins of the two patterns of insecure attachment (that is why, for example, A rather than C type patterns are found).

OTHER RELEVANT RESEARCH

Several other attempts have been made to assess the relationship between maternal behavior and infantile behavior in the Strange Situation. These studies have been less ambitious than many of those reported earlier, and cannot be organized around a common independent variable (such as maltreatment), so their results are included in this one section. All studies reported here assess some version of the general hypothesis that more desirable maternal characteristics and circumstances will be associated with B-type behavior in the Strange Situation.

Responsiveness, Sensitivity, and Social Support

Crockenberg (1981) assessed associations between infant irritability in the neonatal period, maternal responsiveness to distress at 3 months, and maternal reports of social support at 3 months to Strange Situation behavior at 12 months in a sample of 48 dyads. The relationships between social support and Strange Situation behavior and between maternal responsiveness and Strange Situation behavior were significant by chi-square analysis, but the effects of maternal responsiveness were evident only when social support was low and the effects of social support varied depending on the degree of infant irritability. Multiple regression analyses predicting resistance, avoidance, and proximity seeking in the reunion episodes showed that "maternal responsiveness predicted proximity seeking, predicted resistance only when it was extracted prior to social support, and failed to predict avoidance" (Crockenberg, 1981, p.861). Maternal responsiveness thus appeared to be significant, although its effects could only be understood in the context of other important variables. Bates et al. (in press), however, failed to replicate Crockenberg's (1981) finding in this regard. They reported that all attempts to identify significant interactions among predictors of Strange Situation behavior (e.g., maternal behavior, social support, temperament) were unsuccessful.

Durrett, Otaki, and Richards (1984) observed 34 Japanese infants in the Strange Situation at 12 months, and related their behavior to mothers' reports of the amount of emotional support they perceived from the fathers. There were significant effects for attachment category on three of eight subscales as well as on the total scores. In each case, the means for the C and B groups were similar, whereas the A group scores were significantly lower. These results are clearly not consistent with theoretical predictions, and unfortunately the authors did not attempt to explain them.

Bridges, Grolnick, Frodi, and Connell (1984), in a study of 38 dyads, reported that maternal sensitivity rated in a 6-minute play session at 12 months was significantly and predictably related to infant behavior in a 20-month Strange Situation assessment, but sensitivity at 12 months was not related to 12-month Strange Situation behavior. Three other ratings of maternal control style in the same play sessions were not related to Strange Situation classifications at either age, however.

Like Belsky et al. (1984a), Smith and Pederson (1983) sought to operationalize sensitivity in terms of discrete, behavioral measures that could then be related to Strange Situation behavior. Forty-seven mothers and their 12-month-olds were observed in the Strange Situation, directly following this in a 20-minute feeding and play session, and finally in a 3-minute period during which mothers were asked to complete a questionnaire while the infant was in the room. Maternal behaviors reflecting sensitivity to infant cues were scored during the questionnaire period. A priori, "intuitively derived" clusters of maternal responses to infant cues (such as vocalizations and proximity-seeking) were created to reflect "appropriate," "insufficient," and "intrusive" maternal responding, and these behaviors were coded at three-second intervals. Inter-rater agreement was high. Five generally nonindependent summary measures were compared across attachment classifications. In univariate ANOVAs, mothers of A, B, and C infants varied significantly on all five measures: proportion of episodes scored as involving (1) appropriate responding; (2) appropriate responding when active responding required; (3) insufficient responding; (4) intrusive responding; and (5) visual checks on the baby. Mothers of B group infants were significantly higher than mothers of A or C group babies in post hoc comparisons on measures 1, 2, and 5; mothers of C babies were highest on the third measure, and mothers of A babies highest on the fourth measure. All of these findings accord with theoretical expectations, but interpretation is difficult because the assessments were conducted contemporaneously. The direction of influence or causality is uninterpretable for this reason. Even so, Smith and Pederson have offered a promising new approach to the assessment of maternal sensitivity in future research.

Maternal Expressiveness

Estes (1981; see also Estes, Lamb, Thompson, & Dickstein, 1981) reported that the mothers of infants in the B_1 and B_2 subgroups were more "expressively-involved" in their infants' performance during an assessment of sociability at 19 months than were the mothers of infants in the C group or the B_3 and B_4 subgroups. The mothers of A group infants were almost as involved as the mothers of B_1 and B_2 infants, however, and when the three groups were compared, only the mothers of C group infants differed significantly from the A or B group infants' mothers.

Tolan and Tomasini (1977; see also Main, Tomasini, & Tolan, 1979) reexamined the videotapes from Main's (1973) study, which is described more fully in Chapter 9. Forty infants were observed in the Strange Situation at 12 months, and were seen in a play session with mother and an unfamiliar adult at 21 months.[10] Videotapes of the play sessions were repeatedly viewed to allow the rating of maternal sensitivity and acceptance using Ainsworth's scales. A narrative account was also dictated by one of the raters, and was later used for rating maternal anger, aversion to contact, and expressiveness. (It is not clear why these variables were not directly rated from the videotapes.) Two slides of the mother's face were also taken—one at the first sight of her after the playmate entered and one at the first

---

[10]Only 38 were included in Tolan and Tomasini's analyses.

opportunity after toddler–playmate play began—and maternal expressiveness was again rated from these two slides. All ratings not based on slides were significantly and often highly intercorrelated (X = .57, range = .36 to .77; Tolan & Tomasini, 1977). One of the ratings of expressiveness from the slides was correlated with narrative-based ratings of anger and expressiveness; the other rating of expressiveness from the slides was uncorrelated with either of the other expressiveness ratings. Six of the seven ratings revealed significant group differences between B_3 and non-B group infants, but apparently none of the differences was significant when all B group infants were compared with the non-B group infants.

Interpretation of the differences reported is problematic because of the high intercorrelations among the measures, and also because 40% of the B group (i.e., the non-B_3 babies) were excluded in statistical analyses. Furthermore, since maternal characteristics were rated 8 months after the Strange Situation, the study does not elucidate the *origins* of infant behavior in the Strange Situation.

Maternal Behavior Profiles

Antonucci and Levitt (1984) observed 147 middle class mothers and infants in a laboratory-based preseparation–separation–reunion sequence at 7 months, and then had 47 return for Strange Situation assessments at 13 months. At 7 months, seven maternal behaviors were recorded using a time-sampling procedure for the preseparation and reunion phases separately, while eight infant behaviors were recorded during the separation, and nine in each of the preseparation and reunion phases. In addition, a dyadic measure of mutual interactions was used. At 13 months, attachments were classified using Ainsworth's categorical system. There were 17 A, 28 B and only 2 C group infants, so the C-group infants were dropped from the analyses.

There were few differences between the 7-month behavior profiles of mothers whose infants were later classified in the A and B groups. In the preseparation, the B group mothers vocalized more, while in the reunion they looked, touched, and played more and engaged in neutral behavior less. The infant behavior measures revealed no group differences for the preseparation and separation variables, and only two for the reunion episodes; B group infants looked more and touched more. The B group mother–infant dyads also engaged in more mutual interaction, although only in the reunion episode. In light of the large number of statistical tests conducted, these differences are only suggestive.

Principal component factor analyses of infant and maternal behaviors were then used to help select discrete behavior measures for inclusion in multiple discriminant function analyses, with Strange Situation classifications as the criterion variable. In only one analysis (infant separation behaviors) did a variable achieve a loading of more than .25 on the canonical function (looking, -.82) and the success rates for the different functions were quite low: 69%, 73%, 67%, 73%, 78%, and 76% for the mother preseparation, mother–reunion, infant preseparation, infant separation, infant reunion 1, and infant reunion 2 analyses, respectively. The chance success rate was 62%, and in only one case did there appear to be significant prediction from a 7 month function (mother reunion) to 13-month Strange Situation behavior. At best, therefore, these data suggest some modest continuity in behavior, but do not directly address hypotheses concerning the causal relationship between prior interaction and Strange Situation behavior. Indeed, their analyses indicated that both early maternal and infant behaviors were related to later Strange Situation behaviors, but no specific early influences were strongly predictive.

Maternal Personality

Rosenberg (1975)[11] reported that mothers of B group 12-month-olds scored higher on Cohler, Weiss, and Grunebaum's (1970) Reciprocity Factor on the Maternal Attitude Scale than did mothers of A group infants, and were also rated higher on "Maternal Reciprocity-Sensitivity" and engaged in more reciprocal interaction states during a 6-minute free play preceding the Strange Situation. These differences, were not replicated during a 6-minute "directed play" situation, however, and there were no differences on ratings of "infant social responsiveness" in either session.

Like Kiser et al. (1983), Tronick, Ricks, and Cohn (1982) used face-to-face play sessions to study the interactive antecedents of Strange Situation behavior. A small sample of mother–infant dyads were observed during playful and maternal still-face sequences when infants were 3, 6, and 9 months, and were assessed in the Strange Situation at one year. During the still-face sequence at 6 months, infants later deemed securely-attached showed many more "positive elicits" (i.e., vocalizing, smiling, etc.) while infants later classified in A or C groups showed more "no elicits" to the mother's expressionless demeanor. This pattern was not evident at 3- and 9-months however, and thus raises questions about the generality and reliability of the 6-month findings. Maternal behavior was also rated during the 6-month exchanges, but no attachment group differences were reported.

Following the Strange Situation assessment, Tronick et al. (1982) also obtained from the mothers information about their self-concepts and childhood relationships with parents and peers. Compared to the mothers of

---

[11]Rosenberg (1975) used a classification procedure similar, but not identical to, that employed by D. B. Connell (see chapter 12 for further details). Rosenberg also compared data for mothers and infants in the A and C classifications.

A and C group infants, the mothers of B group infants rated themselves as significantly higher on self-esteem, competence and "likability" (there were no differences on defensiveness), and perceived themselves as having been more accepted by parents and peers and as having parents who were more likely to encourage their independence. Similarly, Weber, Levitt, and Clark (1984) reported that the mothers of B and non-B group infants differed in their self-ratings of temperamental characteristics using the Dimensions Of Temperament Survey (Lerner, Palermo, Spiro, & Nesselroade, 1982), with mothers of A babies obtaining higher scores for reactivity than mothers of B and C group infants. Taken together, these findings suggest that the mothers of B group infants may have somewhat more positive self-perceptions than other mothers, but the relationships between these and patterns of infant Strange Situation behavior remain to be explained.

Neonatal Risk Status

Finally, there are now several reports showing no relationship between "at risk" neonatal circumstances and later behavior in the Strange Situation. Rode, Chang, Fisch, and Sroufe (1981) studied 24 middle class infants (20 premature and 4 seriously ill full-terms) and found a distribution across categories (3 A, 17 B, and 4 C group) not significantly different from that typically found in U.S. samples (e.g., Ainsworth et al., 1978). An inventory of specific risk factors also did not distinguish the A, B, and C groups. Goldberg, Perrotta, and Minde (1984), in a study of 56 low-birth weight infants, reported comparable results. Likewise, Frodi (1983), in a study of 20 preterm and 20 full-term infants, again from middle-class families, reported distributions of 2 A, 15 B, and 3 C group classifications in the full term group and 3, 15, and 2 respectively in the preterm group. Again these distributions did not differ significantly. Field, Dempsey, and Shuman (1981) and Holmes, Ruble, Kowalski, and Lavesen (1984) obtained similar findings. Because there is no compelling reason to expect that preterm infants and infants separated neonatally from their mothers *should* differ in the quality of infant–mother attachment (Lamb & Hwang, 1982; Lamb, 1982d) these findings are not very surprising.

However, it is noteworthy that most of the studies cited above were conducted with middle-class families in which any detrimental effects of prematurity on the infant–mother relationship are buffered by the availability of social support. In addition, most of the infants studied did not experience chronic or severe health problems at birth. When prematurity is accompanied by additional difficulties, there may be longer-term effects on the mother–infant relationship. Some support for this conclusion is found in a recent study by Plunkett, Meisels, Stiefel, Pasick, and Roloff (1984), who studied 62 premature infants with either transient or chronic Respiratory Distress Syndrome (RDS). The 17 infants in the "high risk" premature group (chronic RDS) had a much different distribution of attachment classifications (6% A, 53% B, 41% C) than did a "low risk" (without RDS) group (27% A, 64% B, 9% C), and a "moderate risk" (transient RDS) group (18% A, 53% B, 29% C). Thus the effects of prematurity on later Strange Situation behavior may vary depending on whether it is accompanied by other risk factors.

Results of another study also indicated that more severe risk status early in the first year may predict later non-B attachment status. Gordon and Jameson (1979) observed 12 infants who had been diagnosed as suffering from nonorganic failure to thrive (FTT) in the first year using a modified Strange Situation procedure (involving only one separation) when the infants were between 12 and 19 months of age. Their responses were compared with those of a control group of infants who were matched on age, race, sex, socioeconomic status, and age and length of prior hospitalization for reasons other than FTT. Six of the 12 FTT infants were given non-B classifications compared with only 2 of the 12 matched controls. Based on subsequent interviews with mothers of infants in the FTT group, Gordon and Jameson speculated that the developmental delays and temperamental characteristics of these infants may have affected prior patterns of mother–infant interaction. However, maternal characteristics may also be relevant in instances of nonorganic FTT (e.g., Fischoff, Whitten, & Pettit, 1970). Unfortunately, no other assessments of infant or maternal behavior were reported.

Other Maternal Characteristics

Matas, Arend, and Sroufe (1978) reported that the mothers of 23 infants classified in the B group at 18 months provided more support and better quality assistance during tool-use tasks when the children were 24 months of age than did the mothers of 15 A and C group infants. These findings were later replicated by Sroufe and Rosenberg (1982), who studied infants and mothers from Egeland's longitudinal study.

Several researchers have sought to relate daycare experience to Strange Situation behavior, although most have used much older children and/or substantially-modified versions of Ainsworth's scoring system. Thus these studies are not reviewed here, and interested readers are referred to Belsky and Steinberg (1978) and Clarke–Stewart and Fein (1983) for reviews of the relevant literature.

Summary

The results of the many studies described in this section provide general support for the hypothesis that more desirable maternal characteristics are correlated with B-type behavior in the Strange Situation. In a variety of studies, the mothers of B group infants have been rated more responsive, more expressive, more supportive, more sensitive and more attentive to their infants than the mothers of A and C group infants. The mothers of B group infants also rated themselves more positively on a number of personality variables, including self-esteem, competence, and likability. In only a few cases, however, did researchers either search for or find differential correlates of A and C group status. While supporting the general hypothesis that desirable maternal characteristics are associated with B-type Strange Situation behavior, therefore, the findings reported here do not elucidate the specific patterns of maternal behavior that are of formative significance, the processes whereby the effects are mediated, or the differential origins of A- and C-type behavior.

CONCLUSION

In this lengthy chapter, we have reviewed all available information concerning the relationship between parental behavior and parent–child interaction at home, during the first year, and patterns of infant Strange Situation behavior at one year of age or later. The more limited data bearing on the relationship between temperament and Strange Situation behavior is reviewed in the next chapter.

The evidence reviewed in this chapter paints a fairly consistent picture. Briefly stated, it is clear that the infant's prior experiential history outside the Strange Situation does relate in a predictable and consistent fashion to Strange Situation behavior. Overall, there is good reason to believe that mothers who behave in a fashion considered sensitive or socially-desirable by Americans tend to have infants who later exhibit B-type behavior in the Strange Situation. The maternal correlates include characteristics like positive responding to the infant's demands, consistency, warmth, and a degree of harmony in mother–infant interaction. By contrast, major deviations from these patterns of behavior seem to increase the likelihood of A- and C-type attachments. Further, the studies conducted on maltreated infants, those on the differences between mother– and father–infant attachments (see Chapter 6), and those on the effects of changing caretaking arrangements or family circumstances (see Chapter 8), all suggest that variations in the infant's experiential history with a specific caretaker do influence Strange Situation behavior in a consistent and predictable fashion.

However, researchers have *not* shown what *specific* aspects of parental behavior are of formative importance. When one seeks to determine what specific aspects of caretaker behavior are critical, the evidence is inconclusive because (1) there are few *specific* replications from one study to the next, (2) there are too many—mostly nonindependent—measures in most studies, and patterns of significant and nonsignificant group differences do not fit into a theoretically coherent pattern; (3) significant effects are often unreliable across multiple assessments in the first year; and (4) some of the clearest evidence comes from comparisons between extreme groups (e.g., abused and non-abused infants) rather than from studies exploring variations within the normal range. In addition, most researchers have inappropriately used a retrospective rather than prospective analytic design in their study of antecedent influences, making it less certain whether group differences would emerge if antecedents were used to predict classifications, rather than the reverse. Another serious limitation is that researchers have failed to identify distinct and replicable antecedents of the A and C patterns of insecure behavior. These patterns of infant behavior in the Strange Situation are so clearly different that the failure to explain how their origins differ not only from B-group infants but also from one another is surely significant. Similarly, given Ainsworth et al.'s (1971) observation that "the subgroups...[offer]...a much more significant basis of classification of individual differences than...the more broadly defined main groups" (p. 22), it is noteworthy that specific antecedents of subgroup patterns have not been identified—and, indeed, many researchers have not even examined them.

Establishing a relatively consistent association between B-type Strange Situation behavior and desirable caretaking characteristics (and A- and C-type behavior with marked departures from those characteristics) is no small achievement, and this evidence speaks to the validity of the Strange Situation procedure. Thus far, however, the data do not permit us to make more specific statements about *how* particular caretaking practices contribute to the three distinct patterns of infant Strange Situation behavior described by Ainsworth. Since one can hypothesize a range of processes by which these are linked—such as the reinforcement of particular social skills in the baby, the development of a sense of personal efficacy, and the acquisition of (specific or generalized) social expectations—it is unfortunate that we have so little useful information for assessing these alternatives. The formulations of evolutionary biology will be of little help here, because these questions address the proximate (rather than ultimate) processes by which caretaking influences affect infant socioemotional behavior.

Part of the reason for our difficulty in specifying how particular caretaking practices are influential is the generality and imprecision with which such practices have typically been defined and assessed by researchers. Even when separate rating scales are used to assess constructs like maternal sensitivity, cooperativeness and accessibility, for example, the potential for halo effects and the high intercorrelations among these measures strongly suggest that a broader dimension of "good" vs. "bad" mothering is actually being assessed. Furthermore, these variations in caretaking practices are often treated as if they were personality traits, since they are assessed in a manner which presumes substantial cross-situational and cross-time consistency. Because of changing infant competencies, however, parental "cooperativeness" (for example) is likely to require much different skills from the parents of 3- and 9-month olds. Indeed, no researcher has asked whether variations in caretaking characteristics might vary significantly as infant needs and abilities change, and to do so would seriously complicate research in this area. Thus while the transcontextual approach used by many investigators has the advantage of providing a more inclusive (and possibly more sensitive) appraisal of parenting behaviors, it entails questionable assumptions about the consistency of these behaviors and does not take us closer to the goal of identifying how and why these practices may affect infant behavior.

To this end, the more recent attempts of researchers like Belsky et al., Smith and Peterson, and Bates et al. to operationally define caretaker sensitivity in more precise, behaviorially-based ways may provide promising new methods for studying these influences in future research. While the approaches used by each of these researchers may provide a more limited assessment of caretaker influences than do the broader, transcontextual rating scales, they permit the testing of more specific hypotheses concerning the effects of particular kinds of caretaker influences, and also enable researchers to assess their consistency cross-situationally and across time. Thus these methods may prove useful in advancing the research beyond the consideration of global parenting attributes.

We also do not have much evidence indicating that it is the quality of maternal behavior or dyadic interaction in an earlier formative period that influences Strange Situation behavior, rather than contemporaneous patterns of parent–infant interaction. Related to this point, Bates et al. (in press) have conducted home observations both prior to (at 6 months) and contemporaneous with the 13-month Strange Situation assessments, and reported some significant continuity over time in patterns of parental behavior, which was greater than the continuity in infant behavior. Furthermore, the relationships between Strange Situation and home behavior were as strong for the 6-month as for the 13-month observations. One interpretation of these findings is that Strange Situation behavior is more strongly affected by variations in the *current* patterns of dyadic harmony than by experiences in an earlier formative period. Thus early caretaking patterns would predict later Strange Situation behavior only when there is continuity in these interactive patterns. We would therefore expect to find stronger associations with Strange Situation behavior as assessments of dyadic interaction are conducted closer in time to the attachment assessment, as Belsky's data indicate. This would also explain why Egeland and Farber (1982, 1984), whose subjects faced many events and stresses in the first year which were likely to affect the quality of dyadic interaction, were essentially unable to predict subsequent Strange Situation behavior from earlier measures of mother, infant, and dyad. It is also consistent with the repeated findings that risk status in the neonatal period is unassociated with variations in Strange Situation behavior at one year. On the other hand, Grossmann and Grossmann's data are not consistent with this interpretation, unless we assume that the behavior rated as insensitive at 10 months should not be considered "insensitive" because it reflects certain cultural norms. We consider the importance of continuity in caretaking arrangements and family circumstances more fully in Section III (Chapters 8, 9, and 10).

Because theorists and researchers have considered the A, B, and C groups to be homogeneous groups (indeed, the A and C categories are often combined), they have assumed that there is only one possible formative pathway to each pattern of infant behavior. It is quite possible, however, that very different factors may be associated with what is ostensibly the same pattern of Strange Situation behavior. Stated differently, one infant may "avoid" because she is being trained to be independent, another may avoid because he is not stressed by the procedure, while another may "avoid" because she fears or doubts her mother's likely response. In short, there are multiple pathways to A, B, and C patterns of Strange Situation behavior. If this is the case, it would help explain why researchers have been unable to identify specific patterns of parental behavior consistently associated with major portions of the variance in Strange Situation behavior. To some extent, greater attention to subgroup variations by researchers would help to address this issue. More generally, however, it may be necessary to devote greater attention to distinguishing the alternative antecedents of each classification pattern, taking into account characteristics of the infant (see Chapter 6), caretaking patterns, and cultural norms. We discuss this issue more thoroughly in succeeding chapters, and we also return to this issue in the final section of the book.

Consistent with practices in most studies of developmental psychology, researchers reporting statistically significant results seldom indicate how great a proportion of the variance has been explained, but in most cases the proportion of variance explained appears to have been small. In addition, many studies use a large number of measures, with emphasis devoted to those few which yield significant group differences between attachment classifications. It is thus often difficult to integrate significant and nonsignificant findings into a coherent conceptual framework, or to determine the extent to which the multiple measures tap independent sources of variation in parental behavior. Multivariate procedures, which address some of these issues, certainly deserve greater utilization than in the past.

In addition, these difficulties in interpreting the evidence may be due, in part, to the tendency of researchers to focus their attention on a very limited set of potential antecedents—specifically, prior patterns of mother–infant interaction. However, the studies reviewed in this chapter and elsewhere in this volume suggest other sources of influences, including the functioning of the family system and, in particular, the quality of the marital relationship (Goldberg & Easterbrooks, 1984), the impact of stressful events upon the family (Minneapolis Study of Disadvantaged Families), as well as the cultural context (the German, Japanese, and Israel studies). Clearly, infant characteristics also merit attention—particularly with respect to their interaction with other factors. Similar patterns of mothering may, for example, have different outcomes for infants with different characteristics. Thus while prior patterns of mother–infant interaction may explain some variance in subsequent Strange Situation behavior, the amount of unexplained variance and the jumbled array of findings presented in this chapter compels researchers to broaden their study to consider the multiple antecedents of A, B, and C group behavior.

Until more persuasive data are available, therefore, it would behoove reviewers and theorists to remember that Ainsworth's exciting hypotheses about the specific antecedents of Strange Situation behavior remain unproven except in their most general form, which itself does not elucidate formative processes or mechanisms. It is unfortunate that Ainsworth's important exploratory study has been so widely misconstrued as an hypothesis-testing study, as this has led many developmentalists to believe that our knowledge in this area is much more substantial than it actually is.

6
TEMPERAMENT, ATTACHMENT, AND STRANGE SITUATION BEHAVIOR

INTRODUCTION

Although many different implicit and explicit definitions of temperament have been offered, most researchers agree today that individual differences in temperament refer to relatively enduring aspects of behavioral style that have some constitutional basis (Campos, Barrett, Lamb, Goldsmith, & Stenberg, 1983; Goldsmith & Campos, 1982). Because of the pervasive influence of such stylistic differences, it seems reasonable to ask whether temperamental differences influence Strange Situation behavior. There are, in fact, several ways in which temperament and attachment might be related. Some (e.g., Kagan, 1982) have sought to portray temperamental differences rather than differences in maternal behavior as the major sources of individual differences in Strange Situation behavior, but it is possible for temperament to have a significant effect on Strange Situation behavior without contradicting the attachment theorists' emphasis on interactional quality as the basis of Strange Situation behavior.

Those who have suggested that temperamental differences have a major influence on Strange Situation behavior have come from outside attachment theory. For example, Goldsmith and Campos (1982) have argued that temperamental characteristics may influence the ease with which caretakers can respond appropriately to infant signals either directly (e.g., a "difficult" baby is harder to manage) or indirectly through the interaction of infant and adult characteristics (e.g., a "difficult" baby may be easier for some parents to manage than others). Thus temperament might affect the harmony of dyadic interaction and thus the infant's Strange Situation behavior.

A more radical perspective on temperament-attachment relationships has been offered by Chess and Thomas (1982), who have argued that temperamental dimensions of approach/withdrawal, adaptability, quality of mood, and intensity may account for many of the individual differences in Strange Situation behavior, and may also explain many of the predictive associations between early attachment and later socioemotional functioning (see also Rothbart & Derryberry, 1981). Thus, for example, a baby with a negative mood may behave resistantly in the Strange Situation and later be noncompliant with mother and unsociable with peers or unfamiliar adults in follow-up assessments. In a similar vein, Kagan (1982) has suggested that variations in Strange Situation behavior may be attributed to a temperamental tendency to be distressed by unfamiliar or unexpected events. Kagan thus proposed that A group infants do not become upset during the separation episodes and consequently do not seek proximity upon mother's return, whereas C Group babies are so easily and intensely distressed by the procedure that they are difficult to soothe during reunion episodes. By contrast, B group infants, are believed to have an intermediate proneness to distress. As a result, they are upset by the separations but are able to regain comfort and emotional equilibrium by seeking proximity/contact to their caretakers on reunion.

In extreme form, these arguments might suggest that Strange Situation behavior provides little or no information about mother–infant interaction, although none of these theorists has adopted this view. Rather, they propose that temperament plays a major role—perhaps along with interactive harmony and other factors—in shaping patterns of Strange Situation behavior.

Because they have emphasized the formative importance of parent–infant interaction, by contrast, attachment theorists have tended to minimize the direct role played by endogenous infant characteristics (such as temperament) in the development of individual differences in infant–parent security. Attachment theorists, perhaps prompted by Bell's (1968) influential critique, acknowledge that infant characteristics and maternal characteristics together affect the quality of mother–infant interaction, and thus patterns of Strange Situation behavior. Infant characteristics (such as temperament) are presumed to interact in complex ways with maternal characteristics (such as sensitivity) to create a unique and characteristic style of interaction which in turn determines individual differences in Strange Situation behavior. However, the influence of infant characteristics on attachment formation has been discussed in such a way as to minimize its significance, presumably because of the central importance accorded to "maternal sensitivity" within attachment theory. Although attachment theorists acknowledge that infants are born with distinct behavioral styles, they propose that it is the mother's *accommodation* to these characteristics during the first year which determines individual differences in the interactive quality of the dyad and, consequently, individual differences in Strange Situation behavior. Greater emphasis is placed on maternal rather than infant accommodation because of the mother's greater behavioral and cognitive sophistication. As a result, the mother's contributions to differences in Strange Situation behavior are viewed as the primary source of variance (see Ainsworth, 1979a, 1979b Sroufe, in press).

Unfortunately, most research studies to date (Crockenberg's [1981] study is an important exception) have been designed to test only the strongest and more direct effects of temperamental characteristics on Strange Situation behavior, and thus we have little information about possible indirect influences.

Not all attachment theorists share the view that infant temperament only has a limited influence on individual differences in infant–adult attachment. For example, in his social-cognitive interpretation of Strange Situation behavior, Lamb (1981a, 1981b) suggested that differences in infantile attentiveness might influence the degree to which its working model of the parent was influenced by subtle differences in the parent's behavior and responsiveness. Alternatively, Sroufe (in press) has argued that temperamental characteristics may affect subclassification assignment, but not overall (i.e., A vs. B vs. C) classifications.

In the next sections, we review the available evidence concerning the relationship between temperament and Strange Situation behavior. Three types of studies are relevant here: studies on the similarities/differences between infant–mother and infant–father attachments; studies relating parental perceptions of infant temperament to Strange Situation behavior; and research relating to direct observational measures of infant temperament.

INTRA-INDIVIDUAL CONSISTENCY IN STRANGE SITUATION BEHAVIOR

Indirect support for the argument that Strange Situation behavior is determined by prior patterns of interaction between the individual and the specific adult—rather than by infant characteristics, whether constitutionally or experientially determined—has frequently been derived from studies in which the same infants are observed more than once in the Strange Situation, each time with a different attachment figure.

In the first such study, Lamb (1978) observed 12-month-old infants in the Strange Situation with their mothers and fathers. The sessions were only one week apart, but there were no order effects. Half were seen with mother first; half with father. There was no significant similarity between the distribution of infants across the three major groups (A, B, C) with their mothers and fathers. There was a nonsignificant tendency ($p < .06$), however, for infants who were "secure" (B) or "insecure" (A, C) with their mothers to be classified the same way with their fathers also, and vice versa. This hinted at some dependency between the two relationships, but suggested that the determinants of infant–father and infant–mother attachment, as assessed in the Strange Situation, are largely independent.

Even clearer results were obtained in several later studies focused on the same question. Grossmann, Grossmann, Huber, and Wartner (1981) observed 46 German infants in the Strange Situation with their mothers at 12 months and their fathers at 18 months. There was no discernible association between the patterns of infant–father and infant–mother attachment: Similarity for A, B, C classifications was 43% (49% excluding infants who were unclassifiable). Main and Weston (1981) likewise observed 61 infants (from the San Francisco Bay Area) in the Strange Situation at 12 and 18 months. Forty-six were observed first with mothers and 15 with their fathers. Similarity of classifications (A, B, C) was similar to that reported by Grossmann et al. (1981): 44% (51% excluding infants who were unclassifiable). Lamb, Hwang, Frodi, and Frodi (1982) observed 51 Swedish infants in the Strange Situation with each of their parents. The sessions were 2 months apart and the order in which each parent was involved was systematically counterbalanced. As in the other studies, infants were classified differently when seen with their mothers and fathers, although the rate of similarity was somewhat higher (65%). Belsky, Garduque, and Hrncir (1984) observed 53 American infants with one parent at 12- and the other at 13-months of age; again order was counterbalanced and the association between the "security" and "insecurity" of infant–mother and infant–father attachment was 58% (similarity of A, B, C classifications was not reported). Finally, Owen and Chase–Lansdale (1982b) observed 132 American infants with their parents in the Strange Situation in two sessions 1.5 months apart. Similarity in A, B, C classifications with mother and father was 68%, which was highly significant statistically.

Slightly different results were reported by Sagi et al. (in press) in their study of 86 infants from Israeli kibbutzim. Each infant was observed three times in the Strange Situation, once each with mother, father, and metapelet. The sessions were 6 weeks apart and the order of assessment was counterbalanced. Like most other researchers, Sagi et al. reported no significant association between the classification of infant–mother and infant–father attachment (45% for similarity of A, B, C classifications; $N = 78$). There was also no association between the classifications of infants with mothers and metaplot (51% similarity). There was, however, a significant ($p < .001$) tendency for similarity in the classifications of infant–father and infant-metapelet attachments (62% similarity).

TABLE 6.1
Similarity of mother–infant and father–infant attachment classifications

Study	N	Culture	Lag Between Assessments	Proport. Similar: A, B, C	Proport. Similar: Sec. vs. Insec.	Comments
Lamb (1978)	32	U.S.A.	1 week	?	72%	
Belsky, Garduque, & Hrncir (1984)	53	U.S.A.	1 month	?	58%	Proportion similar figure are based on a subsample of 45.
Owen & Chase-Lansdale (1982b)	132	U.S.A.	1.5 months	68%	70%	Similarity was influenced by father involvement, maternal employment, and baby's gender
Lamb, Hwang, Frodi & Frodi (1982)	51	Sweden	2 months	65%	65%	
Sagi, Lamb, Lewkowicz, Shoham, Dvir, & Estes (in press)	78	Israel	1.5 to 3 mo.	45%	46%	High inter-parental consistency (70%) in whether SS procedure was terminated or not.

Main & Weston (1981)	49	U.S.A.	6 months	51%	51%	Excludes 12 infants deemed "unclassifiable" with one or both (N = 2) parents. Of the total (N = 61) most mothers (45) seen at 12 months; most fathers all at 18 months.
Grossmann, Grossmann, Huber & Wartner (1981)	42	Germany	6 months	48%	50%	Excludes 4 infants deemed "unclassifiable" with one parent. Mothers all seen at 12 months; fathers all at 18 months.

With a few exceptions, therefore, the research in this area—which is summarized on Table 6.1—yields a consistent conclusion: Infants behave differently in the Strange Situation when observed with different attachment figures. However, the display of data on this table highlights an interesting pattern that has seldom been noted. Specifically, although few studies reported statistically significant intra-individual consistency, Table 6.1 shows that the degree of similarity was highest when the two assessments were temporally closest together (i.e., 72%: Lamb, 1978), and lowest when the inter-assessment interval was longest (44%: Main & Weston, 1981; 43%: Grossmann et al., 1981), even though the studies that involved the longest temporal separations between assessments involved samples in which there is likely to be substantial stability over time in the classification of infants with the same attachment figures (see Chapter 8 for a further discussion). In both cases, unfortunately, mothers were usually seen first (12 months) and fathers second (18 months) so we do not know whether developmental and/or order effects may have been influential. The ideal study would involve four groups of infants, each seen twice in the Strange Situation: Group 1, mother at time 1 and time 2; Group 2, father at time 1 and time 2; Group 3, mother at time 1, father at time 2; and Group 4, father at time 1, mother at time 2; but such a study has yet to be attempted. However, the results of other studies suggest that developmental changes and order effects should not have a substantial effect, and in neither case would the results strengthen claims regarding the importance of temperament. The pattern evident in Table 6.1 suggests that there may be a tendency for infants to behave somewhat similarly with different attachment figures, although this similarity is attenuated when there is opportunity for intervening events to affect patterns of Strange Situation behavior. However, the existing data are equivocal in support of this conclusion, and further study is thus needed.

This intriguing pattern aside, the implication of the data reported in this section is that the Strange Situation taps aspects of specific relationships, rather than just enduring infant characteristics (whether of constitutional or experiential origins). These studies provide some of the most consistent evidence concerning the effects (or lack of effects) of temperament on Strange Situation behavior; they suggest that temperamental differences *do not* have a strong *direct* effect on Strange Situation behavior.

PARENT-REPORT MEASURES OF TEMPERAMENT

Researchers who have studied the relationship between Strange Situation behavior and parent-report measures of infant temperament have also concluded that temperament does not have a strong, direct influence on

Strange Situation behavior. In contemporaneous assessments of tempera-ment and attachment, Thompson and Lamb (1982), using Rothbart's (1981) Infant Behavior Questionnaire, found no significant differences in the temperamental characteristics of A, B, and C group infants at either 12 1/2 or 19 1/2 months, despite the fact that temperament was significantly associated with stranger sociability scores at each age. Frodi (1983) reported different results; she found that the mothers of C group babies rated their infants as significantly more difficult on an inventory developed by Pederson, Anderson, & Cain (1976) than did mothers of A and B group babies. As if to underscore the lack of clarity concerning relationships with temperament, however, Owen and Chase–Lansdale (1982b) found that fathers of infants who were classified in the B group (with their fathers) rated their 12 month olds *more difficult* on the Toddler Temperament Scale (Fullard, McDevitt, & Carey, 1978) than did the fathers of non B group infants! A similar tendency was observed between mother–infant attach-ments and maternal perceptions of infant temperament. By contrast, Smith and Pederson (1983) reported no association between maternal perceptions of temperament on this measure and Strange Situation classification with mothers. Finally, Weber, Levitt, and Clark (1984) obtained maternal ratings of *both* maternal and infant temperament on the DOTS (Lerner, Palermo, Spiro, & Nesselroade, 1982) and related them to 13-month Strange Situation classifications. Again, there were no significant differ-ences in infant temperament according to attachment status although there were significant differences in maternal temperament associated with attachment classifications.

Studies relating Strange Situation behavior to earlier assessments of temperament have, on the whole, reported similar results. Belsky (personal communication) assessed maternal perceptions of tem-perament at 3 and 9 months using the five-factor Dimensions of Temperament Survey for Infants (DOTS-Infants: Lerner, Belsky, & Windle, 1983) and found no associations with either mother–infant or father–infant attachment classifications at one year. Similarly, Egeland and Farber (1982, 1984), in their socioeconomically disadvantaged sample, found no associations between 6-month scores on the nine dimensions of temperament of the Infant Temperament Questionnaire (Carey, 1970) and either 12- or 18-month attachment classifications. Finally, Maslin and Bates (1983) found that maternal perceptions of infant difficulty at 6 months as measured on the Infant Characteristics Questionnaire (Bates, Freeland, & Lounsbury, 1979) were minimally useful compared with other variables in predicting 13-month attachment classifications. The same was true of the three remaining ICQ scales and the nine scales of the Carey measure (Bates et al., in press).

Other researchers have studied the relationships between parent-report measures of temperament and the seven episode-by-episode interactive measures (e.g., proximity-seeking, resistance, etc.) which form the basis for the Strange Situation classifications. In Belsky's study (personal communication), interactive ratings for the two reunion episodes with mother and father (combined) yielded few significant associations with parental reports of the infant's temperament at both 3 and 9 months (five out of 80 correlations), none of which were consistent for both parents. Similarly, Bradshaw, Goldsmith, and Campos (1984) found very few significant correlations (1 out of 24 correlations) between IBQ (Rothbart, 1981) dimensions and reunion-episode interactive ratings in the Strange Situation. Finally, Weber, Levitt, and Clark (1984) found few significant correlations between the DOTS dimensions of infant temperament and mother-directed interactive behavior during either preseparation (three of 24 correlations significant) or reunion (two of 30 correlations significant) episodes. The same, incidentally, was generally true of dimensions of maternal temperament.

Taken together, these data indicate that variations in temperament as assessed using parent report questionnaires may not play a direct role in determining infant reactions in the Strange Situation. They also do not support claims regarding indirect influences of temperament on attachment, although they do not rule out the possibility that an interaction between maternal and infantile temperament determines the "goodness of fit" between them, and thus the quality of their interaction. Even if the findings were clearer, however, they would have to be interpreted cautiously. Vaughn, Taraldson, Crichton, and Egeland (1981) have argued that parent-report measures of infant temperament are highly subjective because they offer a description of infant behavior from the parent's perspective, rather than an objective account of the infant's characteristics. Vaughn et al. (1981), in fact, have argued that maternal personality (e.g., aggression, anxiety, social desirability) has a stronger (albeit weak) relationship to reported infant temperament than do more objective measures of infant temperament (such as infant social responsiveness in feeding and play)! This is especially important in attempts to relate temperament to Strange Situation behavior, which is itself affected by variations in parental attitudes, stresses, and background (see Chapters 5 and 8 for further detail). In considering temperament-attachment relationships, therefore, it is important to employ more objective, behaviorally-based assessments of infant behavioral style that are less subject to these kinds of subjective influences and may provide less gross and more sensitive measures of infant temperament. Negative results are always difficult to interpret, of course, but at the very least, research involving parent-report measures has thus far failed to support hypotheses concerning a direct link between temperament and Strange Situation behavior.

DIRECT OBSERVATIONAL MEASURES OF
TEMPERAMENT

Researchers who have employed more direct, observational measures of infant temperament paint a much more mixed picture of the relationships between temperament and attachment than do those who have relied on parent-report measures. In part, this is because several different research strategies have been employed in attempts to relate objective measures of temperament to Strange Situation classifications. First, some researchers have assessed the organization of neonatal behavior, and related the resulting measures with Strange Situation behavior. Second, other researchers have described individual differences in infant behavior in the course of home observations conducted during the first year, and then related these measures to Strange Situation classifications. Finally, some investigators have sought to relate individual differences in infant emotional behavior in the Strange Situation to the classifications. Let us consider examples of each of these approaches in turn.

Neonatal Assessments

Waters, Vaughn and Egeland (1980) administered 7-day and 10-day Neonatal Behavioral Assessment Scales (NBAS) (Brazelton, 1973) to a subsample ($N = 100$) of infants from the Minneapolis Study of Disadvantaged Families. These infants were subsequently observed in the Strange Situation at 12 months. Waters et al. reported that seven of the 27 items from the first (day-7) Brazelton assessments distinguished B from C group infants ($N = 26$). Group A infants were not compared. Most differences had to do with orientation, motor maturity, and regulation, with the C group infants being lower in muscle tone, attentiveness, and orientation than the B group infants. However, the same differences were *not* evident when the second (day-10) Brazelton scores were related to Strange Situation classifications, since by this time the performance of the C group infants had improved. Unfortunately, mean values for the day-10 assessment were not reported so it was impossible to determine whether similar patterns of group differences were apparent in the two assessments.

Egeland and Farber (1984) subsequently analyzed data from the whole sample, and did not replicate the results reported by Waters et al.: NBAS scores were unrelated to 12-month attachment classifications. Compared with Waters et al., Egeland and Farber (1984) used factor scores rather than individual item scores, considered the whole sample rather than a subsample, and combined scores from the two Brazelton assessments instead of treating them separately. Even allowing for these differences, there is a surprising lack of convergence between their results and those earlier reported by Waters et al. (1980). Since Waters et al. were not able to obtain the same results with both Brazelton assessments, and Egeland and Farber reported no reliable relationships between Brazelton scores and Strange Situation behavior, there is no evidence that neonatal assessments are related in any direct or consistent way to later Strange Situation behavior. Paradoxically, Egeland and Farber (1982) reported that two of three factor scores derived from nurses' ratings of infants in the neonatal nursery *were* significantly associated with 12-month attachment status; C's were rated as less active and alert and B's as easier to care for. None of these neonatal factors was associated with 18-month attachment classifications, however.

Crockenberg (1981) also sought to relate BNBAS scores to later Strange Situation behavior. She found that a cluster of items assessing irritability during the 5-day and 10-day NBAS assessments *did* predict non-B group classification at one year—but only for mother–infant dyads who reported low social support. The relationship did not hold for the complete sample, however, again suggesting that there was no direct relationship between individual differences in neonatal behavior and later Strange Situation behavior.

Attachment researchers in other countries have also looked for behavioral indicators of temperamental characteristics that may predict later attachment classifications. Grossmann and Grossmann (1983; Grossmann, Grossmann, Spangler, Suess, & Unzner, in press) obtained NBAS assessments for their German sample on three occasions during the first two weeks after birth, and compared these scores with attachment classifications at one year. For two out of three assessments, B group infants obtained somewhat higher ($p < .09$) scores than avoidant infants on an orientation factor. (Resistant infants—of whom there were few [$N = 6$]—did not differ from either group.) In addition, on one of the three assessments avoidant infants obtained significantly higher scores than resistant infants on an irritability factor, but no other group comparisons were significant. When scores for each factor were averaged across the three assessments, however, there were *no* significant A–B–C group differences. Despite this, Grossmann and Grossmann (1983) concluded that "the newborn orientation responses were equally good predictors of secure attachment in the Strange Situation as our maternal sensitivity scores at 2 and at 6 months of age" (p. 9). Note, however, the unreliability of the associations, and the fact that the direction of the group differences ran counter to the direction of differences earlier reported by Waters et al. (1980).

Miyake and his colleagues (Miyake, Chen, Ujiie, Tajima, Satoh, & Takahashi, 1981-82; Miyake, Chen, & Campos, in press) have, in their longitudinal studies of 29 middle-class Japanese infants, made the most ambitious efforts to identify early aspects of behavioral style that predict later attachment classification. In their study, Strange Situation observations at one year were preceded by: (1) assessments of newborn distress reactive to the interruption of sucking (see Bell, Weller, & Waldrop, 1971); (2) 2-hour home observations of infant behavior at 1 and 3 months of age; (3) a 13-minute assessment of stranger reactions and separation distress and an assessment of mother–infant interaction at 7½ months; and (4) a 10-minute free-play session with the mother at 11 months. These assessments revealed several differences between B group and resistant infants earlier in the first year (there were no infants deemed avoidant in this Japanese sample). Specifically, although newborns who were later rated C or "pseudo-C" in the Strange Situation exhibited a significantly longer rise-time to distress than did future B group infants (suggesting that the future C-like infants were *less* irritable), they were later judged to be significantly more fearful on both the stranger-approach and separation assessments at 7½ months, and they spent less time at play in order to retreat to the mother at 11 months. Miyake and his colleagues also concluded that there was a moderate degree of consistency in individual differences on these measures over the first year by inspection of contingency tables arraying these data.

    Miyake et al.'s study is noteworthy because, unlike the other studies described in this subsection, it does not involve the implicit and questionable assumption that differences in neonatal behavior are reflections of temperamental differences. Their research design involves clear recognition of the need for multi-situational assessments of infantile characteristics, particularly individual differences in infantile emotionality. However, Miyake et al. did not obtain strong support for the argument that temperamental variations play a primary role in determining Strange Situation behavior: The sample size was small, expectable group differences were not evident on several measures (e.g., 8–10 measures of infant behavior relating to affect and activity during the home observations), and the direction of differences on some others was counterintuitive (see above). The data are suggestive, nonetheless, and Miyake et al. hope that results obtained in a second, hypothesis-testing, sample will replicate those results reported for the first cohort.

Home Observational Measures of Infant Behavior

Ainsworth and colleagues (1978) noted that in the original Baltimore sample, infants later classified in either the A or C groups on the basis of their Strange Situation behavior cried significantly more during the first and fourth quarter-year observations than did B group infants. Infants in the A and C groups did not, however, differ significantly from each other. As

Ainsworth et al. noted, however, these measures of crying were confounded with variations in maternal responsiveness (see Bell & Ainsworth, 1972), and thus may not have yielded reliable inferences concerning early infant characteristics per se. Similarly, Blehar, Lieberman, and Ainsworth's (1977) findings that infants later classified in the B_3 group on the basis of Strange Situation behavior showed more smiling and "bouncing" and less fussing than A and C group infants in face-to-face play with mother during the first quarter-year are also difficult to interpret, since relevant maternal behavior again differed.

Belsky, Rovine, and Taylor (1984) have, however, reported findings which were consistent with some, but not all, aspects of Ainsworth's report. In their longitudinal investigation of mother and infant behavior at home, they found that the amount of infant distress at 3 and 9 months (but not at 1 month) was significantly associated with 12-month attachment status; A and C group infants evinced more distress than those in the B group. However, the pattern of results differed at each age, with A group infants highest in distress at 3 months and C group infants highest at 9 months. Interestingly, their cross-lag panel correlations indicated that maternal involvement during the preceding observation predicted crying in the subsequent observation, but crying and involvement were not correlated during the same observation. Even so, variations in infant crying were also autocorrelated across each observation. Thus differences in crying showed some temporal stability but were also influenced by differences in maternal behavior.

In their longitudinal study, Bates et al. (in press) found no significant associations between 13-month attachment status and four factor scores relating to infant behavior during a 6-month home observation. Only one of four infant factors (infant object communication) from a 13-month home observation was associated with attachment status. Finally, Antonucci and Levitt (1984) found very few associations between 13-month attachment classification and infant behavior during a laboratory-based preseparation–separation–reunion sequence at 7 months. Overall, therefore, there is no consistent evidence that infantile characteristics as assessed during earlier home observations, predict later variations in Strange Situation behavior.

Emotionality in the Strange Situation

Several researchers have studied the role that emotional arousal plays in Strange Situation behavior in order to better understand emotion-attachment interrelationships, and these data can provide a useful perspective on proposals that differences in a temperamentally-based "proneness to distress" may underlie Strange Situation behavior (Kagan, 1982). Not surprisingly, resistant (i.e., C group) infants, on average, show the most, avoidant (i.e., A group) infants the least, and B group infants an intermediate amount of separation distress (Ainsworth et al., 1978; Grossmann, Schwan, & Grossmann, in press), but these group differences mask substantial individual variation in separation reactions *within* each classification. Some avoidant infants (particularly those in the A_2 subgroup), for example, show marked separation distress, while some B group babies (particularly those in the B_1 and B_2 subgroups) do not become upset at all during separation episodes. Thus, when Thompson and Lamb (1984a) studied the relationships between attachment classification and emotional arousal in the Strange Situation, they found it useful to divide the B group infants into two subgroup clusters (i.e., $B_{1,2}$ and $B_3,4$) to explore the diversity of emotional reactions manifest by B group infants (Ainsworth et al., 1978). Thompson and Lamb (1984a) identified two patterns of emotional responding. Infants in group A and the B_1 and B_2 subgroups exhibited mild separation distress with a long latency to onset but a quick recovery during reunions. By contrast, infants in group C and the B_3 and B_4 subgroups displayed intense separation distress with a brief latency but prolonged recovery time. Subsequent analyses by Connell and Thompson (1984) indicated that emotional reactions in the Strange Situation predicted social interactive behavior more than the reverse, suggesting that emotionality may play an important causal role in underlying infant reunion behavior. Similar results were subsequently reported by Gaensbauer, Connell, and Schultz (1983) and by Frodi and Thompson (in preparation). The fact that the patterns of emotional responses did not correspond to the "secure" vs. "insecure" (i.e., B vs. A/C) distinction indicates that while emotional arousal and Strange Situation behavior may be related, assignment to Strange Situation groups is not determined solely by variations in the intensity of separation distress, as Kagan (1982) has proposed.

Instead, the results of these three studies suggest that differences in the intensity of emotional arousal may underlie a single dimension of infant reunion behavior whose poles are anchored by strong contact-maintaining on the one end and distance interaction at the other. Thus with increasing distress, infants become less satisfied with greeting the caregiver by distal modes (e.g., smiling, vocalizing, etc.) and instead require close physical contact in order to be comforted. However, the *quality* of both the distance interaction or the contact-seeking behavior—that is, whether or not distance interaction is accompanied by clear-cut avoidance, and whether or not contact-seeking is combined with angry resistance—cannot be accounted for solely by variations in the intensity of distress; causes of these differences must thus be sought elsewhere (for example, in the quality of previous caretaking experiences). Thus to the extent that individual differences in the "proneness to distress" are temperamentally based and affect Strange

Situation behavior, they seem to influence only a particular aspect of reunion behavior—specifically, the desire for close, physical contact with the attachment figure.

In any event, there is no clear evidence from any of these studies that the intensity of separation distress in the Strange Situation is, in fact, temperamentally determined. Thompson and Lamb (1984a) found that emotion-attachment interrelationships were consistent in repeated Strange Situation observations at $12\frac{1}{2}$ and $19\frac{1}{2}$ months, even though many infants showed different separation reactions and were assigned different attachment classifications in the two assessments. Jacobsen and Wille (1984a) reported that separation reactions in the Strange Situation were associated with the amount of prior infant–mother separation. In addition, there is suggestive evidence that cultural variations in child-rearing practices may predispose infants in some cultures (e.g., Japan) to experience markedly more and in some cultures (e.g., N. Germany) markedly less separation distress than is typical for American infants, and this is likely to affect the quality of their reunion behaviors (see Chapter 11 for fuller details). Furthermore, Ainsworth et al. (1978) reported that when infants were observed in the Strange Situation with their mothers twice within a two-week period, they manifested much more distress during the second assessment—enough, in fact, to shift some infants from A and $B_{1,2}$ classifications into $B_{3,4}$ and C classifications. Thus although variations in the intensity of separation distress clearly influence reunion behavior in the Strange Situation and *may* be affected by aspects of temperament, earlier experiences also have an important influence on emotional reactions to separation and reunion.

CONCLUSION

As we indicated at the outset, researchers' interest in the effects of infant characteristics (like temperament) on Strange Situation behavior derives from a desire to better understand infantile influences on developing attachment relationships. Such research is especially important in view of the rather vague associations between maternal characteristics and Strange Situation behavior reported in the previous chapter. The findings summarized here and in Chapter 5 suggest that, in addition to exploring the formative influences of parental practices, researchers might be wise to study the ways in which these practices *interact with* infant characteristics in affecting attachment relationships. Since infants themselves differ, any parental behavior may have different effects depending on the infants' behavioral styles, and thus temperamental characteristics may have an important—but complexly indirect—influence on Strange Situation behavior.

Unfortunately, most studies in this area have been designed in such a way that their results can only elucidate the direct effects of temperament on Strange Situation behavior, rather than indirect or interactive effects. Since most theorists expect complex interactive effects, and most studies have explored direct or main effects, it is perhaps not surprising that the results obtained have been so disconfirmatory. In fact, all the research strategies reported here have yielded findings inconsistent with hypotheses concerning direct relationships between aspects of temperament and Strange Situation behavior. Evidence concerning both the consistency of infant–mother and infant–father attachments and the occurrence of changes in attachment status over time also suggest that temperament does not have a strong influence on Strange Situation behavior. Parent-report measures of infant temperament have not shown strong associations with attachment status, and even though there are interpretational problems with such measures, the evidence is no less inconclusive because of them. Likewise, neither assessments of neonatal behavior nor other measures of infant behavior later in the first year consistently predict individual differences in Strange Situation behavior, although some suggestive associations have been reported by Belsky et al. (1984). Studies conducted in Germany and Japan also offered suggestions concerning the influence of temperament on attachment, but in neither case were the findings unambiguous. Finally, studies of emotion-attachment relationships do not support Kagan's (1982) notion that assignment to the A, B, and C categories largely depends on temperamentally-based variations in the intensity of separation reactions: Infants in some of the "secure" and "insecure" subgroups manifest similar degrees of distress, and it has yet to be demonstrated that differences in separation are attributable primarily to temperamental rather than experiential origins.

The problem with much of this evidence is that it addresses only the most direct effects of temperament on attachment, and thus fails to address any hypotheses concerning more indirect, interactive influences. To evaluate more complex models, future studies must be designed to assess infant characteristics both within and outside of interactive situations beginning early in the first year in order to better understand the child's contributions to interactive harmony. In longitudinal analyses, stability of infant characteristics and their changing influence on adult–infant interaction over the first year could be appraised. Another challenging task is to devise observational assessments of the behavioral style so that future studies are less reliant on parent-report measures. Finally, as we indicated earlier, temperamental influences must be studied in the context, not only of parental characteristics, but also of the broader life conditions of the family. For example, temperamental difficulty may have a more potent influence on attachment status when the parent–infant dyad experiences social stress and few sources of support, as Crockenberg's (1981) findings seem to indicate.

These are clearly challenging tasks, and involve more complicated research designs than those necessary to examine the direct effects of temperament on attachment. Yet they are central to researchers' attempts to understand the antecedents of Strange Situation behavior, in the context of the multiple influences on the mother–infant relationship, including those emanating from within the baby. This is especially important in view of the weakness of the findings concerning maternal antecedents, and mandates future studies of the development of mother–infant attachments involving more complex reciprocal influences within the dyad.

7

INTEGRATION: THE ORIGINS AND INTERPRETATION OF STRANGE SITUATION BEHAVIOR

In this section, we have reviewed both theoretical and empirical issues pertaining to the interpretation of Strange Situation behavior. Let us start by summarizing briefly the conclusions reached in Chapters 4, 5, and 6 respectively.

First, we argued in Chapter 4 that the principles of evolutionary biology do not provide a reason to assert that there is a single optimal pattern of infant behavior that develops when the child is reared in a specific optimal fashion. Nor is there a single adaptive pattern of parental behavior entailing consistent sensitivity to infant cues. Rather, there are likely to be multiple pathways and multiple outcomes as infants and parents make the most of their ecological conditions. Behavioral flexibility rather than stereotyping seems mandated by natural selection. Although evolutionary biology has not been a primary concern for attachment theorists since Bowlby, we have suggested some useful questions it does raise for researchers interested in this topic. In particular, it broadened our view of the potential meaning of A, B, and C patterns of Strange Situation behavior, moving us away from global "adaptive" and "maladaptive" designations to a perspective on each pattern as a unique conditional strategy.

Second, we showed that the relationship between prior patterns of parent–infant interaction and subsequent Strange Situation behavior is not at all clearly defined. Many studies have in fact demonstrated that B-type behavior in the Strange Situation tends to be associated with patterns of dyadic interaction or parental behavior that might be considered harmonious and that Americans consider desirable. Although most researchers describe these patterns of behavior as "sensitive," however, the actual behavioral indices or manifestations of "sensitivity" vary dramatically from one study to the next, so we still have little idea what patterns of behavior are actually of formative significance, and which are formatively irrelevant constructs. In addition, specific behavioral measures of parenting have yielded fewer associations with attachment status than have broader rating scales, further clouding what is meant by the parental sensitivity construct. Obviously, this is a crucial issue for those who would attempt to *explain* the processes or mechanisms by which prior parent–infant interaction is related to subsequent Strange Situation behavior.

Strange Situation behavior may be influenced by temperament in at least three ways. First, dimensions of temperament may affect patterns of reaction to the Strange Situation directly, inasmuch as temperament affects factors such as proneness to distress, approach reactions to novel events and novel people, soothability, and engagement with toys. Note, however, that there is currently little empirical support for this hypothesis, because we do not know whether the individual differences in these dimensions are of temperamental origin. Second, constitutional differences in behavioral/emotional style or temperament presumably affect the nature of parent–infant interaction depending on the goodness of fit between parental characteristics and infantile temperament (e.g., Thomas & Chess, 1977). Thus an irritable infant may be difficult for most parents to rear, although some may cope better than others. As Crockenberg (1981), Lamb and Easterbrooks (1981), and Belsky (1984) have suggested, the ability to do so may depend not simply on parental personality/temperament as many might believe, but also on the extent to which the parent's social situation supports or taxes the parent's coping capacities. Third, individual differences in temperament may affect the infant's cognitive understanding or interpretation of the parent's behavioral style during formatively important periods (e.g., Lamb, 1981a, 1981b). Thus, for example, an infant who is distractible and inattentive (perhaps due to distress) may fail to recognize the predictability or unpredictability of the adult's responsiveness. To the extent that variations in Strange Situation behavior reflect variations in the child's expectation about the adult's likely behavior—a plausible though largely unverified hypothesis—then temperament may affect Strange Situation behavior as well.

As we showed in Chapter 6, there is no strong evidence that variations in infant temperament have a direct, straightforward effect on the Strange Situation classifications. The more complex indirect interactive relationships between temperament and attachment have remained largely unexplored, although such theoretical speculations concerning temperament-attachment relationships are most prominent. It seems reasonable to expect that temperament *may* interact with parental characteristics, living conditions, and other factors affecting the development of attachment relationships, but until the relevant multivariate longitudinal studies are completed, we will not know the nature of these interactive associations. The best conclusion currently supported by the data is that temperament may affect Strange Situation behavior but not—with some important exceptions, as discussed below—those variations that are captured by the Strange Situation classification system on which much of our discussion in this book is focused.

In future attempts to relate Strange Situation behavior to prior and contemporaneous patterns of infant–parent interaction, there is a clear need for hypothesis-driven research in which multiple independent studies are conducted using the same variables and in which characteristics of infant, parent, interaction patterns, and social circumstances are repeatedly assessed (using various measures of each relevant construct) so that one can reliably assess the interrelation among these, and determine whether changes occur in these constructs over time in a systematic and explicable fashion. The need for such longitudinal studies is also documented in Chapter 9; suffice it to say that the "security of attachment" *ought* to change in response to changes in patterns of dyadic interaction, which *should* in turn change in response to developmentally or ecologically-driven changes in the propensities of either partner. This is not an unrealistic research task. Statisticians and methodologists have recently developed the procedures— including partial least squares analysis (Wold, 1982) and structural equation modeling (Joreskog & Sorbom, 1977, 1981; McArdle, in press)—to permit the evaluation of complex causal models involving imperfectly measurable constructs. These techniques should be of great help in exploring the origins of Strange Situation behavior and of individual differences in attachment more generally.

Several issues deserve explicit attention in future research endeavors of this sort. First, researchers need to include in their studies observation of both prior and contemporaneous parent–child interaction, so that we can systematically assess the extent to which Strange Situation behavior reflects the *current* status of the parent–child relationship (which varies, to greater or lesser extent, over time) rather than patterns of interaction at some *earlier*, formative period. We suggest later that the data point more toward the former interpretation and this may have substantial implications for our understanding of the origins of attachment patterns, as well as the design of clinical interventions for disturbed parent–child relationships.

Second, one reason for the surprisingly small and quite general relationships found between parental behavior and Strange Situation behavior may be the reliance on a closed-ended classification system that prevents researchers from distinguishing "good" and "bad" examples within any category, and fosters the inappropriate belief that we are dealing with homogeneous groups of infants. In fact, patterns of Strange Situation behavior may emerge from variable interactions among parental practices, infant characteristics, and cultural norms (see Chapter 11). It is important to recognize that there may be multiple pathways to "A-ness" (or "B-ness," or "C-ness") and that we cannot assume that all A group infants have experienced the same antecedent patterns of care. Considerations from evolutionary biology support this view. Likewise, we should perhaps recognize *degrees* of "A-ness," for example, as a means of improving the empirical fit between Strange Situation behavior and corresponding patterns of parent–child interaction, as well as better understanding the variable origins of A-type Strange Situation behavior.

Most generally, attachment theorists need to avoid the simple equations of "attachment security" with Strange Situation behavior. Security of attachment (or, more generally, the harmoniousness of infant–parent interaction) appears to be among the factors affecting Strange Situation behavior, but so too may be aspects of the child's temperament and immediately prior experiences unrelated to the long-term quality of dyadic interaction. In order to specify and assess the relative importance of the antecedents of attachment security, it will be necessary to employ multiple convergent measures of attachment security (including the Strange Situation) and multiple convergent measures of each of the likely antecedent factors.

Currently, the data suggest that socially-desirable parental behavior is associated in the United States with socially-desirable infantile behavior, specifically B-type behavior in the Strange Situation. Similar patterns do not appear as consistently in other cultures, although support for this assertion is not yet strong (see Chapter 11). If it proves to be true, however, this cross-cultural disparity may have crucial implications for the interpretation of Strange Situation behavior and studies concerned with the origins of individual differences in Strange Situation behavior. These findings would mean that some unmeasured characteristic (such as familiarity with strangers or separation from the parents) actually had causal significance, or that in some (as yet unspecified) fashion, cultural values shape not simply patterns of parental behavior (which they obviously do) but also the ways in which preverbal and cognitively-limited infants understand and respond to their experiences. Thus, for example, German infants may interpret their parents' encouragement of independence much differently than Japanese infants would interpret the same behavior.

Of course, such a pattern of results would further complicate attempts to specify uniquely-suited universal patterns of childrearing with uniquely-specifiable effects on child development. Even if this were not the case, however, we feel comfortable asserting that such an hypothesis is implausible given our understanding of behavioral biology. It seems more likely that infants develop conditional strategies of behaving toward their parents—strategies that maximize their chances of surviving to reproductive maturity in the context of the environment created in part by their parents (and others involved in their rearing). This would imply that individual differences in infant–adult attachment would be juvenile adaptations. If patterns of attachment do have implications for personality and behavior after maturity is reached, therefore, these would be coincidental or accidental, rather than outcomes for which the behavior was designed (evolutionarily-speaking) in the first place. Behavioral ecology may be useful in helping us specify what sorts of environments we might expect to be associated with particular patterns of attachment, and in so doing, it would help us to formulate testable hypotheses about the relationship between parental behavior and conditional infant strategies. This would best be achieved by focusing on prototypical index cases rather than marginal cases: clearcut avoidance (type 1), clearcut contact seeking (type 2), and clearcut angry rejection (type 3), for example. What circumstances might we expect to produce such patterns of infantile behavior in response to the stress of separation?

In this, as in many other cases, our task is hampered by the sole reliance on separation–reunion situations for studying individual differences in infant attachment behavior. We would surely be better able to specify the conditions associated with particular patterns of infant behavior if we could specify in a multi-situational fashion the patterns of infant behavior we are seeking to explain. We need to assess individual differences in the harmoniousness of infant–parent interaction across multiple contexts to identify most of the major dimensions along which infants are likely to vary in meaningful and interpretable fashion.

At present, in sum, we see three major issues that must guide future research on the antecedents of individual differences in attachment. First, it is important to distinguish between Strange Situation behavior and the security of attachment, which is likely only one of the factors affecting Strange Situation behavior. Second, we need as a result to develop multisituational procedures for assessing the quality of infant–parent attachment relationships over time. Third, attempts to explore the antecedents of individual differences in infant–parent relationships must involve multiple assessments of each of the putative formative factors, including parental behavior, infantile characteristics, and factors in their social ecology.

III STABILITY AND PREDICTION

8 THE TEMPORAL STABILITY OF ATTACHMENT CLASSIFICATIONS

INTRODUCTION

Claims concerning the stability of attachment classifications are not as central to at least some attachment theorists as are assertions about their antecedents or interpretations. To be sure, it has been claimed (e.g., Waters, 1983) that evidence of high stability is of crucial importance to the interpretability of Strange Situation behaviors, since these classifications are presumed to reflect consistent dimensions of mother–infant interaction. Others (e.g., Thompson & Lamb, 1984b; Thompson, Lamb, & Estes, 1982, 1983; Vaughn, Egeland, Sroufe, & Waters, 1979), however, have argued that if the classifications accurately reflect a dyad's interactive quality, they *should* change when events or circumstances occur which influence the quality of dyadic interaction. If the security of attachment did not change in the face of stressful events or changes likely to affect the quality of interaction, there would be reason to doubt that the Strange Situation is a sensitive index of the parent–infant relationship. Thus the reliability and validity of the Strange Situation procedure can be demonstrated by both high and low levels of temporal stability, provided that changes in classification status are meaningfully related to the kinds of circumstances that may affect adult–infant interaction. Evidence for such external correlates contributes to the validity of the Strange Situation procedure and the interpretability of changes in attachment status. Interestingly, however, one can observe a change over time in the implicit goal of researchers. Following an initial concern about demonstrating that Strange Situation classifications were, or at least could be, stable over time, most researchers

TABLE 8.1
Temporal stability of mother–infant attachment classifications

Study	Social Class Status	N	Age at Time 1	Age at Time 2	Overall Classif. Stability	B group Stability	non-B group Stability
Waters (1978)	middle-income	50	12 mos.	18 mos.	96%	100%	90%
Vaughn, Egeland, Sroufe & Waters (1979)[1]	lower-income	100	12 mos.	18 mos.	62%	82%	38%
Egeland & Farber (1984)[1] (see also Farber, 1981)	lower-income	189	12 mos.	18 mos.	60%	74%	41%
Egeland & Sroufe (1981)[1]							
a) inadequate care	lower-income	25	12 mos.	18 mos.	48%	78%	31%
b) excellent care	lower-income	32	12 mos.	18 mos.	81%	92%	50%
Thompson, Lamb, & Estes (1982)	middle-income	43	12 1/2 mos.	19 1/2 mos.	53%	67%	23%
Frodi, Grolnick & Bridges (1984)	middle-income	38	12 mos.	20 mos.	66%	77%	25%
Owen, Easter-brooks, Chase-Lansdale, & Goldberg (1983, 1984)	middle-income	59	12 mos.	20 mos.	78%[2]	no report	no report
Connell (1976)[3]	middle-income	47	12 mos.	18 mos.	81%	87%	70%
Main & Weston (1981)	middle-income	15	12 mos.	18 mos.	73%[4]	no report	no report

SHORT-TERM STABILITY STUDIES

Ainsworth, Blehar, Waters & Wall (1978) (sample 3)	middle-income	23	50 wks.	52 wks.	56%	86%	11%
Goossens, van IJzendoorn, Kroonenberg & Tavecchio (1984) (Dutch)	middle income	39	18 mos.	19 mos.	—Same observational context— 95% 100% 88% —Different observational context— 55% 75% 25%		

[1]These samples are drawn from the same sample and include many of the same subjects.
[2]Stability of father–infant attachments ($N=53$) over the same period was 62%.
[3]Infants were classified using a modified version of Ainsworth's system (see text).
[4]Stability of father–infant attachments ($N=15$) over the same period was 87%.

are now concerned about defining when, and under what circumstances, we should expect stability, and when we would predict instability or change.

Since 1978, there have been several studies focused on the stability of Strange Situation classifications, and their findings are dicussed in this chapter. The key characteristics of the studies are summarized in Table 8.1, while further details are discussed in the pages that follow.

DEMONSTRATING TEMPORAL STABILITY

In the first study to examine the temporal stability of attachment classifications, Waters (1978) sought to show that, contrary to Masters and Wellman's (1974) conclusion, some measures of mother–infant interaction *could* show stability over time if they reflected the appropriate level of behavioral organization. Such a finding was extremely important at a time when there was great skepticism about the reliability of any measures of infant–parent interaction (see Chapter 3). Waters correctly perceived the need to demonstrate that some measures were reliable in test–retest studies and his demonstration thus set the stage for the explosion of research on attachment that followed.

In his study, Waters confirmed that time-sampled counts or ratings of discrete behaviors in the Strange Situation (e.g., looking, smiling) correlated poorly over a 6-month period (12 to 18 months), but showed that Ainsworth's interactive rating scores (e.g., proximity-seeking, resistance) were more highly correlated over time. Most impressively, 48 out of 50 infants (96%) obtained the same attachment classification at both ages. (Stability of subgroup classifications was 53%.) Thus using the global classification scheme, Waters reported impressive stability over time, even though discrete behaviors were poorly correlated over the two assessments.

The interpretation and generalizability of these findings depends, of course, on the nature of the sample. Waters (1977, 1978) described the sample as lower middle to upper middle class with all families intact and all mothers between 22 and 30 years of age. However, Vaughn, Egeland, Sroufe, and Waters (1979), later described Waters' sample as stable in paternal employment, residence and marital status during the study. This report noted:

> Waters (1978) selected stable middle-class families deliberately. Attachment relationships were viewed as arising from and being maintained by interaction and were expected to be most stable when environmental supports for interaction were stable and when unanticipated changes in stress were minimized. (Vaughn et al., 1979, p. 971).

Such precautions seem reasonable, given Waters' desire to show that measures of mother–infant interaction *could* show stability, but they place limits on the generalizability of Waters' estimate of stability. Waters (1983) has since indicated that no special sample recruitment procedures were employed, but the lack of information about family circumstances and life events between the two assessments makes the stability figure from his study difficult to interpret or generalize.

EFFECTS OF STRESSFUL LIFE EVENTS AND CHANGING FAMILY CIRCUMSTANCES

Lower Income Families

The effects of changing family circumstances on the stability of attachment classification were illustrated by Vaughn et al. (1979), who studied socioeconomically disadvantaged, lower-income families from the Minneapolis Study of Disadvantaged Families. The majority of families earned incomes at or below poverty levels, and only about half the mothers were living with a male partner at the time of the 18-month assessment. Thus these families were more likely to experience unexpected and stressful changes in life circumstances. When 100 of the 267 mothers and infants in the sample were observed in the Strange Situation at 12 and 18 months, only 62% obtained the same classification at both ages.

Like Waters (1978), Vaughn et al. (1979) reported that their sample showed significant temporal stability in attachment classifications, despite widely varying stability estimates (i.e., 96% vs. 62%). Both used Cohen's Kappa statistic (Cohen, 1960, 1968; Fleiss, Cohen, & Everitt, 1969) to test significance. An alternative statistic for this purpose would be *lambda* (Goodman & Kruskal, 1954), which is an index of predictive association. Lambda is designed to reflect the reduction in the probability of error in specifying one categorical variable (e.g., 18-month attachment classification) given knowledge of another categorical variable (e.g., 12-month classification). In Waters' (1978) sample, knowledge of the 12-month classifications reduced predictive error of the 18-month classifications by an impressive 89%. In the Vaughn et al. (1979) sample, however, knowledge of the 12-month classifications improved prediction of 18-month classifications by only 3%.

Vaughn and his colleagues also obtained information from mothers concerning changes in life circumstances occurring between the two assessments. From a 44-item checklist inventory completed by the mothers (adapted by Egeland, Breitenbucher, Dodd, Pastor, & Rosenberg [1979] from Cochrane & Robertson, 1973), Vaughn et al. (1979) calculated weighted ratings of the severity of life stresses experienced by mothers between the 12-month and 18-month observations. For example, a routine move to a new home during this period received a score of 1; a move precipitated by fire, property destruction or other life-threatening circumstances received a score of 3. The kinds of events involved ranged from severe stresses (e.g.,a jail sentence for a member of the family; involvement in a physical fight; a suicide attempt by a family member, etc.) to relatively minor changes in life circumstances (e.g., promotion or change of responsibilities at work; new neighbor; "serious restriction of social life"; increase in number of arguments with spouse, etc.). The total scores could thus reflect a small number of highly stressful events or a larger number of milder life changes.

Vaughn and his colleagues compared four groups: (1) infants who changed from B group to non-B group status ($N = 10$); (2) infants who changed from non-B to B group status ($N = 21$); (3) infants who obtained B-group classifications at both ages ($N = 45$); and (4) infants who obtained non-B group classifications at both ages ($N = 24$). One significant difference between these groups was reported: Mothers of infants in group (1) obtained significantly higher life-stress scores ($M = 10.00$) than the mothers in group (3) ($M = 4.87$). Mean scores for the other two groups fell between these two; there were no differences between families in which infants changed from non-B to B group classifications and those in which the infants obtained non-B classifications at both ages. In sum, life stresses appeared to affect Strange Situation behavior, though not as reliably as one might expect.

In a subsequent report on the sample from which the Vaughn et al. subsample was drawn, Egeland and Farber (1984; see also Farber, 1981) assessed attachment stability for an additional 89 mother–infant pairs combined with the 100 families studied by Vaughn et al. (1979). These 189 families (71% of the original sample of 267) constituted the entire corpus of infants seen twice in the Strange Situation. Stability of major-group classification status for this combined sample was 60%. This figure may actually overestimate the degree of classification stability in the sample, however, since Egeland and Sroufe (1981b) reported that the majority of infant–mother dyads who dropped out of the original sample of 267 were insecurely attached. Other researchers have found that A and C group infants are more likely to change classification than are B group infants (see Table 8.1). The stability of subgroup classifications was not reported.

Instead of life stresses, Egeland and Farber (1984) sought to relate changes in the Strange Situation classifications to multiple measures of mother, infant, and mother–infant interaction obtained both prenatally and at various points in the baby's first year. Of more than 100 measures (i.e., at least 36 measures of maternal characteristics; 27 measures of infant characteristics derived from nurses' ratings, 7-day and 10-day Brazelton NBAS scores, 6-month temperament ratings and 9-month Bayley scores; and 54 ratings of mother–infant interaction during feedings at 3 and 6 months and play at 6 months), only a few ratings of early maternal personality were consistently associated with changes in the Strange Situation behavior. These were not predicted and it is not clear why we would expect early maternal characteristics to be solely influential. Compared to the mothers of infants who obtained B group classifications at both 12 and 18 months, the mothers of babies who changed from the B group to the A or C groups were prenatally more aggressive, suspicious (same differences found 3 months post partum), and less prone to social desirability tendencies. Compared to the mothers of infants who were classified in the A or C groups in both assessments, the mothers of babies who changed from non-B to B group classification statuses were more aggressive prenatally. (Group comparisons were different, however, when stable A's were compared with A's who became B's, and when stable C's were compared with C's who became B's.) There were no other significant findings consistent for infants in both the non-B groups. In light of the large number of statistical tests and the small number of significant group differences these findings must be considered only suggestive until replicated.[1]

In a third report from this sample, Egeland and Sroufe (1981a, 1981b) selected two groups from this disadvantaged sample: one group containing mothers identified as being seriously neglectful or abusive of their infants (inadequate care group, $N = 31$), and the other group comprising mothers considered by the researchers to be providing high-quality care (excellent care group, $N = 33$). The assignment to groups was based on scores from a Child Care Rating Scale (Egeland & Brunnquell, 1979). Besides the quality of infant care, however, mothers in these groups differed in other ways also: Women in the inadequate care group were younger, less well educated and more frequently unmarried than women in the excellent care group, although infants in the two groups did not differ significantly at birth. When Strange Situation observations at 12 and 18 months were compared, 12 out of 25 infants in the inadequate care group (48%) obtained the same classification in both assessments, compared with 26 out of 32 infants in the excellent care group (81%). No information was provided about specific external correlates of changes in attachment status.

In an independent study, Schneider–Rosen, Braunwald, Carlson, and Cicchetti (in press) reported on the stability of attachment classifications among infants from lower-income, socioeconomically disadvantaged backgrounds who either had or had not been maltreated by their parents.

---

[1]In their report, Egeland and Farber (1984) separately compared the following groups: (a) stable B vs. B to A; (b) stable B vs. B to C; (c) stable A vs. A to B; and (d) stable C vs. C to B. In our summary, we have discussed only the data relevant to the groups compared by Vaughn et al. (1979) in their earlier analyses of data from this sample, that is: stable B; stable non-B; non-B to B; and B to non-B. Egeland and Farber (1984) suggest no a priori justifications for the new analytic strategy, which makes it harder to compare findings across studies and reports.

Twenty-four infants (10 maltreated and 14 comparison) were observed in the Strange Situation at both 12 and 18 months. Only half the maltreated infants received the same classification at each age, compared to 71% of the infants in the comparison group. Thirty-two infants (16 maltreated and 16 comparison) were observed at both 18 and 24 months. Again, only half the maltreated infants obtained the same overall attachment classification, compared to 81% of the infants in the comparison group. No specific external correlates of stability or change in attachment status were reported for either group.

This study is also noteworthy since it is the only one in which consistent classification criteria were *not* applied in the 12-, 18-, and 24-month Strange Situation assessments. Instead, these researchers used Ainsworth's classification criteria for 12-month-olds, and then modified these criteria slightly to encompass the changing abilities of the older children. While this somewhat complicates interpretation of their stability estimates, Schneider–Rosen et al. (in press) provided some support for the validity of their revised classification criteria. They noted that the distribution of nonmaltreated infants among the A, B, and C groups at the older ages accorded with the distributions obtained by other researchers using the standard classification criteria.

Middle Class Families

Waters (1978) had shown that high stability of attachment classification could be demonstrated in a middle-class sample, while various analyses of the Minneapolis data had shown high instability in a disadvantaged sample. Together, these findings raised questions about the potential for and likelihood of changes in attachment behavior in middle class samples in which parents were subjected to stressful life events or changing circumstances.

To address this question, Thompson, Lamb, and Estes (1982) examined the stability of attachment in a middle-class sample of 43 dyads. They sought not only to see whether life events affected the stability of attachment classifications, but also to determine which *kinds* of changes in life conditions were related to changes in Strange Situation behavior between 12½ and 19½ months of age. To their surprise, they found greater instability than did Vaughn et al.: Only 53% of their sample obtained the same attachment classifications at 12½ and 19½ months. Stability of subgroup classifications was 26%. Using the lambda statistic, there was essentially no gain in predictive accuracy attributable to knowledge of the earlier classifications.

Thompson et al. (1982) used maternal questionnaires to obtain information about general family conditions, caretaking arrangements, and several kinds of specific experiences for mother and baby (e.g., separations of one day or longer) occurring throughout the baby's lifetime, not just between the two assessments. Two related events that influence mother–infant interaction—maternal employment and the onset of "regular nonmaternal care"—were significantly associated with changes in the Strange Situation attachment classifications. By contrast, single critical experiences (such as separations), and changes in general family conditions (such as moving to a new home) were not associated with changes in attachment status. The evidence regarding these external correlates of changing attachment status must be interpreted cautiously, however, since the relevant life events or circumstances were of low frequency, the sample was small, and because maternal employment and nonmaternal care were nonindependent events.

These findings differed from those of Vaughn et al. (1979) in two ways. First, Thompson et al. found that changing family circumstances were associated with changes in attachment status from B to non-B groups as well as the reverse—in other words, with bidirectional changes in attachment status. In contrast, family changes and stresses in Vaughn et al.'s sample were associated with changes from the B to non-B groups, but not with shifts in the reverse direction. Thompson et al. (1982, 1983; Thompson & Lamb, 1984b) suggested that this difference may be due to the different types of stresses faced by families in the two samples. The severe stresses encountered by disadvantaged families may permit few really constructive resolutions and thus may bias the baby toward attachment insecurity in the face of stress, whereas the less traumatic events or transitions encountered by middle-class families may permit a wider range of constructive responses, some of which may have beneficial effects on the quality of mother–infant interaction and thus result in a shift into the B group. Second, Thompson et al. (1982) reported that maternal employment and nonmaternal care beginning during the *first* year were also associated with changes in Strange Situation attachment classifications during the *second* year. Vaughn et al. (1979) did not report data concerning family changes and stresses in the first year. Thompson et al. (1982, 1983) suggested that short-term changes in mother–infant interaction in the first year may have influenced the initial Strange Situation assessments, but not the follow-up at 19½ months. For example, the initial Strange Situation assessment may have been affected by the child's anxiety over the transition to nonmaternal care earlier in the year, but this effect would have dissipated by the time of the 19½ month assessment (see Blanchard & Main, 1979). If this interpretation is correct, it would indicate that Strange Situation assessments are sensitive to short-lived fluctuations in mother–infant interaction as well as to more enduring characteristics.

In two other studies, researchers have examined the stability of attachment classifications in middle class samples over an inter-assessment period of several months. In one of these studies, Frodi, Grolnick, and Bridges (1984) observed 41 mother–infant dyads in both a structured play session and subsequently the Strange Situation at 12 months; 38 of these dyads returned for identical assessments at 20 months. Maternal "control style" and sensitivity were rated from the play observations at each age, and a questionnaire completed by the mothers at 20 months was used to identify changes in family circumstances between the two assessments. Frodi et al. found that 66% of their sample obtained the same overall (i.e., major group) attachment classification at each age. Although a composite index of changes in family circumstances did not differentiate the four stability groups (i.e., B-group classifications in both assessments, change from B to non-B group, change from non-B to B group, and non-B group status in both assessments), these groups were significantly different on other measures. Specifically, the mothers of infants who either moved into the B group or were classified in the B group on both occasions were rated as less controlling and more sensitive during the 12-month play session, suggesting that maternal attitudes toward the child's growing autonomy in the second year may have fostered the development of secure attachments.

In the other study, Owen, Easterbrooks, Chase–Lansdale and Goldberg (1983, 1984) studied the stability of infant–mother and infant–father attachments from 12 to 20 months in an initial sample of 137 middle-class families. However, only 59 families (43%) participated in both observations with mother, whereas 53 were observed at each age with father. Observations with each parent occurred three to six weeks apart at each age. Owen et al. reported that 78% of the infant–mother dyads obtained the same overall classification at each age, compared with 62% of the infant–father dyads. There were seven families in which mother returned to work between the two assessments, and—contrary to Thompson et al.'s (1982) findings—none of these infants shifted from one attachment group to another. However, the extraordinarily high rate of subject attrition between the two assessments, and the exclusive focus on firstborn children from highly-educated, upper-middle-class families may limit the generalizability of these findings. In addition, as Owen et al. (1984) noted, the design excluded the short-term effects of maternal employment on attachment status, which Thompson et al. (1982) implicated in their discussion of temporal instability. Thus it is difficult to compare the results of these two studies. No other external correlates of attachment stability were studied by Owen et al.

Summary

The results of research on the effects of changing circumstances and stressful life events paint a somewhat inconsistent picture. In all studies, estimates of temporal stability were lower than that initially reported by Waters (1978), and in both middle class and lower income families, changing circumstances and stressful life events have been associated with changes over time in Strange Situation behavior (e.g., Vaughn et al., 1979; Thompson et al., 1982). However, other studies with middle class samples have failed to report such findings (perhaps because of wide variations in assessment and analytic procedures), and one found a relationship between maternal personality characteristics and stability in Strange Situation behavior. Perhaps the problem lies in a failure to quantify accurately the subjectively-perceived stressfulness of different events for different families in different circumstances. In any event, it is clear that stability in Strange Situation classifications cannot be assumed, and that changing family circumstances and caretaking arrangements can affect classifications, and thus temporal stability.

SHORT-TERM STABILITY AND CHANGE

A somewhat different picture is painted by studies on the stability of attachment classifications over periods of one month or less. In the first study concerned with this issue, the 23 infants from Sample 3 described by Ainsworth et al. (1978) were observed with their mothers in the Strange Situation at 50 weeks and again at 52 weeks of age. Ainsworth et al. (1978) reported that only 56% of the sample obtained the same overall classification on both occasions. Examination of the episode-by-episode interactive ratings revealed that there was more proximity- and contact-seeking, searching, and crying and less avoidance in the second of the assessments, suggesting that the changes in classification may have occurred because the infants were more stressed during the second assessment because of their recent experience in the same procedure. Even so, correlational analyses revealed consistent individual differences on the interactive ratings between the two observations.

Subsequently, Goossens, van IJzendoorn, Kroonenberg, and Tavecchio (1984) observed 39 Dutch children in the Strange Situation on two occasions one month apart. Children were 18 months old at the first observation. Observational context was systematically varied in this study, with roughly equal numbers of infants assigned to each of four conditions for the two observations: home–home, home–laboratory, laboratory–home, and laboratory–laboratory. Goossens et al. found that overall (i.e., major group) classifications were highly stable when infants were observed in the same context (95% of the babies obtained the same classification), but were much lower (55% stability) when the context changed. Correlations of scores on the interactive ratings of infant behavior in the reunion episodes revealed a similar pattern of results. In general, there were slightly more shifts from non-B to B group classifications over time than in the reverse direction. Interestingly, however, these researchers found no evidence for either context effects (i.e., the laboratory context did not elicit more stress than home) or order effects (the second observation was not more stressful than the first) in their analyses of the interactive measures (see also Goossens, van IJzendoorn, Tavecchio, & Swaan, 1984).

These short-term stability studies suggest that one of the factors affecting the stability of Strange Situation classifications over brief spans is the child's memory of the earlier assessment, although evidence is mixed concerning the importance of this factor. Ainsworth et al.'s findings suggest that the psychological impact of the second assessment may create greater stress and thus provide a less reliable indicator of the security of attachment. The great instability across different contexts in Goossen et al.'s study also suggests the importance of ensuring the psychological equivalence of different assessments for the Strange Situation to yield valid and reliable classifications of infant–adult attachment. The implication, which is elaborated more fully in Chapter 11, is that when different infants perceive the Strange Situation procedure differently, the results obtained are not comparable and may not reflect individual differences in the same underlying construct.

STABILITY ESTIMATES WITH MODIFIED CLASSIFICATION PROCEDURES

Thus far, we have reviewed studies in which researchers have adhered rather closely to the classification system developed by Ainsworth and her colleagues. Researchers in two other studies, however, have explored the stability of attachment classifications during the second year using modified versions of Ainsworth's system. Because of variations in scoring and sampling procedures, however, their estimates of temporal stability cannot be directly compared with those already discussed.

D. B. Connell (1976) examined the stability of attachment classifications from 12 to 18 months in a sample of 47 middle-class infants and their mothers. (There were 55 dyads in the initial sample.) To classify infants at each age, he used Ainsworth's data to compute weighted equations by which infants could be classified on the basis of various discrete behavior measures and the conventional episode-by-episode interactive ratings. Through a succession of cluster analytic techniques and other procedures, Connell reduced the large number of measures employed by Ainsworth to a subset of variables (mostly interactive ratings) which best discriminated among infants in the three attachment classifications. However, Connell eliminated from Ainsworth's sample infants in the B_1 and B_4 subgroups because they tended to cluster with A group and C group infants, respectively. The rest of her sample was divided into a "design" set (used to create the weighted equations) and a "test" set (used to assess predictive accuracy). The latter exercise proved satisfactory, so Connell then applied these equations to the interactive scores obtained by the infants in his own sample to derive attachment classifications. The resulting distribution of infants across groups at each age was unusual (i.e., 30% or more were in the A group, compared with 15–20% in most studies; 4% at each age were placed in the C group compared with 10–15% in other studies) and this may have resulted from his unusual classification procedure. Connell's decision to eliminate meaningful variance by excluding the B_1 and B_4 classification options makes his finding that 81% of the infants were similarly classified at both ages difficult to evaluate.

Main and Weston (1981) also examined the stability of attachment classifications from 12 to 18 months. Out of a total sample of 61 families, 15 infants were observed in the Strange Situation at both 12 and 18 months with their mothers, and an additional 15 were observed with their fathers at each age. In rating infant behavior in the Strange Situation, Main and Weston created a new classification category consisting of infants who were "difficult to classify" using Ainsworth's system. They reported that the majority of these "unclassifiable" infants would have been deemed securely-attached using Ainsworth's criteria, but seemed insecure to the raters. Like Connell, then, Main and Weston may have increased their stability estimate by creating a new category for those infants whose classification by definition was more prone to error. Main and Weston also employed sample selection procedures that may have affected the estimate of stability. Families were selected on the basis of maternal race, parental occupation, infant birth weight, birth complications, and maternal age. No infants spending more than 25 hours weekly in day-care were included, and only 18% of the mothers worked even part-time. Main and Weston (1981) acknowledged that these criteria may have reduced the number of non-B group infants in their sample, and by reducing or eliminating families characterized by circumstances that were related to changes in attachment status in the Thompson et al. (1982) study (i.e., maternal employment and nonmaternal care), Main and Weston may have increased the likelihood of stability also. The 73% estimate of stability for mothers and 87% for fathers is thus of uncertain generalizability.

CONCLUSION

Several conclusions are suggested by the research reviewed in this chapter. First, it is apparent that estimates of temporal stability in attachment status can and do vary widely across studies, making it difficult to specify a "normative" stability estimate for test–retest studies. Although measurement problems could account for some of this variance, the bulk of the evidence indicates that patterns of Strange Situation behavior reflect the *current*—but not necessarily *enduring*—status of the parent–infant relationship. A baby whose behavior leads to its classification in the insecure A group, for example, need not remain that way; it may shift to the secure B group as circumstances and patterns of interaction change. Similarly, an infant initially classified in the secure B group may not always remain so—although, as we discuss in the following, there tends to be greater temporal stability in B group than in A and C group classifications. In general, then, these studies indicate that the quality of attachment relationships—as these are indexed by Strange Situation behavior—are much more open to change than developmentalists had formerly believed.

Second, changes in attachment status are related in meaningful ways to factors that may affect the consistency of parent–infant interaction, although the specific external correlates of change in attachment status remain to be clarified. Researchers have yet to specify reliably when and under what circumstances changes in attachment classifications are most likely to occur. While there is some evidence that stability is somewhat lower in socioeconomically disadvantaged samples than in middle-class samples, this difference may be due largely to differences in the quality (cf. Egeland & Sroufe, 1981) and/or consistency (for example, compare Waters', 1978, findings with those reported by Thompson et al., 1982) of infant care. Thus whereas the lowest reported stability estimate (47%; Egeland & Sroufe, 1981) was for a sample identified as seriously abusive or neglectful, the highest estimate (96%, Waters, 1978) was obtained in a highly stable, middle class sample. Several studies have indicated, for both middle and lower income families, that when the life circumstances of mother and baby change, there is likely to be change in the classification of Strange Situation behavior. Using different assessment methods, however, other researchers have failed to replicate these findings. Further, changes and stresses in caretaking conditions may not be the only factors underlying changes in Strange Situation behavior. Frodi et al. (1984) related maternal personality characteristics to observed changes in attachment status, suggesting that the socioemotional resources of the mother (perhaps as they interact with family changes and stresses) may affect consistency of mother–infant attachment status. Why personality characteristics (which are presumed to be stable) should produce *changes* in attachment status needs to be explained better, however. Unfortunately, much of the evidence concerning the external correlates of change in attachment status is weak, inconsistent, or interpretationally vague. In addition, some studies examining the early antecedents of stability and change in attachment status (e.g., prenatal assessments of maternal personality characteristics; see Egeland & Farber, 1984) have inappropriately used a retrospective rather than prospective mode of data analysis. That is, attachment stability groupings have been used to predict antecedent events or conditions, rather than the reverse. Taken together, however, the studies reviewed here provide suggestive evidence that behavior in the Strange Situation is sensitive to aspects of infant care that are presumed to influence the security of attachment (see Chapter 5), and thus they help demonstrate the validity of the Strange Situation procedure.

Nevertheless, further research is needed to clarify the circumstances and influences that can result in changes in Strange Situation behavior, and to identify the intervening processes by which these changes come about. To do this, researchers must move beyond simple test–retest designs with concurrent assessments of family circumstances to more detailed longitudinal studies of parent–infant interaction both within and outside the Strange Situation. Researchers have simply *presumed* that patterns of childcare change with the onset of family stress or altered life circumstances, and that these changes in patterns of childcare produce changes in Strange Situation behavior. No researchers, however, have directly observed parent–infant interaction at the time of each Strange Situation assessment in order to verify this assumption, and there may be alternative explanations. For example, the association between changing family circumstances and changing attachment status may occur not because of a direct link between the two, but because they are both associated with changes in another variable, such as marital quality (cf. Belsky, 1981). (Among other things, this would also explain why changing family and childcare circumstances are not always associated with changes in Strange Situation classifications.) As a result, detailed short-term longitudinal studies are required to specify more precisely the variables and processes that mediate changes in Strange Situation behavior over time.

Third, inspection of Table 8.1 reveals that B group classifications are consistently more stable over time than are A and C group classifications. (The one exception is the maltreated group studied by Schneider–Rosen et al., in press.) In many cases, the differences between the two stability coefficients were large. Several explanations for this phenomenon have been offered. Bowlby (1969, p. 347), for example, has suggested that attachment insecurity may be developmentally less robust than attachment security because of the greater stress that insecurity places on parent–child interaction. Thus, once infant and parent have achieved the mutual accomodations that contribute to a secure relationship, these interactive patterns may be more easily maintained by the dyad than patterns that reflect a failure to achieve a satisfactory accomodation. Alternatively, Campos, Barrett, Lamb, Goldsmith and Stenberg (1983) have suggested that the greater stability of the B group classifications may be a methodological artifact of the rating system. Specifically, they suggest that since older infants are likely to be less stressed by the procedure (and thus manifest fewer signs of insecurity), than are the 12-month-olds for whom the procedure was designed, there may be a spurious elevation of temporal stability for infants who were initially classified in the B group. However, since both of the short-term stability studies—Ainsworth et al. (1978) with 12-month-olds and Goossens et al. (1984a, 1984b) with 18-month-olds—also showed greater stability for the B group classifications, this explanation may be incomplete. Third, it is important to note that because the B group classifications are more common, they will appear more stable over time than the A and C group classifications, even if the classifications are assigned on a random basis. In all, the origins and importance of the greater temporal stability of B group classifications remain to be explored in future reseach.

Finally, one of the most interesting—and disturbing—characteristics of research on this topic is that no investigator has examined developmental changes in Strange Situation behavior during the second year. Schneider–Rosen et al.'s (in press) attempts to develop modified classification criteria for 18- and 24-month-olds is a step in the right direction, although this was based on conceptual rather than empirical grounds. However, most researchers have implicitly assumed that the nature of the attachment behavioral system and the behavioral manifestations of attachment relationships are very nearly identical in 12- and 18-month-old infants (i.e., Kagan's [1971] "complete continuity"), and thus that, for example, resistance means the same thing at both ages. This assumption runs counter to a number of theoretical perspectives suggesting that important changes in socioemotional development occur during the second year. For example, Mahler's theory of separation-individuation (see Mahler, Pine, & Bergman, 1975) indicates that the latter half of the second year brings marked shifts in the toddler's feelings about the parent, which derive from a growing awareness of psychological independence. Most pertinently, she also specifically indicates that resistant behaviors are part of the normal individuation process, and do not necessarily reflect insecure attachments. In addition, it is reasonable to expect that with increasing age, interaction with the parent becomes increasingly mediated by distal signaling rather than proximity and contact seeking. It is thus time for a broadening of research goals and interests in this field, so that developmental hypotheses of this sort can be explored. It is ironic that so many researchers have the data needed to accomplish this, but with the focus on stability of individual differences rather than normative developmental change, relevant analyses have not been reported (or even performed). In addition researchers may have been too hasty to dispose of the data obtained from discrete behavior codings and the interactive rating scales, while focusing exclusively on the Strange Situation classifications. The former may be especially useful for studying developmental changes in attachment behaviors.

9 PREDICTIVE VALIDITY OF STRANGE SITUATION CLASSIFICATIONS

INTRODUCTION

The Strange Situation procedure has become popular in part because of claims that Strange Situation behavior predicts important aspects of the child's behavior as much as several years later. Since few assessments of infant characteristics have impressive predictive validity, these claims have understandably excited developmentalists, but the empirical support for them has never been evaluated in systematic fashion. The goal of this chapter is to provide such a review. There is now a great deal of evidence available concerning the sequelae of Strange Situation behavior, and the conclusions they support are, in most respects, better documented than those reached in any other chapter. As will become apparent, however, research on this topic is not without its problems. Readers will note that a variety of outcome measures have been explored, with relatively little clear theorizing about the appropriateness of specific dependent measures or their conceptual link to earlier patterns of Strange Situation behavior. Most researchers have implicitly tested the rather imprecise hypothesis that "secure" (i.e., B group) attachment presages "better" performance and adjustment (broadly defined) in the tasks and challenges encountered in later months or years than does A type or C type behavior in the Strange Situation.

Two broad implicit hypotheses can be entertained to guide the search for the predictive correlates of Strange Situation behavior. First, theorists such as Sroufe (1978, 1983) emphasize the formative importance of the quality of parent–infant interaction in the first year (reflected in Strange Situation behavior) in shaping later patterns of adjustment and competence. Thus

> the behavioral organization evolved with respect to an early developmental
> issue lays the ground work for subsequent behavioral organizations....The
> nature of the earlier behavioral organization, with attachment promoting
> exploration, makes the smooth movement to more autonomous functioning
> virtually inevitable (Sroufe, 1983, p. 46).

While major disruptions in the child's environment may affect the continuity of behavioral organization, the emphasis here is on the self-perpetuating processes from within the child by which earlier patterns become maintained and consolidated.

Second, one could propose that the effects of early parent–infant interaction are likely to be most clearly evident when there is continuity in the quality of care and interaction. In such circumstances, the apparent effects of early patterns of interaction may be maintained by consistency in the quality of care, such that later effects may be attributable to *either* previous *or* contemporaneous influences. This second perspective implies that predictive validity can only be investigated and understood when one records early formative influences, contemporaneous influences, and intervening factors known to be associated with changes in the patterns of care. One important implication, therefore, is that when rearing conditions change, early influences may have little or no predictive value. In its most extreme form, this hypothesis holds that Strange Situation behavior, like any of the outcome measures reported here, simply reflects the current status (in terms of discordance or harmoniousness) of the parent–child relationship. If the relationship status at the time of the Strange Situation and at the time of the outcome assessment is qualitatively similar, then there should be "predictive validity." However, if the status of the relationship changes over time, then there will be little or no apparent "predictive validity" for the Strange Situation assessment. Thus the locus of stability is in caretaking conditions, not in the infant.

It is important to distinguish between these two hypotheses because although many researchers and commentators believe that the first hypothesis has been verified, we believe that the evidence reviewed in this chapter is more consistent with the second.

THE MINNEAPOLIS MIDDLE-CLASS SAMPLE

The most widely-cited studies concerned with the predictive validity of Strange Situation classifications were conducted in Minneapolis by Sroufe and his colleagues. These studies have involved either of two samples: a middle-income sample recruited by Matas, Arend, and Sroufe (1978) or the sample of disadvantaged families studied by Egeland and Farber (1982, 1984) and Vaughn et al. (1979).

In the early study involving the first sample, Matas et al. (1978) related security of attachment at 18 months to measures of the child's and mother's behavior at 24 months in play, problem-solving, and clean-up situations. "Thirty-seven of the [48] subjects were randomly selected; 11 were selected because they were in the non-normative attachment groups...of another larger sample" (p. 549). All were drawn from a list of parents who volunteered to participate in studies shortly after their infants were born. Such families are likely to be stable middle-class families (especially if they can still be located 18 months later) as was indicated by high temporal stability (100%) in attachment classification at 12 and 18 months in a subsample of 14. At 24 months, raters scored: (1) the frequency of symbolic play bouts during free play; (2) oppositional behavior during clean up; (3) angry behavior during clean-up; (4) 10 variables during the problem-solving task (including frequencies of help-seeking, whining/crying, aggressive behavior, frustration behavior, and verbal negativism as well as proportional measures of ignoring, time away from task, active noncompliance, attempted compliance, and compliance); (5) three ratings of behavior during problem-solving (enthusiasm, positive affect, and negative affect) and (6) ratings of the mothers' supportive presence and quality of assistance during the problem-solving tasks. Many of these measures were, of course, nonindependent. There were no significant group differences in DQ between B group and A or C group infants.

The B group infants engaged in more symbolic play than both avoidant and resistant infants. In the problem-solving situation, the B group infants were more enthusiastic and compliant than non-B group infants, they also ignored less and exhibited fewer frustration behaviors, showed more positive affect, and engaged in less negativism, crying/whining, aggression toward mother and negative affect. The avoidant and B group infants also differed in the expected direction on 5 of 7 measures tested, but there were no reported comparisons between B and C group infants, despite the theoretical importance of such comparisons. In all, 10 of 18 infant behaviors and both maternal ratings revealed significant group differences between B and non-B groups. Factor analysis of the infant and maternal variables yielded 5 factors ("competence," "temperament," "DQ," and 2 unnamed factors), the first and third of which were related to security of attachment in the expected direction.[1]

---

[1]The two maternal ratings, compliance, and the negative of ignoring were the major loadings on the first factor, while DQ and the negative of aggression were key loadings on the third factor.

These results are certainly both impressive and interesting, although they raise questions about the locus of the stability. Is it that B group infants become "better adapted" toddlers, or simply that the mothers who fostered "secure" behavior at 18 months continue to provide an appropriate rearing context for the child 6 months later? It is impossible to tell, since the sample is one in which there is likely to be continuity in the quality of care. Interestingly, the group differences in maternal behavior at 24 months were greater than the differences between groups of infants at this age on measures that were coded similarly. Thus a more parsimonious interpretation of these findings is that at both 18- and 24-month assessments, mothers are fostering either competent behaviors in their infants or more negative reactions. At the very least, it would be valuable to know whether group differences in infant behavior remain when differences correlated with the contemporaneous maternal ratings are partialled out. It is also noteworthy that none of the measures were reported to distinguish between the A and C group infants.[2]

Waters, Wippman, and Sroufe (1979) further studied thirty-six 18-month-olds drawn from the sample studied by Matas et al. (1978). Five mother-directed behaviors indicating positive interaction, various combinations of these behaviors, and three nonindependent ratings of "affective sharing" were scored from episode 1 of the Strange Situation. Additional ratings of affective sharing were obtained in a 10-minute free-play session at 24 months from 45 infants (including 30 of those involved in the first phase) whose attachments were assessed at 18 months. The B group infants were more likely to smile at their mothers at 18 months than were A and C group infants, but there were no significant differences in the frequencies of showing or giving toys or looking at mother. Various combinations of these behaviors also revealed no significant group differences. There were significant differences between the B and non-B groups in affective sharing at both 18 and 24 months, but there is no mention of differences between avoidant and resistant infants on any of the measures.

Arend, Gove, and Sroufe (1979) later relocated 26 of Matas et al.'s sample when they were between 54 and 70 months of age. Twelve were initially classified in the B and 14 in the non-B (8 A, 6 C) groups at 18 months, suggesting selective attrition of the B group infants. Each child was described using a 100-item Q-set by a nursery school or kindergarten teacher

[2]Easterbrooks and Lamb (see Lamb 1982b) later attempted to replicate these findings in a sample of 36-month-olds. Neither measures of child behavior in the problem-solving context nor measures of peer sociability were related to Strange Situation behavior, perhaps because the modified Strange Situation devised for use with 3-year-olds (the mother turned off the lights when she left the room) was not appropriate for assessing patterns of attachment among children of this age.

who had known the child at least 8 months. Block and Block (1979) had derived composite Q-sort definitions of both ego-resiliency and ego-undercontrol with which the child's scores on the relevant items were correlated to yield ego-resiliency and ego-control scores. In addition, each child took a 90-minute battery of tests tapping interpersonal problem-solving (2 scores), imaginativeness and originality, structure, planfulness (3 scores), level of aspiration (3 scores), motor inhibition (4 scores), curiosity (5 scores—3 of which were not used in the composites), and delay of gratification (5 scores). From these scores, two composite measures were derived, following Block and Block's procedure, to measure ego-resiliency and ego-control.

The two independent measures of ego-resiliency and ego-control were modestly but significantly correlated with each other, whereas the scores for resiliency did not correlate with those for control. Both the Q-sort and laboratory measures showed the B group children to be more ego-resilient than the A or C group children. A composite score comprising the four infant measures (but not the maternal measures) loading highest on the Matas et al. competence factor was significantly correlated with the laboratory measure of resiliency ($r = .47$), and marginally correlated with the teacher-derived resiliency score ($r = .37$, p .06). The 24-month maternal ratings from the Matas et al. study were significantly correlated with the laboratory measure of resiliency. There were no overall group differences on the ego-control dimension—perhaps, as the authors claim, because both overcontrol and undercontrol are undesirable, meaning that one would expect to find B group children neither high nor low on this dimension. A post hoc analysis revealed that the resistant (C group) infants were high and the avoidant (A group) infants low on ego-control; the B group infants fell in-between with a mean close to that of the C group children. The three additional measures of curiosity all showed the B group children to be more curious; two of these measures were significantly correlated with the teacher-derived measure of ego-resiliency. No other differences were reported on the remaining 20 measures from the laboratory assessment.

Once again, there were few differences between avoidant and resistant infants but reliable differences between B group and non-B group infants. The interpretation of these differences is problematic, however, since this was a select, stable middle-class sample, and Arend et al. candidly discussed the importance of continuity in patterns of caretaking influencing the predictive utility of attachment classification. Can we thus attribute later differences to earlier patterns of infant–mother interaction, or are they maintained by continuing differences in parental behavior? Quite plausibly, this continuity in rearing conditions is critical, as suggested by many of the findings reported in this section.

THE MINNEAPOLIS STUDY OF DISADVANTAGED FAMILIES

Much more extensive attempts have been made to assess predictive validity using the sample of disadvantaged families described by Egeland and Farber (1982, 1984) and Vaughn et al. (1979). In the first follow-up study, Pastor (1980, 1981) observed 62 of the children in the sample at 20 to 23 months of age in a study of dyadic peer interaction. Subjects were included only when the child obtained the same attachment classification at both 12 and 18 months (Pastor, 1980). Twelve A, 13 B, and 12 C group infants were selected as target infants. Each was paired with another child (always a B group toddler) who was considered the control member of the dyad. Twelve of the B subjects were included twice, though not as target children. A Bayley assessment at 24 months revealed no group differences in DQ.

Six 5-point rating scales (overall sociability, orientation to peer, orientation to mother, activity level, mother supportiveness, and mother directiveness) were scored from videotapes by naive observers. Inter-observer reliability was not specified, other than that it was "significantly better than chance by the Lawlis–Lu chi-square test $p < .01$)" (p. 329). Twelve discrete categories of peer-directed behavior and 16 of mother–child interaction were also coded. Two proximity and three looking measures were also used. Four of the six ratings revealed significant group differences, with the B group children scoring higher on overall sociability, orientation to peer, orientation to mother, and mother supportiveness than the A and C group infants, between whom no differences were found. Three of the 12 discrete measures of peer-directed behavior revealed differences, with A and B group children making more social bids and ignoring fewer offers by peers than those in group C, while B group children redirected their own activities after an object struggle more than A group children did. Six of the 16 discrete measures of mother–child interaction revealed significant differences, but in only two cases (proportion of the time that mother rejected a bid; proportion of the time that child complied) were the B group children distinguished from both of the insecure groups. Since few of the discrete behavior measures were independent of one another, and there were only three significant group differences on fully independent measures, these data suggest equivocal group differences on the discrete behavior measures. The only major group differences, therefore, were on several broader rating scales.

Later, Sroufe and Rosenberg (1982) attempted to replicate Matas et al.'s findings using subjects from this socioeconomically disadvantaged sample. Infants who were classified in the B group at 18 months were later (24 months) more enthusiastic, affectively positive, compliant, spent less time away from the task, showed less negative affect, and received more positive scores on two global ratings than those who were classified in either the A or C groups. They also showed more enthusiasm and "affective sharing" during play. The tenor of the results matches Matas et al.'s (1978) findings, although there were few specific replications. Of even greater concern is the fact that there were only three measures distinguishing between 24-month-olds who fell in the B or non B groups at 12 months. Presumably, this was because many of these subjects experienced changes in attachment status between 12 and 18 months (Vaughn et al. 1979). In fact, when a subset of children from this sample with stable attachments from 12 to 18 months were analyzed, prediction from 12 to 24 months was increased. Thus, when viewed in the context of Pastor's (1981) findings, these findings underscore the fact that attachment classifications may have substantial predictive validity only when there is continuity in the quality of care and/or Strange Situation behavior.

This interpretation is supported by the findings reported by Erickson and Crichton (1981) using the same data. They reported that the B group infants were more compliant at 24 months than the A and C group infants, but apparently *only when there was stability between 12 and 18 months in Strange Situation behavior*. The avoidant and resistant infants did not differ from one another.

Erickson and Farber (1983) reported on a further assessment of the children in this sample when they were 42 months old and were observed with their mothers in four teaching tasks. Children were rated on at least eight 7-point scales by two raters whose scores were summed (reliability information was not reported). On four measures, significant differences were obtained between infants who were classified in the B group in both 12- and 18-month assessments and those who were consistently in A or C groups. A's and B's were significantly more persistent, enthusiastic and compliant, but relied less on mother for support than C's did. There were no significant A–B differences, and no group differences on measures of negativism, affection, or avoidance of mother, or the child's overall experience of the session.

A later follow-up of subjects in the same sample occurred when the children were around 4 to 5 years of age. Arguing that "the quality of the child's earlier adaptation will influence its adaptation with respect to subsequent issues" (Sroufe, 1979, p. 838), Sroufe (1983; see also Sroufe, Fox, & Pancake, 1983) invited 40 of the children to participate in a special nursery school program.[3] The children were divided into two groups. One (group 2 attending a 20 week session) contained 25 children, with equal

---

[3]The reports mention 40 children (25 in group 2) in their Method sections. This is because one boy in class 2 moved and was replaced by another. There were thus complete data available on 38 children, 39 children in the classes at any one time, and 40 supplying data for most analyses.

numbers classified in the A, B, and C groups when seen in the Strange Situation at 18 months. Twenty-one of the 25 were selected because they had the same classification at both 12 and 18 months; the others changed classification between 12 and 18 months, but there was "consistency" between the 18-month Strange Situation and 24-month tool use assessments in these three cases, thus reflecting apparent stability in their socioemotional functioning. Nine of the 15 children in group 1 (who attended a 12 week session) had the same classification at 12 and 18 months (7 B's, 2 A's), 2 shifted from one non-B classification to the other over time and the remaining 4 received a non-B classification in one assessment and a B group classification in the other. Three of the latter were later placed in the C group for certain analyses (Sroufe et al., 1983, p. 1620). One other child was deemed "mixed," and because no final decision could be made about his classification status, he was excluded from some analyses. Overall, therefore, the subsample was a highly stable subset of Egeland's sample (Sroufe, 1983, p. 53). The groups were equated on IQ, age, race and (for group 2) sex. In the discussion that follows, all details are drawn from Sroufe's (1983) report. Additional analyses reported by Sroufe et al. (1983) are discussed separately.

An enormous amount of data was gathered using a variety of procedures, including teacher Q-sorts[4] yielding five scores; six rank orderings and 16 ratings by the teachers; a listing by the teachers of each child's friends; observations of "attention structure" in peer interactions; three frequency or proportion measures of peer interaction; judgments regarding friendship pairs; two assessments of sociometric status; 11 measures of behavior toward the teachers and of the teachers' behavior; and 60 specific behavioral measures that were analyzed individually as well as in the context of three item clusters. In all, at least 110 measures (many of them nonindependent) were collected from a sample of 40 children. Teachers were blind with respect to attachment status and specific hypotheses. Interobserver reliabilities were moderate to low (Sroufe et al., 1983).

When data from both groups were combined, several measures yielded significant differences between the B and the non-B group infants. The B group infants were scored higher on the ego-resiliency and self-esteem Q-sorts (which intercorrelated highly, $r = .85$), teacher ratings of agency, positive affect, lower on negative affect, lower in dependency on multiple ratings thereof (see Sroufe et al., 1983, and below) and on an index of their seating relative to the teacher, and higher on the composite measures of positive and negative behaviors, although few of the 60 specific behavioral items ("bizarre behavior" and "wandering" are two that are mentioned)

---

[4]Usually more than one teacher rated each child. For 72% of the cases, average intercorrelations among the Q-sorts exceeded .50.

revealed significant differences. The B group infants were also ranked higher in social competence, number of friends, popularity (on sociometric instruments), and on ratings of social skills, compliance, and empathy. None of these measures were reported to yield differences between the A and C groups. However, on the basis of informal written comments by the teachers, it was later possible to distinguish the A and C groups; the A's were deemed hostile, isolated, and disconnected, while the C's were rated impulsive and helpless. Sroufe (1983) does not say whether descriptions of the B's were similarly classified, and whether they were ever misclassified, but a B class was not even available when the raters were determining whether the teachers' impressions were A-like or C-like. A and C group infants were also distinguished on the basis of classifications made using the 5 "most characteristic" items from the Block Q-sorts, and another set of classifications based on teacher responses recorded on descriptive check-lists. The fact that these measures provided the only way of distinguishing between A's and C's is problematic because we would expect to find clear differences on more specific, behaviorally-based measures between infants who behave so differently in the Strange Situation (see, for example, Sroufe, 1983, p.51).

Nevertheless, this study appeared to yield strong evidence of differences between the B and non-B group children—differences evident on a number of the measures. However, the specific subsample was carefully selected from the larger sample to ensure stability of attachment classifications. As suggested in the previous chapter, this means that there was probably substantial continuity in the quality of care, whether good or bad. It is thus impossible to tell whether the differences among preschoolers are due to differences in earlier rather than contemporaneous patterns of parent–child relationships, since continuity in parent–child interaction may extend to the preschool years also. Indeed, Sroufe (1983) himself acknowledges that "selection [for stable attachments] was deliberate…to increase the likelihood of continuity across this substantial age span" (p.53). This issue is extremely important, given the tendency to attribute later differences in child behavior to *earlier* patterns of maternal behavior and mother–child interaction. This interpretation could be sustained only if there were associations between 12- or 18-month classifications and later behavior in samples in which marked discontinuity in quality of care was evident, or which were unselected in this respect. Since Vaughn et al. (1979) reported that stable attachments were related in this sample to the frequency and severity of life stress in the family, it is reasonable to conclude that prediction of later infant behavior was improved by studying only those infants whose attachments were stable and whose families thus experienced less stress and more stable circumstances.

Further, in light of differences between the first and second class groups (e.g., age, classroom experience, and proportions of B and non-B group children), the decision to combine them for some analyses is questionable. Results are sometimes reported for separate classes, and sometimes only for the combined sample. No mention is made of the independence or nonindependence of the measures, although many measures seem highly interrelated, and some of the data are not reported. This makes evaluation of the findings difficult. Finally, since many of the significant effects emerged from the teacher ratings, the possibility of halo effects producing differences on multiple ratings must be considered.

In a later report, Sroufe et al. (1983) focused explicitly on the dependency data gathered in the study just reported. This involved daily rank orderings by the teachers, with the rankings later combined into a composite; ratings on 12 items from Block and Block's (1979) Q-sort that pertained to dependency (again the various ratings were combined across teachers into a composite); ratings by two teachers (again a composite) on a 7-point dependency scale, Beller's (1955) dependency scales, revised to include 8 sub-scales; behavioral observation using 5 child-initiated and 3 teacher-initiated variables (plus 3 composites), and 3 scores, based on repeated observations, for proximity and contact to teacher during large group song and story times. Altogether, 24 measures were used in this study.

On the composite rankings, the A and C group children (combined) were significantly more dependent than the B group children in both classes, although there were no differences between the A and C groups. The same was true of the global ratings. On the composite Beller scale, there was no significant group difference when data from the two classes were analyzed separately, but there was a difference in the predicted direction when data from the two classes were combined. Sroufe et al. (1983) explained this in terms of the different directions of effects on the 8 subscales, although on only 2 subscales were there significant differences between B and non-B groups for both classes: "Help seeking in self management" (A, C B) and "positive attention seeking" (B A, C). Q-sort ratings also revealed significant differences between B and non-B group children for group 1 and the total sample. Consistent with the analyses reported by Sroufe (1983), none of the teacher-based measures yielded significant differences between the A and C groups, despite clear and consistent differences between B and non-B groups on these measures of dependency.

The seating chart data yielded 3 (albeit nonindependent) measures of the child's seating locations, and all showed the non-B group children spending less time close to or sitting on one of the teachers. None of the 11 other behavioral measures yielded significant differences when data from the two classes were considered separately, and only two nonindependent measures—teacher guidance and a composite of total teacher initiated behaviors—yielded trends in the expected direction (p .10) when the two groups were combined (see Table 5, page 1623).[5] Thus differences between B and non-B children were obtained primarily on multiple teacher ratings and not on discrete observational measures, again raising the possibility of halo effects producing differences on multiple teacher-derived measures. Again, there were no significant A vs. C group differences on most of these measures. Profiles of the relative intensity of child- and teacher-initiated interactions likewise yielded nonsignificant group differences. Data analyses of at least 11 variables across 8 different contexts (i.e., 88 analyses) for the class-2 children only revealed that (1) A's were significantly higher than C's in social help seeking in large group activities; (2) A's and C's (combined) elicited more teacher initiated contact in this context then B's; (3) As were nonsignificantly ($p<06$) higher in social help seeking during outdoor play than C's were: and (4) C's tended to receive more support "give-solicit" from teachers, more total teacher–child contact, and more total teacher-initiated contact in spontaneous group activities than A's. In several cases, however, the overall F tests were nonsignificant, rendering questionable the conduct of contrast analyses. In any event, these differences are too few and based on too small a proportion of expected differences to be very informative.

In a subsequent report by Erickson, Sroufe, and Egeland (in press), data for the 40 children described by Sroufe (1983) were combined with data concerning an additional 56 children from the Minneapolis Study of Disadvantaged Families in other daycare settings throughout the Minneapolis area (these chidren were also 4 1/2 to 5 years of age). On the basis of observations on two half-days, researchers rated these children on seven 7-point scales; these were "conferenced" to yield a single score for each child (no reliability information was reported). Teachers also completed Behar and Stringfield's (1974) 30-item Preschool Behavior Questionnaire (PBQ) and a 31-item Behavior Problem Scale (BPS) developed by Erickson and Egeland (1981). Factor analyses of these questionnaires yielded 5 major factors for each inventory.

When the 60 children from this group of 96 who had the same attachment classifications (10 were A's, 10 were C's, and 40 were B's) at 12- and 18-months were compared on these variables, four of the seven observational variables (agency, dependency, social skills and compliance), yielded significant differences in the predicted direction, although B group infants were distinguished from one of the non-B groups on only two out of four sets of pairwise contrasts, and were distinguished from both non-B groups on no measures. Although these findings were generally consistent with those of Sroufe (1983), Erickson et al. (in press) found no differences on measures of

---

[5]There appear to be some inconsistencies between text and tables in Sroufe et al.'s report. We have relied upon the tables in such cases.

positive and negative affect, in contrast to Sroufe (1983). Two of the five PBQ factors ("hostility" and "gives up, cries") and two of the five BPS factors ("exhibitionalistic—impulsive" and "withdrawal") also yielded significant group differences, although in no case were B infants distinguished from both A and C group infants in pairwise contrasts. In general, however, mean differences were in the expected direction.

Next, on the basis of these measures, all 96 children were surveyed to identify four extreme comparison groups: one designated as "acting out" (N = 17), another as "attention problems" (N = 3), a third as "withdrawn" (N = 7), and a fourth as children who were "virtually free from behavior problems and functioning competently in preschool" (N = 22). The second group was eliminated from subsequent analyses because of its small size. A contingency table analysis involving the remaining groups found a significant relationship with attachment status: Infants placed in the B group at both 12 and 18 months were most often placed in the 4th group (no behavior problems), those in non-B groups at both ages having a higher proportion in the "withdrawn" group, and infants considered "mixed" in attachment status (B group at one age and non-B at another) scattered throughout the three behavior groups. These data clearly showed, therefore, that *stable* attachment status was related to later indices, not B-group status at any single point in time.

The authors acknowledged, however, that even the association between early attachment status and subsequent behavior was quite imperfect: that is, a number of B group infants later evinced behavior problems as preschoolers and vice versa. In attempting to explain why, Erickson et al. (in press) compared (1) children who were given B group classifications *at 18-months* who either did (a) or did not (b) have later behavior problems, and similarly contrasted (2) children who were in non-B groups at 18-months who either did (a) or did not (b) have behavior problems in preschool. The dependent measures were drawn from the 24-month problem-solving situations, 42-month teaching tasks, a Caldwell HOME Inventory (Caldwell, 1979) at 30 months, as well as a range of other child and maternal assessments. Out of more than 100 such comparisons, those which best predicted later behavior problems were 11 child and maternal variables drawn from the 42-month teaching task, three items from the 30-month HOME inventory, and three child language measures. By contrast, very few of the child and maternal variables from the 24-month observation, none of the Life Events Scale Data (at 30-, 42-, and 48-months), and very few maternal personality measures distinguished children who showed subsequent behavior problems from those who did not within each attachment group. Further, most of the variables which distinguished children within the B group also distinguished children within the non-B group.

Although the shift in analytic strategy from comparisons of children who showed stable attachment classifications to comparisons of children classified differently at 18 months makes the interpretation of the results somewhat difficult, several conclusions may be drawn from this interesting report. First, although early attachment status was associated with later behavior problems in preschool, this was true *only* when attachment status was stable in the second year, implying continuity in quality of caretaking. Second, attachment status, even when stable, was not a highly efficient predictor of preschool behavior problems. Other antecedents associated with later problems were often so associated regardless of attachment status, making independent contributions of their own. Thus as Lewis, Feiring, McGuffog, and Jaskir (1984) have suggested, early attachment may be only one of a range of factors that combine and interact to predict later problems. Third, those variables most reliably associated with preschool behavior problems independent of attachment status were drawn from assessments made at about the same time as the preschool observations. In other words, short-term associations were strongest and most informative.

Taken together, these predictive studies from the Minneapolis Study of Disadvantaged Families illustrate some of the theoretical and analytical difficulties encountered in trying to make long-term predictions on the basis of attachment classifications in infancy. Among these are (1) the changeability of early attachment status, which means that predictive efficiency is heightened when one compares infants who obtained the same classification on multiple occasions and who thus probably experienced greater continuity in care, (2) the importance of other factors that may function either independently of or in interaction with early attachment status, and (3) the heterogeneity of the outcome to which predictions are made.[6] All of these factors complicate attempts to attribute later outcomes

---

[6] On this issue, comments by Egeland (1983) on his attempts to identify the antecedents of "compliance" and "noncompliance" in preschoolers are informative.

> Surprisingly, there were very few group differences....even using a number of caretaking, cognitive, and life circumstances variables in combination, we were not able to predict the child's membership in the compliant or noncompliant groups using multiple discriminant function analyses. The reason I was unable to find any social/emotional, cognitive, or caretaking correlates to compliance in preschool children was that these factors were highly variable for the noncompliant group....It appears that the factors related to compliant behavior in preschool are a secure attachment and good quality caretaking, a past developmental history of competence and compliance, and at least a minimum of cognitive and linguistic skills. These same factors (or lack thereof) are not necessarily critical, however, in the development of noncompliance in preschool children. Many of the children in the noncompliant group were securely attached, had a past history of competence, and had the necessary cognitive and linguistic skills. (pp. 133–134)

to the formative influence of early attachments and, as we have suggested, assign greater importance to the continuity of caretaking conditions that may support and perpetuate early influences.

EXPLORATORY AND COGNITIVE COMPETENCE AND PROBLEM-SOLVING

The two longitudinal studies in Minneapolis do not represent the only attempts to explore the predictive validity of attachment classifications. In fact, although the predictive validity of the Strange Situation was not investigated in Ainsworth's longitudinal study, several students of Ainsworth pioneered research on this topic. The first was Silvia Bell (1970). who assessed 33 infants at home on tests of object and person (typically mother) permanence three times between 8 1/2 and 11 months of age. In this study, the hypothesis was that sensitive maternal behavior would foster both B-type Strange Situation behavior and cognitive development—particularly, awareness of person permanence, since mother was associated with such positive experiences.

One week after the third assessment of object and person permanence, the infants were observed in the Strange Situation. In all but 3 cases, there were discrepancies between person permanence and object permanence scores on one or more of the testing sessions, with 18 infants showing discrepancies every time. Twenty-three subjects "showed a preponderance toward discrepancies in favor of person permanence...[positive decalage]...Seven subjects...tended to show discrepancies in the opposite direction...[negative decalage]...three babies [showed] no significant differences by the third testing session" (p. 301). In the Strange Situation, 24 infants behaved in the B pattern, 5 in the A pattern and 4 in the C pattern. "Babies in Group B were the only ones to show a positive decalage, and all but one of them had such a decalage. All but one of the babies in Groups A and C had a negative decalage" (p. 303). Babies in the positive decalage group had significantly higher object concept scores at every test session than those in the negative decalage groups.

Unfortunately, these strikingly clear results are seriously compromised by the fact that all of the Strange Situation classifications were based on narratives dictated by Bell who was also the person responsible for the assessments of object and person permanence. The potential for unintentional bias was thus substantial. In addition, task demands for the assessments of object and person permanence were not equivalent (cf. Jackson, Campos, & Fischer, 1978), nor was the person permanence task equivalent across infants (i.e., in whether mother or stranger was employed).

Levitt, Antonucci, and Clark (1984) attempted to replicate Bell's (1970) findings in a study involving thirty-nine 13-month-old infants. In response to Jackson et al.'s (1978) criticisms, familiarized female research assistants (rather than the mothers) served as the hidden persons, and both person and object were hidden behind curtains in large boxes. After the tests of object and person permanence, the Strange Situation was performed. Of the infants, 3 of the 14 A group, 4 of the 24 B group, and the only C group member reached ceiling on the object and person permanence scales and were thus excluded from further analyses. These analyses showed that A's scored marginally higher on the object than on the person permanence scale (p < .07), whereas B's scored at essentially the same level on both scales. There was no difference between A and B group infants on the overall level of concept attainment. These results thus failed to confirm Bell's findings.

Other aspects of cognitive and linguistic development have also been related to Strange Situation behavior classifications. As in Bell's study, it is hypothesized frequently that sensitive, responsive parenting should promote both B-type Strange Situation behavior and cognitive development, since appropriate cognitive stimulation is involved. In addition, infants who are able to use their parents as secure bases from which to explore, should explore more often and more effectively, gaining cognitive competence and mastery of the environment through exploration (see Ainsworth & Bell, 1974, for a review of these hypotheses).

Another Ainsworth student, Thomas Pentz (1975), observed 31 mothers and children in the Strange Situation when the children were 28 months old, and assessed language acquisition at both 28 and 36 months. No significant relationship was found between Strange Situation behavior and language acquisition. There are three reasons why this may have been the case. First, the Strange Situation may not be valid for assessing "security of attachment" in 28-month-olds since it was developed for use with 12-month-olds. Second, the hypothesis linking maternal sensitivity (indirectly inferred from the Strange Situation behavior of the child) to language development may be incorrect, or the indirect means of testing it may have obscured whatever relationship exists. Third, the groups may have been too small and heterogeneous to permit a sensitive test of the hypothesis.

Tracy, Farish, and Bretherton (1980) studied the relationship between Strange Situation behavior (13 months), and exploratory competence (12 months) in a sample of 40 infants. Only one of 16 tests of exploratory competence (8 each for B vs. A and B vs. A + C comparisons) revealed a significant group difference: About the number one would expect by chance. Interestingly, only 2 of 16 contrast tests of differences in mother-directed behaviors in the exploratory context yielded significant differences, suggesting low transcontextual consistency as well. Similar issues were explored by Belsky, Garduque, and Hrncir (1984; see also

Belsky & Garduque, 1982, for a preliminary report) in a sample of 61 infants seen first in a play session and subsequently in the Strange Situation with one parent at 12 months and the other at 13 months. Two of 6 measures of play showed that the B group infants, when compared with the non-B group infants, engaged in more "transitional" play (a type of play that shows a curvilinear relationship with age from 7 to 24 months; see Belsky & Most, 1981) and showed less disparity between the highest level of play generated spontaneously and the highest level that could be elicited by an experimenter (i.e., "executive capacity"). Thus, the B group infants could exercise their competencies in play more easily in an unstructured play situation than could A and C group infants. There were, however, no significant group differences in the sophistication of play displayed in either free play or elicited play situations. Linear trend analyses revealed that the B group infants performed significantly better than A group infants who in turn performed better than C group infants on one (executive capacity) of 6 measures of the quality of play, although means ranked in the same, predicted order on the other five measures of play. Further analyses revealed that B group infants were more executively competent than those classified in the A and C groups during Strange Situation observations with the mothers, regardless of the security/insecurity of the infant–father attachment. These findings are more impressive than Tracy et al.'s, and suggest that in contemporaneous assessments, B group infants play more easily and comfortably in free play situations than do non-B infants.

Hazen and Durrett (1982) explored the relationships between Strange Situation behavior, exploratory competence, and cognitive mapping in a sample of 28 children who were seen in the Strange Situation at 12 months and in a laboratory playhouse between 30 and 34 months of age. Hazen and Durrett reported that "the children who had been classified as securely attached were more active explorers and higher in cognitive mapping abilities than those classified as anxiously attached" (p. 757), but their findings do not support this strong conclusion. First, the B_1 and B_4 subgroups, traditionally deemed "secure," were combined with the A and C groups respectively, and were considered *insecurely* attached for purposes of analysis. We do not know whether significant differences would have emerged if the A, B, and C groups were compared, as would be necessary to support Hazen and Durrett's conclusion. Second, on only one of five measures of exploration and one of three measures of cognitive mapping did the B_2 and B_3 infants' scores differ from those of both the "avoidant" (A_1, A_2, B_1) and "resistant" (B_4, C_1, C_2) infants. There were no group differences on three measures, and differences between the "secure" and only one of the "anxious" groups on three others. Contrary to Hazen and Durrett's conclusion, therefore, the report contained no unambiguous evidence regarding the predictive validity of the three conventional Strange Situation groups.

Bates and his colleagues (in press; Frankel & Bates, 1983) obtained results consistent with those of Matas et al. (1978). Five factors emerged from an analysis of the maternal and child ratings and frequency measures obtained in the Matas problem-solving situations at 24 months of age, but composite scores based on the major factor (discordant interaction) were the only ones that came close (p .10) to distinguishing the A–B–C groups based on 13 month Strange Situation observations. However 5 of the 9 individual variables on which Matas et al. found significant differences yielded confirmatory findings: (1) quality of maternal assistance, (2) maternal supportive presence, (3) percent of time child away from task (p .10 in both studies), (4) "saying No," and (5) incidence of aggressive behavior. All differences were in the same direction as reported by Matas et al. (1978). As in Matas et al.'s study, the findings here suggested that the A and C group infants and their mothers interact less harmoniously and less effectively in later problem-solving tasks than B group dyads do. Thus the results do not necessarily mean that attachment security has a direct effect on the child's later personality. Rather, viewed in the context of the data reported in chapters 5 and 8, they may indicate that conflicted dyads remain somewhat conflicted dyads, with the cause of conflict in either partner or in their living circumstances.

Similar conclusions were suggested when Frankel and Bates (1983) tried to relate measures of behavior in the Matas problem solving situations to observations of mothers and infants at home when the infants were 6, 13, and 24 months of age. Correlations between the 5 problem-situation factors and 3 infant and 5 maternal behavior factors from the 6-month observations were examined first (Frankel & Bates, 1983). Only 6 of the resulting 40 correlations were significant, and in only 1 case was the correlation significant or near significant for both boys and girls. At 13 months, there were 4 infant and 4 maternal behavior factors derived from the home observation data; 12 of the resulting 40 correlations were statistically significant (1 for both boys and girls). Surprisingly, correlations between factors from contemporaneous home observational and problem-solving observations at 24 months were the weakest. With 6 infant and 3 maternal factors from home observations, a total of 45 correlations were thus computed, of which only 4 were statistically significant—none for both boys and girls. An additional 2 of 25 correlations related to codings of conflict sequences in the home at 24 months were also statistically significant. Taken together, these data reveal very weak relationships over time between discordant or disharmonious home interaction patterns and mother–child interaction in the 24-month problem-solving tasks. However, it is noteworthy that there was a consistent, albeit weak, tendency for more positive interaction at home to be associated with more positive interaction in the problem solving context.

In a follow-up of Grossmann et al.'s (1981) Bielefeld sample when they were three years of age, Lutkenhaus (1984) observed 44 of the original 49 children at home in a competitive ring-stacking task, with the investigator posing as a competitor. In this task, the B group children looked at the competitor's tower less in the success than in the failure trial, whereas the A group children looked at the competitor's tower slightly more often in the success trial. Other analyses focused on speed of stacking and facial expressions during this competitive task and revealed no main effects for attachment status but some interactions between attachment status and task parameters. Unfortunately, interpretation of these results is problematic in view of the absence of any a priori hypotheses about group effects or interactions, the failure of the findings to show any internal coherence, and by the fact that there were significant A, B, C group differences in their initial greeting of the stranger, suggesting that variance in initial sociability may have been the basis of other group differences.

In sum, no reliable predictive association between attachment status and later exploratory or cognitive competence or problem-solving ability has yet been demonstrated. The strongest associations between these constructs occur either when the assessments are contemporaneous, or when predictive assessments occur with the same adult partner, such as mother. In the latter case, the association over time could be due to stability in adult rather than child characteristics, or to their interactive harmony, rather than to some stable attribute of the child.

COOPERATION AND COMPLIANCE

Other researchers have explored the relationships between security of attachment and the child's cooperation and compliance. The first such study was conducted by Main (1973; see report by Main, 1983), who observed 40 infants in the Strange Situation at 12 months and related their behavior in this context to performance in a Bayley test session at 20.5 months and in a 50-minute long play session with a somewhat familiar woman at 21 months. The child was also retested on a subset of Bayley items two weeks after the 20.5 month session. Strange Situation classifications were performed using dictated narrative accounts rated by individuals who had no knowledge of the child's performance at 20 1/2 and 21 months. No information about observer reliability was reported. Nearly half of the infants who were tested on the Bayley (and also had their "cooperation" and "game-like spirit" rated) were assessed by an individual familiar with the Strange Situation classifications, but no bias in favor of the hypothesis was discerned. Ratings of play session behavior were conducted by individuals who had no other knowledge of the infants. Three scores were derived from the Bayley assessment (Developmental Quotient, cooperation, game-like spirit) and 17 from the play session (six pertaining to exploration, five to play with the unfamiliar adult, and six to the semiotic function). Scores in the Bayley test cluster and the semiotic function cluster were highly intercorrelated, as were several of the exploration measures. Three measures of maternal behavior were derived from an analysis of free play behavior at 21 months. These measures of maternal behavior revealed no group differences, although additional ratings of the transcripts and videotapes later indicated substantial group differences in maternal behavior (Main et al., 1979; Londerville & Main, 1981).

For the purpose of analysis, A and C group infants were grouped together in one group ($N = 15$). According to Main (1983), all of the Bayley test measures, four of the six exploration measures, four of the five playmate play measures (plus one at $p < .10$), and three of the six semiotic function measures showed significant B vs. non-B differences in one-tailed tests. All differences favored the B group infants, who were more playful, exploratory, sociable, and cognitively competent.

Although impressive, Main's findings are rendered somewhat difficult to interpret because of the significant B vs. non-B group differences in DQ. Since such differences have not been found in any other studies (Matas, Arend, & Sroufe, 1978; Joffe, 1981; Pastor, 1981; Egeland & Farber, 1982[7]; Waters, Wippman, & Sroufe, 1979), the groups being compared may not have been good samples of the relevant populations. As Sroufe (1983) observes: "well functioning children may be relatively high or low on intelligence and many severely limited children have adequate intelligence" (p. 42), so the confound in Main's study may be of great importance. This precaution is especially pertinent in light of the common correlation between DQ and sociability or cooperation (Lamb, 1982a), and the probable association between DQ and the measure of exploratory competence in this study. At the very least, it would be necessary to control (by covariation procedures) for differences in DQ and *then* examine group differences on the other measures. Indeed, high correlations between DQ, cooperation, and game-like spirit in Main's data suggest that DQ was associated with cooperation and sociability in her study also. In the absence of such analyses, we cannot say whether Main found differences between

[7]Egeland and Farber (1982) reported that babies classified in the C group at 12 months obtained lower Bayley scores at 9 months than those classified in the B group, but there was no significant B vs non-B group difference and no significant relationship between Bayley scores and 18-month Strange Situation classifications.

children who were developmentally different, or whether there were indeed differences attributable to differences in the quality of infant–mother attachment, as assessed in the Strange Situation.

Main's data were also reanalyzed by Londerville and Main (1981), who focused on maternal training methods and filial compliance in the Bayley assessment and play sessions at 21 months. (Four subjects from the earlier study were excluded.) The variables included were: Strange Situation classifications; resistance to mother in the Strange Situation; resistance to stranger in the Strange Situation; four measures of maternal behavior in the play session (tone of voice; forcefulness of physical interventions; number of verbal commands; number of physical interventions); and 9 toddler variables (sex; number of siblings; DQ; cooperation with tester; compliance with mother; active disobedience; evidence of internalized controls; a "baby rescue" measure of compliance; and a maternal report of troublesomeness). Intercoder agreement was high and coders were blind to scores on other measures and Strange Situation classifications. Twenty-two infants were placed in the B, seven in the A, and three in the C group, four were unclassifiable but "nonsecure." Again, unfortunately, the non-B group infants were placed together in a single "insecure" group. With the exception of sex and number of siblings, all individual toddler variables as well as a composite measure were significantly related in the generally expected direction to Strange Situation behavior; B group infants were more compliant and cooperative and less disobedient but more troublesome than the A, C, and unclassifiable group infants combined. Two of the four maternal variables—tone of voice and forcefulness of physical interventions—were likewise related to Strange Situation behavior in the predicted direction, with mothers of B group infants using warmer tones and being less forceful. Resistance to stranger was unrelated to compliance, but resistance to mother at 12 months was negatively related to cooperation with the Bayley tester and compliance with the mother. Like Main's (1973, 1983) results, however, these findings are difficult to interpret in the absence of statistical controls for the effects of DQ.

In their longitudinal study, Bates et al. (in press) also observed many of their infant subjects at home at 24 months with their mothers, 11 months after the Strange Situation assessments. Strange Situation behavior did not predict scores on 24-month constructs, which were similar to those constructs assessed at 6 and 13 months, which did predict Strange Situation behavior (e.g., maternal affectionate caretaking). Consistent with the findings reported by Londerville and Main (1981), and Matas et al. (1978) however, B group classification predicted lower scores on a Mother Negative Control factor at 24 months ($r = -.24$, $p = .04$, one-tail), although there were no differences on a Child Trouble factor. A and C group classification predicted ($r = -.33$, $p = .01$, one-tail) child resistance to maternal control on one of five "conflict sequence" composite scores. Scores on a factor (Reciprocal Interaction) that was a composite of scores derived from post-observation ratings were predicted by attachment security ($r = -.24$, $p = .04$ one-tailed), but scores on 5 other composite measures based on ratings on the post-observation-questionnaire (POQ) and 6 other factors based on molecular observational codes were not predicted by attachment security. Maslin (1983) reported no relationship between Strange Situation behavior and a factor measuring child compliance at 24 months. Overall, these findings suggest that B group infants from middle class, somewhat stable families later have somewhat more harmonious relationships with their mothers, but are not necessarily more compliant with them than A and C group infants are. These predictive relationships were also not very strong.

Miyake et al. (1981–82) also investigated the predictive validity of Strange Situation behavior in their sample of 29 first-born, middle class Japanese infants. Their specific interest was in infant compliance with maternal demands. In a problem-solving situation at 16 months and a delay of gratification procedure at 20 months, the proportion of obedient responses relative to disobedient responses was significantly higher for B-type than for C and pseudo-C type infants at both 16 and 20 months. At 16 months, however, there were no group differences in the frequencies of maternal commands, infant obedient responses, and infant disobedient responses, and at 20 months there were no group differences in the number of infant requests/demands, the number of maternal responses/commands or the number of either obedient responses. Thus these findings are loosely consistent with those of Londerville and Main (1981) and Matas et al. (1978) although Miyake et al. were unable to replicate Londerville and Main's findings on the specific measures they employed.

Taken together, these attempts to predict cooperation and compliance suggest that B group infants may later get along better with their mothers than non-B infants, although confident conclusions are limited by the failure to replicate specific findings from study to study, the possibility of a covariate—DQ—underlying both attachment and cooperation/compliance constructs, and the failure to study predictable variations in cooperation/ compliance within the insecure classifications. It is also difficult to infer causality from these studies. All investigators have studied compliance with mothers and most have also found that mothers of B and non-B infants themselves behaved differently during the assessments of compliance. Because the mothers were also participants in the earlier Strange Situation assessments, any predictive associations between attachment status and later compliance may be due to maternal behavior in both settings. It thus becomes imperative in future research to either examine compliance with other adults or control for variations in maternal behavior in both assessment contexts.

BEHAVIOR PROBLEMS

Two large longitudinal projects—those initiated by Bates (Bates et al., in press) and Lewis (Lewis, Feiring, McGuffog, & Jaskir, 1984)—have explored the relationship between Strange Situation behavior and later behavior problems.

In their longitudinal study, Bates et al. (in press) attempted to relate scores on their attachment security index at 13 months with measures of behavior problems at 36 months. They used Behar's (1977) Preschool Behavior Questionnaire (PBQ), which has scales for: Anxious behavior, Hostile behavior, and Hyperactive behavior. Interestingly, the perceptions of mothers and of secondary caregivers (e.g., teachers, relatives) of the same children on the PBQ were not significantly correlated, leaving doubt about precisely what is measured by these ratings.

Predictor variables were divided into 8 predictor domains. Perhaps because many of the PBQ ratings themselves tapped maternal perceptions, early maternal perceptions were the best predictors of behavior problems, while attachment variables, especially A–B–C attachment classifications, were among the worst. Indeed, they were essentially unrelated to the PBQ ratings by either mothers or secondary caretakers. One of the attachment behavior measures emerged as a significant predictor in a secondary regression analysis: The more an infant avoided proximity in the reunion episodes, the more likely a high rating for anxiety by secondary caregivers. Because variables were selected for inclusion in part on the basis of the first order analyses, however, these results are hard to evaluate.

Bates et al. suggest that their failure to replicate Sroufe's (1983) findings concerning the relationship between A and C group classification and later behavior problems could be due to the fact that Sroufe's subjects came from backgrounds in which they faced much more severe stresses than did Bates' middle-class subjects. Another possibility is that Bates' parent report measure of behavior problems is less reliable and valid than Sroufe's. However, since Sroufe's findings did not provide strong evidence of the prediction of behavior problems from early attachment classifications alone, it is not necessary to view Bates study as a non-replication, as Bates et al. did. Rather, the Minneapolis study underscores the importance of continuity of early attachments (and thus, most likely, of caretaking) as mediating predictive relationships, while both studies (see Erickson et al., in press) suggest that other variables may be at least as important as early attachment status in predicting preschool behavior problems.

Lewis et al.'s (1984) attachment classifications were based, not on behavior in the typical Strange Situation, but on the basis of reactions to reunion in a laboratory playroom following a single brief (3-minute) separation[8]. One hundred and thirteen infants were seen in this context at 12 months and were later evaluated when they were 6 years of age using Achenbach's (1978) Child Behavior Profile (CBP), which yields a total score, scores on two broad-band factors (internalizing and externalizing) and several narrow-band behavioral problem scales (9 for girls and 9 others for boys). In addition, cognitive functioning was assessed at 3, 12, 24, and 36 months, demographic data by repeated interviewing, "birth planning" and other factors by maternal questionnaire, the child's social network using an adapted version of Pattison's (1975) Psychosocial Network Inventory, and changing psychosocial circumstances and life stresses were tapped using a Life Events Questionnaire. Distribution of the subjects in terms of attachment classifications and the incidence of behavior problems was consistent with that reported in other studies (Ainsworth et al., 1978; Achenbach & Edelbrock, 1978, 1981).

Analyses of variance revealed that B group males had the least and C group males the most behavior problems on the total CBP, with A, B, and C groups significantly distinguished from each other. For girls there was a nonsignificant trend indicating that B group and A group children showed the *most* and C group children the *least* behavior problems. On the Internalizing scales, the males again ranked B < A < C, but there were no significant effects for girls. However, on the Externalizing scale, there was a significant effect for girls (C < A, and C < B) but not for boys. On the narrow-band scales, there were no group differences at all for girls, but significant effects for boys in pairwise contrasts on schizoid behavior problems (A > B), depression (C > B), social withdrawal (C > B), uncommunicative behavior (A > B and C > B), and somatic complaints (A > B and C > B).

Next Lewis et al. (1984) used CBP percentile criteria developed by Achenbach and Edelbrock (1981) to identify children as "at risk" for developing psychopathology. Contingency-table analyses showed that A and C group male infants were significantly more likely to manifest risk for later psychopathology by these criteria, whereas among girls, this was not true. Viewed prospectively, 40% of the A and C group males were deemed at risk for later psychopathology, compared with 15% of the A, B, and C group girls and about 6% of B group males. Thus early attachment classifications were predictors of later "at risk" status for boys but not for girls.

---

[8]Although this represents a substantial modification of the traditional Strange Situation procedure, both Waters et al. (1979) and Lamb et al. (1985) have presented evidence suggesting that such modified procedures provide assessments whose validity is comparable to that of traditional Strange Situation assessments.

Lewis et al. (1984) then proceded to ask why 60% of the boys who were classified in the A or C groups as infants did *not* develop risk status for psychopathology. A discriminant function analysis was used to discriminate those non-B infants who either did or did not show later risk status on the CBP as 6-year-olds. This analysis involved 7 predictor variables and indicated that those boys who experienced "negative environmental factors" (in order of importance: whether the child's birth was unplanned, a large number of life stress events in the child's lifetime, second-born birth status, and a small number of friends) were more likely to develop risk for psychopathology. The function using these environmental variables correctly reclassified 75% of the non-B infants into "risk" and "non-risk" groups. Interestingly, however, Lewis et al. concluded that B group boys exposed to the same negative environment factors apparently did not develop psychopathology, although this finding may have been a statistical artifact of the discriminant function analysis, in which only two B group infants were in the "risk" group.

These results thus suggested that early attachment classifications, in interaction with subsequent experiences, influence whether or not children will later manifest risk for psychopathology—at least for boys—although the unpredicted sex differences in results are perplexing. As Lewis et al. summarized:

> Such findings lend support to [the notion of] an interactive process wherein poor early attachment predisposes a boy to psychopathology if he is also subject to environmental stress. Thus, insecurely attached males are more vulnerable to environmental stress (p. 133).

Their data further "suggest that a early secure attachment renders males somewhat impervious to the effects of stress and places them at low risk for psychopathology" (p. 134), although this may be a less reliable conclusion for the reason noted above. However, Lewis et al.'s provocative conclusion—consistent with the findings of Bates et al. (in press)—is that "infants neither are made invulnerable by secure attachments nor are they doomed by insecure attachments to later psychopathology" (p. 134).

SOCIABILITY WITH UNFAMILIAR ADULTS

Several investigators have studied the relationship between Strange Situation behavior and the quality of interaction with unfamiliar adults. Main and Weston (1981), for example, observed 61 infants in the Strange Situation with their mothers and fathers at 12 and 18 months of age. Forty-six of the infants were seen first with their mothers, and 15 with their fathers. One week before the 12-month Strange Situation, 44 children were seen in a play session (with their mothers present) in which a clown attempted to evoke 3 types of emotional reactions (apprehension, delight, and "concerned attention"). The infants' degree of "relatedness" to the clown and of "conflict behavior" during the session were rated from the videotapes by naive coders. Only 1 of 23 infants who were classified in the B group with their mothers showed conflict behavior, compared with 11 (56%) of the 21 A and C group or "unclassified" infants. B group infants were also highest on the stranger "relatedness" measure, although there was no statistical test of the difference. However, there were apparently no significant differences in relatedness or conflict between avoidant, resistant or "unclassified nonsecure" infants. It was found that Strange Situation behavior with mother overrode the relationship with father in regard to relatedness, with similar trends apparent for conflict behavior; in both cases, performance was better for those classified B than for those classified in the A or C groups with their mothers, regardless of the babies' attachment status with their fathers. Interpretation of these findings is difficult, however, as (1) in every case, these behaviors were rated one week before the assessment of mother–infant attachment and 6 months before the assessment of father–infant attachment and (2) mothers (but not fathers) were present in the clown/play sessions. This may explain, therefore, the preeminence of attachment status with mother over that with father in predicting behavior with the stranger. It is also important to note that the relationships reported are between near-contemporaneous assessments, with conflict behavior and relatedness assessed one week *before* the Strange Situation with mother. Overall, therefore, this study provides evidence regarding the construct validity or external correlates of Strange Situation behavior. The information is limited, however, by the lack of detail regarding the constructs assessed, and the confounds in the procedure noted earlier.

Thompson and Lamb (1983b) observed 43 middle class infants and their mothers in the Strange Situation at 12 1/2 and 19 1/2 months. Immediately prior to each Strange Situation, infants were observed in a brief standardized procedure designed to assess sociability toward unfamiliar adults modified from that developed by Stevenson & Lamb (1979). Following Easterbrooks and Lamb (1979), Thompson and Lamb (1983b) distinguished B_1B_2 from B_3B_4 infants for analytic purposes. At each age, the B_1 and B_2 infants were most sociable and the C_2 and B_3B_4 infants least sociable, even though, given the frequency of changes in classification (see chapter 8), different infants fell in each of the groups each time. When the attachment classifications changed over time, the sociability scores at each age were not significantly correlated ($r = -.18$), but they were highly correlated ($r = .74$) when the attachment classification was the same at both ages. These findings thus suggest that prediction of later socioemotional behavior may depend upon concurrent stability in attachment status or patterns of parent–child interaction, rather than arising from characteristics intrinsic to the child.

Lamb, Hwang, Frodi, and Frodi (1982) also related stranger sociability to Strange Situation classifications in a sample of 51 Swedish infants and their parents. Infants were seen with one parent at 11 months and the other at 13 months; order of assessment was counterbalanced. For half of the infants, sociability was assessed twice (before each Strange Situation) with male strangers and for the other half, female strangers were employed. The two sociability scores were summed for analysis, as they were significantly (though not highly, $r = .39$) correlated. As predicted (Easterbrooks & Lamb, 1979; Thompson & Lamb, 1983b), infants who had B_1B_2 relationships with their fathers were slightly but significantly more sociable than those with B_3B_4 or A relationships. There was also a tendency for infants who were classified in the B group with their fathers to be more sociable than those who were placed in either the A or C groups. There was no significant relationship between infant–mother attachment classifications and the child's sociability. There was no effect for degree of parental involvement in caretaking, and, contrary to Main and Weston's (1981) findings, no evidence that those who were classified in either B or non-B groups with *both* parents were especially high or low (respectively) in sociability. Infants were, however, significantly more sociable with female than with male strangers.

Lamb's (1979) procedure, to Strange Situation behavior in a sample of 20 preterm and 20 fullterm infants. There was no difference between the term and preterm infants in number of B or non-B attachment classifications or in the mean sociability scores. There was also no A, B, C group difference on the composite sociability scores, although one of the 6 component measures showed that B group infants were more sociable when the stranger first entered. Unfortunately, Frodi (1983) did not break down the B group into the B_1B_2 and B_3B_4 clusters studied by Thompson and Lamb (1983b) and Lamb, Hwang, Frodi, and Frodi (1982).

Nakano (1982–83) also examined the relationship between Strange Situation classification (at 12 and 23 months) and stranger reactions at 23 months in a subgroup of Japanese infants from Miyake et al.'s (1981–82, in press) study. Unfortunately, the subgroup comprised only 7 girls (3 of whom changed classification between 12 and 23 months) and was thus too small to permit any reliable analyses.

Taken together, these studies offer some suggestion that B group infants are more sociable in their initial encounter with adult strangers, although this difference is not highly reliable, since more than one investigator has failed to find this effect. Interestingly, no study (except Nakano's) has involved attempts to study the relationship between mother–infant attachment and stranger sociability predictively—all have relied upon contemporaneous or near-contemporaneous assessments. Equally significantly, no investigator has found A and C group differences in stranger sociability, despite the fact that A babies tend to be more sociable with the stranger in the Strange Situation (but see Thompson & Lamb, 1983b). Thus these studies raise more questions for future investigations than they resolve.

SOCIABILITY AND SOCIAL COMPETENCE WITH PEERS

In addition to Pastor (1980, 1981), whose work was discussed earlier, several researchers have studied the relationship between security of attachment and later interactive skills with peers. Lieberman (1977) attempted to relate the quality of the infant–mother relationship to preschoolers' social competence with peers. The study involved forty 3-year-olds and thus, like Pentz's, must be criticized for using a procedure (the Strange Situation) that is potentially invalid for children of this age. However, instead of A, B, C classifications, several composite measures of attachment security were derived by principal components analysis of variables from both home and Strange Situation observations. The first factor comprised behaviors indicating absence of anxiety on the part of the child and a relaxed maternal demeanor during the home observation. The second factor comprised "anxious mother-oriented versus toy-oriented behavior in the strange situation. The third component [sociability] represented expansive sociability versus social withdrawal in the strange situation" (p. 1283). Ratings of maternal attitudes and scores on a composite measure based on the first component were related to the peer competence measures drawn from a 15-minute free-play session. None of the composite measures based on Strange Situation behavior were similarly related, which may confirm our concerns about the inappropriateness of this procedure for assessing 3-year-olds. Since both the 3-year Strange Situation and the home-based measure of attachment security are of unknown validity, these data provide equivocal evidence concerning the relationship between security of attachment and peer competence. However, Lieberman's attempts to develop measures of the quality of child–parent attachment that are not solely based on the classification of behavior in the Strange Situation are commendable.

More impressive findings concerning the relationship between Strange Situation behavior and peer competence were reported by Waters et al. (1979), who used films of thirty-two, 15-month-olds and their mothers in a novel situation involving 5–10 minutes of free play, the entrance of a stranger, a 1-minute separation, and then a mother–infant reunion. To rate

security of attachment, information about reunion behavior was supplemented by measures of separation and pre-separation behavior.
Unfortunately, the avoidant and resistant infants were placed together in a
single "anxious" group for purposes of analyses. "Secure" and "anxious"
groups did not differ on Bayley Scale assessments of DQ at 14 months or on
Stanford–Binet assessments at 36 months.

When the children were 3½ years old, naive observers performed Q-sort
assessments on the basis of a 5-week observation in a preschool setting. The
mean of the scores assigned by two independent raters (interrater $r = .61$)
was employed in group comparisons using

> two 12-item criterion Q-scales...assembled rationally and without reference to
> the attachment data from the 72 item Q set. The first 12-item set (peer
> competence) included all reliable items referring to initiative, skill, and
> engagement in interaction with peers...The second 12-item set (ego-strength/
> effectance) included all reliable items referring to personal and motivational
> assets that do not assume an interactive context (Waters et al., 1979, p. 826).

However, three items were later reassigned because they correlated better
with the set other than that to which they were initially assigned. Composite
scores were computed by summing scores on the items in each set. The two
composite scores were highly correlated ($r = .61$). Eleven of the 12 peer
competence items, as well as the composite score, distinguished the two
attachment groups. In addition, 5 of the 12 ego strength/effectance items
distinguished the two groups, as did the summary score. There is thus
evidence of group differences, especially in peer competence, two years
after group assignment. However, it is important to note that in the original
study for which this sample was recruited, families were specifically selected
on the grounds that their circumstances were likely to remain stable
throughout the duration of the study (see Bronson, 1981). As we have
earlier indicated, this consistency in caretaking circumstances is likely to
heighten predictive relationships with earlier attachment status.

In their study, Easterbrooks and Lamb (1979) focused on differences
between infants in the B_1 or B_2, B_3, and B_4 subgroups within the "secure"
(B) group in order to test the validity of these subgroup distinctions as
predictors of peer interactional skills. No A or C group infants were studied.
All observations took place when the infants were 18 months old; "focal"
infants from three groups ($B_1, 2$, B_3, B_4) were observed in an unfamiliar
playroom for 30 minutes with an unfamiliar "foil" playmate who was always
drawn from either the B_1 or B_2 subgroup to ensure comparable playmates
for all subjects. Of 21 discrete behavior measures and 3 composite measures
of peer interaction, there were significant overall group differences on 2 of
the discrete measures and 2 of the composite measures, with the focal $B_1 B_2$

infants spending more time interacting with and being close to their peers than focal B_3 and B_4 infants. Pairwise contrasts revealed significant B_1 B_2 vs. B_3 differences on 7 measures (including all 4 of those showing overall differences) and B_1 B_2 vs. B_4 differences on 5 measures, including 2 of the 4 showing overall differences. As expected, the B_1 B_2 infants also spent less time in the peer session touching and being near their mothers, indicating that there was some trans-situational consistency in their responses to mothers, since these infants are also noted for distal interaction in the Strange Situation. These differences in mother-directed behavior, however, make it difficult to interpret the group differences on peer interaction measures. The groups may not actually have differed in social competence; rather, different reactions to the unfamiliar situation may have produced patterns of mother–child interaction that simply precluded or potentiated peer interaction. It would be important to know whether group differences on the peer interaction measures remained when variance attributable to differences in mother-directed behavior was partialled out.

Jacobsen, Wille, Tianen, and Aytch (1983) observed 107 infants in the Strange Situation at 18 months and then observed 15 As, 15 Bs, and 15 Cs interacting for 25 minutes with an unfamiliar same-sex B infant at 23.5 months. Group differences on 5 of 11 measures of child behavior were found. Surprisingly, however, the B and A group infants engaged in more onlooker behavior than did the C group infants, who engaged in more solitary play and more positive interaction with peers than either B or A group infants; indeed the B infants engaged in the *least* positive interaction with peers. The A infants engaged in the most positive interaction with their mothers. Unfortunately, the significance of the pairwise comparison was not reported for any of these analyses. Even in their absence, however, it is clear that Pastor's (1980, 1981) and Waters, Wippman, and Sroufe's (1979) findings concerning the greater peer competence of B group toddlers were not replicated.

Subsequently, Jacobson and Wille (1984) reported observing 19 of the 107 children (7 A group, 6 B group, and 6 C group at 18 months) as focal partners in 25-minute peer play sessions at 24 and 35 months, always with a B group same-sex unfamiliar playmate. Six measures of each child's behavior in the dyadic context were then analyzed. There were no significant group differences among focal children in either assessment, but on one measure (number of positive responses), playmates paired with B group focal children scored higher than C group or A group children when data from both observations were pooled. There were also some significant Age by Attachment group interactions in behavior directed to focal children that were unpredicted and difficult to interpret. Given the small sample size, the inconsistency of the results at 2 and 3 years, the small number of significant effects, and the absence of clear group differences in the behavior of target or focal children, it is difficult to interpret these findings.

Overall, therefore, associations between prior Strange Situation classifications and later indices of social competence or engagement with peers are equivocal. Apart from the impressive findings of Waters et al., no other investigators have identified clear, reliable associations between attachment status and peer competence in studies of either contemporaneous or predictive relationships.

SELF RECOGNITION

Tajima (1982–83) followed up 26 of Miyake et al.'s (1981–82) 29 Japanese subjects when they were 16 months old, and 23 of them once again when they were 20 months old. On each occasion, Tajima employed Lewis and Brooks–Gunn's (1979) procedure for assessing self-recognition in the mirror. This involves noting self-referent behavior after applying rouge to the baby's face. At 16 months, 40% of the C infants recognized themselves, compared to 12.5% of the B group infants, but this difference was not statistically significant (p .10). At 20 months, however, 75% of the C infants and 26.5% of the B group infants manifested self-recognition (p .05). At both ages, therefore, the findings ran counter to what would have been predicted.

Schneider–Rosen and Cicchetti (1984) also examined the relationship between Strange Situation behavior and visual self-recognition (using the same procedure as Tajima) in a sample of thirty-seven 19-month-olds. Eighteen of them had been maltreated, while the remaining 19 were matched, lower-income controls. Fifteen of the infants were capable of visual self-recognition; 73% of whom were classified in the B and 27% in the non-B groups. This difference was statistically significant. The difference in self-recognition between the maltreated (5 of 18) and nonmaltreated (10 of 19) toddlers was not reliable. However, 74% of the nonmaltreated toddlers expressed positive affect following observation of their rouge-marked noses, compared with only 22% of the maltreated infants—a statistically significant difference. The presumably earlier attainment of the capacity for visual self-recognition among the B group infants is consistent with the interpretation that these infants are able to explore their physical and social environment more fully and more trustfully, and that this exploration promotes the emergence of the skills underlying the capacity for visual self-recognition. The results, however, run counter to those reported by Tajima. Further research is thus needed to clarify the relationship, if any, between Strange Situation behavior and visual self-recognition.

CONCLUSION

The investigators whose work is reviewed in this chapter have attempted to relate Strange Situation behavior in infancy to a host of sequelae, including compliant cooperation with mother, aspects of personality functioning, sociability, and cognitive competence. While most have looked at the predictive correlates of early attachment status, a number have instead studied contemporaneous correlates, providing evidence more pertinent to the construct validity of the Strange Situation than to its predictive validity. Whether studying contemporaneous or predictive associations, however, researchers have generally failed to identify clear, replicable associations between Strange Situation behavior and other aspects of socioemotional functioning attributable to enduring characteristics of the infant. Instead, the evidence to date suggests that continuity in infant behavior may be equally attributable to consistency in caretaking conditions that perpetuate early characteristics in later assessments, or to consistency in parental behavior in both the Strange Situation and follow-up observations.

The clearest evidence for the long-term predictive validity of Strange Situation classifications comes from the ambitious Minneapolis studies, in which children have been studied through the preschool years. However, we have noted that in many of these studies, stability over time in family or childcare circumstances either could be assumed (due to sample characteristics) or was actually ensured by subject selection procedures (such as selecting children who had earlier obtained the same attachment classifications at 12 and 18 months which, according to Vaughn et al., 1979, was associated with reduced life stress). The fact that the strongest evidence for predictive validity is obtained from such studies affects the generalizability of these findings, and has important implications for their interpretation. These data do *not* support the hypothesis that experiences during an early formative period in the first year necessarily have long-term implications for the child. Rather, it seems that *when* there is continuity in parent–child interaction and in other circumstances likely to influence child development (inferred from stability of attachment classifications, sample characteristics, or the absence of major intervening changes in family or caretaking conditions), early patterns of child behavior are likely to be maintained. The implication, therefore, is that recent rather than early patterns of child–parent interaction may be the bases of observed differences in child behavior in follow-up assessments.

Of course, our alternative interpretation of these findings is itself conjectural, since none of these studies has provided explicit information about the stability of family or caretaking circumstances in the period between the Strange Situation and the follow-up assessment. Even so, our assumption that such stability is likely to exist is supported by these researchers' acknowledgments (1) that selection of subjects for consistent early patterns of attachment was explicitly intended to maximize predictive relationships (e.g., Sroufe, 1983, p.53), and (2) that in the face of major changes in life circumstances, the predictive associations they found are not likely to be found (e.g., Sroufe, 1978; Erickson et al., in press). These acknowledgments have important implications for the interpretation of these findings, since they suggest that the locus of stability in such predictive relationships could be in the caretaking environment, rather than in the child. Clearly, the viability of these alternative explanations point to the need for further detailed longitudinal studies in which concurrent changes in family conditions and caretaking circumstances—and their effects on parent–child interaction—are assessed in the period between the Strange Situation and later assessments.

A second problem with much of this research is that the same adult often participates in both the early Strange Situation assessment and in the follow-up procedure. This is true of the widely-cited study by Matas et al. (1978), all of the studies of cooperation and compliance, and most of the studies concerning exploratory/cognitive competence, peer interaction skills, and stranger sociability. While it is often difficult to obtain valid assessments of early socioemotional behavior without the supportive presence of a parent, studies so designed introduce an important confound into the evidence for predictive validity, since many have found that the mothers of B, A, and C group infants also differ in follow-up assessments. Since the mother was also a participant in the initial Strange Situation and we know that variations in maternal behavior influence the infant's Strange Situation behavior, it is reasonable to ask whether evidence of consistency in infant behavior over time is due to stable infant characteristics, or to the consistent supportiveness or nonsupportiveness of the parent. Main and Weston (1981) found, in fact, that when a different parent participated in the Strange Situation and the external assessment, there were substantially weaker relationships. Unfortunately, no researcher has statistically controlled for variations in the adult's behavior in examining A, B, and C group differences in later behavior, although some have the data for accomplishing this. Distinguishing the effects of parent and infant contributions to later prediction of infant behavior remains, therefore, an issue for further empirical exploration.

Thirdly, it is remarkable that very few researchers have found reliable differences between A and C group infants, even though these should be found if Strange Situation classifications have predictive validity. As Sroufe wrote:

A reasonable and testable prediction is that the various patterns of adaptation shown by avoidant infants will represent meaningful developmental outcomes and that the set of patterns shown by avoidant children will be distinct (probabilistically) from the set of patterns shown by resistant infants (1983, p. 51; italics in original).

Despite this, few researchers have found support for this prediction and, indeed, it is rarely remarked upon. Most strikingly, many researchers have not even *sought* to explore such differences, instead grouping the A and C pattern infants into a single "insecure" group. In most cases, this occurs despite the fact that one would expect significant differences between A and C infants in the follow-up assessments. The failure to identify specific, replicable differences between these groups is of crucial importance in assessing the predictive validity of Strange Situation behavior.

Another key issue is the reliance on analytic and methodological procedures that potentially bias the results in favor of finding differences between children earlier classified in the B or non-B groups. Selective sample recruitment is but one example of a general tendency. Another problem characteristic of much research in this area is that many measures are employed, but attention is focused almost exclusively on those revealing group differences. No concern is typically expressed about the number of measures that *fail* to reveal the hypothesized group differences, or about the inconsistencies between significant and nonsignificant findings in terms of the general formulations being tested. Thus an incomplete overall picture of the findings is often presented and discussed in research reports, implying stronger evidence for the predictive validity of Strange Situation behavior than actually exists.

Much of the difficulty here lies in the vagueness of hypotheses and poorly-defined rating scales, which allow researchers to explain in a post hoc fashion why comparable measures revealed contradictory findings, or why only a subsample of the measures revealed differences consistent with the hypotheses. As we indicated at the outset of this chapter, many researchers in this area seem to approach the issue of predictive validity with no more specific expectation than that B group children will be "better" at later ages than will A or C group children. In some respects, this nonspecific formulation is easy to prove when many measures of later functioning are employed, but the results of the research reviewed here indicate that this kind of "shotgun" strategy has not been successful in identifying the *specific sequelae* of early patterns of Strange Situation behavior. Researchers need to consider more carefully what specific aspects of later socioemotional functioning *should* be affected by earlier attachment status (e.g., *why* should we expect Strange Situation behavior to predict cognitive performance?), leading to the design of more precise follow-up assessments employing a limited number of carefully-designed measures. Rather than expecting attachment status to predict multiple indices of "good" functioning at later ages, in other words, it is time to develop more specific hypotheses concerning the aspects of later behavior that attachment status should—and should not—predict well. Discriminant as well as convergent validity should be an important research goal. This kind of research strategy is not only likely to yield clearer, stronger evidence concerning later differences between B and non B groups, but may also provide a better way of identifying the sequelae of A and C group status also.

Finally, the reliance on broad rating scales is problematic in much of this research because of the potential for generalized halo effects that influence multiple observer ratings, resulting in an apparent array of significant group differences. In some cases (e.g., Easterbrooks & Lamb, 1979), furthermore, nominally blind raters, familiar with the Strange Situation classification system, could easily guess the classification status of the subjects they were observing by assuming some trans-contextual consistency in infant behaviors. This is especially problematic when behavior in the two contexts is assessed roughly contemporaneously. This is why we have emphasized throughout this review the number of significant group differences that were apparent on broader rating scales contrasted with more discrete, behavioral-ly-based, time-sampled or frequency-count measures. Although broader ratings have the advantage of incorporating diverse information into an overall assessment, they are subject to biasing influences that are not as great a concern with more discrete measures. Optimally, of course, the two kinds of measures should converge in their overall findings, although this has often not been the case in the research we have reviewed.

Despite these qualifications, it is important to note that B and non-B group infants do seem to differ in important ways outside the Strange Situation. There is some evidence for example, that B group infants show greater exploratory competence (e.g., Arend et al., 1979; Bates et al., in press; Belsky et al., 1984), are more sociable with unfamiliar adults (e.g., Main & Weston, 1981; Thompson & Lamb, 1983b), and may also get along better with peers (e.g., Waters et al., 1979) than non-B infants, although these findings have not been replicated consistently by independent investigators. What makes this sprawling literature both so enticing and so frustrating is that it does not permit us to explain *why* these differences are apparent. Are they due to the quality (and, in some instances, stability) of the child's overall rearing conditions? Can they be attributed to the supportive presence of a parent at each assessment? Do they derive from the child's own cognitions (e.g., social expectations, perceptions of personal agency, etc.) which may or may not change or remain the same depending on the stability or variability of childrearing circumstances? We simply cannot answer these questions today because studies in this area were not designed to address them. The necessary research could be conducted relatively easily, however, and we hope that they will attract the attention of researchers in the future.

In sum, although there do appear to be some reliable relationships between Strange Situation behavior and other child characteristics—at least in B vs. non-B group comparisons—such relationships appear to be significant only when there is continuity in caretaking conditions (or when the assessments are contemporaneous). Thus early influences or experiences *in interaction* with indices of the stability and quality of environmental conditions may *combine* to predict later socioemotional functioning (see Lewis et al., 1984). Such a relationship would contrast with notions of early formative or sensitive periods, and is consistent with findings from the animal studies from which "critical period" notions have been borrowed by developmental psychologists (see Denenberg, 1984; Klopfer, 1984). Beyond this general statement concerning the relationship between early attachment and later outcomes given stable circumstances in the interim, however, there is little we can say confidently about the *specific* effects of early attachment status. We hope the issues raised in this chapter motivate researchers to embark on a new series of studies using more clearly-defined hypotheses, specific measures, and nonconfounded designs to yield clearer findings regarding predictive validity.

10 INTEGRATION: STABILITY AND PREDICTION

As the data-rich chapters in this section indicate, the temporal stability and the predictive validity of attachment classifications have been well-studied issues. The available evidence concerning these topics, although not always as conclusively consistent with the authors' interpretations as they would like, also paints a reasonably consistent picture. In this brief integrative chapter, we indicate how we believe the findings should be summarized, and then discuss the implications of this appraisal both for the understanding of Strange Situation behavior and for the understanding of early socioemotional experiences more generally.

As we showed in Chapter 8, one cannot specify a universal coefficient of stability for Strange Situation attachment classifications. Studies to date have yielded estimates ranging from near perfect stability to the amount of "stability" one would expect to find by chance. Contrary to the common immediate reaction to data of this sort, neither the variability in stability estimates, nor the fact that all subsequent stability coefficients have been lower than Waters' initial study suggested are of great importance. The key issue is: Is there anything systematic about the instances of instability or change that enables us to predict them a priori? Although there is a clear need for additional hypothesis-testing longitudinal studies, there is some evidence that the instability is sometimes predictable, with changes in attachment classification occurring when there have been changes in life stresses or family circumstances likely to affect the quality of care afforded the infant and/or the patterns of parent–child interaction. In such instances, the systematic or lawful patterns of change in classifications (varying depending on changing life events) constitute evidence that Strange

Situation behavior does in fact validly reflect variations in the quality of parent–child interaction and relationships (see also Section II). Unfortunately, the mechanisms by which such experiences affect Strange Situation behavior remain unexplained, and we do not know why changing family circumstances do not always affect Strange Situation behavior nor why changing circumstances have bidirectional effects on Strange Situation behavior. As we have suggested, certain factors (e.g., quality of the marital relationship; family resources) may mediate the impact of these circumstances on attachment stability, and these hypotheses also deserve further study.

The fact that patterns of Strange Situation behavior can and in some circumstances do change not only bears on the construct validity of the Strange Situation classifications; it also has profound implications for the interpretation of research on the predictive validity of Strange Situation behavior. In those contexts when the stability of Strange Situation classification is known to be high or can be assumed to be high, Strange Situation classifications are often related to indices of sociability with unfamiliar adults, compliance, problem solving behavior, subsequent behavior problems and indices of personality functioning. There is also evidence for some effect on sociability with peers. Evidence concerning the association between Strange Situation behavior and subsequent behavior problems is not always strong (see Bates et al., in press), although data from one such follow-up study (Lewis et al., 1984) yielded some suggestive and theoretically interesting findings.

Lewis et al.'s report, in fact, raises important questions about the frameworks we might adopt in attempting to explain any demonstrated predictive validity for Strange Situation classifications. Lewis et al. reported that, at least among boys, A and C group children were at greater risk for evincing psychopathology at age 6. Whether or not they did so, argued Lewis et al., depended on whether they were subsequently exposed to negative life experiences; if they were, then the chances of pathology were higher. Unfortunately, negative life experiences were not directly measured, so this interpretation requires further investigation. Lewis et al. also suggested that boys may be more vulnerable to both the buffering and destabilizing effects of variations in early experiences than girls are. Other studies concerned with similar situations have not found such buffering, but it is an intriguing question with great significance, deserving of more attention than it has been afforded to date. The findings suggest that child characteristics—in the form of individual differences in vulnerability to pathogenic circumstances—may play an important role in mediating the effects of early experience (as tapped by Strange Situation assessments) on later personal functioning.

To be sure, this constellation of results has not been sought or found in any other studies, so we cannot say how robust it will prove to be. Most other studies, as noted earlier, have limited their focus to samples in which negative life events were less likely to occur, so the specific interaction between prior attachment status and subsequent life experiences has not been studied. Such studies also often leave unanswered questions concerning the source of whatever predictive validity is demonstrated: Are the later group differences attributable to differences in earlier patterns of parent–child interaction, or are they due to the *current* status of the parent–child relationship which, because of the stable samples selected, resembles the earlier status and thus gives the appearance of formative significance to the earlier patterns of interaction?

Lewis et al.'s findings are thus important because they suggest that *both* factors are important. Poor parent–child relationships—to the extent that they are reflected in the Strange Situation classifications—do not guarantee poor outcomes: They predict difficulty only when the child later encounters stressful events, and they may make the child unusually susceptible to such influences.

Such a conclusion is entirely consistent with the notion of "homeorhesis" used by Bowlby (1973, pp. 366–369)—after Waddington, 1957—to describe consistency and change in personality functioning in early development. According to Bowlby, processes of evolutionary adaptation ensure greater flexibility in accomodating to environmental contingencies in early than in later development. With increasing age, "homeorhetic processes" reduce environmental lability so as to promote greater individual consistency. Bowlby viewed homeorhetic processes as being more influential beginning in later childhood or adolescence. He suggested that these processes are of two kinds. First, environmental stability provides consistent support for development. Second, processes within the organism (e.g., representational models of self and others; defensive processes) also serve to perpetuate individual characteristics. Bowlby's formulation is thus consistent with the findings we have reviewed in Chapters 8 and 9—and with the results of the Lewis et al. (1984) study—in at least two ways. First, it affirms the sensitivity of the infant and young child to environmental changes and stresses that may affect the stability and predictability of socioemotional functioning. Second, it indicates that such stability and prediction are products of *both* environmental conditions and intra-individual processes.

Of course, this pattern of results has been reported only in relation to one type of outcome measure (behavior problems) in only one study. Furthermore, it seems unreasonable to assume a priori that the same relationship between early attachment and subsequent behavior patterns should hold regardless of the specific outcome at issue. Indeed, behavioral ecology would suggest variations in the degrees of early experientially determined fixedness depending on the fitness implications of the specific outcomes. In some areas, in other words, fixedness may be beneficial, whereas in other areas, flexibility would be advantageous. As a result, we might expect buffering against environmental impact on some aspects of personal functioning (where flexibility might be disadvantageous) and sensitivity to environmental impact with respect to these aspects of development where flexibility would be desirable. Thus we do not know either whether Lewis et al.'s formulation will be consistent with data from other research on the relationship between attachment and behavior problems or whether the same formulation could be applied to other research on the sequelae of individual differences in Strange Situation behavior.

It is unfortunate that the studies of predictive validity undertaken thus far—with few exceptions—have simply tested the implicit and rather loose notion that desirable (i.e., B group) Strange Situation behavior is likely to be associated with desirable outcomes. But why some outcomes and not others? What is or are the mechanisms whereby early interactive patterns are related to aspects of later performance? The absence of a clearly articulated theoretical framework is a continuing impediment to the advance of understanding in this area. Indeed, the lack of clarity with respect to characterization of the long-term impact of Strange Situation behavior is not unrelated to some of the interpretational problems discussed in the previous section. We are unlikely to understand how Strange Situation behavior is related to later functioning until we know what aspects of prior interactional experience affect Strange Situation behavior. Likewise, we are unlikely to learn much about the differential long-term implications of A and C group status until we have a clear idea of their differential origins and so have a basis on which to posit subsequent relationships.

Running through all of these questions is another more basic question: What are we to make of individual differences in Strange Situation behavior? As we have shown in the previous section, individual differences in the harmony of parent–infant interaction appear to be related to the pattern of infantile behavior in the Strange Situation whereas there is no clear evidence regarding the role of temperament in shaping Strange Situation behavior. Further, the relationship between parental behavior and Strange Situation behavior appears to be quite weak, and this raises questions both about the possible influence of other factors (such as aspects of prior experiential history that may be less directly related to the quality of infant–parent interaction) and about whether the 8-category classification system now in widespread use provides the most powerful way of assessing individual differences that are meaningfully related to prior or contemporaneous experiences. The same question naturally arises in relation to the association between Strange Situation behavior and *subsequent* infantile performance: Could prediction be better if a different classification system was employed?

In the chapters that follow, we cast new light on the interpretation of Strange Situation behavior through a focus on cross-cultural research, and then look closely at the statistical properties of the existing classification system and alternative analytic strategies.

IV CROSS NATIONAL RESEARCH

11 CROSS-CULTURAL STUDIES USING THE STRANGE SITUATION

INTRODUCTION

As the Strange Situation has come into prominence as a procedure for assessing individual differences in parent–infant attachments, there have been several attempts to use it in countries other than the U.S. Undoubtedly fostered by the widespread claims from American studies regarding the reliable external correlates (antecedents and consequences) of Strange Situation behavior, these attempts were based in part on formulations from evolutionary biology suggesting the transcultural applicability of the classification scheme. Thus they have proven very important to our developing understanding and interpretation of Strange Situation behavior. This is because the findings obtained have forced researchers to ask themselves why the distribution of infants across attachment classifications in other countries is not in accord with that of American infants. In attempting to answer this question, they have suggested that national group differences in infant temperament and in child-rearing patterns which may be unrelated to parental sensitivity (such as those variations in prior experience that affect the stressfulness of the procedure) may affect Strange Situation behavior. Not surprisingly, this has inevitably led them to wonder about the extent to which the same factors affect the behavior of American babies as well. To the extent that these factors influence Strange Situation behavior, of course, the assumption that individual differences in Strange Situation behavior in the U.S. necessarily and primarily reflect individual differences in prior parental behavior becomes increasingly less persuasive. Likewise, researchers have been forced to question the assumptions that (1) similar patterns of Strange Situation behavior necessarily have the same origins and the same relationship to future behavior in different cultures, and thus that (2) "Strange Situation behavior" is isomorphic with "security of attachment." Such issues clearly get to the heart of current theorizing involving the Strange Situation and offer the greatest promise of advancing our understanding of the origins and implications of early individual differences in infant–parent attachments.

Research using the Strange Situation outside the United States began in the late 1970's with longitudinal studies conducted in West Germany (Klaus and Karin Grossmann) and Sweden (Michael Lamb, Ann Frodi, Philip Hwang, and Majt Frodi). It has since been used in Israel (Abraham Sagi, Lamb, and their coworkers), the Netherlands (Marinus von IJzendoorn and his colleagues), Japan (Kazuo Miyake and his colleagues), and in other parts of West Germany (the Grossmanns, Kuno Beller).[1] The goal of this chapter is to review these studies, with special emphasis on the implications of their findings for the understanding of Strange Situation behavior. Some of the studies have also been discussed earlier in this book, and in such cases detailed findings are not repeated here.

For the most part, interest in the cross-cultural data has been piqued by evidence concerning a distribution across Strange Situation groups and subgroups that in many cases deviates substantially from the distribution considered typical in the United States.[2] For this reason, we present in Table 11.1 details concerning the distributions found in the U.S., Israel, Japan, The Netherlands, Sweden and West Germany.

Several conclusions are immediately apparent from the data presented in this table. First, the distribution of infants among the A, B, and C classifications clearly varies markedly across cultural contexts, indicating that the distributions obtained by Ainsworth et al. (1978) and other American researchers may not, in fact, be normative for all countries. Second, with one exception (Grossmann et al.'s [1981] study of infants in Bielefeld, West Germany), the B classification is modal in all cultural contexts. It is the distribution of infants between the A and C groups that varies markedly, suggesting that the findings of these cross-cultural studies may be especially useful in exploring the differential origins of A and C type behavior. Third, the distribution of infants among categories varies not only between cultures but also *within* cultures with different distributions obtained for independent samples in Israel, West Germany, and Japan.

---

[1]Beller's research has only been reported in oral form at a convention (Beller, 1984). As we do not have access to a written report, we do not discuss his study here.
[2]The distribution reported by Ainsworth et al. (1978) on the basis of four small studies (Ainsworth et al., 1974; Bell, 1970; Ainsworth et al., 1978; Main, 1973) comprising a total of 106 infants is usually employed as the standard against which distributions obtained in other studies are compared.

TABLE 11.1
Distribution of infants across attachment categories (in percentages)

Country	A_1	A_2	B_1	B_2	B_3	B_4	C_1	C_2	N
U.S.A.[a]	11	9	9	10	42	4	6	7	106
Japan[b]-Sapporo	0	0	7	31	17	3	14	10	25
Japan[c]-Sapporo	0	0	14	21	25	18	11	11	28
Japan[d]-Tokyo	11	3	3	11	22	31	11	8	36
W. Germany[e]- Bielefeld	39	10	0	20	10	2	8	4	46
W. Germany[f]- Regensburg	20	23	14	20	11	7	2	2	44
Sweden[g]	8	14	12	18	40	6	2	2	51
Israel[h]-kibbutz	0	8	2	25	20	8	24	9	82
Israel[h]-city	0	3	17	31	28	6	14	3	36
The Netherlands[i]	9	15	26	15	15	16	2	2	136

[a]Ainsworth et al. (1978). Note that 1 infant was placed in the A group, without subgroup assignment. The B_4 subgroup option was not available in the first subsample ($N = 23$).

[b]Miyake et al. (in press, unpublished data). Three of the 29 infants (10%) were classified as "pseudo-C", and 1 (3%) was classified in the B group without subgroup assignment.

[c]Miyake and Campos (personal communication of unpublished data). In addition, one infant was assigned to the C group without subgroup assignment.

[d]Durrett, Otaki, and Richards (1984). In addition, 3 infants could not be classified.

[e]Grossmann et al. (1981). In addition, 3 of 49 infants could not be classified into any of the groups.

[f]Karin Grossmann (personal communication). In the table, we combine data from 11 infants seen with their mothers at 12 months and 33 infants seen with their mothers at 18 months. In addition, 4 infants seen with their mothers at 18 months were deemed unclassifiable.

[g]Lamb, Hwang, Frodi, & Frodi (1982) and unpublished data.

[h]Sagi et al. (in press) and unpublished data. In addition 1 of 83 infants in the kibbutz sample could not be classified.

[i]van IJzendoorn et al. (1984).

Since in two of these cases the same researchers obtained both samples, the differences are not easily attributable to procedural or coding variations, although sampling error is a possibility with such small sample sizes. Likewise, the cultural variations are probably not due to measurement variability, because all non-American researchers have sought to ensure comparability with American practices. Variations in classification distributions have also been noted by some American researchers (e.g. Antonucci & Levitt, 1984; Easterbrooks & Lamb, 1979; Main & Weston, 1981)

WEST GERMANY

The first attempt to employ the Strange Situation outside the United States was undertaken by the Grossmanns in Bielefeld, an industrial town in North-central West Germany. Details of the study were provided in Chapters 5 and 6, because it constituted a deliberate attempt to replicate

Ainsworth's findings concerning the antecedents of Strange Situation behavior and to determine whether indices of neonatal behavioral organization were related to Strange Situation behavior. As reported in Chapter 5, the various ratings of maternal and infant behavior at home were interrelated in Bielefeld as they were in Baltimore. The mothers of infants later classified in the B group were rated more sensitive when the infants were 2 months of age than were the mothers of future C group infants, and the B group mothers were rated more sensitive than both A and C group mothers at 6 months. (Findings for measures of acceptance and cooperation have not been reported.) There were, however, some anomalous findings. First, variations in maternal sensitivity at 10 months were not related to Strange Situation behavior at 12 months: mothers of A, C, and B group infants were equally sensitive at this point. Second, the inter-group variation in maternal sensitivity at earlier ages was much less than it had been in Baltimore, with a maximum average range of 2 rather than 4 points on the 9-point sensitivity scale. This diminution of variability was especially pronounced at 10 months. Third, there were a surprisingly large number of German infants assigned to the avoidant (A) group—49% as opposed to 20–25% in most American studies (Ainsworth et al., 1978). A similarly anomalous distribution was obtained when the infants were observed with their fathers at 18 months of age (Grossmann et al., 1981). Fourth, measures of maternal sensitivity and acceptance did not correlate highly in the Bielefeld sample as they had in Ainsworth's study.

   Grossmann and Grossmann's findings are fascinating and intriguing. Because theirs was a detailed longitudinal study, furthermore, it was possible to explore the ramifications of their results by considering (1) the relationship to antecedent patterns of interaction; (2) the behavior of infants in the Strange Situation in greater detail than the classifications permit; and (3) the predictive validity of the Strange Situation classifications. Let us consider each of these issues in turn.

The Antecedents of Strange Situation Behavior

In seeking to explain why so many of the Bielefeld infants behaved avoidantly, the Grossmanns noted that North German mothers are concerned about independence training at a much earlier age than are American mothers. Those behaviors designed to foster independence may thus have been rated as rejecting and insensitive by observers applying Ainsworth's rating scales. However, because *all* of the German mothers appeared to be engaged in independence training in earnest by 10 months, as the Grossmanns noted, group differences in "maternal sensitivity," were no longer evident at 10 months. The question this raises for the Grossmanns and for us thus becomes: Can the earlier group differences in maternal behavior be considered differences in maternal sensitivity, when later scores were attributed to "independence training" rather than sensitivity? And what of the fact that the German mothers were not, on average, rated as more insensitive than American mothers in the fourth quarter?

Ainsworth (1983) concluded that, whatever their motivations, the mothers of avoidant German infants were indeed insensitive, and as the Grossmanns pointed out, "maternal sensitivity" and selected infant behaviors at home were intercorrelated at 10 months as they were in Baltimore.

> The infants of sensitive mothers cried less than infants of insensitive mothers, they sought close bodily contact more often, responded more promptly to being picked up and protested less often when being put down again (Grossmann, Grossmann, Spangler, Suess, & Unzner, in press, ms p.23). Grossmann et al. (in press, ms. p.29) thus concluded "we can now be sure that all of us mean the same phenomenon when we speak of maternal sensitivity."

Earlier in the manuscript, however, the Grossmanns (Grossmann et al., in press) wrote that "most of the Bielefeld avoidant infants (group A) did not experience insensitive mothering during the first year of life" (Grossmann et al., in press, ms. p.2). Why, then, were they avoidant? Alternatively, if we assume that the increased "insensitivity" (qua independence training) of the German mothers explains the disproportionate number of avoidant-insecure infants in this sample, we must then explain why some infants still behaved in the B-fashion when there were no significant B vs. non B group differences in sensitivity at 10 months and relatively small differences earlier. One interpretation of the findings is that infant behavior in the Strange Situation was determined by variations in maternal sensitivity early in the first year, regardless of variations in subsequent maternal behavior. This interpretation has two implications: (1) that early patterns of infant–mother interaction have a formative influence that is more important than later experiences or events, and (2) that nearly half of the West German mothers in this sample were consistently insensitive, in terms of Ainsworth's definition and ratings. The first implication runs directly counter to Belsky et al.'s (1984a) findings (see Chapter 5) and to the findings of several studies focused on the effects of life events and stress on patterns of Strange Situation behavior (see Chapter 8). Together, they suggest that later rather than earlier interactive influences may have the major impact on Strange Situation behavior. The second implication is not consistent with the Grossmanns' assertion (noted earlier) that most of the A group mothers were not insensitive, and also raises questions about the appropriateness of employing one culture's definition of desirable maternal behavior in a different cultural context. Researchers should feel uncomfortable doing this without evidence that the behavior has the same meaning—in terms of its predictive and construct validity—in the specific culture.

How, therefore, can the high proportion of A group infants in this sample be explained? The Grossmanns (1983) argue that increased demands to behave in a culturally appropriate fashion (i.e., independently) produced avoidant behavior in the Strange Situation, with "our infants' behavior patterns of avoidance in the Strange Situation [being] an indication of the difficulty of coping with demands that the infants have not learned to cope with yet" (p.6). "Initial avoidance of attachment figures appears to be a first indicator of infant's application of cultural rules, as well as their acceptance of demands and requirements which are not neglectful" (p.7). Thus factors other than insensitively rejecting parental behavior appear to be associated with Strange Situation behavior, notably, an apparent interaction between cultural norms and infant competencies. In addition, aspects of parental behavior other than insensitivity may be rated as indices of insensitivity on Ainsworth's rating scales, including behaviors which may be culturally normative in countries other than the U.S.A.[3] Grossmann et al. (in press) note, in fact, that "insensitivity for the purpose of enforcing cultural norms is not the same as a rejecting attitude toward the child which was the case in the Baltimore sample" (ms. p.30).

In addition to parentally-enforced cultural demands, dimensions of constitutionally-based infant characteristics may have influenced the behavior of the Bielefeld infants in the Strange Situation. Grossmann and Grossmann (1983) reported that 12 of 16 infants classified in the B group on the basis of interaction with their mothers in the Strange Situation were "good orienters" neonatally, as assessed on Brazelton's NBAS, compared with only 9 of 24 A group infants. Newborn orienting capacities were also associated with the classification of infant–father attachment, although details of this association have not been provided. Grossmann and Grossmann (1983) simply stated that "Of 25 good orienters, 13 have a secure attachment classification to the father; only 7 were not good orienters" (p. 10). These findings were not strong, however, (see Chapter 6).

---

[3]The Grossmans also assessed a sample of 50 South German infants and mothers in the Strange Situation at 12 months of age. These families, all from Regensburg (Baveria), yielded a distribution across categories more similar to that typically found in the U.S., but the A group was still unusually large. Although various interpretations have been offered for these differences, we believe that, in the absence of information about patterns of parental behavior in Regensburg, and without stronger evidence concerning the relationship between parental behavior and Strange Situation behavior in either city, such speculation is premature. In any event, the distributions obtained in the two samples appear more similar to one another than to the normative U.S. distribution (see Table 11.1).

Detailed Analyses of Strange Situation Behavior

Other analyses that bear upon interpretation of the avoidant behavior in the Bielefeld sample were reported by Grossmann, Schwan and Grossmann (in press) who reanalyzed the Strange Situation videotapes, focusing on behavior in the initial episode (1) and the two reunion episodes (4 and 7). A detailed coding distinguished 20 different modes of orientation toward or away from the parent or objects; the beginning and end of behavioral sequences; 5 different consequences of behavioral acts; 6 expressive gestures; 9 facial expressions of emotion; 11 types of vocalization; and 2 expressive behaviors that had either facial and vocal, or gestural and active components. Inter-rater reliabilities were generally good. The results were complex, but were summarized by Grossmann et al. (in press) as follows:

> B classification does not mean secure and cheerful appearance of the infants after reunion with their mothers. There were no correlation with mood and play groupings. There were happy as well as unhappy infants classified A as well as B. They differed in how they expressed their feelings and how they addressed themselves to their mothers....[some of the A group infants] managed the Strange Situation rather well, and 3 infants did not display any indication of distress or impairment in mood and quality of play. Characteristically some of them ignored their mothers in episodes [4] and [7]. But some greeted their mothers and vocalized happily. But there were also those who reacted by absolute passivity and remained expressionless after the separation, with mood and play very much depressed. *Only these latter infants were close to the description of the "avoidantly insecure" A-category found in* [*U.S. studies*]....Nearly all infants classified B were openly and directly involved in signal exchange with their mothers, particularly when they needed them badly. The infants classified A were inhomogenious. When in good mood, some remained concentrated on objects and some engaged in direct communication. In poor mood, however, all infants classified A avoided direct communication....In general, signals directed to the mothers were more dampened with infants classified A than B. This was due to [a subgroup within the As]. Other [A] infants...were quite competent in their communications. *Therefore, A classification in our sample seems insufficient for an evaluation of the emotional security and stability of the infants in general. To use the term "insecurity of attachment" outside the context of the Strange Situation is a severe risk. Such an* [inference][4] *would certainly have been unfounded for our sample, and it has to be refuted on the basis of results generated on the basis of the method presented here.* (ms. pp.61–62; italics added).

This conclusion underscores the needs (1) to distinguish between the

---

[4]The manuscript says "influence," but the context suggests that "inference" is meant.

constructs of "security of attachment" and Strange Situation classification, (2) appreciate the cross-cultural diversity in A, B, and C patterns of behavior, and (3) to develop alternative measurement systems for capturing meaningful variations in Strange Situation behavior (such as the emotion measures used in this study). These issues are also addressed in later chapters.

Another interesting finding observed in the Bielefeld data is that within the B group, the subgroups that used distal and proximity-oriented behavior (B_1 and B_2) predominated, whereas the proximity- and contact-oriented B_3 subgroup is typically modal in the U.S. (see Table 11.1). Thus there was a cultural difference in the distribution of infants over groups and subgroups: the high distress, high contact-seeking subgroups (C's, B_4's, B_3's combined) predominate in the U.S., whereas the low distress, low contact-seeking subgroups (A's, B_1's, B_2's combined) predominated in Bielefeld.

Predictive Validity

Members of Grossmann and Grossmann's research team have since attempted to determine whether avoidant Strange Situation behavior indeed has the same relation to later child behavior that it has in the U.S.. Such research on predictive validity would help clarify the interpretation of "avoidant" infant behavior in the Bielefeld context.

In one recent report, Lutkenhaus (1984) observed 44 of the Bielefeld children at home when they were three years old. An investigator made narrative notes concerning the child's initial reaction to the male investigator and later rated the children on a 7-point scale according to their readiness to interact with him. The A group children were significantly less ready to engage the visitor than were either B or C group children, who did not differ from one another.[5] These findings paralleled those reported by Main and Weston (1981) in a sample of American infants, and thus suggest that avoidant behavior may have the same implications in West Germany and the U.S. On the other hand, Grossmann et al's., (in press) statements regarding the nonhomogeneity of the A group (see above), and the fact that differences in willingness to engage the visitor may have different origins in different cultures (e.g., maternal insensitivity vs. independence training) suggest that these cross-cultural similarities need to be interpreted cautiously.

---

[5]Lutkenhaus also reported results of observations in a subsequent competitive task, but as these data are not readily interpretable and do not parallel findings obtained in the U.S., discussion is only provided in Chapter 9.

Summary

The Grossmanns' study is the most extensive to be conducted outside the U.S., and its findings are very important both when viewed alone and when considered in the context of studies conducted in other countries. As indicated earlier, the results imply that, in addition to maternal sensitivity, cultural goals and values as well as temperamental dispositions must be considered when attempting to explain and understand Strange Situation behavior. The Grossmanns have shown that within the conventional classification groups there may be considerable heterogeneity with respect to behaviors reflecting attachment security, underscoring the likelihood that similarities in Strange Situation behavior (as indexed solely by assignment to the same group or category) do not necessarily imply that the behavior has the same origins or meaning. The study undertaken by the Grossmanns thus plays an important role in underscoring the need to distinguish between security of attachment and Strange Situation behavior. The other studies discussed in the following confirm the validity of this distinction.

SWEDEN

The distribution across attachment categories obtained by Lamb, Hwang, Frodi, and Frodi (1982) in Goteborg (Sweden) was quite similar to that reported by Ainsworth et al. (1978) and the deviation from the more typical U.S. distribution was not statistically significant. Like the Bielefeld infants, however, these Swedish infants appeared to show less distress in the Strange Situation than American infants typically do (unpublished data). For some reason, therefore, the Strange Situation appeared to perturb these German and Swedish babies less than it typically stresses American infants.

Lamb and his colleagues, however, were singularly unsuccessful in their attempts to identify antecedents of Strange Situation behavior in these Swedish families (unpublished data). Neither measures of parental attitudes and values taken both pre- and postnatally nor measures of parental behavior, infant behavior, and parent–child interaction in observations when the infants were 3 and 8 months of age were related to Strange Situation categories. Newborn behavior was not assessed, but parental reports of infant temperament at 5 months of age were not related to Strange Situation behavior. These findings leave us uncertain about what if anything the Strange Situation behavior of Swedish infants really means. The possibility that it may not mean very much—and thus may not tap some fundamentally important aspect of the developing infant's personality or the infant–parent attachment—is strengthened by the report that Strange

Situation classifications with mothers were unrelated to measures of infant sociability with unfamiliar adults (contrary to findings obtained in the U.S. and Israel) and that Strange Situation behavior with fathers was only weakly associated with stranger sociability (See Chapter 9 for further details).

THE NETHERLANDS

Mothers and infants from yet another Northern European city (Leiden, The Netherlands) were studied by van IJzendoorn, Tavecchio, Goossens, Vergeer, and Swaan (1983). The distribution of these 62 toddlers across attachment categories was more similar to that found in the United States by Ainsworth (Ainsworth et al., 1978) than to that found in Bielefeld by the Grossmanns (1982, 1983), but because the latter samples involved one-year-olds whereas van IJzendoorn et al.'s involved two-year-olds, this comparison may be of limited value. Some validation of the procedure's utility with older infants was provided by van IJzendoorn et al. (1983), however. On a newly-developed scale designed to assess "perceived security" by parental report,[6] the B_4 and C group infants combined ($N = 13$) obtained significantly lower scores than the A_1 and A_2, or B_1, B_2, and B_3 infants. There were no differences between A group and $B_{1,2,3}$ group children. Although detailed data were not presented, the authors suggested that the B_4 and C children were similar with respect to "perceived security"—a finding that raises questions about the appropriateness of considering B_4 children to be members of the secure B group. Correlational analyses revealed that high levels of perceived security as reported by the parents was associated with low levels of contact maintenance and proximity seeking in the Strange Situation.

Because the incidence of B_4 classifications in the Netherlands seemed unusually high, van IJzendoorn, Goossens, Kroonenberg, and Tavecchio (1984) further researched the correlates of this categorization. In an enlarged sample of 136 mother–child pairs, in which the mean age of the children was 21 months, 22[7] were assigned to the B_4 category. Some ($N = 24$) of the 136 mothers and children were observed in two 4-minute free play sessions during which maternal sensitivity was rated using Ainsworth et al.'s (1974) rating scale, and 77 of the parents also provided information via questionnaires on a number of background characteristics. In the Strange

---

[6]The Perceived Security Scale asks that parents rate the intensity of the child's distress responses to separations ranging from half an hour to "a few days," unfamiliar settings, and unfamiliar people.

[7]The text indicates that there were 21 assigned to the B_4 subgroup; the tables suggest that there were 22. In this, as in other cases, we have assumed the tabular material to be correct.

Situation, the mean scores of avoidance in the Dutch sample were somewhat higher than in the U.S. (Ainsworth et al., 1978), but on the other interactive rating scales the means in the two countries were quite similar.

In the Strange Situation reunion episodes, the B_4 children most resembled the C group ($N = 5$) in terms of proximity-seeking, contact maintaining, and resistance, while being unlike most of the other B group children on these dimensions. (There were some similarities between B_3 and B_4 infants.) The B_4's were similar to the other B group children primarily in the low incidence of avoidance. Likewise, on measures of exploratory manipulation, the B_4 toddlers were the first to diverge from the other B group infants, behaving like the C group toddlers from the first reunion on. The inability to use the attachment figure as a secure base from which to explore and the similarity between B_4 and C group infants raised questions in these researchers' minds about the appropriateness of considering the B_4 infants to be securely-attached. In the free play session, on the other hand, the mothers of B group children (B_4 included) were rated more sensitive than the mothers of A and C group children (combined). Because subgroup N's were small, however, it was not possible to test the reliability of $B_{1,2,3}$ vs. B_4 vs. C group differences statistically.

Van IJzendoorn et al. (1984) attempted to discriminate the $B_{1,2,3}$ infants from the B_4 children with discriminant analyses using the background variables as predictors for infants with employed mothers and infants with unemployed mothers separately. Among children with employed mothers ($N = 28$), B_4 children ($N = 4$) seemed more likely to come from higher social status families, to be boys, and to have mothers who (1) played more and engaged in less caretaking relative to their partners, (2) were slightly more satisfied with the parental division of labor and (3) tended to agree with their partners more regarding the division of labor than were $B_{1,2,3}$ infants and their mothers. Items relating to prior separation did not discriminate. In families in which mothers were not employed ($N = 31$), B_4 children ($N = 12$) came from higher SES families, were heavier at birth, were less likely to have been hospitalized, had experienced more separations from their parents, spent less time with babysitters, and had mothers who engaged in less play with their children than their partners did. Because the samples were so small, however, and the number of variables was so large (13) these findings must be considered merely suggestive until replicated. It is also not clear why the correlates of the B_4 classification should be different in the presence/absence of maternal employment.

Overall, therefore, the Dutch research has been quite inconclusive. On the one hand, van IJzendoorn and his colleagues have demonstrated that the B_4 infants' behavior differs in important ways from the behavior of infants in the other B subgroups. On the other hand, they have been unable to either identify distinguishing features in the backgrounds of B_4 and $B_{1,2,3}$ infants or explain why the incidence of B_4 infants seems higher in the Netherlands than in any other culture studied.

ISRAEL

Sagi and his colleagues (in press) studied 86 infants on Israeli kibbutzim with central living quarters for children. As mentioned in Chapter 5, each infant was seen in the Strange Situation three times—once each with mother, father, and the metapelet (caretaker) primarily responsible for his or her care. Sessions were scheduled 6 weeks apart in counterbalanced order, although there were no order effects. Like van IJzendoorn and his colleagues, Sagi et al. felt uncomfortable about including the B_4 infants in the "secure" B category, and so considered them as a separate group.[8] Sagi et al. found that the distribution across attachment categories (A, B, B_4, C) for infant–mother and infant–metapelet assessments differed significantly from the distribution reported by Ainsworth et al. (1978) for samples in the U.S. Specifically, the Israeli sample contained more infants in the B_4 and C groups and fewer infants in the avoidant and remaining B-groups than did the American sample. The distribution for fathers did not differ significantly from that reported by Ainsworth et al. (1978), although the same pattern was evident. Significantly fewer infants in the kibbutz sample were assigned to the B group with their mothers than were a group of Israeli city children, but unfortunately the small sample of city children ($N = 36$) precluded comparison across the four category clusters (A, B, B_4, C) considered in the kibbutz sample. As in the kibbutz sample, the distribution across categories in the city sample differed somewhat from the typical U.S. distribution in the relative proportions of avoidant, resistant, and B_4 (dependent) classifications, although there was no significant difference in the relative proportions of B and non-B group classifications. Although there may be some cultural difference between Israeli and American children in the frequency of certain attachment categories, however, the kibbutz childrearing arrangements thus seemed to have an additional independent effect.

As noted in Chapter 5, one explanation proposed by Sagi and his colleagues to explain the distribution across attachment classifications was that kibbutz child-care arrangements fostered insecurity. They pointed out that such arrangements entail multiple caretakers and conditions in which infants' cries may go unanswered for long periods of time (especially at

---

[8]Later analyses substantiated these reservations. Sagi et al. (in preparation) found that the B_4 infants resembled the C group infants with respect to stranger sociability more closely than they resembled the $B_{1,2,3}$ infants.

night), and thus that the higher proportion of C group attachments would be consistent with predictions from attachment theory. They also noted a tendency for the individual metaplot to have several infants with "similar" attachments to them, suggesting that quality of care was influential.

Instead of variations in the quality of care, however, the distribution of infants across attachment categories could perhaps be explained by differences in the psychological impact or interpretation of the Strange Situation procedure. According to Sagi et al., a considerable number (35%) of the sessions on the kibbutz had to be terminated prematurely or modified by eliminating episodes 3 and 4 because the infants were inconsolably distressed. Most of these infants were later classified in the C category. Interestingly, there was significant consistency over the three assessments for each child (i.e., with mother, father, and metapelet) in whether or not the sessions needed to be terminated or abbreviated. When Sagi et al. excluded from consideration those infants whose sessions were abbreviated, the distribution across attachment categories for mother–infant, father–infant, and metapelet–infant sessions did not deviate significantly from the distribution reported by Ainsworth et al. (1978). Thus the overall deviation in the distribution across categories in the total sample was accounted for by a group of infants who consistently manifested unusual degrees of distress and were extremely difficult to soothe.

Sagi et al. suggested that this was because the kibbutz-reared infants as a group were unusually distressed by strangers. Prior to each Strange Situation session, the researchers assessed the infants' sociability twice (with a male and a female stranger) using what is, to American infants, an innocuous and nonintrusive procedure. The mean sociability scores were substantially lower (even when corrected for some differences in scoring) than those obtained with American infants (Thompson & Lamb, 1982; Stevenson & Lamb, 1979; Sagi, Lamb, & Gardner, in prep.). Furthermore, the subsequent appearance of another stranger in episode 2 of the Strange Situation provoked considerable distress on the part of many infants—most notably those whose Strange Situation sessions had to be abbreviated or modified. As a result, Sagi et al. (in press, in prep.), argued that for this large subgroup of their subjects, and probably also for Israeli kibbutz infants on average, the Strange Situation procedure was substantially more stressful than it is for most American infants.

The implication of this for interpretation of the Strange Situation classifications is profound. If the kibbutz infants were indeed reacting to more stressful circumstances, one cannot simply compare their behavior to that of American infants who are, in essence, responding to a psychological-ly different experience. And even though the greater distress evinced by the kibbutz infants may be another indication of their insecurity, this is only one of several possible explanations. Another possible interpretation is that these infants were more distressed by strangers because they lived in fairly small, closed groups in which they were, as a consequence, seldom exposed to real strangers (see Konner, 1972). American infants, by contrast, frequently see strangers in supermarkets, pediatric clinics, playgrounds, housing projects, and the like. This factor may also explain why the distribution across classifications in the Israeli city samples was closer to U.S. norms, since there was likely to be greater similarity in their experiential histories. It is also possible that these Israeli infants were temperamentally prone to high distress and inconsolability, and that this was exacerbated by childrearing practices on the kibbutzim. All of these factors may have worked together to create the unusual responses on the part of many kibbutz-reared Israeli infants to the Strange Situation procedure.

The central and most important implication of Sagi et al.'s findings is that, if a procedure is to provide a valid and comparable assessment of infants and/or infant–adult relationships in different cultures, it is crucial that the experience be psychologically similar for all infants, or that we know how and why the experiences are dissimilar and can adjust our judgements to take the dissimilarities into account. The Strange Situation procedure was designed to assess the manner in which infants use attachment figures as sources of comfort and security when faced with mild to moderate stresses induced by events that have everyday analogues. If, however, encountering and later being left with a total stranger have little everyday meaning for some infants—as may be true with Sagi et al.'s kibbutz-reared infants—then their behavior in the Strange Situation cannot be interpreted in the same way as that of American infants unless we have good, well-articulated and empirically-based reasons (i.e., validity studies) for doing so. In other words, we must first learn what the Strange Situation episodes mean to infants in any given culture before attempting to use them as indices of infant–adult attachment.

Sagi et al.'s findings have implications not only for cross-cultural research projects but for intracultural uses as well. They suggest that whenever the Strange Situation procedure represents a psychologically different experi- ence for some infants than for others, we cannot assume that the differences in Strange Situation behavior are entirely due to differences in security of attachment. The differences may in part be due to differences in individual patterns of infant–adult interaction, but they may also be due to constitutional differences in temperament, current state of health, or other differences in past experience (e.g., degree of exposure to strangers) that affect the child's response to and interpretation of the Strange Situation.

Sagi et al.'s findings suggest, although they do not demonstrate, that all of these factors may affect Strange Situation behavior. First, they showed that there was high stability over repeated assessments of stranger sociability (Sagi et al., in preparation), and that there was consistency over repeated assessments (albeit with different attachment figures) in whether the Strange Situation sessions were completed or modified/terminated prematurely. Since most kibbutz-reared infants presumably had similarly rare experience with strangers, yet only some were consistently upset by them, some other factor—either insecurity, specific aspects of prior experiences, or temperamental characteristics, or other factors—must have functioned interactively, with this lack of experience with strangers more influential in some cases than in others. Second, most of the infants whose sessions were terminated/modified were later classified in either the C or B_4 groups. This is consistent with the argument that dependent or resistant classifications may co-occur with negative reactions to strangers (see Chapter 9), but there is no empirical or a priori reason to assume that the direction of effects is from attachment "insecurity" to high stranger anxiety rather than the reverse. Indeed, as pointed out earlier, it seemed as if high stranger anxiety produced the distress that in turn led to classification in the B_4 or C categories, and, indeed, this is consistent with the characterization of these classifications offered by Ainsworth et al. (1978). Third, the fact that infants with the same caretaker tended to be classified similarly with respect to Strange Situation behavior (see Chapter 5) indicates that prior patterns of infant–adult interaction *may* have influenced the Strange Situation behavior of these Israeli infants. However, no other questionnaire data concerning factors likely to influence attachment behavior (e.g., caretaker instability or motivation, major separation) were related to Strange Situation behavior.

Overall, therefore, this study suggests that many factors *may* affect Strange Situation behavior; consequently, it may be premature to assume that because infants behave similarly in the Strange Situation, they behave similarly for the same reasons, and thus have similar types of attachments. Importantly, this probably applies to all uses of the Strange Situation, regardless of cultural or subcultural context.

JAPAN

Similar issues were raised by Miyake et al.'s (1981–82, in press) research in Japan. These researchers, studying 29 middle class primiparous Japanese mothers and their infants, reported an unusually high number of C group infants ($N = 10$, or 34% of the sample); the remainder were B group. Three of the 10 C group babies were dubbed "pseudo-C" infants, for whom the best classification, in terms of the existing classification system, appeared to fall somewhere between the B_4 and C subgroups. As with Sagi et al.'s (in press) Israeli subjects, the Strange Situation procedure appeared to arouse more stress among these Japanese infants than it typically does in the U.S.—again suggesting that the Strange Situation may have a psychologically different meaning to infants in different cultures. The stressfulness of the Strange Situation procedure could be attributed to cultural differences in rearing practices and/or to temperamental differences. (See Li-Repac, 1982, for similar findings in Chinese and Chinese–American samples.) Although the supporting evidence is only suggestive, Miyake and his colleagues have chosen to emphasize temperamental factors, arguing that

> "Analysis of their behaviors in other situations suggested that there is a strong temperamental variable that is stable and preserved from the newborn period through to 23 months of age and that tends to be associated with the type C infant" (Miyake et al., 1981–82, p.27).

In the newborn period, 6 out of 7 C's and 8 out of 12 B's were upset by the removal of a pacifier; at 1 and 3 months, 3 of 12 B's compared with 4 out of 7 C's showed high levels of distress or thumbsucking during unstructured home observations; at 7 months, 6 of 7 C's, compared with 3 out of 8 B's, showed fear at the entrance of a stranger, while 4 of 8 B's and 6 of 7 C's were fearful at separation from the mother. At 11 months future C's ran to their mothers more (and so played less) in a free play context than did future B's. All these findings suggested to Miyake et al. a temperamental predisposition to C-ness, particularly as there were fewer group differences in maternal behavior. At 7 months, mothers interrupted the "free play" of future C's more than did the mothers of future B's. The latter mothers were also more responsive, but there were no group differences in level of overall stimulation or in levels of "effective stimulation."

Although there are repeated hints regarding the possible importance of temperamental differences in explaining differences in Strange Situation behavior, however, it is important to note that some of the group differences did not reach conventional levels of significance and that some other measures did not reveal the group differences (e.g., C's showed longer rather than shorter, rise times in neonatal assessments and showed less rather than more crying in the 7-month assessments) one would expect if temperamental differences were indeed of major importance (see Chapter 5 for further details). Thus Miyake et al.'s findings remain provocative, yet speculative, until replicated. Fortunately, these researchers have initiated a replication study that may help verify some of their suggestions. Indeed, preliminary reports reveal the same distribution across attachment categories in the second cohort.

Differences between the childrearing practices of Japanese and American parents may also help account for the different Strange Situation behavior patterns of Japanese and American babies. The key difference in rearing practices may have been the Japanese infants' unfamiliarity with even brief separations from their mothers.[9] Because Japanese infants are rarely if ever separated from their mothers, even at night (e.g., Caudill & Weinstein, 1969; Lebra, 1976; Vogel, 1963), this may explain why they were unusually stressed by the brief separations involved in the Strange Situation procedure.[10] Again, this points to the importance of ensuring that the procedure represents a psychologically comparable and similar experience for different infants (both intra- and inter-culturally) and to the fact that factors other than variations in maternal sensitivity may affect Strange Situation behavior. Just because two infants behave similarly in the Strange Situation (for example, an Israeli C and a Japanese C) does not mean that they do so for the same reason. In the absence of culturally-specific validation, therefore, we cannot assume that the same behavior denotes similar qualities of attachment security.

The same issues were raised earlier with respect to the behavior of Israeli and German infants. In Israel, many infants seemed unusually distressed by encounters with strangers, and the "incompetence" of their attachment behavior may have been due to the magnitude of their stress rather than the quality of their attachments. In Germany, by contrast, many (but not all) of the A group infants appeared unstressed by the procedure. Grossmann et al.'s (in press) detailed behavioral analyses indicated that some of these infants gave no evidence of insecurity, even though they were classified in the A group along with infants who did appear insecure. Again, the implication is that the Strange Situation classifications may capture variations in behavior other than attachment security. Furthermore, when different infants are placed in the same category even though their behavioral similarities have different origins, attempts to explore the antecedent or predictive validity of "attachment security" are compromised. The heterogeneity of some of the Ainsworth classification groups is an issue that we explore more thoroughly in Section V.

Within-cultural variability may also complicate the explanation of Strange Situation behavior. In the case of Japan, Durrett, Otaki, and Richards (1984) reported that for a sample of 34 infant–mother dyads from Tokyo, attachment classifications were distributed in a manner more similar to that obtained by Ainsworth et al. (1978) for American dyads than by Miyake et al. (in press) in their Japanese studies. Durrett et al. predicted that Japanese mothers who perceived their husbands to be supportive would

---

[9]Another possible source of influence might have been the unusually high degree of concern on the part of the Japanese mothers about behaving appropriately in a University laboratory context. Their unease may have unsettled their children as well.

[10]Miyake et al. (in press) reported that the infants in their study were (according to the mothers' reports) left alone or with another adult an average of 2.5 times monthly.

tend to have B group infants, but this was not confirmed. Instead, mothers of B and C group infants had high scores on subscale measures of spousal pride, enjoyment, and sensitivity and on the composite support measure, whereas mothers of A infants consistently had the lower scores. Thus paternal support may have affected the development of infant–mother attachments, but not in the predicted manner. No other correlates of attachment status were reported, making it difficult to evaluate the difference between the Tokyo and Sapporo samples with respect to the distribution of infants' across attachment classifications. Interestingly, Durrett et al. reported that nearly half the B group infants in their sample were classified in the B_4 subgroup, which is consistent with Miyake et al.'s findings concerning the predominence of $B_3/$ B_4/C classifications.

As had van IJzendoorn et al. (1983, 1984) in The Netherlands, and Sagi et al. (in press) in Israel, Miyake et al. felt uncomfortable including the B_4 infants in the "secure" B group. Three of Miyake et al.'s Japanese infants fell between the B_4 and C categories and, considered relative to U.S. norms, their behavior certainly did not appear "secure." In some of their reports, therefore, these infants were labeled "pseudo-C" and were considered insecure. Sagi et al. likewise combined the B_4 infants with the C group or excluded them from consideration for analytic purposes. On the measures of sociability, interestingly, the scores of B_4 infants resembled those of C group infants more than other B group infants, confirming their special status (Sagi et al., in prep.). In The Netherlands, the B_4 infants' behavior resembled the C infants more than other B's in most respects save the absence of resistance (van IJzendoorn et al., 1984). Their mothers, however, were more sensitive than the C mothers and about as sensitive as the B group mothers. Thus these multicultural studies have helped identify the unusual status of the B_4 subgroup, one that is so small in most U.S. studies that it is typically not possible to examine it separately.[11] The various analyses discussed in Section IV help further to define the characteristics of this subgroup.

CONCLUSION

Whatever the relationship between maternal sensitivity and Strange Sitaution behavior in the United States, the findings of studies done abroad suggest that factors other than maternal sensitivity may have a powerful effect on infant behavior in the Strange Situation. Because this underscores

---

[11]Recall, too, that the B_4 subgroup was not included in Ainsworth's initial longitudinal study. As far as the U.S. is concerned, we only have Silvia Bell's impressions to support the claim that these mothers were sensitive but that recent destabilizing events (e.g., separations) had temporarily affected what were essentially secure relationships.

that "Strange Situation behavior" and "security of attachment" may on occasion be distinct constructs, it raises profound questions about interpretation of Strange Situation behavior—wherever the research is conducted. In particular, the findings reviewed in this chapter suggest that the baby's temperament and prior experiential history may affect Strange Situation behavior independently of attachment security.

As suggested in Chapter 6, there is some indication—although no conclusive evidence—that constitutional differences in temperament *may* affect Strange Situation behavior. To the extent that there are temperamental differences between infants in different cultures, as Miyake et al. and other researchers suggest, this has implications for comparisons across cultures. To the extent that there are variations *within* cultures too, this may have more far-reaching implications. The problem with temperamentally-based explanations, however, is that researchers in the U.S. and other nations have yet to offer clear, definitive evidence of temperamental influences when the evidence does not submit to more parsimonious alternative explanations (Sroufe, in press). Thus, whereas it is hard to deny that temperament should be considered as a potential influence, new research is needed to demonstrate its importance (see Chapter 6).

The evidence regarding the effects of prior experiential history—other than maternal sensitivity and the quality of prior dyadic interaction—seems clearer. The Strange Situation was designed to provide a context for observing how infants organize their attachment behavior around attachment figures when *mildly* or *moderately* distressed. All infants—regardless of attachment security—appear to use their attachment figures appropriately in some circumstances, however, so it is important that infants experience qualitatively and psychologically similar degrees of stress in the Strange Situation, otherwise their behavior is not comparable. When the brief separations are especially unusual and stressful for some infants (as they apparently were for the Japanese infants), or when the separations are not stressful (as they apparently were for the German and Swedish infants), or when the stranger is an unusually threatening event (as for the Israeli children), the infants' experiences of the Strange Situation are psychologically different and their behavior may thus differ from that of American infants. It may be different because there are differences in security, but it may be different for other reasons too, so we cannot assume that the behavior observed has the same meaning it has when observed in the U.S. Stated differently, Strange Situation behavior may reflect differences in security of attachment, as Ainsworth and her colleagues have argued, but it may also reflect differences in temperament, and differences in the familiarity, stressfulness, or interpretation of the procedure on the part of infants and parents. The latter factors may be significantly influenced by cultural proscriptions concerning childrearing practices, as the German,

Japanese, and Israeli studies seem to indicate. Interestingly, these studies suggest that such proscriptions may vary within as well as between cultures.

Researchers have yet to parse out the relative importance of these factors, even though this is critically important to the understanding of Strange Situation behavior, and thus to use of the Strange Situation procedure as an index measure in developmental research. To complicate matters further, it seems likely that the relative importance of these factors will vary across cultures (or sub-cultures) and probably within cultures as well. For example, temperamental factors may have a greater influence on Strange Situation behavior in samples in which prior background experiences make the procedure nonstressful, as the Grossmann analysis of A-type infant behavior seems to indicate. Recognition of this fact calls for a radically different approach to the use of the Strange Situation in the study of socioemotional development and the development of alternative procedures for assessing individual differences in attachment. We explore both of these issues more thoroughly in the next two sections.

V ALTERNATIVE ANALYTIC APPROACHES

12

MEASURING INDIVIDUAL DIFFERENCES IN STRANGE SITUATION BEHAVIOR

INTRODUCTION

As the preceding chapters suggest, Ainsworth's classification system has provided a foundation for a large body of research, in all of which it has been assumed that there exist clear differences among groups of infants defined by the A, B, and C categories. The A–B–C classification system has recently been questioned on several grounds (Campos, Barrett, Lamb, Goldsmith, & Stenberg, 1983; Connell & Goldsmith, 1982; Gardner & Thompson, 1983; Lamb et al., 1984), however. First, it has been argued that "security of attachment" may not be the only factor influencing infant behavior in the Strange Situation. Because other aspects of socioemotional functioning, such as temperamental differences (Goldsmith & Campos, 1982) may be influential, exclusive focus on the A, B, C categories, which are interpreted as measuring only security of attachment, may obscure other important contributions to Strange Situation behavior. Second, individual differences in Strange Situation behavior may be better represented by variations along continuous dimensions rather than the discrete categorical differences presupposed by the A, B, C group typology. This possibility is suggested in part by what seem to be continuities underlying the definitions of the subgroups: for example, the distal to proximal interactive style continuum along which the B subgroups can be arrayed, and the possible "borderline secure" status of the B_1 and B_4 subgroups proposed by some (e.g., Goldberg et al., 1984; Hazen & Durrett, 1982; van IJzendoorn et al., 1983). Third, it has been argued that there is little a priori reason to expect that individual differences in Strange Situation behavior will be discrete rather than continuous, since natural selection is more likely to have fostered behavioral continua rather than discrete types of behavior (Lamb et al., 1984 and Chapter 4). Finally, if a valid multidimensional set of continuous measures could be developed to represent individual differences in Strange Situation behavior, it would be of substantial utility in research on early socioemotional development. Continuous variables have many desirable statistical properties not shared by categorical variables. For example, they are likely to produce higher predictive validity coefficients. In addition, continuous variables are far more tractable in the structural equation modeling techniques that are essential for addressing the complex longitudinal questions currently needed in Strange Situation research (see Chapters 7, 10, and 14).

For these four reasons, Connell and Goldsmith (1982) and Lamb and his colleagues (1984) have called for the investigation of alternative means of summarizing behavioral data from the Strange Situation. One suggestion was that researchers develop and employ continuous dimensions based on factor analyses of Strange Situation interactive measures. Examples of such investigations are presented in Chapter 13. In this chapter we evaluate the A–B–C typological system for representing individual differences in Strange Situation behavior.

CRITERIA FOR SUCCESSFUL TYPOLOGICAL MEASUREMENT SYSTEMS

If a typological system (like the existing classification procedure) provides the best means of representing individual differences in Strange Situation behavior, it should meet at least three criteria. First, the infants should fall into clearly defined types, with little overlap between the groups. That is, members of one group (or subgroup) should resemble each other on theoretically relevant variables more than they resemble members of other groups. If the groups overlap and blend into one another, it suggests that the individual differences would be represented better by a continuous measurement system. Second, infants who are similarly classified should be characterized by the same behavioral markers in different samples. Much interest has been sparked by recent studies suggesting that the distribution of babies across the A, B, and C categories varies from culture to culture (see Chapter 11), but interpretation of these differences necessarily depends on the assumption that the behavioral markers used to distinguish different groups are consistently applied across samples. Third, a successful typology should adequately summarize individual differences on the theoretically relevant observational variables from the Strange Situation. This criterion can be operationalized by looking at the proportion of variance in the relevant observational variables explained by the A-, B-, C-typology. The application of the first two of these criteria is explored in this chapter; the third is taken up in Chapter 13.

PREVIOUS RELEVANT RESEARCH

In addition to the analyses presented in this chapter, three attempts have been made to evaluate the extent to which the criteria for adequate typological and continual representation of individual differences have been met. First D. B. Connell (1976) undertook cluster and discriminant analyses of data from Ainsworth's Baltimore sample (Ainsworth et al., 1971). Second, Ainsworth and her colleagues (1978) themselves undertook a multiple discriminant analysis of the same data (Ainsworth et al., 1978). Finally, J. P. Connell (see Chapter 13) developed structural models for a large composite data set comprising observational measures from several samples. In this chapter, we review the findings and statistical techniques employed by D. B. Connell and Ainsworth et al.; J. P. Connell himself reviews his findings and procedures in the next chapter.

Both D. B. Connell and Ainsworth and her colleagues based their analyses on data from 106 one-year-olds (of which Connell used 104) seen by Ainsworth and her colleagues in the Strange Situation. Seventy-five measures were available on these infants, and Ainsworth et al. used 73. These variables included ratings of the infants' interactive behavior in each episode, and several more discrete measures of behaviors such as crying, vocalization, looking, and smiling at mother, also recorded on an episode-by-episode basis.

D. B. Connell

D. B. Connell (1976) used factor, cluster, and multiple discriminant analyses to determine whether infants could be correctly reclassified into their A, B, or C groups using these variables. Concerned by the small ratio of subjects to variables, Connell began by including only those 20 variables on which there were substantial mean differences between groups. Most of these were Ainsworth's interactive scales. From these, Connell extracted two orthogonal factors from the correlation matrix of the variables. He then plotted factor scores for each subject and examined the plot (redrawn as Figure 12.1) for clustering. The more closely together infants from the same Ainsworth group were clustered, the more valid the typological system would appear to be. In the figure, subjects in groups B_2 and B_3 are labeled "B," while those in groups B_1, B_4, A, and C have their own labels. The dimensions represented in the plot (i.e., the factors) were not identified by Connell.

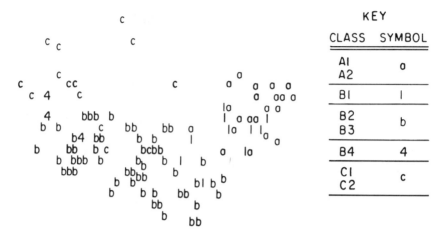

FIG. 12.1.   Cluster analysis from D. B. Connell (1976).The dimensions represent the principal components of 20 variables.

Inspection of Figure 12.1 shows that the C group infants were widely dispersed, intermingled with infants from the B_4 and $B_{2,3}$ groups. Further, although the A's were quite tightly clustered, the interior of the cluster contained a large number of B_1 infants. Evidently, the borders between the A/B and B/C groups were not well defined in this analysis. Connell recognized that the B_1 and B_4 subgroups were problematic and thus dropped them from further analyses.

D. B. Connell then divided the remaining subjects ($N = 91$) into a design set ($N = 65$), from which he developed classification functions, and a cross-validation set ($N = 26$) on which the functions could be tested using multiple discriminant function analysis (Hand, 1981; Huberty, 1984). Classification functions are weighted sums of variable scores on individuals that are used to predict the group memberships of the individuals. The percentage of individuals correctly reclassified into their original groups on the basis of the discriminant functions provides a measure of the extent to which there is sufficient information in the observational data to identify the group membership of infants on a subject–by–subject basis. D. B. Connell reported that 96% of the cross-validation subjects were successfully reclassified using his discriminant functions. The results of such reclassifications, however, must be interpreted carefully. Successful classification using discriminant functions does not imply that the classifications initially used in development of the discriminant functions give the best account of the individual differences in observed infant behavior, since this analytic approach assumes the classifications in calculating the discriminant functions to predict them. It does suggest, however, that *given the classifications*, the interactive measures can be used to predict group membership efficiently.

Ainsworth, Blehar, Waters, and Wall (1978)

Ainsworth et al. (1978) wished to use multiple discriminant analysis to "test the hypothesis that the behaviors highlighted in the instructions for classification are indeed the major behaviors in which the three groups differ" (P.96). As had D. B. Connell, Ainsworth et al. reduced the number of measures prior to performing the discriminant analysis. To do this, they eliminated variables on which the groups did not differ significantly in univariate tests and which did not contribute significantly to discriminant functions distinguishing the A from the B or C from the B groups. The remaining 22 variables were then employed in the discriminant analysis. They included proximity seeking, contact maintaining, avoidance, and resistance in the two reunion episodes with mother; four measures of exploratory behavior; measures of crying in five episodes; and five measures of interaction with the stranger.

Ainsworth and her colleagues found that they were able to successfully reclassify 92% of their subjects in the discriminant function analysis. They thus concluded that "the ways in which the infants in our sample were classified is consistent with the stated specifications" (Ainsworth et al., 1978, p.115), although the discriminant functions weighted five measures of interaction with the stranger that are not highlighted in the instructions for classification.

Evaluation

Although these results are interesting, it is difficult to generalize from either D. B. Connell's or Ainsworth et al.'s analyses for several reasons. Connell selectively excluded the B_1 infants who actually resembled A infants more than other B infants, and the B_4 infants who more closely resembled C infants. Consequently, he based his discriminant analysis on a data set from which he had already removed those infants who were likely to be difficult to classify correctly. This strategy probably exaggerated the success of the reclassification exercise and precluded generalization of this estimate of success to the traditional classification system, which includes B_1 and B_4 infants. Interestingly, the subjects excluded were from the subgroups that should be most difficult to classify if the behavioral dimensions underlying the Strange Situation classification system are continuous rather than categorical.

The results of Ainsworth et al.'s analyses suggested that the A–B–C-groups can be successfully discriminated on the basis of other measures of

Strange Situation behavior, but their methodology can be improved upon in two regards. First, a cross-validation sample was not employed, due to the large number of measures being analyzed and consequent concern about the subjects-to-variable ratio. As Huberty (1984) notes, however, when classification functions are applied to the data from which they were developed, the rate of correct reclassification overestimates the true "hit" rate. Second, both D. B. Connell and Ainsworth reduced the number of variables employed in order to increase the ratio of subjects to variables and thus avoid capitalizing on chance differences between groups. It is possible, however, that the variable selection procedures they employed might themselves tend to capitalize on chance. Selecting variables on the basis of significant univariate differences (rather than theoretical relevance to attachment classification) only displaces the potential role of chance from the multiple discriminant analysis to the univariate analyses. In addition, the variables selected for further analysis were chosen empirically rather than theoretically, resulting in the inclusion of variables that are of limited relevance to the classification criteria. Such analyses thus provide a poor test of whether the A–B–C groups accurately reflect individual variation in the behaviors most relevant to attachment system functioning.

NEW ANALYSES OF STRANGE SITUATION DATA SETS

The analyses reported here and in related reports (Gardner, Lamb, & Thompson, in preparation; Gardner & Thompson, 1983) evaluate the traditional typological system for representing individual differences in Strange Situation behavior. Using four samples of data, we focus on individual differences in infant behaviors during reunions with the mother in the Strange Situation, since theoretical accounts describe these as the most critical dimensions for determining security of attachment (Ainsworth et al., 1978). The data come from three cultures, the United States, Sweden, and Israel, and our analyses address two issues. First, we present cross-validating discriminant analyses of Strange Situation data to determine whether the A, B, and C groups are characterized by similar behavioral markers in Swedish, Israeli, and American data sets. Second, we use cluster analysis to determine whether, on the basis of individual differences in various measures of Strange Situation behavior, infants aggregate in distinct groups that resemble the A, B, and C groups.

  The four data sets used in this study were: (1) 43 infants from Michigan seen in the Strange Situation with their mothers at 12½ months (Thompson, Lamb, & Estes, 1982), (2) 59 infants from Pennsylvania seen with their mothers at 11 or 13 months (Belsky, Rovine, & Taylor, 1984), (3) 51 infants from Sweden seen with their mothers at 11 or 13 months (Lamb, Hwang,

Frodi, & Frodi, 1982), and (4) 63 infants from Israeli kibbutzim seen with their mothers between 11 and 14 months of age (Sagi et al., in press).[1,2] The total N is 216.

In order to limit the variable set in a theoretically motivated way while maintaining a high subjects-to-variables ratio, we focused our analyses on five 7-point rating scales scored from videotaped records of the two reunion episodes. The scales, which were introduced more fully in chapter 3, were: *proximity* and contact seeking; *contact-maintaining*; *resistance*; *avoidance*; and *distance interaction*. These variables provide operationalized and relatively objective criteria against which the adequacy of the global A, B, and C group classifications may be assessed. Moreover, normative accounts of Strange Situation behavior describe the behavior of prototypical group representatives in terms of their manifestation of these behaviors in the reunion episodes, and raters are guided by these measures when they classify the infant into one of the classification groups. The infants' scores on these variables were averaged across reunion episodes to increase the reliability of the measures.

DISCRIMINANT FUNCTION ANALYSES

To determine whether the A, B, and C group classifications reflect the same behavioral markers across samples, discriminant functions were derived for each of the four samples. The classification functions were derived using prior probabilities of group membership of .17 for A, .69 for B, and .14 for C, reflecting the proportions of each group within the pooled sample. Each function was applied to both the data set from which it was derived and the data from the other three samples for purposes of cross-validation.

The results of the discriminant analyses are shown in Table 12.1, which contains 16 matrices recording frequencies of accurate reclassifications obtained when the infants in each data set (represented by the rows) were classified using each of the four sets of classification functions (represented by the columns). For example, the matrix in the second row and first column represents the results of classifying the Pennsylvanian infants using the Michigan classification functions. The matrices on the diagonal of the table therefore represent the reclassification of infants using functions developed

---

[1]We are grateful to these investigators for allowing us to conduct analyses of their data.
[2]In the Israeli kibbutz sample, a total of 85 infants were seen with their mothers but for several of them the Strange Situation procedure had to be modified because the infants were extremely distressed. Thus, twenty-two infants had to be excluded from our analyses, either because they could not be classified into one of the traditional groups or because some of the reunion data were missing.

TABLE 12.1
Results of Discriminant Analysis for Four Strange Situation Data Sets

Data Sets	Michigan A	B	C	Pennsylvania A	B	C	Sweden A	B	C	Israel A	B	C
Michigan												
A	6	1	0	5	2	0	6	1	0	7	0	0
B	1	29	0	1	29	0	1	24	5	4	26	0
C	0	1	5	0	1	5	1	0	5	1	1	4
Pennsylvania												
A	9	1	2	11	1	0	9	0	3	12	0	0
B	3	36	0	1	36	2	2	27	10	5	34	0
C	0	1	7	0	1	7	1	0	7	4	0	4
Sweden												
A	8	1	2	6	4	1	10	0	1	11	0	0
B	5	32	1	0	38	0	0	38	0	7	30	1
C	1	0	1	1	0	1	0	0	2	1	0	1
Israel												
A	4	0	2	5	0	1	4	0	2	6	0	0
B	2	33	5	1	37	2	1	36	3	1	38	1
C	0	0	17	0	0	17	0	1	16	0	0	17

Classification Functions (column group header spanning Michigan, Pennsylvania, Sweden, Israel)

from the same data set, whereas the cross-validation results appear in the off-diagonal matrices. Within each matrix the rows represent the classification of the infants using the Ainsworth system, while the columns represent the classifications obtained from the functions. Diagonal elements in the matrices represent "hits" (e.g., A's reclassified as A's) whereas off-diagonal elements represent "misses" (i.e., incorrect reclassifications).

Table 12.2, showing the percentage of correct reclassifications obtained in each application of the classification functions, revealing that the interactive scales contain sufficient information to correctly reclassify

TABLE 12.2
Percentages of Correct Reclassifications

Data Sets	Michigan	Pennsylvania	Sweden	Israel
Michigan	93%	91%	81%	86%
Pennsylvania	88%	91%	73%	85%
Sweden	80%	88%	98%	82%
Israel	86%	94%	89%	97%

Classification Functions (column group header spanning Michigan, Pennsylvania, Sweden, Israel)

infants in the great majority of cases. In the cross-validation analyses, percentages of correct reclassifications range from 73% (Pennsylvanian children classified using Swedish functions) to 94% (Israeli children classified using Pennsylvanian functions). All these percentages are significantly better than chance (minimum $z = 2.92$, $p < .006$).

An informative statistic concerning the accuracy of the reclassifications is the percentage improvement over chance (Huberty, 1984):

$$I = 100 \times \frac{F_o - F_e}{N - F_e},$$

where F_o is the frequency of "hits" observed during the classification analysis, F_e is the frequency of "hits" expected by chance alone, and N is the sample size. Thus, $I = 100\%$ when reclassification is perfect, and zero when it is no better than chance. Percentage improvement statistics for each analysis are reported in Table 12.3, and show that the reclassification is substantially better than chance in every case. On the whole, the cross-validation analyses show that the classification system can be well predicted based on theoretically relevant individual differences in infant behavior in four samples from three cultures.

Errors do occur, however, and it is possible to see a systematic pattern in them. First, in the within-culture cross-validation (i.e., when the Michigan classification functions are cross-validated on the Pennsylvanian data set and vice versa), the average hit rate is 89.5%, and the average percentage improvement over chance is 78%. All the other cross-validations are across cultures, and here the average hit rate and average percentage improvement over chance are somewhat lower, 84.4% and 65.9% respectively. For these four samples, at least, cross-validation thus works somewhat better within culture than across cultures.

Examination of Table 12.1 clearly illustrates the problem: The Israeli and Swedish classifications functions cross-validate less well than the Michigan

TABLE 12.3
Percentage Improvement Over Chance in Classification

Data Sets	Classification Functions			
	Michigan	Pennsylvania	Sweden	Israel
Michigan	85%	80%	60%	70%
Pennsylvania	76%	83%	46%	70%
Sweden	50%	70%	95%	55%
Israel	72%	88%	78%	94%

or Pennsylvanian functions. Interestingly, the Israeli and Swedish functions produce characteristic and distinctive patterns of errors. The Israeli functions tend to misclassify C and particularly B group infants from other cultures as A's. This is understandable: Infants in the Israeli sample displayed more resistance than infants from the other three samples ($M = 2.6$ for the Israelis vs. $M = 1.8$ for the other cultures, $p < .00002$). This is not just because there were proportionately more C group babies in the Israeli data set: Infants in both the B and C groups had higher mean scores for resistance than did infants in the same groups in the other cultures. Thus due to what may be a shift in the culturally typical levels of resistant behavior in the Strange Situation, some B group children from other cultures more closely resemble A group infants in Israel. The Swedish functions tended to commit the complementary errors: misclassifying A and B group children as C's. This may be due to a limited data base: The Swedish data set contains only two C group children. In addition, however, the Swedish children on the whole differ from children in the other two cultures. They are more avoidant ($M = 2.9$ vs. $M = 2.4$, $p < .01$), and tend to maintain contact less ($M = 2.8$ vs. $M = 3.6$, $p < .01$) than Israeli and American infants. Not surprisingly, then, some B group children in other cultures more closely resemble C group than B group Swedish infants.

This pattern of errors could have three explanations. First, it is possible that the measures were poorly applied in Sweden and Israel. This seems unlikely, since when the functions were applied to the data from which they were derived, they reclassified infants very well (98% and 97% hit rates for Swedish and Israeli samples respectively). Second, raters in different cultures could be misusing the scales and systematically assigning different ratings in different cultures to similar behaviors. This seems unlikely, since the rating scales in the Ainsworth system are anchored to relatively explicit behavioral descriptions and the same person (Michael Lamb), along with individuals he trained, conducted the Michigan, Swedish, and Israeli ratings and classifications. By contrast, the Michigan and Pennsylvania data, which cross-validate well, were rated by different and completely independent groups of raters.

A third and more interesting explanation is that the A, B, and C patterns have somewhat different behavioral referents in different cultures, as evidenced by the systematic pattern of classification function errors. Raters viewing children in different cultures may interpret similar ratings somewhat differently in deciding upon the attachment group classifications, perhaps because different significance is attached to aspects of parent–infant interaction in different cultures. One result of this would be a tendency on the part of judges to make their classifications on a sample-relative basis, classifying children into groups depending on how they look relative to a sample norm rather than to an absolute norm.

Discriminant analyses also yield important information in the composition of the discriminant functions themselves. Discriminant functions are linear combinations of the original variables that form dimensions on which the groups defined by categorical variables are maximally separated. Variables heavily weighted in the discriminant functions therefore contribute more strongly to the separation of the groups.

The standardized discriminant functions from the pooled sample of 216 infants are presented in Table 12.4. To the right of the standardized discriminant function coefficients is an index recommended by Huberty (1984) for measuring the importance of each variable in a discriminant function,

$$h = (b_{ij})^2 - (1 - R_i^2),$$

where b_{ij} is the standardized discriminant function coefficient for variable i on discriminant function j, and R_i is the multiple correlation of variable i with the other variables in the set. The h statistic takes into account the intercorrelation of the variables when determining the contribution of any one to separation of the groups: Variables that are highly intercorrelated with others already present in the set are given less weight, whereas those that contribute independent information are given more. In surveying Table 12.4, it may be seen that the first discriminant function is defined primarily by the infants' resistance, while the second function is defined almost entirely by avoidance. This implies that the information contained in the A–B–C group classification system essentially reflects variations on these two variables.

TABLE 12.4
Standardized Discriminant Functions for the Pooled Sample

| | Discriminant Functions | | | |
| | Function 1 | | Function 2 | |
Variable	Discriminant Coefficients	Huberty's Index	Discriminant Coefficients	Huberty's Index
Avoidance	.252	.046	.885	.564
Resistance	1.023	.835	−.349	.097
Distance Interaction	−.491	.190	−.101	.008
Contact-maintaining	−.288	.031	−.030	.000
Proximity-seeking	−.269	.036	.015	.000

CLUSTER ANALYSES

We obtain a different perspective on the validity of the typological classification system by employing cluster analytic techniques. The question discriminant analysis addresses is: *Given the A, B, and C groups*, can we find an optimally weighted sum of variables that discriminates among them? Cluster analysis asks: *Given the data*, do the infants fall into clear and distinct groups (specifically, the A, B, and C groups)? Since discriminant analysis assumes the existence of the groups, and seeks ways to discriminate among them, it cannot detect other—perhaps more plausible—groupings. Unlike discriminant analysis, cluster analysis takes a sample of subjects of *unknown* classification and groups the subjects into clusters indicated by the measurements (Hand, 1981; Sneath & Sokal, 1973). Interestingly, informal cluster analytical procedures appear to have been used in the original development of the A–B–C system. According to Ainsworth and her colleagues, the classification system was developed "by grouping infants whose behavior in all episodes was alike in as many respects as possible. This purely empirical exercise yielded seven clusters of infants" (Ainsworth, et al., 1978, pg. 58) and these seven clusters were sorted into the A, B, and C groups. An eighth cluster (B_4) was later identified (Bell, 1970).

Clustering methods coalesce individuals into clusters on the basis of the similarity of their profiles of scores. If the groups in the Ainsworth classification system accurately capture the individual differences among infants in the Strange Situation, then the classes found through cluster analytic techniques should correspond closely to the Ainsworth groups. If they do not, we should find that the empirically derived clusters contain mixtures of the Ainsworth groups, indicating that some infants in one group resemble infants from other groups more than other members of their assigned group.

We applied hierarchical cluster analytic techniques to the 5 interactive variables employed in the discriminant analyses. Infants from all 4 samples were clustered twice, with the similarity between clusters being measured by the euclidian distance between the profiles of means for each cluster ("centroid linkage"). In the first cluster analysis, the data were standardized using the *pooled* means and standard deviations. Thus mean and variance differences between the different samples (e.g., the tendency towards greater resistance on the part of Israeli infants) were taken into account in forming clusters. In the second cluster analysis, each sample was individually standardized before being pooled, so that mean and variance differences between samples did not affect the formation of clusters. By pooling data from different cultures, we are not assuming that the Strange Situation procedure or the A–B–C classification system are equally valid across cultures. Including children from different cultures in a single cluster

Clusters

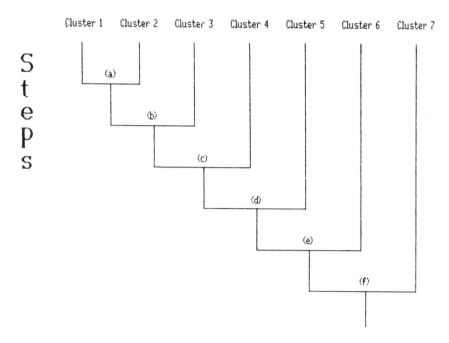

FIG. 12.2.   Clustering pattern obtained in the first cluster analysis.

analysis gives us an interesting perspective on the cross-cultural validity of the A–B–C classification system. If this system is independent of culture, the clusters derived should be based on A, B, and C group memberships. If cultural differences result in different styles of attachment behavior, however, then the clusters may reflect the infants' cultural memberships.

At the beginning of a hierarchical cluster analysis each case is considered to be a separate cluster. The analysis proceeds stepwise, with the two most similar clusters being joined to form a new cluster at each step, ending when all the subjects are in a single cluster. The results, in a sense, represent the history of this clustering process, reflecting relative differences in the degrees of similarity. Figure 12.2 presents a tree representing the results of the first cluster analysis up to the point where the 216 infants had been grouped into 7 clusters.[3] The top of the figure shows the seven clusters before any further combinations of clusters occurred.

---

[3]Figure 12.2 has been simplified by deleting two "clusters," each containing only one infant: an Israeli C_2 that entered the mega-cluster between steps (d) and (e), and an Israeli C_1 that entered the mega-cluster on the (true) final step (i.e., after step [f]).

TABLE 12.5
Membership of Clusters with Pooled Sample Standardization

Cluster	A1	A2	B1	B2	B3	B4	C1	C2	Proportion of cluster belonging to each sample	
1	0	2	10	37	29	1	0	0	32%	Swedish
									30%	Israeli
									19%	Michigan
									19%	Penn.
2	0	1	0	3	12	4	6	1	52%	Israeli
									26%	Michigan
									15%	Swedish
									7%	Penn.
3	0	0	2	4	3	0	0	0	56%	Swedish
									33%	Israeli
									11%	Michigan
4	10	17	6	2	1	0	0	2	32%	Penn.
									32%	Swedish
									21%	Swedish
									15%	Michigan
5	0	5	0	0	0	0	5	3	31%	Penn.
									31%	Israeli
									23%	Swedish
									15%	Michigan
6	0	1	0	4	13	14	7	0	64%	Penn.
									26%	Michigan
									5%	Swedish
									5%	Israeli
7	0	0	0	0	1	1	7	0	100%	Israeli

The membership of each cluster is listed in Table 12.5. The largest is cluster 1, consisting primarily of B_1, B_2, and B_3 infants, whereas cluster 2 consists primarily of B_3's, B_4's, and C_1's. This implies that a substantial group of "secure" B_3's resemble a group of "anxious" C_1's and intermediate B_4's more than they resemble the secure B's in, for example, cluster 1. Similarly mixed groups are seen in cluster 6, which consists primarily of B_3's, B_4's, and C_1's, and cluster 4, containing A_1's, A_2's, and B_1's. These mixtures are understandable, however. In clusters 2 and 6, the proximity-seeking B_3's and the (possibly insecure but proximity seeking) B_4's are grouped with the actively resistant (and proximity-seeking) C_1's. In cluster 4, the distally-interacting non-proximity-seeking B_1's are grouped with the non-proximity-seeking A's. Thus proximity-seeking behavior and distance interaction seem to be two modes by which infants are aggregrated. An exception to this patterning is evident in cluster 5, consisting of 5 A_2's and 8 C's! That these children resemble each other more than they resemble other A's or C's suggests that there may be a relatively rare group of infants displaying *both* avoidance and resistance. Finally, four of the seven clusters primarily contain infants from a single sample (most notably the Israeli C_1's in cluster 7) suggesting that sample differences play a substantial role in defining the clusters.

The subsequent steps of the cluster analysis simply involve the progressive absorption of the other clusters into cluster 1. Steps (a) and (b) add cluster 2 and 3 to cluster 1, forming a core group of B's (along with some C_1's from cluster 2). It might be expected that the next cluster to join would be cluster 6, which also consists primarily of infants in the B_3, B_4, and C_1 subgroups. Instead, however, cluster 4, consisting primarily of A's and B_1's, is the next to join, implying that these A's and B_1's resemble the large cluster of B's more than the infants in cluster 6. The A and C group mixture in cluster 5 joins in step (d), followed by cluster 6 in step (e). The last to join is cluster 7, a group of (presumably) highly resistant Israeli C's.

By examining the history of the clustering, one observes that at no point in the sequence are there three substantial groups resembling the traditional A, B, and C groups. The A's are concentrated into their own group (with some B_1's), however, and the emerging mega-cluster is initially defined by B's, primarily from the proximal end of the B_1 to B_4 spectrum. The other B infants, however, are scattered among the other clusters. Moreover, the C group infants, particularly the C_2's, show very little tendency to cluster together. In summary, the clusters seem understandable and interpretable in terms of a proximal vs. distal interactive dimension but they do not closely coincide with the traditional classification groupings. This suggests that the observational data contain a substantial amount of information not captured by the A–B–C typology.

In the second cluster analysis, data from each sample were standardized with respect to the sample mean and variance before being pooled. This removes important information from the data set, and hence the analysis is less desirable in most ways than the analysis just presented. The strategy was employed nonetheless, however, because we wanted to investigate the possibility that judges make their classifications on a "sample-relative" basis: classifying children into groups depending on how they look relative to a sample norm rather than to an absolute norm. If this is the case, the second cluster analysis should produce results that resemble the traditional Ainsworth pattern more than the results of the first did.

The cluster tree for this analysis is presented in Figure 12.3,[4] with the cluster memberships listed in Table 12.6. Examination of Table 12.6 shows that clusters are again defined primarily by the traditional subgroups rather than groups. Clusters 1 and 7 are mixed groups: Cluster 1 concentrates the A group infants with B_1 and B_2 infants whereas cluster 7 contains all but one C_1 infant, with some B_3 and B_4 infants. The presence of these mixed groups again suggests that the A, B, and C groups tend to overlap and shade into one another, rather than being tightly coherent, discrete groups. The other clusters subdivide the B infants: Cluster 3 consists primarily of infants from the B_1 and B_2 subgroups; clusters 4 and 5 primarily consist of infants from the B_2 and B_3 subgroups; whereas clusters 2 and 6 contain only infants from the B_3 and B_4 subgroups. Examination of the sample composition column helps explain the separation between clusters 2 and 6: Cluster 2 consists predominately of American infants, while cluster 6 consists entirely of Swedish and Israeli infants. This suggests that the sample-specific standardization of the data did not succeed in removing all differences between the samples. The separation between clusters 4 and 5 is not so easily explained, but examination of Figure 12.3 shows that they are joined early in the subsequent steps of the clustering processes.

Inspection of Figure 12.3 shows that steps (a), (b), and (c) of the clustering sequence join together clusters 3, 4, 5, and 6. If we freeze the clustering process here, we find clusters and mega-clusters that somewhat resemble the A, B, and C groups (see Table 12.7). The fusion of clusters 3, 4, 5, and 6 formed a large cluster composed almost entirely of B infants and modally defined by B_2 and B_3 infants. Besides this large cluster, there remain cluster 2 (B_3 and B_4 infants, mostly American), cluster 1 (A_1, A_2, B_1, and B_2 infants), and cluster 7 (C_1, B_4, and B_3 infants). Excepting cluster 2, the infants roughly fall into groups modally defined by A, B, and C groups, respectively. The anomaly posed by cluster 2 is underlined by the fact that cluster 7 (the "C_1 cluster") fuses with the large ("B") cluster on step (d), indicating that the C_1's resemble the majority of B group infants more than the B_3 and B_4's in cluster 2. Cluster 1, containing the A infants, however, seems more disimilar and enters last.

Several conclusions may be drawn from the results of the two cluster analyses. Most important is the fact that, although the clusters were defined by expectable similarities among the traditional subgroups to an impressive degree (e.g., "contiguous" B subgroups clustered together), we did not find

---

[4]Figure 12.3 has been simplified by deleting 8 subjects who did not fall into larger clusters. An Israeli B_2 and a Swedish A_2 infant entered the larger cluster between steps (e) and (f). An anomalous group of an A_2 and a C_2 from Israel, an A_2 from Sweden, and a C_2 from Michigan entered the large cluster after the last step depicted in the Figure. Following this, a Swedish C_1 and a Michigan C_1 entered on the (true) final step.

TABLE 12.6
Membership of clusters with individual sample standardization

Cluster	A1	A2	B1	B2	B3	B4	C1	C2	Proportion of cluster belonging to each sample	
1	10	16	9	7	2	0	0	3	32% 26% 23% 19%	Israeli Penn. Swedish Michigan
2	0	0	0	0	7	10	0	0	53% 35% 6% 6%	Penn. Michigan Israeli Swedish
3	0	1	9	22	2	2	0	0	39% 28% 17% 17%	Penn. Michigan Swedish Israeli
4	0	3	0	14	34	2	1	0	37% 28% 19% 17%	Swedish Israeli Penn. Michigan
5	0	0	0	4	6	0	0	0	50% 20% 20% 10%	Israeli Swedish Michigan Penn.
6	0	0	0	0	3	1	0	0	50% 50%	Swedish Israeli
7	0	3	0	2	5	5	23	2	40% 30% 15% 15%	Israeli Penn. Michigan Swedish

distinct and clear clusters corresponding to the A, B, and C groups. Explanation of the remarkable contrast between the results of the discriminant analysis, where the A–B–C groups were crisply evident, and the cluster analysis, where they were not, lies in the differences between the procedures. Discriminant analysis filters the information in the data set in order to find predetermined groups, whereas cluster analysis relies upon all the information in the data set. Since the cluster analysis did discern

Clusters

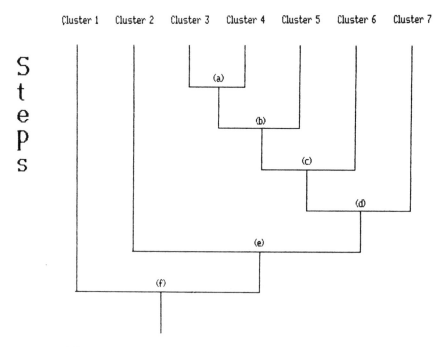

FIG. 12.3.   Clustering pattern obtained in the second cluster analysis.

predictable similarities among the subgroups, we have reason to believe that it responded to systematic variance, rather than noise in the data. The variance that seems to be tapped best by the cluster analyses concerns the extent to which infants use proximity- and contact-seeking interactive modes (i.e., the B_3, B_4, C_1, and C_2 subgroups) or primarily use distal modes (i.e., the B_1, B_2, A_1, and A_2 subgroups). Since it failed to distinguish the A, B, and C groups in the unstandardized data set, however, some inadequacies of the typological system were highlighted as well. First, the analysis revealed substantial overlap among the A, B, and C groups. Only in the standardized data set, in which mean and variance differences between samples had been removed, did we find a picture with noticeable (though highly imperfect) resemblance to the traditional A–B–C trichotomy. Even there, however, the clusters defined by concentrations of A group and C group infants did not respect the A/B or B/C boundaries: Instead, they drew B group (especially B_1 and B_4 subgroups) infants into their clusters. It could be argued, as suggested by Hazen and Durrett (1982) and Goldberg et al. (1984), that the B_1's are a 'borderline' group, with tendencies toward both

TABLE 12.7
Membership of clusters with individual sample standardization:
Midpoint in clustering

Cluster	A1	A2	B1	B2	B3	B4	C1	C2	Proportion of cluster belonging to each sample	
1	10	16	9	7	2	0	0	3	32% 26% 23% 19%	Israeli Penn. Swedish Michigan
2	0	0	0	0	7	10	0	0	53% 35% 6% 6%	Penn. Michigan Israeli Swedish
3+ 4+ 5+ 6	0	4	9	40	45	5	1	0	24% 20% 29% 27%	Penn. Michigan Sweden Israeli
7	0	3	0	2	5	5	23	2	40% 30% 15% 15%	Israeli Penn. Michigan Swedish

avoidance and security. It seems more reasonable, however, to question the value of the traditional typological representation of individual differences in Strange Situation behavior, and to consider whether a set of continuous dimensions would not capture the variation better. This issue is addressed more fully in Chapter 13.

The results of cross-sample and cross-cultural comparisons also have relevance for interpretation of our findings. Particularly in the first cluster analysis, for example, some clusters were dominated by individuals from one or two samples, suggesting that cross-sample differences could be as salient as the A, B, C group differences. The second cluster analysis seemed noticeably more congruent with the A–B–C system, suggesting that where an infant stands with respect to sample-relative norms, as well as where the infant stands with respect to the objective behaviors that are used to define the groups, may influence its classification. If similar levels of "security" or "anxiety" are manifest somewhat differently in different cultures, there are likely to be substantial problems in communicating and interpreting results if attachment classifications reflect somewhat different patterns of behavior across samples and particularly across cultures.

SUMMARY

Whereas the discriminant function analyses suggested that the A–B–C typology can be effectively predicted on the basis of the interactive measures, the cluster analyses cast doubt on the extent to which individual differences in Strange Situation behavior are fully captured by the typological system. The consistent failure of these analyses to yield clusters comprised primarily of infants with a similar group status suggests that, whereas there are some similarities among group members (as demonstrated in the discriminant function analyses), there are other more impressive similarities among infants in different classificaton groups that would lead to a very different clustering. Application of the typological system thus involves ignoring major areas of similarities among infants with respect to their Strange Situation behavior.

These results suggest the advisability of exploring alternative means of representing individual differences in Strange Situation behavior: Specifically, can one employ multivariate analytic procedures to develop a discrete number of continuous variables that represent meaningful individual differences in Strange Situation behavior? That question is explored in Chapter 13, written for this volume by J. P. Connell.

13

A COMPONENT PROCESS APPROACH TO THE STUDY OF INDIVIDUAL DIFFERENCES AND DEVELOPMENTAL CHANGE IN ATTACHMENT SYSTEM FUNCTIONING

James P. Connell

University of Rochester

OVERVIEW

The conceptual and methodological approach to the study of mother–infant attachment represented by the work of Ainsworth and her colleagues has promoted the empirical study of this important topic and offered the field a broad heuristic framework. However, the A–B–C classification system for summarizing Strange Situation behavior has been criticized because it promotes overly restrictive notions of what constitute important markers of individual differences in attachment system functioning—i.e., reunion behavior toward the caretaker (Connell & Goldsmith, 1982; Campos et al., 1983; Lamb et al., 1984; this volume)—and because it ignores the possibility of developmental change in the meaning and markers of secure attachment over the second year of life (Connell, 1984) and in different cultures (Sagi, 1984).

As a result of these critiques, some researchers have undertaken a search for alternative (though not necessarily competitive) approaches to the study of attachment system functioning. The "component process" approach presented in this chapter is but one of these alternatives. The ultimate goal of this approach is to determine how intra-organismic, interpersonal, and other contextual factors produce individual differences and age-graded change in attachment system functioning over the life-span.

First, I assume that age-graded change and individual differences in the functioning of the attachment system are influenced by both intra-organismic and interpersonal processes. More specifically, it is assumed that the infant's phenomenological experiences, such as strong emotions, and the sensitivity of the caretaker's responses to infant communications of these emotional experiences play a role in shaping and formulating the goals (e.g., seeking comfort vs. avoiding or rejecting) and regulating the goal-directed actions (e.g., proximity seeking vs. avoidant behavior) of infants toward their parents or caretakers. I have termed these intra-organismic and contextual variables "component processes" of attachment system functioning. My use of the term component processes originates in the model of attachment system functioning shown in Figure 13.1. This model represents an attempt to make more explicit how component processes may relate to each other temporally within a context such as the Strange Situation. The first component in this temporal sequence is the child's ambient affective state, which influences the way the child appraises events like the mother's departure. This "primary appraisal process" involves the infant's intuitive evaluation of the positive or negative consequences of this change in the environment (Arnold, 1970; Lazarus, 1966), and then leads to an affective reaction that "triggers" either a secondary appraisal process (whereby the child internally processes the affective experience and/or refers to the caretaker for further information: Klinnert et al., 1984) or the deployment of social interactive behaviors toward (or away from) the parent. The parent's reactions to both the emotional expression and the social

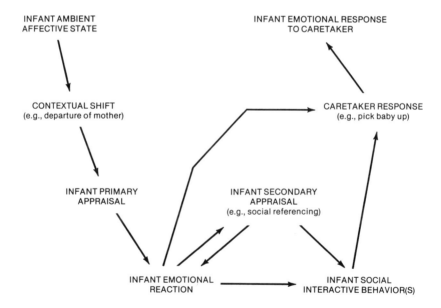

FIG. 13.1   A model of temporal relationship among emotional, social-interactive, and contextual component processes of attachment system functioning.

interactive behaviors constitute the next component process. Last follows the infant's affective state after the parent's response (or lack thereof).

A second assumption is that there are theoretically relevant and predictive dimensions of individual and dyadic differences on each of these component processes and that these are multiply, differentially, and predictably determined. This assumption of multidetermination departs at least implicitly from Ainsworth's approach, in which the quality of attachment is seen to be the primary if not sole organizer of the infant's emotional and social-interactive component processes. While the current approach assumes that the presence of these component processes in early life is evolutionarily predetermined, it also assumes that the canonical and less frequent configurations of the component processes (e.g., those thought to characterize secure and insecure attachments) are not evolutionary predetermined but rather are ontogenetically articulated.

Third, I assume that age-graded changes in the functioning of the attachment system will be reflected by changes in the mean levels, structural organization, and centrality of these component processes. Changes in the mean levels of these processes would, for example, involve increases or decreases in the degree of negative affect shown by infants upon separation, whereas changes in the structural organization of this component process might involve a more differentiated set of emotional reactions in older infants. Changes in centrality could involve either age-graded change in the strength of correlations among the component processes within a particular context (e.g., ambient affective state predicting less variance in affective reactions to separation in older infants) or change in the antecedents or consequences of individual differences in one or more of the component processes (e.g., ambient affective state being more highly correlated with dimensions of temperament in younger than in older infants).

How might this approach further our understanding of attachment system functioning, specifically as manifest by infant behavior in the Strange Situation? The advantages of the proposed approach are that: (1) it is potentially sensitive to all factors organizing emotional and social-interactive behavior, not only security of attachment; (2) *ongoing* emotional and social-interactive processes in the Strange Situation can be assessed; (3) developmental change in the organization of component processes can be examined using the same assessment procedure at different points in time; and (4) the component processes can be related prospectively and retrospectively to external variables including but not restricted to those thought to be related to attachment security. Overall, this approach encourages more detailed and comprehensive theoretical predictions regarding the organization of emotional and social-interactive behavior and its relation to caretaker responsiveness and intra-organismic factors such as temperament, cognitive/perceptual processes, and state variables. The target of both retrospective and prospective hypotheses concerning individual differences in attachment system functioning need no longer be restricted to A–B–C classification status, and developmental change in attachment system functioning can be conceived more broadly than as shifts in or stability of attachment classifications.

EMPIRICAL STUDIES USING THE COMPONENT PROCESS APPROACH

Our first attempt to instantiate empirically these component processes involved examining social-interactive behaviors in the Strange Situation (Connell & Goldsmith, 1982). Specifically, we sought to describe patterns of individual differences in Strange Situation behavior using scores on Ainsworth et al.'s social-interactive scales (i.e., proximity and contact seeking, contact maintaining, resistance, avoidance, distance interaction) for each of the Strange Situation episodes. Data sets were provided by other researchers.

Our first goal was to see if meaningful dimensions of social interactive behavior toward mother and stranger could be extracted by combining scores on these interactive scales into composites using a factor analytic strategy. By empirically deriving dimensions from scores on the interactive scales (instead of using scores on these measures to identify types or groups), we expected to account for more of the reliable variability in social-interactive behavior and also provide a more detailed picture of the ways in which the social-interactive behaviors are organized within each episode. We then hoped to examine relations between these dimensions across Strange Situation episodes in what we termed a "mini-longitudinal" study. This strategy was chosen as a first step toward examining (1) temporal consistencies of the social interactive processes, (2) contextual effects on those processes and (3) relationships between different component processes assessed at different points in time.

Our initial, albeit preliminary, findings were encouraging. We identified a set of factors that appeared to capture the coherences among the social-interactive categories in each episode. We also provided initial evidence for strong relationships between individual differences in infants' reactions to contextual shifts of separation from and reunion with their mothers. The new approach was thus successful in demonstrating interrelationships between scores on the social-interactive and emotional component processes within the attachment system. These findings provided the first evidence that our model (see Figure 13.1) had some validity, since the infant's affective reactions to the contextual shift of separation indeed appeared to motivate their subsequent social-interactive behavior toward the parent. As we summarized our findings:

> to be sure, the underlying causes of the affective reactions [to separation] remain unspecified, as are the processes underlying the translation of affect to subsequent (social-interactive) behavior. However, we believe these initial results offer some support for a theoretical framework which incorporates affective and motivational constructs beyond the quality of attachment (Connell & Goldsmith, 1982, p. 228).

Next, Gaensbauer, Connell, and Schultz (1983) examined these same component processes using data gathered in a slightly different observational setting (including free-play and infant mental testing sessions as well as separation and reunion episodes). The measures of social interaction were taken from Ainsworth et al. (1978) and Ricciuti (1974), supplemented by several more direct and independent measures of infant emotional expression. For the latter, 9-point rating scales assessing the presence and intensity of 6 different categories of emotion—pleasure, interest, fear, anger, sadness, and distress—were rated in consecutive 30-second intervals throughout the (approximately) 45-minute procedure. The goal of this study was to examine directly how contextual influences such as the temporal contiguity of and levels of stress engendered by the different episodes (e.g., separation from mother was assumed to be more stressful than free play with her) affected the consistency and the interrelationships between scores on these component processes both within and across the episodes.

A single hedonic tone dimension (negative to positive emotion) was derived within each episode from factor analyses of the discreet emotion ratings made during that episode, and a single social-interactive dimension (high to low "mother orientation") was derived by factor analyses of scores on the mother-directed social-interactive ratings in each episode.

Correlational analyses indicated moderate to strong relationships (Mean coefficient = .6; range = .4 to .75) between scores on the emotion and social interactive dimensions within episodes. Using path-modeling techniques (Wold, 1970), the relative consistency of the emotion dimension and the social-interactive dimensions was examined across episodes. A greater number of stronger and more noteworthy interrelationships were obtained for the emotion dimensions. The two contextual factors (temporal contiguity and stressfulness) affected the consistency of both component processes, with episodes sharing similar amounts of stress and temporally contiguous episodes yielding higher levels of consistency in both the emotion and social-interactive dimensions than episodes differing in stressfulness and episodes further apart in the sequence. Finally, emotion and social-interaction interrelationships within episodes varied importantly, again depending on the degree of stressfulness. Specifically, in the low stress episodes (e.g., mother approach), high degree of positive affect predicted high mother-orientation whereas in relatively high-stress situations (e.g., stranger approach), high negative arousal predicted high mother-orientation.

These results further validated the component process model, specifically confirming the central motivating role specified for infantile affective responses in the model. Strong relationships were found between emotion and social-interactive behaviors; the emotional context (i.e., high vs. low stressfulness) of the episodes influenced the consistency and interrelationships between the emotional and social-interactive dimensions, and emotion was more consistent across all contexts than was social interactive behavior.

Encouraged by these intriguing findings, we pursued three further issues regarding emotion-attachment interrelationships. First, would we see asymmetric influences between these two components over the course of the Strange Situation: That is, would emotion regulate social interaction to a greater extent than the reverse? Second, we wanted to determine whether there would be change over the second year of life in the patterns of cross-situational consistencies and asymmetric influences. Third, would the asymmetric influences between the two component processes apply also to the stability of individual differences in these processes over a 7-month period? That is, would stability of emotional reactions to contextual shifts (such as those occurring in the Strange Situation) predict stable patterns of social interaction in these same episodes to a greater extent than the reverse. The first question specifically addresses the model's assumption that emotional processes are more central and proximal regulators of social-interactive behaviors than the reverse. If such an asymmetry exists, then the antecedent variables studied when attempting to understand the determinants of attachment system functioning must be expanded to include both biological and experiential contributors to emotional responsiveness. The second question is more explicitly developmental. If the relationship between the emotional and social-interactive component processes change over the second year of life—for example, if *more* social-interactive behavior upon reunion is systematically related to the intensity of emotional reactions to separation at older ages—we can start specifying what it is about the attachment system that develops. Other theorists have implied that the system functions in essentially the same way over this age range, with only the mean levels of particular social-interactive behaviors (e.g., decreases in proximity seeking) and/or the security of the attachment relationship changing over time. The third question addressed in the study concerned the sources of continuity in the component processes. If stable individual differences in emotional reactions to Strange Situation episodes are more predictive of stable patterns of social interaction than the reverse, we may need to reconceptualize continuities in attachment functioning, investigating intra-organismic and interpersonal processes that may account for such "emotional stability."

In order to address these questions, Connell and Thompson (1984) reanalyzed a data set that included ratings for 43 infants on Ainsworth's social-interactive scales as well as independent assessments of the infants' emotional expressions at both 12½ and 19½ months.[1] Vocal and facial emotional reactions were assessed at 15-second intervals throughout the procedure. From these discrete interval-by-interval ratings, the following summary measures were obtained separately for the vocal and facial modalities in every episode, except where indicated: peak distress intensity, minimum distress intensity, latency to distress onset (episode 3), and two indices of emotional recovery (episodes 4, 6, and 7). For the purposes of our study, we focused on data from two separation episodes in which the baby was alone with the stranger (i.e., episodes 3 and 6) and the two reunion episodes (i.e., episodes 4 and 7). Data from the preseparation episodes (i.e., episodes 1 and 2) were not examined because a number of the social-interactive and emotion variables showed low variability, and the "baby alone" separation episode (episode 5) was excluded because no explicitly social interactive behavior can be scored. As suggested by Gaensbauer et al.'s (1983) analyses, the four episodes chosen are all relatively high stress contexts and as such they are contexts in which the functioning of the attachment system should be salient.

Social interactive dimensions were derived separately for the separation and reunion episodes from the correlations among scores on the 5 social interactive scales. As in the previous investigations, factor analytic procedures[2] were performed to estimate the number and determine the composition of the factors within each episode; confirmatory analyses were subsequently used to assess the adequacy of the factor model's goodness-of-fit to the correlations among the social interactive behaviors within each episode.

The resulting social interactive dimensions for each age are shown in Table 13.1 along with the weighting assigned each of the social interactive scales when forming composite scores on the social interactive dimensions (+ or − in front of a variable indicates unit weightings, .5 indicates the score was multiplied by .5 before adding it into the composite). This weighting

---

[1] For a more complete description of the data set and measures obtained, see Thompson and Lamb (1982, 1984a) or Connell and Thompson (1984).

[2] Further detail on this analytic procedure are presented later in this chapter in the discussion of the Connell and Bridges (1984) mega-analyses. For a more general introduction to the structural modeling approach, see Connell and Goldsmith (1982).

procedure is a variant of that recommended by Wackwitz and Horn (1971), and was applied to each of the factors, yielding scores on 8 dimensions at each age, 2 for each of the 4 episodes on which we focused. The factor analyses of scores from the 2 separation episodes at each age yielded very similar results, as did analyses of data from the two reunion episodes. As can be seen in Table 13.1, the factor structures at the 2 ages were quite similar, indicating that the structural organization of the social-interactive processes per se was not markedly different at the two ages. In both separation episodes at both ages, for example, two factors were necessary to account for the pattern of correlations among scores on the five social interactive scales: The factors were labeled "proximity/contact with stranger" and "unsociability with stranger." Infants who obtained high scores on the factor proximity/contact with stranger at both ages sought and maintained proximity to and contact with the stranger relative their peers, whereas a high score on the factor, unsociability with stranger, indicated that the infant was less sociable with the stranger (as manifested by avoidance of and resistance to contact with the stranger as well as lack of positive distance interaction) relative to peers.

The emotion dimensions for each episode were derived by factor-analyzing episode-by-episode scores on the variables described previously. As indicated in Table 13.2, factor analyses yielded a single dimension of high to low negative arousal in each episode at each age. Scores were assigned to each subject for each episode using the procedure followed with the social interactive dimensions. High scores on this dimension indicated a relatively high peak and high minimum negative intensity during the episode and either a short latency to show negative expression (episode 3) or a longer period necessary to recover from negative expression (episodes 4, 6, and 7).

Next, we examined the consistency of scores on the social interactive and emotion dimensions across the four episodes. At both ages, significantly greater consistency (i.e., higher correlations across episodes) was evident in the emotion component, indicating that this component may provide a more reliable index of socio-emotional functioning across situations than the social-interactive dimensions. That is, infants are less idiosyncratic in their patterns of emotional arousal across the episodes of the Strange Situation than they are in their patterns of social-interactive behaviors toward mother and stranger. Not only was the consistency of emotion scores greater than that of the social interactive scores but this consistency also varied less across different types of episodes (mother present vs. stranger present) and different degrees of temporal contiguity (adjacent episodes vs. non-adjacent episodes). Thus, in a relatively stressful situation like the Strange Situation, infants are more likely to show idiosyncratic *shifts* in social interactive strategies from mother to stranger and from one episode to the next than they are to show idiosyncratic shifts in levels of negative arousal

TABLE 13.1

Social Interactive Dimensions Factor Analytically Derived From Two Separation and Two Reunion Episodes (From Connell & Thompson, 1984)

Episode #	Dimension Label	Interactive Category Markers[a]	
		12½ Mos.	19½ Mos.
3,6	a) Proximity/Contact with Stranger (PR/CON STR)	+PS +CM	+PS +CM
	b) Unsociability with Stranger (UNSOC STR)	+PA +CR -DI	+PA +CR -DI
4,7	a) Proximity/Contact vs. Avoidance With Mother (PR/CON vs. AVM)	+PS +.5CM -PA	+PS +CM -.5PA
	b) Resistance vs. Distance Toward Mother (RES vs. DISM)	+CR -DI +.5CM	+CR -DI

[a]All markers unit weighted in forming dimension scores except where indicated.

Note: PS = proximity seeking, CM = contact maintaining, PA = proximity avoidance, DI = positive distance interaction, CR = contact resistance.

231

TABLE 13.2
Emotion Dimensions Factor Analytically Derived From Two Separation
and Two Reunion Episodes (From Connell & Thompson, 1984)

Episode #	Dimension Label	Emotion Dimension Marker[a,b]
4,6,7	Negative Emotion (NEGEMO)	+VPI +VMI + VR1 + VR2 +FR1 +FR2
3,4	Negative Emotion (NEGEMO)	+VPI +VMI -FLA

[a]Markers of the emotion dimension were the same at 12½ and 19½ months.
[b]All markers unit weighted in forming dimension scores.
Note: V and F indicate vocal or facial modality respectively and PI = peak intensity, MI = minimum intensity, R1 = recovery index #1, R2 = recovery index #2, LA = latency to peak intensity.

across the different contexts. The strong cross-situational consistency of the emotional component coupled with the context-boundedness of consistencies in social-interactive processes indicated to us that two infants who show similar shifts in emotional arousal across different types of episodes may engage different types of social-interactive behaviors in response to these emotional reactions. Age-level comparisons indicated that the emotion scores were less consistent at 19½ months than at 12½ months. We interpreted these data to mean that more idiosyncracies in emotional patterning were emerging, which may be due to some of the older infants' acquisition of an ability to "self-right" emotionally over the course of the Strange Situation procedure.

Next, we asked whether asymmetric influences exist such that emotion plays a more central role in regulating social interaction than vice versa. This, of course, would be the prediction emerging from the model in Figure 13.1. Whereas the model and previous research recognize that mutual influences exist (e.g., Klinnert et al., 1984; Stern, 1977), we hypothesized that over the course of the Strange Situation, the infant's emotional reactions in the separation episodes would play a greater role in predicting subsequent social-interactive behavior during reunions than social-interactive behavior during the first reunion would play in predicting later emotional reactions to separation. These hypotheses were examined using multiple regression analyses in which an emotional dimension and a social-interactive dimension were the independent variables and either a later social-interactive dimension or emotion dimension was the dependent variable. The social interactive dimensions used in these analyses were those shown for the reunion episodes in Table 13.1: Proximity/contact to vs. avoidance of mother and resistance vs. distance interaction toward mother. The purpose of the analyses was to see if, for example, later resistance vs.

distance interaction toward mother is influenced by intervening emotional reactions to separation when one controls for earlier levels of the same social-interactive dimension.

Our hypothesis was supported in analyses involving both of the social-interactive dimensions at 19½ months, but only marginally for the resistance vs. distance interaction dimension at 12½ months. However, later negative emotional reactions to separation were not significantly predicted by intervening social interactive behavior with mother when earlier emotional reactions to separation were controlled for. These findings, together with those obtained in the Gaensbauer et al. study suggest first that emotional processes play a central role in establishing a relatively consistent base-line of ongoing activity particularly at the younger age and second that, with age, emotional patterning across situations becomes more idiosyncratic but more broadly and closely linked with individual differences in subsequent social-interactive behaviors. We speculate that this broader and more flexible linkage of the two component processes at 19½ months may contribute to an increased ability to self-right emotionally over the course of the procedure.

Finally, we asked whether asymmetric influences would exist regarding the stability of individual differences in each component process over the 7-month period. To examine this, we formed groups of infants based on the stability (or lack thereof) of their scores on each of the two component processes. To form these groups, we combined relevant scores from the two separation episodes and the two reunion episodes separately for the social-interactive dimensions and across all four episodes for the emotion dimension. Within the "stable emotion group," close to 90% of the variance in scores on the four social-interactive dimensions was shared over the 7-month period. Within the four stable social interaction groups, the average amount of shared variance on the emotion scores was 46% (range 23%–63%). Thus, stability of emotional responsiveness predicted stability of social interaction more than the reverse.

The results of the Gaensbauer et al. and Connell and Thompson investigations provided preliminary empirical and theoretical elaboration of the predicted relationships between infants' emotional experiences and their social-interactive behavior toward their caretakers. The clear implication is that an understanding of individual differences in attachment system functioning will have to include explanations of both (1) individual *differences* in emotional reactivity to contextual variation and (2) individual variations in social interactive strategies deployed following *similar* emotional experiences. The developmental implications of this work are not unrelated to these individual difference questions. The greater individual variation in the temporal patterning of emotional arousal and social-interactive behaviors in older infants as well as the more systematic connections between emotion and later social interaction may indicate that in older infants emotional reactions call up idiosyncratic social-interactive strategies through which they begin to regulate themselves emotionally, whereas younger infants' social-interactive strategies are more stereotypically applied, their emotional reactions more self-perpetuating, and thus their emotional regulation more external in origin.

MEGA-ANALYSIS OF SOCIAL-INTERACTIVE BEHAVIOR IN THE STRANGE SITUATION

The results of the three studies reviewed in the foregoing suggest that the component process approach may be useful for addressing important issues regarding attachment system functioning, specifically (1) the roles played by emotional responsiveness and social interactive behavior and (2) developmental changes in the interrelationships between emotion and social-interactive behavior over the second year of life. The results encouraged us to study these component processes further using data generated in several Strange Situation studies. Before doing so, however, we decided to capitalize on the paradigmatic comparability of these studies (e.g., the fact that they used the same rating system for coding social interactive behaviors) and derive a single set of social interactive dimensions from several data sets. The results of our previous "mini-longitudinal" studies might have been

TABLE 13.3
Description of Data Sets

Researchers	N	Gender Distribution	SES	1st SS Assessment	2nd SS Assessment
Ainsworth et al., 1978	105	59 M., 46 F.	Middle-Class	12–13 mos.	—
Waters, 1978	50	25 M., 25 F.	Lower-to-Upper-Middle-Class	12 mos.	18 mos.
Thompson, 1981	43	21 M., 22 F.	Middle-Class	12 mos.	19 mos.
Belsky, Rovine & Taylor, 1984	60	28 M., 32 F.	Middle-Class	12–13 mos.	—
Frodi et al., 1984	41	24 M., 17 F.	Lower-to-Upper-Middle-Class	12 mos.	20 mos.

compromised by the relatively large number of variables compared to the number of subjects. Thus we thought that by combining data from a number of studies and conducting the analyses described above on data from hundreds of subjects, this concern could be ameliorated appreciably. We also expected that the resulting social interactive dimensions could be used as the basis for future research by us and others on component processes of attachment system functioning. Through the generosity of our colleagues, we obtained twelve data sets involving Strange Situation assessments of infants and mothers. We combined these data into two data sets: one involving 12- to 13-month-old infants ($N = 299$) and one involving 18- to 20-month-old infants ($N = 134$). These data sets and their sources are described in Table 13.3.

Preliminary Analyses

Because we were interested in the social interactive component of the attachment system, we restricted our attention to data from episodes in which social interaction took place and in which the interactive ratings showed adequate variability: episodes 2, 3, 4, 6, and 7. Only the variables scored in all samples (proximity seeking, contact maintaining, avoidance, resistance and distance interaction toward mother and stranger) were included in the preliminary analyses. These variables and the codes used in describing the results of the mega-analyses are presented in Table 13.4.

Variables showing floor effects and inadequate variability across all samples were then eliminated: Specifically, these were resistance and contact maintaining toward stranger and resistance and avoidance toward mother in episode 2 at both ages, as well as distance interaction toward

TABLE 13.4
Social Interactive Category and Episode Codes

Category	Code - Mother	Code - Stranger
Proximity Seeking	PS	PSS
Proximity Avoidance	PA	PAS
Contact Maintaining	CM	CMS
Contact Resistance	CR	CRS
Distance Interaction	DI	DIS

Episode Codes
2 = Preseparation (Mother + Baby + Stranger)
3 = 1st Separation (Stranger + Baby)
4 = 1st Reunion (Mother + Baby)
6 = 2nd Separation (Stranger + Baby)
7 = 2nd Reunion (Mother + Baby)

mother and proximity seeking toward stranger in episode 2 at 12 months only. Because we obtained significant mean level differences among the samples on many of the interactive scale scores, two standardization procedures were employed and the correlations among the variables were then examined: One involved standardizing scores on the interactive variables within each sample, before merging the data sets and computing correlations; the other involved merging the data sets before standardizing the variables using the composite data set. In either case, the patterns of intercorrelations emerging were almost identical: Fewer than 5% of the correlations differed in magnitude by more than .05. For the mega-analysis reported here, we used the standardized scores obtained from the second procedure.

We also examined the variability of the correlations across samples and although certain correlations showed considerable sampling variability, there did not appear to be any consistent pattern to this variation (e.g., one sample's correlations were not consistently lower or higher than the rest). Thus, we proceeded to the mega-analysis under the assumption that we were working with a set of correlations computed on a single population. In subsequent analyses, we plan to test the comparability of the data emerging from the different samples using structural modeling techniques that allow for the factor patterns to be compared directly across multiple groups.

Factor Analyses of the Interactive Categories

Exploratory factor analyses of the correlations among scores on the interactive categories within each episode at each age level were performed using a least squares procedure and an oblique rotation toward simple structure with correlated factors. Based on these results, we then performed maximum likelihood confirmatory factor analyses using the LISREL VI program (Joreskog & Sorbom, 1983). The goal of these analyses was to obtain a theoretically interpretable and parsimonious set of social-interactive dimensions at each age level. We also adjusted the models in order that the factors specified in the models showed adequate goodness-of-fit to the pattern of correlations among the interactive categories. Goodness-of-fit in this context refers to a chi-square statistic that indicates the degree of difference between the pattern of correlations generated by the factor model being specified and the pattern of correlations obtained from the actual data. The larger the chi-square, the greater the discrepancy and the poorer the fit of the factor model.

Two problems were encountered in attempting to achieve this goal. First, although the large sample size increased our confidence in the reliability of the findings, it made it difficult to attain a good statistical fit to the data. This problem is due to the fact that with larger samples the correlations obtained from the sample data are assumed to be closer approximations to the population parameters; therefore, even very small deviations of the correlations generated by the factor model from these correlations based on the large sample adversely affect the goodness-of-fit statistic. Conversely, with small samples, good fits of models are relatively easy to obtain because the sample correlations have large standard errors and, as a result, the model-generated correlations can be more discrepant from these small sample correlations and still have the model show adequate fit. Our second problem was that because a small number of variables were factor analyzed, there were few degrees of freedom available for modifying the model to achieve a better fit before the factor model became "overfit" statistically and/or theoretically unparsimonious. For example, one way to improve the fit to the data is to have more variables load on each factor. This strategy, however, would entail abandoning the notion that conceptually distinct dimensions underlie the organization of the observed behavior—e.g., resistance vs. distance interaction as distinct from proximity/contact vs. avoidance. A second model fitting strategy would involve increasing the *number* of factors in the model; however, with the small number of variables included in our analyses (usually five), one very quickly reaches the point at which the advantages of a factor analytic model (as opposed to simply using scores on the interactive scales themselves) are vitiated as the number of factors rapidly approaches the number of observed variables. These two problems were not trivial and the final models presented here reflect consideration of both.

The social-interactive dimensions emerging from the confirmatory analyses for data from each episode at each age level are presented in Tables 13.5 and 13.6. Also presented in these tables are the standardized factor pattern loadings for each interactive variable loading on the dimensions. Those loadings are interpretable as standardized regression coefficients indicating the degree of relationship between the factor/dimension and the observed variable. All of these coefficients are greater than twice their standard error. Finally, two indices of goodness-of-fit are presented: the chi-square statistic previously discussed (with its degrees of freedom and probability level) and the root mean square residual. The second index was included following the recommendation of Joreskog (1978, personal communication).

As stated earlier, the larger the chi-square, the worse the fit. The probability level indicates the probability that the pattern of correlations that would be generated by the factor model is the same as the pattern of correlations from the actual data. In three of the ten cases tested, this probability was less than $p = .01$. The root mean square residual can be interpreted as the average amount of correlation remaining between the variables that is *not* "explained" by the model. For samples of this size, given

TABLE 13.5

Results of Confirmatory Factor Analyses of Infant Social Interactive Behaviors in Selected Episodes of the Strange Situation (12 to 13 months: $N = 299$)

Epi. #	Dimension Label	Social Interactive Variable and Factor Pattern Loadings	X^2	dF	p	Mean Sq. Residual
2	Stranger Wariness (STRWAR2)	.8 PS2 + .8CM2 + .7 PAS2 – .3 DIS2	26.13	2	.00	.06
3	a) Unsociability with Stranger (UNSOC STR3)	.5 CRS3 + .4 PAS3 –.9 DIS3	7.43	4	.11	.04
	b) Proximity/Contact Toward Stranger (PR/CON STR3)	.5 PSS3 + 1.0 CMS3 – .2 PAS3				
4	a) Proximity/Contact vs. Avoidance Toward Mother (PR/CON vs. AM4)	.9 PS4 + .5 CM4 – .6 PA4	3.34	3	.34	.02
	b) Resistance vs. Distance Toward Mother (RES vs. DISM4)	.5 CM4 + .6 CR4 – .5 DI4				
6	a) Unsociability with Stranger (UNSOC STR6)	.7 CRS6 + .3 PAS6 – .6 DIS6 – .3PSS6	9.89	3	.02	.03

b) Proximity/Contact Toward Stranger (PR/CON STR6)	.6 PSS6 + 1.0 CMS6 – .2 PAS6			
7 a) Proximity/Contact vs. Avoidance Towards Mother (PR/CON vs. AM7)	.8 PS7 + .5 CM7 – .7 PA7	15.52	3	.001
b) Resistance vs. Distance Toward Mother (RES vs. DISM7)	.6 CM7 + .3 CR7 – .8 D17			.06

239

TABLE 13.6

Results of Confirmatory Factor Analyses of Selected Episodes of the Strange Situation (18 to 20 months: $N = 134$)

Epi. #	Dimension Label	Social Interactive Variable and Factor Pattern Loadings	X^2	dF	p	Mean Sq. Residual
2	a) Stranger Wariness (STRWAR2)	.9 PS2 + .6 CM2 + .2 DI2 + .4 PAS2	16.89	3	.01	.06
	b) Sociability with Stranger (SOCIAB STR2)	1.0 DIS2 + .5 PSS2 + .3DI2 − .5 PAS2				
3	a) Unsociability with Stranger (UNSOC STR3)	.6 CRS3 + .7 PAS3 - .8 DIS3 − .3 PSS3	4.90	2	.09	.04
	b) Proximity/Contact Toward Stranger (PR/CON STR3)	.5 PSS3 + .8 CMS3 − .3 PAS3				
4	a) Proximity/Contact vs. Avoidance Toward Mother (PR/CON vs. AM4)	.6 PS4 + .6 CM4 − .7 PA4	7.29	2	.03	.05
	b) Resistance vs. Distance Toward Mother (RES vs. DISM4)	.6 PS4 + .7 CM4 + .4 CR4 − .7 DI4				

240

6	a) Unsociability with Stranger (UNSOC STR6)	$.6$ CRS6 $+ .3$ PAS6 $- 1.0$ DIS6 $- .3$PSS6	3.69	2	.16
	b) Proximity/Contact Toward Stranger (PR/CON STR6)	$.7$ PSS6 $+ .9$ CMS6 $- .3$ PAS6			
7	a) Proximity/Contact vs. Avoidance Toward Mother (PR/CON vs. AM7)	$.7$ PS7 $+ .6$ CM7 $- .6$ PA7	6.89	2	.03
	b) Resistance vs. Distance Toward Mother (RES vs. DISM7)	$.7$ CM7 $+ .4$ PS7 $+ .4$ CR7 $- .9$ DI7			

The rows 6a and 7a also carry values .05 and .06 respectively in the final column.

the magnitude of the original correlations among the variables, this provides a "fairer" estimate of goodness-of-fit than the traditional chi-square test (see earlier discussion of sample size and goodness-of-fit). In no case was this residual greater than .06. This means that in all cases the difference between the correlation generated by the model (i.e., the correlation predicted to occur in the population for which the model was true) and the observed correlation was less than or equal to .06, indicating that adequate fits were obtained for each model.

In sum, 9 dimensions emerged from the patterns of correlations among the 24 interactive variables included in the mega-analysis of the 12-month data set and 10 dimensions from the 26 interactive variables analyzed at 18 to 20 months. Substantive interpretations—particularly of social-interactive dimensions in the reunion episodes (since these bear most directly on the component processes included in the working model)—are incorporated in a later section describing some preliminary developmental investigations using these social-interactive dimensions.

Deriving Scores on the Social-Interactive Dimensions

The weightings presented in Tables 13.5 and 13.6 can be used to form scores on each dimension for individual subjects. (This factor scoring procedure is also a variant of that recommended by Wackwitz, & Horn, 1971). It is probably safe to assume that this sample more adequately represents the population of American infants from lower-to-upper-middle class families than any single sample of smaller size and greater homogeneity. Thus my suggestion to researchers interested in pursuing the component process approach with their own Strange Situation data is that they either use these exact weights to form scores on the social interactive dimensions or at least pay attention to the factor composition which emerged from these mega-analyses.

Social Interactive Dimensions and Patterns of Secure and Insecure attachment

The relationship between the social interactive dimensions presented here and the traditional attachment classifications is portrayed in Table 13.7. Results obtained using the 12–13 month data set are presented in the top half of the table and results obtained using data from 18–20-month-olds are presented in the bottom half. The figures represent the proportions of total sums of squares obtained by regressing scores from each social interactive dimension on the attachment classification grouping listed across the top of the tables. Stated differently, these figures represent the proportions of total variability in scores on the social-interactive dimensions accounted for by mean differences between attachment groupings.

Given the widespread use of the global secure (i.e., B group) vs. insecure (i.e., A plus C group) distinction in attachment research, the column in which B group babies are contrasted with A and C group babies is of particular interest. At 12 to 13 months, security of attachment predicts more than 1% of the variance in only three of the nine dimensions and more than 8% in only one dimension. Approximately 26% of the variance on the proximity/contact vs. avoidance dimension in the second reunion—episode 7—is predicted by this contrast. At 18 to 20 months, less than 9% of the variance is predictable in all dimensions by security vs. insecurity. When a distinction is made between the two insecure groups (i.e., A vs. B vs. C contrasts are made) slightly greater prediction occurs, particularly in the reunion episode. Even in these episodes, however, approximately 64% of the variance in the social-interactive dimensions is *not* predicted using the A–B–C classification system at 12 months and approximately 80% is not predicted at 18 months. Finally, when the eight subclassifications are distinguished, the prediction of scores on the social interactive dimensions again improves, but the average proportion of variance unexplained is still around 65% in the younger samples and 74% in the older samples.

These results do not mean that the traditional classifications do not account for any meaningful variability in infant Strange Situation be-havior—their empirical relationships with other constructs (see Chapter 5 and 9) indicate that some important individual differences are captured by the traditional typology. It is clear, however, that a great deal of reliable variability in social interactive behavior during this procedure is unrelated to the patterns of secure and insecure attachment tapped by the Ainsworth system. And, it appears that this low predictive capacity is more apparent at the older age. My interpretation of these findings is that the unexplained variability in the social-interactive dimensions, while not related to attachment security, is systematic and thus predictable. In fact, the results reported earlier in this chapter demonstrate that the component process of infant emotional variation predicts considerably greater variability in social-interactive dimensions than does security of attachment, per se.

DEVELOPMENTAL CONSIDERATIONS AND CONCLUSIONS

At the outset, I discussed the limitations of the traditional views of attachment system functioning that led me and my colleagues to formulate this alternative methodological and conceptual approach. Specifically, whenever the Strange Situation paradigm and the A–B–C classification system are used in tandem with infants ranging from 12 to 20 months of age, two implicit assumptions are made: (1) that the defining features of an adaptively-functioning attachment system are invariant over this period and

(2) that this system can be validly assessed in the same way near the end of the second year as at the beginning. We have recently examined these two assumptions using the component process approach in two different longitudinal data sets that included assessments of both the social-interactive and emotional components.

In one study (Bridges, Grolnick, Frodi, & Connell, 1984), we examined relationships between independently rated dimensions of social interactive behaviors obtained from the Strange Situation procedure and the same infants' emotional responses in a structured series of toy play tasks with an experimenter before the Strange Situation. At 12 months, we found a significant positive relationship between the emotion dimension (coded for positive to negative emotions) and the social interactive dimension (marked positively by "positive distance interaction" and negatively by "resistance toward mother"). Thus 12-month-old infants who were rated as emotionally positive in the free play situation tended to interact positively with their mothers from a distance and not resist contact with them during the Strange Situation. The 12-month emotion ratings also predicted resistance in the Strange Situation at 20 months, but in the *opposite* direction. The infants with positively rated emotions at 12 months were *more* resistant towards their mothers at 20 months.[3]

In the second study (Connell, Thompson, & Tero, 1984), we examined the relative stability of social interactive versus emotional components of the attachment system, and a similar finding emerged. Of the group of infants who remained emotionally positive from 12½ to 19½ months (i.e., those who stayed above the median on an emotional dimension coded positive to negative and summed across two separation and reunion episodes), 62% shifted from below the median on the resistance vs. distance interaction dimension at time 1 to above the median on this same dimension at time 2. Thus, a significant proportion of infants who consistently showed relatively positive emotional responses in the Strange Situation over the second year of life showed less resistance towards mother than their peers at 12½ months and more resistance at 19½ months.

These preliminary developmental findings indicate that "resistance towards the mother," which is a salient marker of insecure attachment in the Ainsworth classification system and which signifies less adaptive functioning at 12 months, may actually signify more adaptive functioning later in the second year of life. We thus concluded that the two previously-stated assumptions underlying the use of the A–B–C classifications are, at best, tenuous when applied to older infants, and that alternative theoretical views are needed to explain the development of the attachment system. We are currently exploring the usefulness of Mahler, Pine, and Bergman's (1975)

---

[3]It should be noted that the levels of resistance at both ages were moderate.

developmental theory in this regard. The data emerging from our analyses fit with these theorists' view that, over the second year of life, the normal infant moves from a phase in which the mother is used as a secure base for exploration in a relatively conflict-free way (one of Ainsworth's markers of secure attachment) to a phase late in that second year in which infants struggle with their growing understanding of both their mothers' separateness and their own individuality. This struggle, termed "rapprochement," is viewed by Mahler et al. as an important precursor of mature interpersonal relationships and manifests itself in bouts of resistance and ambivalent behavior toward the mother during this period. At this point, it would appear that Mahler et al.'s description of developmental changes in the mother–child relationship over the first 8 months of the second year of life is more compatible with the data than are implicit assumptions of invariance in both the meaning and markers of secure infantile attachment over this period.

These initial studies of infant social-interactive and emotional component processes indicate that our approach to the study of attachment involves more than a shift from a typological to a dimensional view of the same construct. The model presented earlier will eventually allow for factors such as the quality and consistency of the caretaking environment to be treated as a component process of the attachment system along with infant emotions and social-interactive behaviors. With a multidimensional characterization of each component process, the "fits" of alternative models which include longitudinal and contemporaneous relationships among the component processes, as well as their antecedents and consequences, may be estimated using, for example, structural modeling techniques. This dimensional approach to the study of attachment system with its analytical focus on basic processes rather than global clinical indices could also yield a richer idiographic and normative portrayal of the attachment system as it functions in contexts other than the Strange Situation.

In the study of a phenomenon such as attachment which is so central to the understanding of human functioning across the life-span, alternative methodological approaches and theoretical views must be encouraged and developed and should not be cast aside prematurely in favor of a single, predominant approach. The component process approach described in this chapter may be an alternative that can help shed light on substantive questions such as the development and functioning of the attachment system in at-risk populations, in older and younger populations, and in different cultures.

TABLE 13.7

Variability in Social Interactive Dimensions Accounted and Not Accounted for by Attachment Classification Groupings Expressed in Proportional Sums of Squares

| 12–13 months | Attachment Classification Grouping | | | | |
	A vs. C	B vs. AC	A vs. B vs. C	A1 vs. A2 vs. B1 vs. B2 B3 vs. B4 vs. C1 vs. C2	Unexplained
STRWAR2	.0425	.00079	.0433	.1818	.8182
UNSOC STR3 PR/CON STR3	.1142	.0048	.1190	.2883	.7116
	.0094	.0056	.0149	.0620	.9378
RES vs. DISM4 PR/CON vs. AVM4	.1818	.0776	.2594	.4995	.5005
	.1954	.0214	.2168	.4414	.5586
UNSOC STR6 PR/CON STR6	.1703	.0023	.1726	.3172	.6829
	.0018	.0026	.0044	.0203	.9796
RES vs. DISM7 PR/CON vs. AVM7	.1542	.0096	.1637	.5468	.4532
	.1642	.2594	.4236	.7018	.2982

18–20 months

STRWAR2	.0220	.0002	.0221	.2423	.7576
SOCIAB STR2	0000	.0149	.0149	.1246	.8753
UNSOC STR3	.0033	.0265	.0299	.2638	.7362
PR/CON STR3	.0378	.0039	.0417	.1551	.8449
RES vs. DISM4	.1460	.0693	.2152	.4654	.5345
PR/CON vs. AVM4	.2008	.0242	.2250	.4894	.5106
UNSOC STR6	.0485	.0239	.0724	.3162	.6838
PR/CON STR6	.0004	.0069	.0073	.0729	.9271
RES vs. DISM7	.1681	.0838	.2519	.5970	.4030
PR/CON vs. AVM7	.1902	.0273	.2176	.5777	.4223

Table reports the proportion of the total sums of squares due to each attachment classification grouping, SS REG/SS Total. Unexplained variation is calculated by subtracting variance due to subclassifications from unity.

14

NEW DIRECTIONS FOR ATTACHMENT RESEARCH: DESIGN, MEASUREMENT, AND ANALYSIS

In this section we have presented empirical evidence concerning (1) the validity of Ainsworth's categorical representation of individual differences in Strange Situation behavior (Chapter 12) and (2) recent efforts to develop continuous latent variables underlying individual differences in Strange Situation behavior (Chapter 13). In this chapter, we summarize these findings and then offer recommendations concerning design, measurement, and analytic strategies that might benefit future research. Since the bulk of relevant research is longitudinal in character, we have emphasized means of ameliorating some of the problems that plague longitudinal research designs concerned with topics as complex as the development of attachment relationships.

SUMMARY OF CHAPTERS 12 AND 13

In chapter 12, we employed discriminant and cluster analytic methods to determine how well the A–B–C classification system summarized individual differences in Strange Situation behavior. The predictor variables were scores on the social interactive scales during reunion episodes of the Strange Situation. The subjects came from four samples drawn from three cultures. The discriminant analyses showed that the A–B–C typology cross-validated well across samples and across cultures. These analyses also indicated, however, that the A–B–C groups primarily reflect differences in resistance and avoidance, and did not as strongly reflect differences in contact-maintaining, proximity-seeking, or distance interaction. Cluster analyses, using scores on the same five social interactive scales grouped infants in ways that differed substantially from their A–B–C groupings. Clusters were primarily defined by their position along a proximity/contact-seeking vs. distance interaction dimension, with resistance and avoidance apparently contributing less variance. Since these analyses did not yield clusters composed primarily of infants belonging to the same attachment group (or even subgroup), they suggested the need to explore other ways of representing individual differences in Strange Situation behavior (see also Connell & Goldsmith, 1982).

A promising alternative to the A–B–C classification system involves using the scores in the social interactive scales and other measures taken during the Strange Situation to estimate continuous latent variables representing individual differences in component processes of attachment system functioning. Research based on this "component process" approach to understanding Strange Situation behavior was presented in Chapter 13. Using confirmatory factor analytic methods, J. P. Connell derived continuous dimensions to represent separately emotional and social interactive processes in the Strange Situation. Analyses of several data sets indicated that differences in emotional reactivity to stressful events during the procedure play an important role in explaining patterns of social interactive behavior across episodes within the Strange Situation. Moreover, emotional expression in earlier episodes of the Strange Situation uniquely predicted social interactive behavior in a subsequent episode whereas social interaction in earlier episodes did not uniquely predict emotional behavior later on. These results thus suggest that individual differences in Strange Situation behavior may index not only "security of attachment," but other basic psychological processes as well. In particular, Connell's results suggested that the infant's emotional state plays an important role in providing a base line from which individual differences in social interactive strategies may emerge. Furthermore, Connell argues that antecedent and consequent conditions of those component processes may be profitably examined using this approach.

LONGITUDINAL STUDIES IN ATTACHMENT RESEARCH

In this chapter, the discussion focuses on methodological issues in longitudinal studies of the antecedents, stability, and consequences of individual differences in Strange Situation behavior. In the preceding chapters—specifically those in Sections II and III—we have raised several questions concerning the causal relationships among developmental processes that might underlie the observed relationships between caretaking circumstances, characteristics of the infant–parent attachment, Strange Situation behavior, and the child's later developmental achievements. The

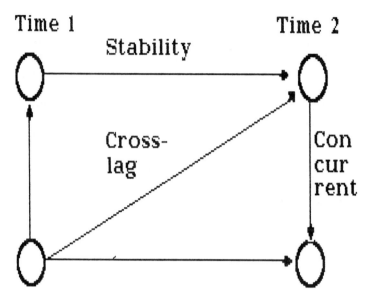

FIG. 14.1   Types of causal relationships.

primary objective of the present discussion is to consider how longitudinal studies should be designed, how measurement systems should be constructed, and how data should be analyzed so as to shed light on the causal relationships underlying these associations. There are several problems with the analysis of variance designs frequently employed in longitudinal studies of Strange Situation behavior and the security of attachment, and these problems lead us to propose that longitudinal panel designs be employed instead. These designs have formidable complexities of their own, however, and we discuss these as well.

Let us begin by illustrating some of these issues. In Figure 14.1, a circle represents a single measurement of single construct. Circles in the same "row" of the graphic are repeated measurements of that construct, while circles in the same "column" are measurements of different constructs in the same time wave.[1] The arrows represent causal relationships between constructs. We also distinguish between three types of causal relationships in longitudinal designs: *stability* arrows depict the influence of a construct in an earlier wave on the same construct in a later wave. *Concurrent* arrows depict the influence of one construct on another construct within the same wave. Finally, *cross-lag* arrows depict the influence of one construct in an earlier wave on a different construct in a later wave.

---

[1]In discussing longitudinal designs, it is customary to refer to each time point at which measurements are collected as a "wave" of measurement.

ANALYSIS OF VARIANCE DESIGNS IN LONGITUDINAL
RESEARCH ON ATTACHMENT

To illustrate the problems involved when ANOVA designs are employed in attachment research, consider studies concerned with the antecedents of Strange Situation behavior. As reviewed in Chapter 5, the data show that some characteristics of early parent–infant interaction have a consistent and predictable relationship to later patterns of Strange Situation behavior. Specifically, mothers whose caretaking styles, personality, and social circumstances are considered desirable by American researchers tend to have babies who later behave in a B-type fashion in the Strange Situation. We concluded, however, that the precise pathways of influence from early parent–infant interaction to later infant behavior cannot at present be discerned. Here we show that this obscurity is in part a result of reliance on ANOVA design strategies.

The relationship between measures of parent–infant interaction and subsequent Strange Situation behavior has often been studied by comparing differences in the mean ratings of sensitivity attained by groups of mothers classified by their infants' later Strange Situation group (e.g., Ainsworth, Bell, & Stayton, 1971). A similar analytic strategy has often been employed in studies relating Strange Situation classifications to other measures of the child's later behavior (e.g., Easterbrooks & Lamb, 1979). Although analysis of variance is actually a statistical method rather than a longitudinal design, reliance on this method seems to have led previous investigators to design their studies to fit the requirements of a one-way ANOVA. This choice is unfortunate for three reasons. First, the analysis of variance approach can lead researchers to over emphasize the results of significance tests, instead of considering the proportion of variance explained by their statistical models. Second, when used to study the antecedents of Strange Situation behavior, analysis of variance designs involve applying retrospective analytic strategies in the context of a prospective design. Third, analysis of variance designs do not allow the assessment of more than one causal relationship (stability, concurrent, or cross-lagged) at a time. They therefore preclude investigation of many important alternative developmental questions.

Significance Tests versus Measures of Explained
Variance

The significance test results frequently reported from analyses of variance indicate whether differences between group means are statistically reliable. They say little about the strength of the relationship between the dependent and independent variables. Measures of the proportion of variance explained would be more informative, particularly in studies reporting very small but statistically significant differences between group means. Such measures are easy to derive even when an analysis of variance design is employed, but unfortunately they are seldom reported.

Inappropriate Retrospective Analyses

The use of analysis of variance procedures when studying the antecedents of infant attachment or Strange Situation behavior forces a retrospective structure onto a prospective design and research hypothesis. For example, when studying the effects of prior parental behavior on infant Strange Situation behavior, the natural roles of independent and dependent variables are reversed: The antecedent variable in the longitudinal design—some measure of parental behavior—becomes the dependent variable in the analysis of variance. The results of the analysis thus present the distribution of scores on the antecedent variable as a function of the infant's subsequent behavior, whereas the hypothesis logically demands information regarding the distribution of scores on measures of the consequent infant behavior as a function of the antecedent parental behavior. There are instances in which the use of retrospective and prospective data-analytic strategies yield much different results from the same data set. Thus this methodological strategy limits our ability to assess and interpret the effects of parental behavior on patterns of parent–infant interaction.

Limitations of ANOVA in Causal Analysis

Most importantly, the analysis of variance design does not allow investigators to contrast alternative hypotheses concerning the causal processes underlying development. The analysis of variance provides information concerning the association between Strange Situation behavior and one putative antecedent or consequent factor. Many different causal processes could explain this association, however. For example, suppose that some investigators measure maternal sensitivity in the context of parent–child interaction at 8 months, and observe the dyads again in the Strange Situation at 12 months. They find that high maternal sensitivity at 8 months predicts B-type behavior at 12 months. All of the following explanations are consistent with this finding.

1. The infant's attachment to the mother is taking shape at 8 months, and the mother's caretaking style has a formative impact on the infant's emerging understanding of the social world. Consequently, this is a sensitive period for social development, during which maternal caretaking style has a

decisive effect on the child's emergent socioemotional style, and this in turn determines the infant's Strange Situation behavior at 12 months. This explanation is depicted in Figure 14.2. Remember that only the constructs in the lower left hand and upper right hand corners are actually measured and included in the analysis.

2. Maternal behavior at 8 months influences only the concurrent behavior of the infant, and has no real effects on later Strange Situation behavior. Similarly, maternal sensitivity at 12 months influences the concurrent behavior of her infant in the Strange Situation. However, maternal sensitivity is a stable individual characteristic, so measures of maternal sensitivity at 8 months predict maternal sensitivity at 12 months, and thus the infant's behavior as well. This explanation is depicted in Figure 14.3.

3. The infant's attachment to the mother emerges at 8 months, and the patterns of behavior tapped by the Strange Situation are determined by endogenous (e.g., temperamental) infantile characteristics. Mothers adapt their behavior to their infants style far more than the reverse, and hence mother's style of interaction with the infant (as assessed at 8 months) is an

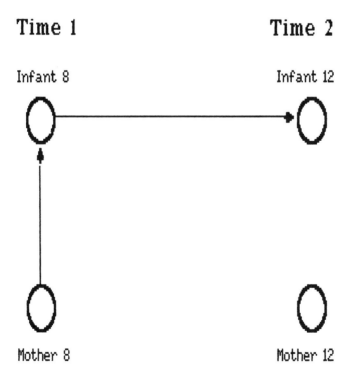

FIG. 14.2   Explanation 1.

Time 1   Time 2

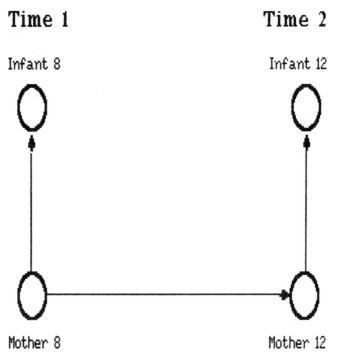

FIG. 14.3   Explanation 2.

effect of rather than a cause of the infant's pattern of attachment behavior. This explanation is depicted in Figure 14.4.

4. The behavior of both mothers and infants is characterized by stability and autonomy, but both are able to adapt their behavioral styles to the demands of the other over the course of the first year. Thus the development of the attachment relationship is a process of convergence and reciprocal determination. This explanation is depicted in Figure 14.5.

The list is not exhaustive, of course. However, all of these explanations, and others like them, are consistent with the demonstration of an association between maternal sensitivity at 8 months and infantile Strange Situation behavior at 12 months in an analysis of variance design. Clearly, reliance on this analytic strategy tells us only about the association between two variables and does not provide any information concerning the causal relationship that might explain the observed correlations. In particular, it is impossible to determine whether antecedent or concurrent maternal behavior influences infant behavior in the Strange Situation, since the concurrent maternal behavior is neither measured nor analyzed. Similarly,

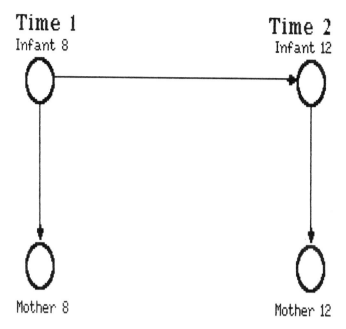

FIG. 14.4   Explanation 3.

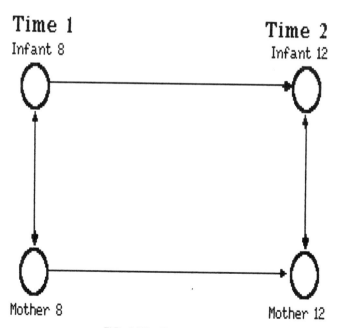

FIG. 14.5   Explanation 4.

it is impossible to assess the direction of effects between mother and infant at either 8 or 12 months. It is easy to see that precisely the same concerns surround the employment of analysis of variance designs in longitudinal studies designed to explore the predictive validity of Strange Situation behavior (see Chapter 9).

Summary

The key issues in longitudinal research on attachment concern the causal processes underlying the stability or instability of Strange Situation behavior, and the nature of its relationship to antecedent and consequent factors. Earlier studies employing analysis of variance designs have made substantial contributions by making the associations or correlations apparent. Analysis of variance designs cannot, however, shed further light on causal relationships involved in the development of individual differences in attachment relationships, and should be replaced in future research by analytic procedures and research designs that allow the exploration of causal relationships.

PANEL MODEL DESIGNS

In order to explore the causal relationships between Strange Situation behavior and its antecedents and consequences, it is better to employ longitudinal panel designs (in which each of the constructs is measured in each wave) rather than analysis of variance designs.[2]

In Figure 14.1, we depicted a two-variable, two-wave longitudinal panel design for studying the relationship between maternal sensitivity and patterns of infantile attachment. For simplicity of exposition, the model depicted includes only two waves, but for many purposes more frequent measurements would be desirable.

In the figure, each variable that is the target of an arrow is regressed on the variables with arrows pointing toward it. An attempt must then be made to "fit" the resulting system of regression equations to the data in order to test the adequacy of hypothetical patterns of causal relationships. The object is to write a system of regression equations that parsimoniously

---

[2]Longitudinal panel research has been discussed more extensively by Duncan (1969, 1972), Jordan (1978), Rogosa (1979), and particularly Kessler and Greenberg (1981), and was recently applied by Aneshensel and Huba (1983). Readers are referred to these sources for further details. It should be clear that in discussing regression approaches to panel analysis, we are not advocating the use of cross-lag correlational analysis. The problems with this technique are discussed by the investigators cited earlier.

accounts for the variation and covariation of the variables in a theoretically meaningful way. However, longitudinal panel models will not necessarily elucidate the causal relations underlying the development of attachments unless researchers pay careful attention to several considerations: (1) the variables should ideally measure all the potential causal influences, (2) each construct should be adequately measured, and (3) if a hypothesis testing study is planned, the investigator must ensure that the regression structure to be tested constitutes an identified model. These points are elaborated below.

All Causally Relevant Constructs Should Be Measured

In any non-experimental study, researchers must strive to avoid misinterpreting patterns of association between variables that result from their common dependence upon other variables that have been omitted from the

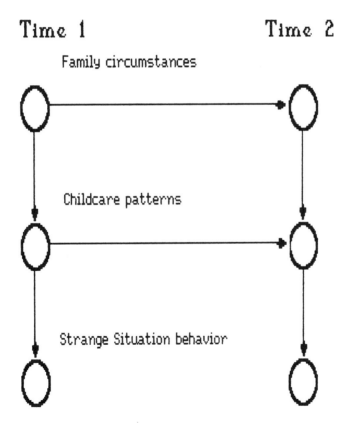

FIG. 14.6 Three-variable, two-wave panel design.

study. As we have suggested earlier in this book, individual differences in Strange Situation behavior are a complex product of many interdependent influences, including: endogenous characteristics of the infant, the history of parent–infant interaction, the family system, and its sociocultural context. As we suggested in Chapters 5, 8, and 9, studies of the antecedents, consequences, or stability of Strange Situation behavior that failed to include potentially important causal influences may have led to an oversimplified view of the continuities or correlations between aspects of the infant's early experience and its later social development. The problem of unmeasured constructs is particularly acute in longitudinal studies employing the analysis of variance design in which only one variable is included in each wave of measurement.

In Chapter 8, for example, our review of research on the stability of Strange Situation behavior during the second year of life suggested that the infant's behavior may be affected by the quality of concurrent patterns of parent–child interaction, which may in turn be affected by changes in family circumstances that influence the patterns of childcare. These patterns of influence are depicted in Figure 14.6. This interpretation suggests that stability in measures of Strange Situation behavior is most likely to occur when there are stable life circumstances and stable patterns of parent–child interaction. However, while there have been longitudinal studies in which Strange Situation behavior and family circumstances have been measured concurrently (e.g., Thompson et al., 1982), the presumed mediating variable (quality of parent–child interaction) has always been omitted. Thus this interpretation has yet to be confirmed empirically.

Each Construct Must Be Adequately Measured

The size of a regression coefficient between two variables reflects not only the strength of the association between the constructs being measured, but also the proportions of measurement error in each measure. Thus the quality of measurement of each construct in each wave of the study affects the assessment of causal relationships between them.

Naturally, assessment of "security of attachment" is of particular concern in this area. A persistent theme of this book has been the need to distinguish between "individual differences in security of attachment" and "individual differences in Strange Situation behavior." The former are the real values attributable to individuals on a hypothetical underlying construct, the latter are data that may reflect not only security of attachment but other influences as well. Many investigators appear to believe that individual differences in Strange Situation behavior are direct measures of the security of infantile attachment, but unfortunately, data based on a single Strange Situation assessment are also influenced by factors (artifacts) that have little known or direct relation to the security of attachment. For example, the infant's behavior may be affected by the idiosyncratic behavior of the stranger or mother, the state of the infant on the day of the observation, experiences prior to the observation, and the reaction of the infant to a particular unfamiliar context. All these factors degrade the quality of assessment to a currently unknown extent, because even if the differences are related in some indirect way to the security of attachment, this relationship cannot be recognized or taken into account unless the effects of these artifacts are explicitly measured.

There is no mystery involved in getting better, more generalizable measurements: One must devise measurement systems that generate scores based upon more information. Latent variables can then be used to concentrate information from several measurements of a construct into a single score. The latent variable measuring a construct will be free of artifacts due to a single context, occasion, and measurement procedure to the extent that its indicators span multiple contexts, occasions, and procedures.

Such strategies will not, of course, ensure that security of attachment is perfectly assessed, because there are a number of factors other than sources of error that might be sources of unexplained variance. The most important of these likely include aspects of temperament (see Chapter 6), cultural differences in experiential histories (see Chapter 11), as well as family circumstances and caretaking arrangements (see Chapters 8 and 9). These factors must also be measured carefully in order to increase the proportion of variance in infant behavior that can be explained.

Hypothesis Testing Studies Must Be Designed to Produce Identified Regression Structures

Testing hypotheses in panel studies is not simply a matter of drawing arrows and computing regression coefficients. To successfully fit a system of equations to a set of data, there must be enough information in the data set to determine a single set of values for the coefficients of the regression equation. This is of particular concern when coefficients among latent variables must be estimated. If there is sufficient information in the data set to yield a single set of values for all coefficients, the model is *identified*; but if more than one set of values is consistent with the data, then the model is *unidentified* (Duncan, 1972; Dupacova & Wold, 1982; Fisher, 1966; Jordan, 1978). Unfortunately, many of the hypotheses that are of interest in the study of developmental processes may remain unidentified using panel models. In particular, a panel model involving all possible stability, cross-lagged, and concurrent causal paths will be unidentified (Jordan, 1978), as it requires the estimation of too many unknown coefficients relative to the information available from the data. Even in panel designs with relatively few coefficients, however, there may be too little information in the data to specify a single value for a particular coefficient.

To identify a model based on panel data, some paths must be excluded from estimation in the model by fixing the values of their regression coefficients (most frequently by fixing them to zero). Setting a coefficient to zero eliminates a causal path from the model. The restrictions on the coefficients must be chosen so that all ambiguities entailed in estimating causal paths from data are eliminated. If the coefficients that are fixed are correctly chosen, the remaining subset of coefficients will be identified and can be unambiguously estimated from the data.[3] Unfortunately, several different subsets of coefficients, representing substantively different causal models, may produce identified models and be equally consistent with the data set. For example, Figures 14.7a and 14.7b represent alternative systems of regressions that could be fitted to a two-wave, two-variable longitudinal data set. In these models, the circled variables have been labeled eta_1 through eta_4. As in the earlier figures, eta_1 and eta_3 might be aspects of infant behavior, while eta_2 and eta_4 could be aspects of maternal behavior. Assume that these eta variables represent latent variables, from which errors of measurement have been removed to some degree. The causal paths represent weights in regression equations: The beta is the weight for the variable at the tail of the arrow in the equation involved in predicting the variable at the arrow's head. Finally, the psi weights represent the variances and covariances of the unobserved disturbances affecting the latent variables. Psi_1 and psi_2 are the simple variances of eta_1 and eta_2, while psi_3 and psi_4 are the residual variances for eta_3 and eta_4. Psi weights with double subscripts represent covariances between the disturbances—as would result, for example, if a third variable affecting both latent variables was omitted from the design. Both Figures 14.7a and 14.7b represent regression systems with 10 terms to estimate: four latent variable disturbance variances, a disturbance covariance, and five regression weights in 14.7a; four variances, two covariances, and four regression weights in 14.7b. Both systems are "just identified," meaning that every coefficient can be estimated, but no others can be. For example, if we augmented the system in Figure 14.7a with a $psi_{3,4}$ coefficient representing a covariance between the disturbances affecting eta_3 and eta_4, the model would no longer be identified.

It can be seen that neither model includes every causal influence that could be operating. For example, neither model includes a cross-lag

---

[3]The identification of structural equation models is a complex and apparently not completely resolved topic. For discussions relevant to longitudinal panel models, see Jordan (1978) and Kessler and Greenberg (1981).

Time 1   Time 2

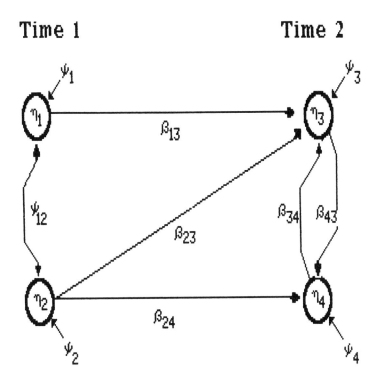

FIG. 14.7a Just identified model with one cross-lag and two concurrent paths.

influence of early infantile behavior on later maternal behavior. The system
in Figure 14.7b implies that there is a contemporaneous influence of infants
on mothers at time 2, but no contemporaneous influence of mothers on
infants. Figure 14.7a has a bidirectional influences at time 2, but it does not
allow for covariances between the unmeasured disturbances effecting eta_3
and eta_4. This means that all the influences of mother on baby (and
vice-versa) that affect the etas are also measured by the etas. In each case,
these models leave out pathways of influence that may be required by the
theory that the researcher would like to test. Moreover, coefficients cannot
be fixed in a model simply for analytical convenience—a coefficient
representing a potential causal relationship should not be excluded from
estimation if the influence it represents may be present in the data. Finally,
as if to add insult to injury, statistical tests will not determine which of the
models (14.7a or 14.7b) best fits the data. These models can only be
compared with even more restricted "nested" models: that is, regression
systems including a proper subset of the coefficients in the less restricted
model.

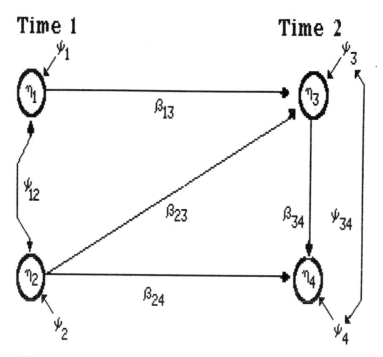

FIG. 14.7b   Just identified model with one cross-lag and one concurrent path.

It is apparent that there are no guarantees that every causal hypothesis will prove to be testable. Thus it is important to carefully examine the regression systems representing the theoretical models of interest during the design phase of the study. It may be possible to design the study so that the researcher can later impose a scheme of restrictions sufficient to identify the desired model. As Kessler and Greenberg (1981) show, it may also be possible to improve the identifiability of the model by increasing the number of waves of measurement, or by carefully choosing the constructs to be measured.

Summary

Longitudinal panel designs have the potential to make major contributions to attachment research, particularly when they are analyzed using a system of regression equations on latent variables. However, these designs require careful planning to ensure that all components of the causal system are measured. Moreover, each construct should be measured in such a way that the scores are highly generalizable and contribute to an accurate estimation of the causal relations in the system. Latent variables concentrating information from multiple occasions, contexts, and procedures are particularly appropriate for this purpose. Questions remain, however, concerning the longitudinal designs most appropriate for testing complex developmental processes involving stability, concurrent, and cross-lagged relationships between constructs. An appreciation of the measurement and design challenges and pitfalls in longitudinal studies of attachment leads us once again to urge caution in interpreting the existing, highly limited evidence.

ANALYTICAL METHODS

We have focused this discussion on the design and measurement requirements for causally interpretable longitudinal studies, without specifying methods of analysis. This reflects our conviction that design and measurement are the most important issues, since analytical methods in themselves add nothing to the causally relevant information present in the data. Any successful attempt to model the system of causal relations underlying the development of attachment also imposes requirements on methods of analysis, however. For example, when one intends to model a complex system, it is inappropriate to divide the analysis into a host of subanalyses, each encompassing only a few of its parts. At some point in the modeling process, all causally linked components need to be analyzed together. Similarly, if latent variables are used to distinguish real from spurious components of variance in the data, then it is necessary to employ an analytic method that can accomodate them. Several methods can be used to analyze regressions involving latent variables, and the choice among them must be made carefully.

The most widely known program for analyzing regression equations relating latent variables is LISREL (Joreskog, 1979; Joreskog & Sorbom, 1977). LISREL provides maximum likelihood estimates of the coefficients that indicate the dependence of the measured variables on the underlying latent variables (for discussions of structural equation models, see Browne, 1982, and McArdle, in press). The maximum likelihood function used in the estimation procedure also provides a goodness of fit statistic, which is distributed according to the chi-square distribution when the data can be assumed to be multivariately normal. These features make LISREL attractive for many investigations, but for several reasons it should not be an automatic choice for longitudinal studies of attachment.

First, since LISREL assumes that the latent variables are continuously distributed, it is inappropriate for models in which one or more constructs are believed to be categorical. Although LISREL can analyze categorical variables, this usage is sensible only when these data are viewed as indicators of underlying continuous latent variables. Thus it is not useful for data sets including the traditional A–B–C classifications in which the underlying construct (security of attachment) is assumed to be categorical. This difficulty can be negotiated in several ways. For example, the A–B–C classification can be discarded, with individual differences in Strange Situation behavior represented instead as continuous latent variables, as suggested by J. P. Connell in Chapter 13. Researchers could then use the LISREL methodology. Alternatively, researchers wishing to retain the typological data could explore recent work on the use of structural equation models in studies involving both categorical and continous data (Muthen, 1983, 1984). Muthen's method, however, assumes that the categorical variables are ordinal and represent the partitioning of underlying continua: This is not true of the purely nominal A–B–C typology. Muthen's method would therefore require modification of the current classification system, perhaps by collapsing it to a secure/insecure dichotomy. When all the "observed" variables and latent variables in the data set are categorical, researchers may wish to investigate the latent variable models for categorical data presented, for example, by Clogg (1981) and Mooijaart (1982).

A second possible objection to LISREL concerns the nature of the maximum likelihood estimation. Some analysts (e.g., Bookstein, 1982) feel that unless the underlying distributional and structural assumptions of the model are closely met, LISREL is likely to be "super-optimal," in that it explains too much variance in a given system, making the model conform to the idiosyncracies of a given sample, instead of being broadly generalizable. This should be of special concern in longitudinal studies, with detailed observational data, in which large samples are often hard to obtain. LISREL estimates can also be unstable when small samples are employed. In a Monte Carlo study of comparatively simple factor analysis problems, Boomsma (1982) reported that LISREL analyses of samples smaller than 100 are prone to estimation problems such as negative variances, failure to converge, and that they may thus yield misleading conclusions.

Finally, LISREL may be sensitive to deviations from the assumption of multivariate normality: Unlike standard univariate linear models, the test statistics in LISREL do *not* appear to be robust with respect to major deviations from normality (Joreskog & Sorbom, 1981).

An alternative procedure for analyzing regressions involving latent variables while being less vulnerable to these problems is Partial Least Squares analysis (PLS; see Bookstein, 1982, Lohmoller, 1984; and Wold, 1982). PLS makes no assumptions concerning the distribution of the data (and does not, therefore, provide an ordinary significance or goodness-of-fit test). Moreover, it does not attempt to maximize the fit of the model to an individual sample of data, and may therefore result in a more robust, generalizable model. Finally, PLS is based on an interative series of least squares regressions, and though it results in a model of a complete system, it does not attempt to analyze the entire system simultaneously at any point in the estimation process. As a result, PLS avoids the identification problems implicit in maximum likelihood methods. Less attractively, PLS does not compute standard errors for its coefficients. Models are evaluated by a cross-validation test procedure that is even more unfamiliar to social scientists than the goodness-of-fit procedure in LISREL. Finally, compared with LISREL, PLS does not provide the researcher with as rich an armory of methods for specifying causal models. In particular, since no distributional assumptions are made, it is impossible to place restrictions on the covariances among residual components in the model. This limitation can be viewed as either restritive or realistic, depending on the analysts' confidence in their theories and data. Nevertheless, PLS is a methodology worthy of closer investigation by attachment researchers.

Summary

For several years, multivariate regression analyses using latent variables have been termed LISREL analyses and we can expect these methods to be widely used in the coming years. Although LISREL is a powerful and important tool, it has limitations as well. In particular, LISREL implies stringent assumptions concerning the distribution of the data (continuous and multivariately normal), and it requires large samples. Researchers would do well to investigate a rapidly developing set of alternatives to LISREL, including methods for the analysis of categorical "observed" and latent variables and Partial Least Squares methods.

Our discussion has focused on one use of latent variable models in the study of attachment—longitudinal panel models—but there our many other possible uses for latent variable models.

For example, factor models can be estimated simultaneously in several groups, with the coefficients representing the structure of the latent variables being either constrained to be equal or allowed to vary across groups (Joreskog, 1971). By examining whether there is a substantial improvement in fit when the constraints forcing the equality of coefficients across groups are relaxed, the analyst can ascertain whether or not a given factor model is valid in more than one population.

Such multiple group factor analytic methods may be particularly useful in cross-cultural studies of infant attachment. They could help determine whether similar clusters of behaviors—say, several ratings of emotional expression serving as indicators of a 'reactivity' construct—fulfill similar expressive and social-interactional functions in different cultures. Assuming that a similar latent variable structure can be found in two or more samples from different cultures, the analyst can proceed to the next step of estimating group means on the latent variables (Sorbom, 1974). Supposing that a given cluster of behaviors does serve a similar function in several cultures, this analysis asks whether they are employed at different levels of intensity or frequency—for example, are infants in one culture more emotionally reactive than those of another?

Factor structure and factor means may change across time as well as across groups. As infants gain new communicative skills and new understanding of the social world, the specific behaviors used in emotional expression and social interaction change rapidly. There is little reason to suppose that the same behaviors will serve similar functions in the attachment system at different periods of development, and it is also important to study how the behaviors relevant to components of the attachment system change as infants develop. Thus researchers may wish to investigate methods for modeling developmental changes in the structure and level of latent variables (see, for example Baltes & Nesselroade, 1970; Emmerich, 1968; Nesselroade, 1970).

SUMMARY

The developmental processes linking early experience, attachment behavior, and later social and cognitive developmental outcomes comprise a complex system of interdependent variables spanning many contexts. As our discussion indicates, the design and measurement requirements of any study hoping to capture the system will be of comparable complexity. Attachment researchers have often measured different constructs on different occasions, providing little opportunity to explore alternative hypotheses concerning developmental processes. The analysis of variance designs that have been used in the past do not provide sufficient information to formulate and test statistically any causal hypotheses concerning the development of attachment.

As a multivariate and primarily longitudinal research domain, research on the development of attachment must take advantage of recent developments in multivariate methodology. We have suggested in these chapters that panel designs and latent variable measurements can open many important questions for research, although use of these stategies requires researchers to develop new measurement techniques for assessing attachment (or its age-appropriate equivalent) at multiple stages of development. Moreover, we need multiple cross-contextual measures to provide convergent evidence concerning attachment. At the same time, substantial problems must be resolved concerning the optimal design and analysis of panel models. Methodological research is needed to determine whether some designs might allow researchers to test identified systems of regression equations modeling hypotheses concerning combinations of concurrent, cross-lagged, and stability relations. More information is also needed on the merits of alternative analytical schemes, such as the LISREL and PLS modeling procedures for analyzing systems of regressions involving latent variables.

VI FUTURE DIRECTIONS

15

FUTURE DIRECTIONS FOR RESEARCH ON STRANGE SITUATION BEHAVIOR

INTRODUCTION

We have attempted in this book to provide a succinct but thorough review of available evidence concerning the origins and implications of individual difference in patterns of attachment behavior in the Strange Situation. This exercise has left us with a clearer sense of the research landscape than we had before; an awareness of what we know, what we do not know, and what issues seem crucially important as we (as a subdiscipline) plan future research endeavors. In the three sections of this brief closing chapter, we aim to gather together the strands developed in the preceding chapters. In the first, we summarize the major conclusions emerging from our review of the literature to date. Second, we address key issues arising from our integration that seem to represent crucially important interpretive lacunae. Finally, we identify some promising and important areas for future empirical research.

SUMMARY OF THE EVIDENCE

After reviewing the literature, we find that the strong claims regarding the antecedents, interpretation, temporal stability, and predictive validity of Strange Situation behavior are only partly supported by the empirical and theoretical literature. In almost every case, we have found it necessary not only to qualify but also to restate more conservatively the relevant hypotheses or conclusions earlier posed or reached by proponents of the Strange Situation procedure.

271

The evidence regarding the antecedents of Strange Situation behavior falls farthest short of the popular claims. In fact, we found no consistent evidence that *particular* variations in parental behavior within the normal range are systematically associated with specific patterns of Strange Situation behavior, although the results of several studies all suggest that more socially desirable maternal behavior is associated with B group infant behavior in the Strange Situation. The lack of consistency from study to study and from assessment to assessment precludes insight into the *specific* patterns of maternal behavior that are of formative significance with respect to *specific* patterns of child behavior and socioemotional development, however. Thus we do not obtain much insight into the particular processes determining how maternal behavior influences the child's socioemotional functioning.

Further evidence that parental behavior does in some way affect Strange Situation behavior comes from studies showing that changes in family circumstances and caretaking arrangements can produce changes in patterns of Strange Situation behavior. There is also some evidence that extremely deviant patterns of childrearing, such as neglectful and abusive parental behavior, are associated with increases in the probability of "insecure" or non-B group attachment behavior. On the other hand, so too are cultural variations in rearing practices, which suggests that there may be multiple possible antecedents of distinct patterns of Strange Situation behavior. Evidence concerning temperamental influences, although very weak, also contributes to an overall conclusion that there are multiple pathways to A, B, and C patterns of Strange Situation behavior. In addition, if mothers behave consistently over time (as some researchers have found), one needs to ask whether antecedent or concurrent patterns of parental behavior underlie Strange Situation behavior.

Clearly, we need more and better research if we are to say anything specific about the antecedents of Strange Situation behavior. Most conspicuously lacking is evidence concerning the differential origins and sequelae of the two "insecure" patterns of Strange Situation behavior—the avoidant and resistant patterns—or compelling arguments why such manifestly different patterns of behavior should *not* have different antecedents and different implications. Relevant findings, like those of Ainsworth (in the Baltimore Longitudinal Study) and Belsky (in the Pennsylvania Infant and Family Development Project), clearly deserve attempts at replication, using clearly-defined hypotheses and specific measures.

That Strange Situation behavior may be meaningful, and thus worthy of interpretation, is suggested by the results of studies focused on the stability and predictive validity of Strange Situation behavior. These studies show that Strange Situation classifications *can*, in some circumstances, be extremely stable over time, and when stable, are often correlated with aspects of later child behavior. However, when family circumstances and caretaking arrangements change, so too (in at least some cases) do the patterns of Strange Situation behavior. These findings have at least four implications. First, they suggest that Strange Situation behavior can indeed be affected by patterns of infant–parent interaction, even if the specific dimensions of importance remain unidentified. Second, they mean that the Strange Situation may tap the *current* status of the infant–parent relationship, not necessarily some characteristic of interaction during an early formative period. Third, they imply that there is a great deal of flexibility in attachment system functioning. Fourth, they suggest that predictions of later behavior are likely to be successful only when there is continuity in the family circumstances and caretaking arrangements that maintain specific patterns of child behavior, or when something is known of the conditions in which the child has lived between the time of the Strange Situation and the time of the later assessment. Predictive validity has most often been studied, and has only been demonstrated with any real success, in cases where such stability could either be assumed, was actually ensured by sample selection procedures, and/or when the same adult participated with the child in early and follow-up assessments. As a result, the term "predictive validity" is not wholly appropriate; the later behavior may be determined, not only by earlier patterns of attachment, but also by current patterns of parent–child interaction. Because these patterns are stable over time, they are also associated with specific prior patterns of Strange Situation behavior. Indeed, there is now some suggestive evidence that early experiences (to the extent that their effects are tapped by the Strange Situation) may *interact* with later experiences to determine the child's subsequent performance. More detailed interpretation is precluded by the fact that researchers have yet to determine how and which patterns of parent–infant interaction relate to later child characteristics. In addition, as we noted in the preceding chapter, studies have not been designed and/or analyzed in a sufficiently sophisticated manner to permit tests of alternative causal models. Finally, the *specific* factors underlying changes in attachment status remain largely unidentified, partly because researchers have focused their attention on family events per se rather than their psychological significance for mother and infant.

Nevertheless, knowledge of Strange Situation behavior, knowledge of continuity or discontinuity in family/caretaking circumstances, and information about intervening events in the child's life taken together do allow us to explain some of the variance in later child behavior. What we now need are findings that improve our ability to interpret Strange Situation behavior. This demands not only hypothesis-driven studies focused on the antecedents and consequences of Strange Situation behavior, but also a reconceptualization of the Strange Situation procedure and the construct of attachment security. Our review suggests several potentially valuable new directions, and these are discussed later in this chapter.

In undertaking this reconceptualization, however, we need to discard the notion that one pattern of Strange Situation behavior is evolutionarily adaptive while others are maladaptive. In the view of most contemporary behavioral biologists, fixed action patterns and predetermined behavior patterns are likely to be much less significant than access to a flexible array of behavioral strategies chosen depending on environmental and physiological constraints so as to maximize inclusive fitness. Evolutionary biology thus demands an evaluation not only of biologically-influenced predispositions but also of the contingencies provided by the specific environments or 'niches' in which individuals might manifest these predispositions. Without a careful analysis of the fit between behavior patterns and niches, it is impossible to determine which patterns might be adaptive and which not.

At this point, it is doubtful whether we have either the data or the theoretical sophistication needed to determine the adaptive significance of variations in human ecology. Thus confident statements about the global adaptive significance of patterns of attachment behavior are, at present, unwarranted. This conclusion, incidentally, also has implications for research on the sequelae of patterns of Strange Situation behavior, since it indicates that the B-pattern may not render these infants "better adapted" in a global sense for any and all developmental tasks. Furthermore, it is unlikely that ultimate explanations derived from speculations about behavior that would have been adaptive in "the environment of evolutionary adaptedness" will ever be sufficient in themselves to explain the patterns of behavior one sees in the Strange Situation.

Unfortunately, theorists have mistakenly assumed that because ethological theory permitted a profound conceptual breakthrough in the understanding of normative patterns of behavior, the principles of evolutionary biology considered in isolation are likely to provide equivalent insight into the origins of individual differences in infant development. Attachment theory took a great stride forward when John Bowlby synthesized ideas from ethology, psychoanalysis, and cybernetics. This encourages us to hope that new insights can be gained if we once again undertake the daunting task of synthesizing contemporary evolutionary and psychological theory. In evolutionary theory, at least, there are important theoretical resources that developmentalists have yet to mine: for example, life-span evolutionary theory (Stearns, 1976, 1977) or parent–offspring conflict theory (Parker & MacNair, 1979). Patience will be critical: Even if interesting hypotheses are developed, it may be a long time before feasible empirical tests can be devised. To date, behavioral biology has not advanced our understanding of individual differences in infant attachment not because it has failed, but because it has yet to be applied appropriately.

KEY ISSUES

Index vs. Construct

Perhaps the most important issue in this review pertains to the distinction between Strange Situation behavior and security of attachment, or stated differently, the distinction between the index and the construct.

On the one hand, there is suggestive (and consistent) evidence that the quality of parent–child interaction is related to Strange Situation behavior in a reliable fashion, with more desirable patterns of parental behavior being associated with B group patterns of Strange Situation behavior. Thus B-type behavior can be said to index more harmonious parent–child relationships, and thus might be deemed indicative of "secure" infant–adult attachment.

On the other hand, variations in the patterns of parent–child interaction only account for a small portion of the variance in Strange Situation behavior, and they do not coherently and consistently predict variations in Strange Situation behavior. Most important in this regard is the fact that the different antecedents of A and C group patterns remain largely unexplained. Also, it is becoming clear that factors other than the quality of parent–child interaction may affect Strange Situation behavior: Independence training in North Germany, unfamiliarity with strangers in Israeli kibbutz-reared children, and unfamiliarity even with brief separations among Japanese infants reflect the influence of cultural variations in normative early experiences. Further, detailed codings of emotional reactions in the Strange Situation consistently demonstrate that these account for variation in Strange Situation behavior not tapped by the attachment classifications. In addition, the impact on Strange Situation behavior of endogenous infant characteristics like temperament, father involvement, the quality of the marital relationship, and family conditions related to stress and social support are all suggested by the available findings.

These factors remind us that the Strange Situation was designed to observe individual differences in infant response to moderately escalating amounts of stress. For this procedure to be valid, however, the infants being compared must experience similar degrees of distress. If they do not, it becomes impossible to say whether the behavioral variations observed are attributable to variations in the intensity of the distress experienced or to variations in the quality of the infant–parent relationship. In such circumstances, furthermore, it does little good to note that variations in the quality of the relationship may explain differences in the intensity and quality of the distress experienced in the Strange Situation; they *may* indeed (see, however, Thompson & Lamb, 1984a), but other factors may do so also. This is a crucial point, we believe, for it renders dangerous any attempts to infer the quality of a relationship, particularly in divergent social and cultural contexts, from variations in Strange Situation behavior alone. Researchers might do well to explore the validity of Strange Situation measures based on procedures individually calibrated to equate the intensity of the distress (say, by prolonging or shortening separations until the infant exhibits 30 seconds of continuous crying, or by varying the intrusiveness of the stranger).

Because of the common tendency to consider the index (Strange Situation classifications) and construct (security of attachment) to be isomorphic, it is often forgotten that there may be many roads to A-ness, B-ness, or C-ness. Variations in parental behavior may explain the classification of some children, but congenital characteristics (e.g., Down Syndrome; see Thompson, Cicchetti, Lamb, & Malkin, 1985), variations in other aspects of early history (e.g., familiarity with strangers or separations [see Chapter 11]), and perhaps aspects of temperament (see Chapter 6) may be more important in other cases. Simply because two infants behave similarly in the Strange Situation, we cannot assume that there have been similarities in their experiences with their parents, nor that there will be similarities in their subsequent developmental trajectories.

Measurement Issues

Like the other points made in this section, the clear implication is that the Strange Situation cannot and should not be used as a sole indicator of the quality of parent–child relations. However, the traditional research strategy, dubbed the "hourglass" design by Connell and Goldsmith (1982), examines the correlates of Strange Situation behavior through relationships with a set of antecedent measures and a set of predicted outcome measures. Because the Strange Situation classifications are the only measures at the fulcrum of this associative network, the research is always limited. What is needed are multiple measures that are taken together to yield a new composite index of quality of infant–adult attachment that gains reliability and validity by avoiding exclusive reliance on behavior observed in one context on one occasion. The availability of such a powerful measure of the quality of parent–child relationships would not only enhance our ability to specify antecedents and consequences, but would obviously be of clinical utility as well.

As mentioned earlier in the book, one reason for the small proportion of variance in either antecedent or consequent measures accounted for by

Strange Situation behavioral classifications may well be the reliance upon a categorical scoring system. Even with the recently developed practice of labeling some children "unclassifiable," the use of a threefold categorical system inevitably results in a situation in which some infants are good and others poor exemplars of a category. The inclusion of such heterogenous groups within any category almost certainly reduces the validity of the categories, and reduces the amount of variance likely to be explained when one seeks external correlates. One could explore the antecedents and consequences of the categories by including only prototypical exemplars in research, but that would necessarily limit generalizability and might result in elimination from consideration of a great deal of the variability which researchers should seek to explain. Simply increasing the number of classification categories also would not alleviate many of these problems. Continuous multiaspect, multimeasure, multisituation composite variables would, we submit, provide more robust, more reliable, and more valid indices of the quality of parent–child relationships than would the existing unidimensional classification system. Among the situations one would want to sample are: naturalistic observations; encounters with strange adults in the presence and absence of attachment figures; reactions to separations from and reunions with attachment figures in the presence and absence of other attachment figures and in the presence and absence of other potential stressors; introductions to novel toys and environments; introductions to unfamiliar animals (such as dogs) in the presence and absence of attachment figures; and behavior in relation to attachment and non-attachment figures in a variety of caretaking contexts such as feeding, play, and soothing. Some of the data-analytic procedures discussed in the previous chapter could subsequently be used to identify consistent dimensions of parent–child interaction across these situations.

Conceptualization of Development

Another major issue, alluded to earlier, has to do with conceptualization of early experience effects. Developmental psychologists have a long history of seeking simple answers to this question, striving to show that early experiences are either all-important or quite unimportant. The truth, we suspect, lies somewhere between these two extremes, and there is a growing body of evidence, gathered using the Strange Situation procedure, that underscores this conclusion. Interestingly, a similar conclusion is suggested by experimental research with animals, where we find the traditional conceptualization in terms of "critical periods" yielding to a more dynamic and fluid view of developmental processes (Denenberg, 1979, 1982). Early experiences do have an impact, it seems, but it is an impact that can be ameliorated or exacerbated by subsequent experiences. Further, the earlier and later sources of influence work together in a multiplicative or interactive rather than additive fashion.

The research reviewed in Section IV provides ample support for this conclusion. To the extent that Strange Situation classifications capture variation in the quality of parent–child relationships, we saw that the ability to predict future behavior was only robust when there was likely to be stability in the quality of parent–child relations. Predictions were weaker or nonsignificant when the quality of parent–child relationships was likely to change. Unfortunately, researchers have yet to undertake the types of studies needed to specify how much of the variance in any given outcome measure is accounted for by measures of *early* parent–child interaction, and how much by the *current* status of the relationship. We might expect that the early quality of the relationship helps shape the later quality and that, in relation to at least some outcomes, experiences during an earlier formative period may have specific and direct impact on the later outcome. There is no reason to expect, however, that the effects of early experiences will be equally strong or equivalently mediated with respect to different outcomes; so we need careful conceptualization of developmental processes before longitudinal studies are undertaken. Indeed, if variations in the quality of attachment—particularly those tapped by the existing classification system—represent juvenile adaptations or strategies adopted by individuals to get through infancy and early childhood successfully, they may have no predictive validity whatsoever. This is, therefore, one area in which the formulations of evolutionary biology may be germane.

In their efforts to specify the formative effects of early experiences, attachment researchers have been developmental in orientation. In another respect, however, research in this area has been surprisingly non-developmental in nature. Despite descriptions by Bowlby (1969) and Marvin (1977) of a fourth stage in attachment development (i.e., "goal-corrected partnership"), attachment researchers have made little effort to identify the ways in which child–parent relationships develop and change beyond the first year. Part of the difficulty lies in researchers' reliance on the Strange Situation procedure, the validity of which has been shown for infants within the 10- to 24-month-age-range. Even within this limited period, however, we do not know whether infant behaviors in the Strange Situation have the same meaning at different ages, and despite the number of researchers who have observed infants more than once in the Strange Situation, none have looked closely at such developmental changes. Beyond 24 months, it is likely that the growth of the behavioral repertoire accompanied by the emergence of verbal-mediational and elementary role-taking skills (and thus the ability to apprehend others' subjective states) bring about significant changes in the nature of parent–child interaction and the kinds of "working models" underlying children's conceptions of their parents. In the future, researchers should devote considerably more attention to the nature of developmental changes in attachment relationships, extending their efforts into the toddler and preschool years.

DIRECTIONS FOR FUTURE RESEARCH

The Strange Situation was developed more than two decades ago and in the last decade has become the most important technique employed in research on early socioemotional development. In this book, we have strived both to determine whether research using the Strange Situation has answered the questions that motivated it, and to stimulate further research in this area. We can identify several directions for future research on early attachment relationships.

Conceptualization of Attachment

Perhaps the broadest question worthy of further investigation concerns the basic conceptualization of attachment as articulated by Bowlby (1969). We have throughout this volume accepted Bowlby's assumptions regarding the protective, adaptive value of attachment behavior and we believe this view to be the most coherent and powerful explanatory framework currently available. As a result, we have not questioned the assumptions underlying development of the Strange Situation assessment procedure, most importantly, the notion that stress or fear functions to activate the attachment behavior system, and thus makes apparent individual differences in the functioning of the attachment system. It is possible, however, that individual differences in other aspects of the attachment relationship would be revealed if one focused on affective sharing and socioemotional interaction in more positively-valenced contexts. This underscores the need to observe dyadic functioning in a variety of contexts.

Longitudinal Studies of Parental Behavior, Parent–Child Attachment, and Child Development

In our review, we identified alternative hypotheses concerning the causal paths governing the associations between early Strange Situation behavior and later childhood behavior. On the one hand, the remarkable effectiveness of the Strange Situation in predicting later behavior (relative to any other measures yet developed) could occur because it taps the quality of parent–infant interaction at a sensitive formative period. On the other hand, the continuity between Strange Situation behavior and later child behavior could occur because both are correlated with contemporaneous patterns of parent–infant interaction, and it is the continuity of parental caregiving that explains the prediction. A third, probably more realistic, hypothesis is that early experiences, like constitutional differences, may have direct long-term effects, may shape the child's reactions to subsequent experiences, and may also influence the types of experiences he or she encounters. In this way, early experiences interact with later experiences to shape behavior. The challenge is to specify these interactions more systematically and to conduct hypothesis-testing studies.

Unfortunately, longitudinal investigations using the Strange Situation are rarely designed to compare the merits of rival hypotheses. To contrast the rival hypotheses outlined above we need contemporaneously to assess parental behavior, the quality of parent–infant interaction, Strange Situation behavior, and child behavior on two or more occasions. Moreover, since such longitudinal studies are quasi-experiments rather than true experiments, they must employ measurement systems carefully designed for use in structural regression statistical analyses, LISREL, log-linear analyses, or partial least squares analyses to ensure that alternative causal explanations can be tested (e.g., Bookstein, 1982; Joreskog, 1979; Joreskog & Sorbom, 1977; Nesselroade & Baltes, 1979; Wold, 1982). Because constructs such as temperament and social experience may significantly affect the development of attachment, as well as Strange Situation behavior, these too must be tested through the comparison of rival hypotheses in future research. The field has matured to the point where we need not only exploratory studies, but also systematic attempts to decide between competing hypotheses and theories.

Cross Cultural Research

Increasingly, the Strange Situation is being used outside the U.S. and it is clear that the distribution of infants into classification groups and subgroups differs among cultures. It has accordingly been suggested that infants from different cultures experience the Strange Situation in different ways. Is this difference quantitative (e.g., both American and Israeli infants find the procedure stressful, the Israelis simply find it more stressful), or qualitative (e.g., German infants understand that the separation will be temporary, and do not regard the stranger as a threat)? If the difference is qualitative, is it possible or even desirable to develop culturally-specific assessment procedures that are functionally equivalent and produce comparable indices of attachment in different cultures? This relates to issues discussed in the previous section of this chapter.

Cross-culturally divergent findings also suggest important substantive questions concerning the varied goals and means of childrearing in different cultures. Do parents in different cultures aim to develop different constellations of personality and behavior in their infants? Do they desire different affective qualities in their attachment relationships? If there are different goals, might one not expect different patterns of prediction in different cultures? And, of course, do Strange Situation classifications in other countries have the same relation to antecedent and consequent constructs that they appear to have in the U.S.? International discussion and collaborative research will be essential in addressing these questions.

Development of Continuous Measurement Systems

We also need to explore alternatives to the classification procedure that has hitherto been popular. As detailed earlier, evolutionary biology provides no theoretical justification for distinguishing between these patterns, there is no evidence that the existing groups optimally represent the variance in Strange Situation behavior, and no evidence that any distinctions other than those between "securely-attached" and "insecurely-attached" infants have any validity. Consequently, several researchers are currently attempting to develop measurement systems based on continuous dimensions to summarize individual differences in Strange Situation behavior (Connell, Chapter 13; Connell & Thompson, 1984; Gardner, Lamb, & Thompson, 1984), and some suggestions were presented in Chapters 12 and 14. These represent a few of several possible alternatives for scoring and studying individual differences in Strange Situation behavior; only further research on the antecedents and consequences of differences in these dimensions will show whether or not they represent an improvement over the existing classification system. Unless alternative possibilities are entertained and compared, however, we will never learn how good the existing system is.

To the extent that these continuous measures reflect variations in Strange Situation behavior alone, however, they are unlikely to account for a substantial portion of variance on external measures, even if they are more powerful than the classifications. As repeatedly emphasized, we need to reevaluate our reliance on a single 20-minute session which, however carefully designed and scored, can never hope to capture all significant variance in infant behavior. A scoring system that includes assessment of infant social behavior in a variety of ecologically- and evolutionarily-valid contexts would appear desirable. An appraisal of behavior based on observations in diverse contexts is likely to be more reliable and more valid than assessment in any single context, particularly when individual and cultural variations in broad aspects of childrearing unrelated to the quality of parent–child relationships may bias any assessment based on a single procedure.

The suggestion that we develop continuous measures for summarizing Strange Situation behavior would be, at best, only a beginning to innovative research on the measurement of attachment relationships. We need to develop and integrate measures of behavior in both laboratory and non-laboratory contexts, combining information across contexts to create a more reliable measure of individual or dyadic function, rather than simply correlating Strange Situation behavior and indices of behavior in other contexts, as has been the popular strategy. Such composite measures, which take into account aspects of behavior in diverse contexts, are likely to be more reliable, powerful, and valid than measures of behavior in any one context. Also important is the need to ensure that standardized situations are in fact psychologically comparable for different subjects, whose prior experiences and/or temperament may lead them to perceive apparently similar situations quite differently.

In the past, researchers have avoided "tampering" with a procedure and approach that appeared so successful. As our review has shown, however, the success has been greatly exaggerated. Perhaps realization that the Strange Situation procedure is both informative and fallible will provoke renewed efforts to understand individual differences in infant attachment behavior.

REFERENCES

Achenbach, T. M. (1978). The child behavior profile, I: Boys aged 6–11. *Journal of Consulting and Clinical Psychology*, *46*, 478–488.

Achenbach, T. M., & Edelbrock, C. S. (1978). The classification of child psychopathology: A review and analysis of empirical effects. *Psychological Bulletin*, *85*, 1275–1301.

Achenbach, T. M., & Edelbrock, C. S. (1981). Behavioral problems and competencies reported by parents of normal and disturbed children aged 4 through 16. *Monographs of the Society for Research in Child Development*, *46* (serial number 188).

Ainsworth, M. D. S. (1964). Patterns of attachment behaviors shown by an infant in interaction with his mother. *Merrill–Palmer Quarterly*, *10*, 51–58.

Ainsworth, M. D. S. (1967). *Infancy in Uganda: Infant care and the growth of love*. Baltimore, MD: Johns Hopkins Press.

Ainsworth, M. D. S. (1969). Object relations, dependency, and attachment: A theoretical review of the infant–mother relationship. Child Development, *40*, 969–1025.

Ainsworth, M. D. S. (1972). Attachment and dependency: A comparison. In J. L. Gewirtz (Ed.) *Attachment and Dependency*. Washington, D.C.: V.H. Winston.

Ainsworth, M. D. S. (1973). The development of infant–mother attachment. In B. M. Caldwell & H. N. Ricciuti (Eds.) *Review of child development research* (Vol. 3). Chicago: University of Chicago Press.

Ainsworth, M. D. S. (1974). *The secure base*. Unpublished manuscript, Johns Hopkins University.

Ainsworth, M. D. S. (1979a). Attachment as related to mother–infant interaction. In: *Advances in the Study of Behavior*, (Vol. 9), eds. J. S. Rosenblatt, R. A. Hinde, C. Beer, & M. Busnel. New York: Academic Press.

Ainsworth, M. D. S. (1979b). Infant–mother attachment. *American Psychologist*, *34*, 932–937.

Ainsworth, M. D. S. (1983). Patterns of infant–mother attachment as related to maternal care: Their early history and their contribution to continuity. In D. Magnusson & V. L. Allen (Eds.), *Human development: An interactional perspective*. New York: Academic Press, pp 35–55.

Ainsworth, M. D. S. (1984a). *Adaptation and attachment*. Paper presented to the International Conference on Infant Studies, New York City, April.

Ainsworth, M. D. S. (1984b). Contribution to a symposium on, The Strange Situation: Insights from an international perspective, at the International Conference on Infant Studies, New York, April.

Ainsworth, M. D. S., & Bell, S. M. (1969). Some contemporary patterns of mother–infant interaction in the feeding situation. In A. Ambrose (Ed.), *Stimulation in early infancy*. New York: Academic Press.

Ainsworth, M. D., & Bell, S. M. (1970). Attachment, exploration and separation: Illustrated by the behavior of one-year-olds in a strange situation. *Child Development, 41*, 49–67.

Ainsworth, M. D. S., & Bell, S. M. (1974). Mother–infant interaction and the development of competence. In K. J. Connolly & J. S. Bruner (Eds.), *The growth of competence*. New York: Academic Press.

Ainsworth, M. D. S., Bell, S. M., & Stayton, D. J. (1971). Individual differences in strange situation behavior of one-year-olds. In H. R. Schaffer (Ed.), *The origins of human social relations*. London: Academic.

Ainsworth, M. D. S., Bell, S. M., & Stayton, D. J. (1972). Individual differences in the development of some attachment behaviors. *Merrill–Palmer Quarterly, 18*, 123–143.

Ainsworth, M. D. S., Bell, S. M., & Stayton, D. J. (1974). Infant mother attachment and social development: 'Socialization' as a product of reciprocal responsiveness to signals. In M. P. M. Richards (Ed.), *The integration of a child into a social world*. Cambridge, England: Cambridge University Press.

Ainsworth M. D. S., Blehar, M. C., Waters, E., & Wall, S. (1978). *Patterns of attachment*. Hillsdale, N.J.: Lawrence Erlbaum Associates.

Ainsworth, M. D., & Wittig, B. A. (1969). Attachment and exploratory behavior of one year olds in a strange situation. In B. M. Foss (Ed.), *Determinants of infant behavior* (Vol. 4). London: Methuen.

Alexander, R. D. (1964). The evolution of social behavior. *Annual Review of Ecology and Systematics, 5*, 324–383.

Aneshensel, C., & Huba, G. (1983). Depression, alcohol use, and smoking over one year: A four-wave longitudinal causal model. *Journal of Abnormal Psychology, 92*, 134–150.

Antonucci, T. C., & Levitt, M. J. (1984). Early prediction of attachment security: A multivariate approach. *Infant Behavior and Development, 7*, 1–18.

Arend, R., Gove, F. L., & Sroufe, L. A. (1979). Continuity of individual adaptation from infancy to kindergarten: A predictive study of ego-resiliency and curiosity in preschoolers. *Child Development, 50*, 950–959.

Arnold, M. (1970). Perennial problems in the field of emotion. In M. Arnold (Ed.), *Feelings and emotions*. New York: Academic.

Baltes, P., & Nesselroade, J. (1970). Multivariate longitudinal and cross-sectional sequences for analyzing ontogenetic and generational change. *Developmental Psychology, 2*, 163–168.

Bates, J. E. (1980). The concept of difficult temperament. *Merrill–Palmer Quarterly, 26*, 299–319.

Bates, J.E., Bayles, K., & Kiser, L. (1981). *The generalizability of indexes of mother–infant face-to-face play at age 6 months*. Final report to the Spencer Foundation, January.

Bates, J. E., Freeland, C. A. B., & Lounsbury, M. L. (1979). Measurement of infant difficultness. *Child Development, 50*, 794–802.

Bates, J. E., Maslin, L. A., & Frankel, K. A. (in press). Attachment security, mother–child interaction, and temperament as predictors of behavior problem ratings at age three years. In I. Bretherton & E. Waters (Eds.), *Growing points in attachment theory and research. Monographs of the Society for Research in Child Development*.

Bates, J. E., Olson, S. L., Pettit, G. S., & Bayles, K. (1982). Dimensions of individuality in the mother–infant relationship at 6 months of age. *Child Development, 53*, 446–461.

Behar, L., & Stringfield, S. (1974). A behavior rating scale for the preschool child. *Developmental Psychology, 10*, 601–610.

Behar, L. B. (1977). The preschool behavior questionnaire. *Journal of Abnormal Child Psychology, 5*, 265–275.

Bell, R. Q. (1968). A reinterpretation of the direction of effect in studies of socialization. *Psychological Review, 75*, 81–95.

Bell, R. Q., Weller, G., & Waldrop, M. (1971). Newborn and preschooler: Organization of behavior and relations between periods. *Monographs of the Society for Research in Child Development, 36*, (Serial No. 142).

Bell, S. M. V. (1970). The development of the concept of object as related to infant–mother attachment. *Child Development, 41*, 291–311.

Bell, S. M., & Ainsworth, M. D. (1972). Infant crying and maternal responsiveness. *Child Development, 43*, 1171–1190.

Beller, E. K. (1955). Dependency and independency in young children. *Journal of Genetic Psychology, 87*, 25–35.

Beller, E. K. (1984). *The Strange Situation: Insights from an International Perspective—The Berlin study*. Paper presented to the International Conference on Infant Studies, New York, April.

Belsky, J. (1981) Early human experience: A family perspective. *Developmental Psychology, 17*, 3–23.

Belsky, J. (1984). The determinants of parenting: A process model. *Child Development, 55*, 83–96.

Belsky, J., & Garduque, L. (1982). *The interrelation of attachment and free and elicited play behavior*. Paper presented to the International Conference on Infant Studies, Austin, TX, March.

Belsky, J., & Most, R. (1981). From exploration to play: A cross-sectional study of infant free-play behavior. *Developmental Psychology, 17*, 630–639.

Belsky, J., & Steinberg, L. D. (1978). The effects of day care: A critical review. *Child Development, 49*, 929–949.

Belsky, J., Garduque, L., & Hrncir, E. (1984). Assessing performance, competence, and executive capacity in infant play: Relations to home environment and security of attachment. *Developmental Psychology, 20*, 406–417.

Belsky, J., Rovine, M., & Taylor, D. (1984a). The Pennsylvania Infant and Family Development Project, III: The origins of individual differences in infant–mother attachment: Maternal and infant contributions. *Child Development, 55*, 718–728.

Belsky, J., Taylor, D., & Rovine, M. (1984b). The Pennsylvania Infant and Family Development Project, II: The development of reciprocal interaction in the mother–infant dyad. *Child Development, 55*, 706–717.

Bischof, N. (1975). A systems approach toward the functional connections of attachment and fear. *Child Development, 46*, 801–817.

Blanchard, M., & Main, M. (1979). Avoidance of the attachment figure and social-emotional adjustment in day-care infants. *Developmental Psychology, 15*, 445–446.

Blehar, M. C. (1974). Anxious attachment and defensive reactions associated with day care. *Child Development, 45*, 683–692.

Blehar, M. C., Lieberman, A. F., & Ainsworth, M. D. S. (1977). Early face-to-face interaction and its relation to later infant–mother attachment. *Child Development, 48*, 182–194.

Block, J., & Block, J. H. (1979). The role of ego control and ego resiliency in the organization of behavior. In W. A. Collins (Ed.), *Minnesota Symposia on Child Psychology*, vol. 13. Hillsdale, NJ: Lawrence Erlbaum Associates.

Bookstein, F. (1982). The geometric meaning of soft modeling, with some generalizations. In

K. Joreskog & H. Wold (Eds., *Systems under indirect observation: Causality-Stucture-Prediction*. Part II. New York: North-Holland Publishing Company.

Boomsma, A. (1982). The robustness of LISREL against small sample sizes in factor analysis models. In K. Joreskog & H. Wold (Eds.), *Systems under indirect observation: Causality-Structure-Prediction*. Part I. New York: North-Holland Publishing Company.

Bower, T. G. R. (1974). *Development in infancy*. San Francisco: Freeman.

Bower, T. G. R. (1977). *A primer of infant development*. San Francisco: Freeman.

Bowlby, J. (1946). *Forty-four juvenile thieves, their characters and homelife*. London: Bailliere, Tindall, & Cox.

Bowlby, J. (1951). *Maternal care and mental health*. Geneva: World Health Organization.

Bowlby, J. (1958). The nature of the child's tie to his mother. *International Journal of Psychoanalysis, 39*, 350–373.

Bowlby, J. (1969). *Attachment and loss*. Vol. 1: *Attachment*. New York: Basic.

Bowlby, J. (1973). *Attachment and Loss* (Vol. 2). *Separation: Anxiety and anger*. New York: Basic Books.

Bowlby, J. (1982). Attachment and loss: Retrospect and prospect. *American Journal of Orthopsychiatry, 52*, 664–678.

Bradshaw, D. L., Goldsmith, H. H., & Campos, J. J. (1984). *Attachment, temperament and social referencing: Interrelationships among three domains of infant affective behavior*. Unpublished manuscript, University of Denver, Denver, CO.

Brazelton, T. B. (1973). *Neonatal Behavior Assessment Scale*. Philadelphia: Lippincott.

Bretherton, I. (1985). Attachment theory: Retrospect and prospect. In I. Bretherton and E. Waters (Eds.), *Growing points in attachment theory and research. Monographs of the Society for Research in Child Development*, in press.

Bretherton, I., & Ainsworth, M. (1974). Responses of one-year-olds to a stranger in a strange situation. In M. Lewis & L. Rosenblum (Eds.), *The origins of fear*. New York: Wiley.

Bridges, L. J., Grolnick, W. S., Frodi, A., & Connell, J. P. (1984). *Determinants and correlates of mastery motivation and attachment across the second year: A structural modeling approach*. Paper presented to the Meetings of the International Conference on Infant Studies, New York, New York.

Brim, O. G., & Kagan, J. (Eds.) (1980). *Constancy and change in human development*. Cambridge, MA: Harvard University Press.

Brody, S. (1956). *Patterns of mothering*. New York: International Universities Press.

Bronfenbrenner, U. (1979). *The ecology of human development*. Cambridge MA: Harvard University Press.

Bronson, W. C. (1981). *Toddlers' behaviors with agemates: Issues of interaction, cognition, and affect*. Norwood, NJ: Ablex.

Browne, M. (1982). Covariance structures. In D. M. Hawkins (Ed.), *Topics in applied multivariate analysis*. Cambridge: Cambridge University Press.

Caldwell, B. (1970). *Home observation for measurement of the environment*. Little Rock, AK: Center for early development and education. University of Arkansas.

Campos, J. J., Barrett, K. C., Lamb, M. E., Goldsmith, H. H., & Stenberg, C. (1983). Socioemotional development. In P. H. Mussen (Ed.), *Handbook of Child Psychology*, Vol. II. *Infancy and developmental psychobiology* (ed. by M. M. Haith & J. J. Campos). New York: Wiley.

Carey, W. B. (1970). A simplified method for measuring infant temperament. *Journal of Pediatrics, 70*, 188–194.

Carey, W. B., & McDevitt, S. C. (1977). Revision of the infant temperament questionnaire. *Pediatrics, 61*, 735–739.

Caudill, W., & Weinstein, S. (1969). Maternal care and infant behavior in Japan and America. *Psychiatry, 32*, 12–43.

Charlesworth, B. (1980). *Evolution in age-structured populations.* New York: Cambridge University Press.

Charnov, E. L., & Krebs, J. (1974). On clutch size and fitness. *IBIS, 116,* 27–219.

Charnov, E. L., Gotshall, D. W., & Robinson, J. G. (1978). Sex ratio: Adaptive response to population fluctuations in pandalid shrimp. *Science, 200,* 204–206.

Chess, S., & Thomas, A. (1982). Infant bonding: Mystique and reality. *American Journal of Orthopsychiatry, 52,* 213–222.

Clarke, A. M., & Clarke, A. D. B. (Eds.) (1976). *Early experience: Myth and evidence.* New York: Free Press.

Clarke–Stewart, K. A., & Fein, G. G. (1983). Early childhood programs. In P. H. Mussen (General editor) *Handbook of child psychology,* vol. 2, M. M. Haith and J. J. Campos (Volume editors) *Infancy and developmental psychobiology.* New York: Wiley.

Clogg, C. (1981). New developments in latent structure analysis. In E. Jackson & D. Borgatta, (Eds.), *Factor analysis and measurement in sociological research: A multidimensional perspective.* Beverly Hills: Sage.

Coates, B., Anderson, E. P., & Hartup, W. W. (1972). Interrelations in the attachment behavior of human infants. *Developmental Psychology, 6,* 218–230.

Cochrane, R., & Robertson, A. (1973). The Life Events Inventory: A measure of the relative severity of psycho-social stresses. *Journal of Psychosomatic Research, 17,* 135–139.

Cohen, J. (1960). A coefficient of agreement for nominal scales. *Educational and Psychological Measurement, 20,* 37–46.

Cohen, J. (1968). Weighted kappa: Nominal scale agreement with provision for scaled disagreement or partial credit. *Psychological Bulletin, 70,* 213–220.

Cohler, B. J., Weiss, J. L., & Grunebaum, H. U. (1970) Childcare attitudes and emotional disturbance among mothers of young children. *Genetic Psychology Monographs, 82,* 3–47.

Connell, D. B. (1976). *Individual differences in attachment behavior: Long-term stability and relationships to language development.* Unpublished doctoral dissertation, Syracuse University, Syracuse, NY.

Connell, J. P. (1984). The development and component processes of the attachment system: Some suggestions for their rediscovery. Submitted for publication.

Connell, J. P., & Bridges, L. (1984). *Dimensions of social interaction in the Strange Situation: A mega-analysis.* Unpublished manuscript. University of Rochester.

Connell, J. P., & Goldsmith, H. H. (1982). A structural modeling approach to the study of attachment and Strange Situation behaviors. In R. N. Emde & R. J. Harmon (Eds.), *The development of attachment and affiliative systems.* New York: Plenum Press.

Connell, J. P., & Tero, P. (1984). *A reanalysis of individual differences and developmental change in Strange Situation behaviors.* Paper presented at Meetings of the Society for Research in Child Development, Detroit.

Connell, J. P., & Thompson, R. A. (1984). *Emotion and social interaction in the Strange Situation: Consistencies and asymetric influences in the second year.* Manuscript submitted for publication.

Connell, J. P., & Thompson, R. A., & Tero, P. (1984). *Emotion attachment interrelationships in the Strange Situation: A structural modeling approach.* Paper presented at the International Conference on Infant Studies, New York.

Corter, C. M. (1973). A comparison of the mother's and a stranger's control over the behavior of infants. *Child Development, 44,* 705–713.

Corter, C. M., Rheingold, H. L., & Eckerman, C. O. (1972). Toys delay the infant's following of its mother. *Developmental Psychology, 6,* 138–145.

Crittenden, P. M. (April, 1984). *Maltreated infants: Vulnerability and resilience.* Paper presented at the meeting of the Society for Research in Child Development, Detroit, MI.

Crockenberg, S. B. (1981). Infant irritability, mother responsiveness, and social support influences on the security of infant–mother attachment. *Child Development*, *52*, 857–865.

DeCasper, D., & Fifer, W. (1980). Of human bonding: Newborns prefer their mothers' voices. *Science*, *208*, 1174–1176.

Denenberg, V. H. (1979). Paradigms and paradoxes in the study of behavioral development. In E. Thoman (Ed.), *Origins of the infant's social responsiveness*. Hillsdale, NJ: Lawrence Erlbaum Associates.

Denenberg, V. H. (1982). Early experience in teractive systems, and brain laterality in rodents. In L. A. Bond & J. M. Joffe (Eds.), *Facilitating infant and early childhood development*. Burlington, VT: University Press of New England.

Denenberg, V. H. (1984). Stranger in a strange situation: Comments by a comparative psychologist. *Behavioral and Brain Sciences*, *7*, 150–152.

Dollard, J., & Miller, N. E. (1950). *Personality and psychotherapy*. New York: McGraw Hill.

Duncan, O. D. (1969). Some linear models for two-wave, two-variable panel analysis. *Psychological Bulletin*, *72*, 177–182.

Duncan, O. D. (1972). Unmeasured variables in linear models in panel analysis. In H. L. Costner (Ed.), *Sociological Methodology 1972*. San Francisco: Jossey–Bass.

Dupacova, J., & Wold, H. (1982). On some identification problems in ML modeling of systems with indirect observations. In K. Joreskog & H. Wold (Eds.), *Systems under indirect observation: Causality-structure-prediction*. Part II. New York: North-Holland Publishing Company.

Durrett, M. E., Otaki, M., & Richards, P. (1984). Attachment and the mother's perception of support from the father. *International Journal of Behavioral Development*, *7*, 167–176.

Easterbrooks, M. A., & Goldberg, W. A. (1984). Toddler development in the family: Impact of father involvement and parenting characteristics. *Child Development*, *55*, 740–752.

Easterbrooks, M. A., & Lamb, M. E. (1979). The relationship between quality of infant–mother attachment and infant competence in initial encounters with peers. *Child Development*, *50*, 380–387.

Egeland, B. (1983). Comments on Kopp, Krakow and Vaughn's chapter. In M. Perlmutter (Ed.), *Development and policy concerning children with special needs. Minnesota Symposia on Child Psychology*, Vol. 16. Hillsdale, NJ: Lawrence Erlbaum Associates.

Egeland, B., Breitenbucher, M., Dodd, M., Pastor, D., Rosenberg, D. (1979). *Life stress scale and scoring manual*. Unpublished manuscript, University of Minnesota.

Egeland, B., & Brunnquell, D. (1979). An at-risk approach to the study of child abuse: Some preliminary findings. *Journal of the American Academy of Child Psychiatry*, *18*, 219–235.

Egeland, B., & Farber, E. A. (1982). *Antecedents of infant–mother attachment relationships in economically disadvantaged families*. Unpublished Manuscript, University of Minnesota, Minneapolis, MN.

Egeland, B., & Farber, E. A. (1984). Infant–mother attachment: Factors related to its development and changes over time. *Child Development*, *55*, 753–771.

Egeland, B., & Sroufe, L. A. (1981a). Attachment and early maltreatment. *Child Development*, *52*, 44–52.

Egeland, B., & Sroufe, L. A. (1981b). Developmental sequelae of maltreatment in infancy. In R. Rizley & D. Cicchetti (Eds.), *Developmental perspectives on child maltreatment* (New Directions for Child Development Series No. 11; W. Damon, General Editor). San Francisco: Jossey–Bass.

Eibl–Eibesfeldt, I. (1979). Human ethology: Concepts and implications for the sciences of man. *Behavioral and Brain Sciences*, *2*, 1–57.

Emmerich, W. (1968). Personality development and concepts of structure. *Child Development*, *39*, 671–690.

Engel, G. L. (1971). Attachment behavior, object relation and the dynamic-economic points of view. *International Journal of Psychoanalysis*, *52*, 183–196.

Erickson, M., & Egeland, B. (1981). *Behavior problem scale technical manual.* Unpublished manuscript. University of Minnesota.

Erickson, M. F., & Crichton, L. (1981). *Antecedents of compliance in 2-year-olds from a high-risk sample.* Paper presented to the Society for Research in Child Development, Boston.

Erickson, M. F., & Farber, E. A. (1983). *Infancy to preschool: Continuity of adaptation in high risk children.* Paper presented at the Meetings of the Society for Research in Child Development, Detroit, MI.

Erickson, M. F., Sroufe, L. A., & Egeland, B. (in press). The relationship between quality of attachment and behavior problems in preschool in a high-risk sample. In I. Bretherton & E. Waters (Eds.), *Growing points in attachment theory and research. Monographs of the Society for Research in Child Development.*

Escalona, S. K., & Leitch, M. (1953). *Early phases of personality development.* Evanston, IL: Child Development Publications.

Estes, D. (1981). *Maternal behavior and security of attachment at 12 and 19 months.* Unpublished masters thesis, University of Michigan.

Estes, D., Lamb, M. E., Thompson, R. A., & Dickstein, S. (1981). *Maternal affective quality and security of attachment at 12 and 19 months.* Paper presented to the Society for Research in Child Development, Boston.

Farber, E.A. (1981). *Factors related to changes in infant–mother relationships.* Paper presented to the Society for Research in Child Development, Boston.

Feinman, S. (1984). Correlations in search of a theory: Interpreting the predictive validity of security of attachment. *The Behavioral and Brain Sciences, 7,* 152–153.

Field, T. M., Dempsey, J. R., & Shuman, H. H. (1981). Developmental follow-up of pre- and post-term infants. In S. L. Friedman & M. Sigman (Eds.), *Preterm birth and psychological development.* New York: Academic Press.

Fischoff, J., Whitten, C. F., & Pettit, M. G. (1970). A psychiatric study of mothers of infants with growth failure secondary to maternal deprivation. *Journal of Pediatrics, 79,* 209–215.

Fisher, F. (1966). *The identification problem in econometrics.* New York: McGraw–Hill.

Fliess, J., Cohen, J. & Everitt, B. (1969). Large sample standard errors of kappa and weighted kappa. *Psychological Bulletin, 72,* 323–237.

Frankel, K. F., & Bates, J. E. (1983). *Mother–toddler interactions while solving problems: Correlations with attachment security and interaction at home.* Unpublished manuscript, Indiana University.

Freud, A. (1949). Certain types and stages of social maladjustment. In K. R. Eissler (Ed.), *Searchlights on delinquency.* New York: International Universities Press.

Freud, A. (1965). *Normality and pathology in childhood.* New York: International Universities Press.

Freud, S. (1940). *An outline of psychoanalysis.* New York: Norton.

Frodi, A. (1983). Attachment behavior and sociability with strangers in premature and fullterm infants. *Infant Mental Health Journal, 4,* ??–??.

Frodi, A., & Thompson, R. A. (in prep.). *Affective expressions of premature and fullterm infants in the Strange Situation.* Manuscript in preparation, University of Rochester, Rochester, NY.

Frodi, A., Bridges, L., & Grolnick, W. (1984). *Determinants and correlates of mastery motivation: A short term longitudinal study of infants in their second year.* Unpublished manuscript, University of Rochester.

Frodi, A., Grolnick, W., & Bridges, L. (1984). *Maternal correlates of stability and change in infant–mother attachment.* Unpublished manuscript, University of Rochester, Rochester, NY.

Frodi, A. M., Lamb, M. E., Leavitt, L. A., & Donovan, W. L. (1978). Fathers' and mothers' responses to infant smiles and cries. *Infant Behavior and Development, 1,* 181–198.

Fullard, W., McDevitt, S. C., & Carey, W. B. (1978). *The Toddler Temperament Scale*. Unpublished manuscript, Temple University, Philadelphia, PA.

Gaensbauer, T. J., Connell, J. P., & Schultz, L. A. (1983). Emotion and attachment: Interrelationships in a structured laboratory paradigm. *Developmental Psychology, 19*, 815–831.

Gardner, W. P., Lamb, M. E., & Thompson, R. A. (in prep.). *On the measurement of individual differences in Strange Situation behavior*.

Gardner, W. P., & Thompson, R. A. (1983). *A cluster analytic evaluation of the Strange Situation classification system*. Paper presented at the annual meetings of the Society for Research in Child Development, Detroit.

Gewirtz, J. L. (1972). Attachment, dependency, and a distinction in terms of stimulus control. In J. L. Gewirtz (Ed.), *Attachment and dependency*. Washington: Winston.

Ghiselin, M. T. (1974). *The economy of nature and the evolution of sex*. Berkeley: University of California Press.

Goldberg, W. A., & Easterbrooks, M. A. (1984). The role of marital quality in toddler development. *Developmental Psychology, 20*, 504–514.

Goldberg, S., Perrotta, M., & Minde, K. (1984). *Maternal behavior and attachment in low birthweight twins and singletons*. Poster presentation to the International Conference on Infant Studies, New York, April.

Goldsmith, H. H., & Campos, J. J. (1982). Toward a theory of infant temperament. In R. N. Emde & R. J. Harmon (Eds.), *The development of attachment and affiliative systems*. New York: Plenum.

Goodman, L.A., & Kruskal, W.H. (1954). Measures of association for cross-classifications. *Journal of the American Statistical Association, 49*, 732–764.

Goossens, F. A., van IJzendoorn, M. H., Kroonenberg, P. M., & Tavecchio, L. W. C. (1984). *The stability of attachment across time and context in a Dutch sample*. Unpublished manuscript, University of Leiden, The Netherlands.

Goossens, F. A., van IJzendoorn, M. H., Tavecchio, L. W. C., & Swaan, J. (1984). *The Strange Situation in a Dutch context: The stability of attachment across time and context*. Unpublished manuscript, University of Leiden, The Netherlands.

Gordon, A. H., & Jameson, J. C. (1979). Infant–mother attachment in patients with nonorganic failure to thrive syndrome. *Journal of the American Academy of Child Psychiatry, 18*, 251–259.

Grolnick, W. S., Bridges, L. J., & Frodi, A. (1984). *Correlates of stability and change in infant–mother attachment between 12 and 20 months*. Paper presented to the International Conference on Infant Studies, New York, April.

Gross, M. R., & Charnov, E. L. (1980). Alternative male life histories in bluegill sunfish. *Proceedings of the National Academy of Science* (USA), *77*, 6937–6940.

Grossmann, K., & Grossmann, K. E. (1982). *Maternal sensitivity to infants' signals during the first year as related to the year old's behavior in Ainsworth's Strange Situation in a sample of Northern German families*. Paper presented to the International Conference on Infant Studies, Austin Texas.

Grossmann, K. E., & Grossmann, K. (1983). *Cultural and temperamental aspects of the avoidant attachment behavior patterns in infants*. Paper presented to the Society for Research in Child Development, Detroit.

Grossmann, K. E., Schwan, A., & Grossmann, K. (in press). Infants' communications after brief separation: A reanalysis of Ainsworth's Strange Situation. In P. B. Read & C. E. Izard (Eds.), *Measuring emotions in infants and children* (Vol. 2) New York: Cambridge University Press.

Grossmann, K. E., Grossmann, K., Huber, F., & Wartner, U. (1981). German children's behavior towards their mothers at 12 months and their fathers at 18 months in Ainsworth's Strange Situation. *International Journal of Behavioral Development, 4*, 157–181.

Grossmann, K., Grossmann, K. E., Spangler, G., Suess, G., & Unzner, L. (in press). Maternal sensitivity and newborns' orientation responses as related to quality of attachment in northern Germany. In I. Bretherton & E. Waters (Eds.), *Growing points in attachment theory and research. Monographs of the Society for Research in Child Development.*

Gubernick, D. (1981). Parent and infant attachment in mammals. In D. Gubernick & P. Klopfer (Eds.), *Parental care in mammals.* New York: Plenum.

Hamilton, W. D. (1964). The genetical theory of social behavior. *Journal of Theoretical Biology, 7,* 1–52.

Hand, D. (1981). *Discrimination and classification.* New York: Wiley.

Harlow, H. F. (1958). The nature of love. *American Psychologist, 13,* 673–685.

Harlow, H. F. (1961). The development of affectional patterns in infant monkeys. In B. M. Foss (Ed.), *Determinants of infant behavior* (Vol. I). London: Methuen.

Harlow, H. F., & Zimmerman, R. R. (1959). Affectional responses in the infant monkey. *Science, 130,* 421.

Hartmann, H. (1939; Eng trans 1958). *Ego psychology and the problem of adaptation.* New York: International Universities Press.

Hartmann, H., Kris, E., & Lowenstein, R. M., (1949). Notes on the theory of aggression. *Psychoanalytic Study of the Child, 3,* 9–36.

Hazen, N. G., & Durrett, M. E. (1982). Relationship of security of attachment to exploration and cognitive mapping abilities in 2-year-olds. *Developmental Psychology, 18,* 751–759.

Hinde, R. A. (1982). Attachment: Some conceptual and biological issues. In J. Stevenson–Hinde & C. Murray Parkes (Eds.), *The place of attachment in human behavior.* New York: Basic Books.

Hinde, R. A. (1983). Ethology and child development. In P. H. Mussen (Ed.), *Handbook of Child Psychology.* Vol. II. *Infancy and Developmental Psychobiology* (M. M. Haith & J. J. Campos, Eds.). New York: Wiley.

Holmes, D. L., Ruble, N., Kowalski, J., & Lavesen, B. (1984). *Predicting quality of attachment at one year from neonatal characteristics.* Paper presented at the International Conference on Infant Studies, New York, New York.

Huberty, C. (1984). Issues in the use and interpretation of discriminant analysis. *Psychological Bulletin, 95,* 156–171.

Isaacs, S. (1929). Privation and guilt. *International Journal of Psychoanalysis, 10.*

Jackson, D. N. (1974). *Personality Research Form Manual.* Goshen, NY: Research Psychologist's Press.

Jackson, E., Campos, J., & Fischer, K. (1978). The question of decalage between object permanence and person permanence. *Developmental Psychology, 14,* 1–10.

Jacobsen, J. L., & Wille, D. E. (1984). Influence of attachment and separation experience on separation distress at 18 months. *Developmental Psychology, 20,* 477–484.

Jacobsen, J. L., & Wille, D. E. (1984). *The influence of attachment pattern on peer interaction at 2 and 3 years.* Paper presented to the International Conference on Infant Studies, New York, April.

Jacobson, J. L., Wille, D. E., Tianen, R. L., & Aytch, D. M. (1983). *The influence of infant–mother attachment on toddler sociability with peers.* Paper presented to the Society for Research in Child Development, Detroit.

Joffe, L. (1981). *The quality of mother–infant attachment and its relationship to compliance with maternal commands and prohibitions.* Paper presented to the Society for Research in Child Development, Boston.

Jordan, L. (1978). *Linear structural relations, longitudinal data, and the cross-lag idea.* Paper presented at the meeting of the American Statistical Association, San Diego, CA..

Joreskog, K. (1971). Simultaneous factor analysis in several populations. *Psychometrika, 36,* 409–426.

Joreskog, K. (1979). Statistical estimation of structural models in longitudinal-developmental investigations. In J. Nesselroade & P. Baltes (Eds.), *Longitudinal research in the study of behavioral development*. New York: Academic Press.

Joreskog, K., & Sorbom, D. (1977). Statistical models and methods for the analysis of longitudinal data. In D. Aigner & A. Goldberger (Eds.), *Latent variables in socioeconomic models*. Amsterdam: North Holland Publishers.

Joreskog, K., & Sorbom, D. (1978). *LISREL IV. Analysis of linear structural relationships by the method of maximum likelihood*. Chicago: National Education Resources.

Joreskog, K., & Sorbom, D. (1981). *LISREL V. Analysis of linear structural relations log maximum likelihood and least squares methods*. Chicago: International Educational Services.

Joreskog, K., & Sorbom, D. (1981). *LISREL VI. Analysis of linear structural relations log maximum likelihood and least squares methods*. Chicago: International Educational Services.

Kagan, J. (1971). *Change and continuity in infancy*. New York: Wiley.

Kagan, J. (1982). *Psychological research on the human infant: An evaluative summary*. New York: William T. Grant Foundation.

Kagan, J. (1984). Continuity and change in the opening years of life. In R. N. Emde & R. J. Harmon (Eds.), *Continuities and discontinuities in development*. New York: Plenum.

Kanaya, Y. (1982–83). Analysis of infant's inhibited behaviors shown in peer interaction at 23 months. *Annual Report: Research and Clinical Center for Child Development*, Faculty of Education, Hokkaido University, Sapporo, Japan.

Kessler, R., & Greenberg, D. (1981). *Linear panel analysis: Models of quantitative change*. New York: Academic.

Kiser, L. J., Bates, J. E., Maslin, C. A., & Bayles, K. (1982). *Mother–infant play at six months as a predictor of attachment security at thirteen months*. Unpublished manuscript, Indiana University.

Klein, M. (1923/1948). Infant analysis. In *Contributions to psychoanalysis 1921–1945*. London: Hogarth.

Klein, M. (1932/1975). *The psychoanalysis of children*. New York: Delacorte Press.

Klein, M. (1957). *Envy and gratitude*. London: Tavistock.

Klinnert, M., Campos, J. J., Sorce, J., Emde, R. N., & Svejda, M. (1983). Emotions as behavior regulators: Social referencing in infancy. In R. Plutchik & H. Kellerman (Eds.), *Emotion: Theory, research an experience*. Vol. 2. *Emotions in early development*. New York: Academic.

Klopfer, P. H. (1984). Caugats on the use of evolutionary concepts. *Behavioral and Brain Sciences*, *7*, 156–157.

Konner, M. J. (1972). Aspects of the developmental ethiology of a foraging people. In N. Blurton Jones (Ed.), Ethiological studies of child behavior. Cambridge: Cambridge University Press.

Konner, M. (1977). Evolution of human behavior development. In P. H. Leiderman, S. Tulkin, & A. Rosenfeld (Eds.), *Culture and infancy: Variations in human experience*. New York: Academic Press.

Korner, A. F., & Thoman, E. G. (1970). Visual alertness in neonates as evoked by maternal care. *Journal of Experimental Child Psychology*, *10*, 67–78.

Korner, A. F., & Thoman, E. G. (1972). The relative efficacy of contact and vestibular-proprioceptive stimulation in soothing neonates. *Child Development*, *43*, 443–453.

Krebs, J. R., & Davies, N. B. (1981). *An introduction to behavioural ecology*. Sunderland, MA: Sinauer.

Kuhn, T. (1962). *The structure of scientific revolutions*. Chicago: The University of Chicago Press.

Kuhn, T. (1970). The function of dogma in scientific research. In B. A. Brody (Ed.), *Readings in the philosophy of science*. Englewood Cliffs, NJ: Prentice Hall.

Lamb, M. E. (1974). A defense of the concept of attachment. *Human Development*, *17*, 376–385.

Lamb, M. E. (1976). Proximity seeking attachment behaviors: A critical review of the literature. *Genetic Psychology Monographs*, *93*, 63–89.

Lamb, M. E. (1977a). The development of mother–infant and father–infant attachments in the second year of life. *Developmental Psychology*, *13*, 637–648.

Lamb, M. E. (1977b). Father–infant and mother–infant interaction in the first year of life. *Child Development*, *48*, 167–181.

Lamb, M. E. (1978). Qualitative aspects of mother– and father–infant attachments. *Infant Behavior and Development*, *1*, 265–275.

Lamb, M. E. (1979). Separation and reunion behaviors as criteria of attachment to mothers and fathers. *Early Human Development*, *3/4*, 329–339.

Lamb, M. E. (1981a). The development of social expectations in the first year of life. In M. E. Lamb & L. R. Sherrod (Eds.), *Infant social cognition: Empirical and theoretical considerations*. Hillsdale, NJ: Lawrence Erlbaum Associates.

Lamb, M. E. (1981b). Developing trust and perceived effectance in infancy. In L. P. Lipsitt (Ed.), *Advances in infancy research*, (Vol. 1). Norwood, NJ: Ablex.

Lamb, M. E. (1981c). The development of father–infant relationships. In M. E. Lamb (Ed.), *The role of the father in child development* (Revised edition). New York: Wiley.

Lamb, M. E. (1982a). Individual differences in infant sociability: Their origins and implications for cognitive development. In H. W. Reese & L. P. Lipsitt (Eds.), *Advances in child development and behavior*, (Vol. 16). New York: Academic.

Lamb, M. E. (1982b). Maternal employment and child development: A review. In M. E. Lamb (Ed.), *Nontraditional families: Parenting and child development*. Hillsdale, N.J.: Lawrence Erlbaum Associates.

Lamb, M. E. (1982c). On the familial origins of personality and social style. In L. Laosa & I. Sigel (Eds.), *The family as a learning environment*. New York: Plenum.

Lamb, M. E. (1982d). Early contact and mother–infant bonding: One decade later. *Pediatrics*, *70*, 763–768.

Lamb, M. E., & Easterbrooks, M. A. (1981). Individual differences in parental sensitivity: Origins, components, and consequences. In M. E. Lamb & L. R. Sherrod (Eds.), *Infant social cognition: Empirical and theoretical considerations*. Hillsdale, NJ: Lawrence Erlbaum Associates.

Lamb, M. E., Gaensbauer, T. J., Malkin, C. M., & Shultz, L. (1985). The effects of child abuse and neglect on security of infant–adult attachment. *Infant Behavior and Development*, *7*, in press.

Lamb, M. E., & Hwang, C.–P. (1982). Maternal attachment and mother–neonate bonding: A critical review. In M. E. Lamb & A. L. Brown (Eds.), *Advances in developmental psychology* (Vol. 2). Hillsdale, N.J.: Lawrence Erlbaum Associates, (pp. 1–39).

Lamb, M. E., Hwang, C. P., Frodi, A., & Frodi, M. (1982). Security of mother–and father–infant attachment and its relation to sociability with strangers in traditional and non-traditional Swedish families. *Infant Behavior and Development*, *5*, 355–367.

Lamb, M. E., Pleck, J. H., Charnov, E. L., & Levine, J. A. (in press). A biosocial perspective on paternal behavior and involvement. In J. B. Lancaster, J. Altmann, A. Rossi, & L. Sherrod (Eds.), *Parenting across the lifespan: Biosocial perspectives*. Chicago: Aldine.

Lamb, M. E., Sagi, A., Lewkowicz, K., Shoham, R., & Estes, D. (1982). *Security of infant–mother, –father, and –metapelet attachments in kibbutz-reared infants*. Paper presented to the Denver Psychobiology Research Group Retreat, Estes Park, CO.

Lamb, M. E., Thompson, R. A., Gardner, W. P., Charnov, E. L., & Estes, D. (1984). Security of infantile attachment as assessed in the Strange Situation: Its study and biological interpretation. *Behavioral and Brain Sciences*, *7*, 127–147.

Lazarus, R. S. (1966). *Psychological stress and the coping process*. New York: McGraw Hill.

Lebra, T. S. (1976). *Japanese patterns of behavior*. Honolulu: University of Hawaii Press.

Lerner, J. V., & Lerner, R. M. (1983). Temperament and adaptation across life: Theoretical and empirical issues. in P. B. Baltes & O. G. Brim (Eds.), *Life-span development and behavior*, Vol. 5. New York: Academic.

Lerner, R. M., Belsky, J., & Windle, M. (1983). *The Dimensions of Temperament Survey for Infancy (DOTS - Infancy): Assessment of its psychometric properties*. Unpublished manuscript, Pennsylvania State University, University Park, PA.

Lerner, R. M., Palermo, M., Spiro, A., & Nesselroade, J. R. (1982). Assessing the dimensions of temperamental individuality across the life span: The Dimensions of Temperament Survey (DOTS). *Child Development, 53*, 149–159.

Levitt, M. J., Antonucci, T. C., & Clark, M. C. (1984). Object-person permanence and attachment: Another look. *Merrill–Palmer Quarterly, 30*, 1–10.

Lewis, M. (1972). Parents and children: Sex role development. *School Review, 80*, 229–240.

Lewis, M., & Ban, P. (1971). *Stability of attachment behavior: A transformational analysis*. Paper presented to the Society for Research in Child Development, Minneapolis.

Lewis, M., & Brooks–Gunn, J. (1979). *Social cognition and the acquisition of self*. New York: Plenum.

Lewis, M., & Wilson, C. D. (1972). Infant development in lower class American families. *Human Development, 15*, 112–127.

Lewis, M., Feiring, C., McGuffog, C., & Jaskir, J. (1984). Predicting psychopathology in six-year-olds from early social relations. *Child Development, 55*, 123–136.

Lewis, M., Weinraub, M., & Ban, P. (1972). *Mothers and fathers, girls and boys: Attachment behavior in the first two years of life*. Educational Testing Service Research Bulletin, Princeton, N.J.

Lieberman, A. F. (1977). Preschoolers' competence with a peer: Relations with attachment and peer experience. *Child Development, 48*, 1277–1287.

Li–Repac, D. C. (1982). *The impact of acculturation on the child-rearing attitudes and practices of Chinese–American families: Consequences for the attachment process*. Unpublished doctoral dissertation, University of California–Berkeley.

Lohmoller, J.–B. (1984). *Latent variable partial least squares program manual*. Koln, Federal Republic of Germany: Universitat zu Koln, Zentralarchiv fur empirische sozialforschung.

Londerville, S., & Main, M. (1981). Security of attachment, compliance, and maternal training methods in the second year of life. *Developmental Psychology, 17*, 289–299.

Lorenz, K. (1935/1970). Companions as factors in the bird's environment. In: *Studies in animal and human behavior*. Cambridge, Mass.: Harvard University Press.

Lutkenhaus, P. (1984). *Infant–mother attachment at 12 months and style of interaction with a stranger at the age of three*. Paper presented at the Meeting of the International Conference on Infant Studies, New York, NY.

Lyons–Ruth, K., Connell, J., Grunebaum, H., Botein, S., & Zoll, D. (1983). *Maternal family history, maternal caretaking, and infant attachment in multiproblem families*. Paper presented at the Meetings of the Society for Research in Child Development, Detroit, MI.

Maccoby, E. E., & Feldman, S. (1972). Mother-attachment and stranger reactions in the third year of life. *Monographs of the Society for Research in Child Development, 37*, (No. 1, Serial No. 146).

Maccoby, E. E., & Masters, J. C. (1970). Attachment and dependency. In P. H. Mussen (Ed.), *Carmichael's manual of child psychology* (Ed. 3). Vol. 2. New York: Wiley.

MacNair, M. R., Parker, G. A. (1978). Models of parent–offspring conflict. II. Promiscuity. *Animal Behavior, 26*, 111–122.

Mahler, M. S., Pine, F., & Bergman, A. (1975). *The psychological birth of the human infant*. New York: Basic Books.

Main, M. (1973). *Exploration, play and cognitive functioning as related to child–mother attachment.* Unpublished doctoral dissertation, Johns Hopkins University.

Main, M. (1981). Avoidance in the service of attachment: A working paper. In K. Immelmann, G. Barlow, M. Main, & L. Petrinovich (Eds.), *Behavioral development: The Bielefeld interdisciplinary project.* New York: Cambridge University Press.

Main, M. (1983). Exploration, play, and cognitive functioning related to infant–mother attachment. *Infant Behavior and Development, 6,* 167–174.

Main, M. B., & Stadtman, J. (1981). Infant response to rejection of physical contact by the mother. *Journal of the American Academy of Child Psychiatry, 20,* 292–307.

Main, M. B., & Weston, D. R. (1981). The quality of the toddler's relationship to mother and to father: Related to conflict behavior and the readiness to establish new relationships. *Child Development, 52,* 932–940.

Main, M., & Weston, D. (1982). Avoidance of the attachment figure in infancy: Descriptions and interpretations. In J. Stevenson-Hinde & C. Murray Parkes (Eds.), *The place of attachment in human infancy.* New York: Basic Books.

Main, M. B., Tomasini, L., & Tolan, W. (1979). Differences among mothers of infants judged to differ in security. *Developmental Psychology, 15,* 472–473.

Marvin, R. S. (1977). An ethological-cognitive model for the attenuation of mother–child attachment behavior. In T. M. Alloway, L. Krames, & P. Pliner (Eds.), *Advances in the study of communication and affect (Vol. 3). The development of social attachment.* New York: Plenum Press.

Maslin, C. A. (1983). *Anxious and secure attachments: Antecedents and consequences within the mother–infant system.* Unpublished doctoral dissertation, Indiana University.

Maslin, C. A., & Bates, J. E. (1982). *Anxious attachment as a predictor of disharmony in the mother–toddler relationship.* Paper presented to the International Conference on Infant Studies, Austin, Texas.

Maslin, C. A., & Bates, J. E. (1983). *Anxious and secure attachments: Antecedents and consequences in the mother-infant system.* Manuscript in preparation, Indiana University.

Masters, J. C., & Wellman, H. M. (1974). The study of human infant attachment: A procedural critique. *Psychological Bulletin, 81,* 213–237.

Matas, L., Arend, R. A., & Sroufe, L. A. (1978). Continuity of adaptation in the second year: The relationship between quality of attachment and later competence. *Child Development, 49,* 547–556.

Maynard Smith, J. (1982). *Evolution and the theory of games.* New York: Cambridge University Press.

Maynard Smith, J. (1984). Game theory and the evolution of behaviour. *Behavioral and Brain Sciences, 7,* 95–125.

McArdle, J. J. (in press). Dynamic and structural equation modeling applied to repeated measures anlaysis. In J. R. Nesselroade & R. B. Cattell (Eds.), *The handbook of multivariate experimental psychology.* (2nd Ed.) New York: McGraw-Hill.

McCall, R. B. (1977). Challenges to a science of developmental psychology. *Child Development, 48,* 333–344.

Messer, S. B., & Lewis, M. (1972). Social class and sex differences in the attachment and play behavior of the one-year-old infant. *Merrill–Palmer Quarterly, 18,* 295–306.

Miller, G. A., Galanter, E., & Pribram, K. H. (1960). *Plans and the structure of behavior.* New York: Holt, Rinehart, & Winston.

Miyake, K., Chen, S–J., Ujiie, T., Tajima, N., Satoh, K., & Takahashi, K. (1981–82). Infant's temperamental disposition, mother's mode of interaction, quality of attachment, and infant's receptivity to socialization—interim progress report. In *Annual Report: Research and Clinical Center of Child Development.* Faculty of Education, Hokkaido University, Sapparo, Japan.

Miyake, K., Chen, S.-J., & Campos, J. J. (in press). Infant temperament, mother's mode of interaction, and attachment in Japan: An interim report. In I. Bretherton & E. Waters (Eds.) *Growing points in attachment theory and research. Monographs of the Society for Research in Child Development.*

Mooijaart, A. (1982). Latent structure analysis for categorical variables. In Joreskog, K., & Wold, H. (Eds.), *Systems under indirect observation: causality-structure-prediction.* New York: North-Holland.

Moss, H. A. (1967). Sex, age and state as determinants of mother–infant interaction. *Merrill–Palmer Quarterly, 13,* 19–36.

Murphy, L. B. (1956). *Personality in young children.* New York: Basic Books.

Murray, A. D. (1979). Infant crying as an elicitor of parental behavior: An examination of two models. *Psychological Bulletin, 86,* 191–215.

Muthen, B. (1983). Latent variable structural equation modeling with categorical data. *Journal of Econometrics, 22,* 43–65.

Muthen, B. (1984). A general structural equation model with dichotomous, ordered categorical, and continuous latent variable indicators. *Psychometrika, 49,* 115–132.

Nakano, S. (1982–83). Does quality of attachment in a Strange Situation relate to later competence in a different situation? *Annual Report: Research and Clinical Center for Child Development,* Faculty of Education, Hokkaido University, Sapporo, Japan.

Nesselroade, J. (1970). Application of multivariate strategies to problems of measuring and structuring long-term change. In L. Goulet & P. Baltes (Eds.), *Life-span developmental psychology: Theory and research.* New York: Academic.

Nesselroade, J., & Baltes, P. (1979). (Eds.), *Longitudinal research in the study of behavior and development.* New York: Academic Press.

Olson, S. L., Bates, J. E., & Bayles, K. (1982). Maternal perceptions of infant and toddler behavior: A longitudinal construct validation study. *Infant Behavior and Development, 5,* 397–410.

Owen, M. T., & Chase–Lansdale, L. (April, 1982a). *The "difficult" baby: Parental perceptions and infant attachments.* Paper presented at the meeting of the International Conference on Infant Studies, Austin, TX.

Owen, M. T., & Chase–Lansdale, L. (April, 1982b). *Similarity between infant–mother and infant–father attachments.* Paper presented at the meeting of the SouthWestern Society for Research in Human Development, Galveston, TX.

Owen, M. T., Easterbrooks, M. A., Chase–Lansdale, L., & Goldberg, W. A. (1983). *Infancy into toddlerhood: Effects of maternal employment on infant–mother and infant–father attachments.* Paper presented at the meeting of the Society for Research in Child Development, Detroit, MI.

Owen, M. T., Easterbrooks, M. A., Chase–Lansdale, L., & Goldberg, W. A. (1984). The relation between maternal employment status and the stability of attachments to mother and to father. *Child Development, 55,* 1894–1901.

Parker, G. A., & MacNair, M. R. (1979). Models of parent–offspring conflict IV. Suppression: Evolutionary retaliation by the parent. *Animal Behavior, 27,* 1210–1235.

Pastor, D. L. (April, 1980). *The quality of mother–infant attachment and its relationship to toddlers' initial sociability with peers.* Paper presented at the International Conference on Infant Studies, New Haven.

Pastor, D. L. (1981). The quality of mother–infant attachment and its relationship to toddlers' initial sociability with peers. *Developmental Psychology, 17,* 326–335.

Pastor, D., Vaughn, B., Dodds, M., & Egeland, B. (1981). *The effect of different family patterns on the quality of mother–infant attachment.* Paper presented to the Society for Research in Child Development, Boston.

Pattison, M. (1975). A psychosocial kinship model for family therapy. *American Journal of Psychiatry, 132,* 1246–1251.

Pedersen, F. A., Anderson, B. J., & Cain, R. L. (1976). *A methodology for assessing parental perception of infant temperament*. Paper presented to the Southeastern Conference on Human Development, April.

Pentz, T. (1975). *Facilitation of language acquisition: The role of the mother*. Unpublished doctoral dissertation, Johns Hopkins University.

Pettit, G. L., & Bates, J. E. (1984). Continuity of individual differences in the mother–infant relationships from 6 to 13 months. *Child Development, 55*, 729–739.

Pleck, J. H. (1983). Husbands' paid work and family roles: Current research issues. In H. Lopata & J. H. Pleck (Eds.), *Research in the interweave of social roles (Vol. 3), Families and jobs*. Greenwich, CT.: JAI.

Plunkett, J. W., Meisels, S. J., Stiefel, G. S., Pasick, P. L., & Roloff, D. W. (1984). Patterns of attachment among preterm infants of varying biological risk. In S. J. Meisels (Chair), *Developmental vulnerability of infants born at severely high risk*. Symposium conducted at the Biennial Meeting of the International Conference on Infant Studies, New York, New York.

Rajecki, D. W., Lamb, M. E., & Obmascher, P. (1978). Toward a general theory of infantile attachment: A comparative review of aspects of the social bond. *Behavioral and Brain Sciences, 1*, 417–464.

Reed, G. L., & Leiderman, P. H. (1983). Is imprinting an appropriate model for human infant attachment? *International Journal of Behavioral Development, 6*, 51–69.

Ricciuti, H. N. (1974). Fear and development of social attachments in the first year of life. In M. Lewis & L. A. Rosenblum (Eds.), *The origins of fear*. New York: Wiley.

Ricks, M. H. (1982). *Origins of individual differences in attachment: Maternal, infant, and familial variables*. Paper presented to the International Conference on Infant Studies, Austin, Texas.

Robertson, J., & Bowlby, J. (1952). Responses of young children to separation from their mothers. *Courrier, 2*, 131–142.

Rode, S. S., Chang, P.-N., Fisch, R. O., & Sroufe, L. A. (1981). Attachment patterns of infants separated at birth. *Developmental Psychology, 17*, 188–191.

Rogosa, D. (1979). Causal models in longitudinal research: Rationale, formulation, and interpretation. In J. Nesselroade & P. Baltes (Eds.), *Longitudinal research in the study of behavioral development*. New York: Academic Press.

Rosen, K. S., & Cicchetti, D. (1983). *The relationship between affect and cognition in maltreated infants: Quality of attachment and the development of self-recognition*. Paper presented to the Society for Research in Child Development.

Rosenberg, S. E. (1975). Individual differences in infant attitude: Relationships to mother, infant interaction system variables. *Dissertation Abstracts International, 36*, 1930b.

Rosenthal, M. K. (1973). Attachment and mother–infant interaction: Some research impasse and a suggested change in orientation. *Journal of Child Psychology and Psychiatry, 14*, 201–207.

Rothbart, M. K. (1981). Measurement of temperament in infancy. *Child Development, 52*, 569–578.

Rothbart, M. K., & Derryberry, D. (1981). Development of individual differences in temperament. In M. E. Lamb & A. L. Brown (Eds.), *Advances in developmental psychology*, Vol. 1. Hillsdale, NJ: Lawrence Erlbaum Associates.

Rousseau, J. J. (1962). *Emile*. The Hague: Jean Neaulme.

Rutter, M. (1972). *Maternal deprivation reassessed*. Harmondsworth, Middlesex: Penguin.

Rutter, M. (1979). Maternal deprivation, 1972–1978: New findings, new concepts, new approaches. *Child Development, 50*, 283–305.

Sagi, A. (1984). The Strange Situation procedure: Insights from an International perspective. Symposium presented in the International Conferences on Infant Studies, New York.

Sagi, A., Lamb, M. E., & Gardner, W. (in preparation). *Relationships between Strange*

Situation behavior and stranger sociability among infants on Israeli kibbutzim. Manuscript in preparation, University of Haifa, Israel.

Sagi, A., Lamb, M. E., Estes, D., Shoham, R., Lewkowicz, K., & Dvir, R. (1982). *Security of infant–adult attachment among kibbutz-reared infants*. Paper presented to the International Conference on Infant Studies, Austin, TX.

Sagi, A., Lamb, M. E., Lewkowicz, K., Shoham, R., Dvir, R., & Estes, D., (in press). Security of infant–mother, –father, and –metapelet attachments among Kibbutz-reared Israeli children. In I. Bretherton & E. Waters (Eds.), *Growing points in attachment theory and research. Monographs of the Society for Research in Child Development*.

Schaffer, H. R. (1971). *The growth of sociability*. Harmondsworth, England: Penguin.

Schaffer, H. R. (1963). Some issues for research in the study of attachment behaviour. In B. M. Foss (Ed.), *Determinants of infant behaviour* (Vol. 2). London: Methuen.

Schaffer, H. R., & Callender, W. (1959). Psychological effects of hospitalization in infancy. *Pediatrics, 24*, 528–539.

Schneider–Rosen, K., Braunwald, K. G., Carlson, V., & Cicchetti, D. (in press). Current perspectives in attachment theory: Illustration from the study of maltreated infants. In I. Bretherton & E. Waters (Eds.), *Growing points in attachment theory and research. Monographs of the Society for Research in Child Development*.

Schneider–Rosen, K. & Cicchetti, D. (1984). The relationship between affect and cognition in maltreated infants: Quality of attachment and the development of visual self-recognition. *Child Development, 55*, 648–658.

Schneirla, T.C. (1966). Behavioral development and comparative psychology. *Quarterly Review of Biology, 41*, 283–302.

Smith, P. B., & Pederson, D. R. (1983). *Maternal sensitivity and patterns of infant–mother attachment*. Paper presented at the Meetings of the Society for Research in Child Development, Detroit, MI.

Sneath, P., & Sokal, R. (1973). *Numerical taxonomy: The principles and practice of numerical classification*. San Francisco: Freeman.

Sorbom, D. (1974). A general method for studying differences in factor means and factor structure between groups. *British Journal of Mathematical and Statistical Psychology, 27*, 229–239.

Spanier, G. (1976). Measuring dyadic adjustment: New scales for assessing the quality of marriage and similar dyads. *Journal of Marriage and the Family, 38*, 15–32.

Spence, M. J., & DeCasper, A. J. (1982). *Human fetuses perceive maternal speech*. Paper presented to the International Conference on Infant Studies, Austin, TX, March.

Spitz, R. A. (1950). Possible infantile precursors of psychopathology. *American Journal of Orthopsychiatry, 20*, 240–248.

Sroufe, L. A. (March, 1978). Attachment and the roots of competence. *Human Nature, 1*(10), 50–57.

Sroufe, L. A. (1979). The coherence of individual development. *American Psychologist, 34*, 834–841.

Sroufe, L. A. (1983). Individual patterns of adaptation from infancy to preschool. In M. Perlmutter (Ed.), *Development and policy concerning children with special needs. Minnesota symposium on child psychology* (Vol. 16). Hillsdale, NJ: Lawrence Erlbaum Associates.

Sroufe, L. A. (1985). Attachment classification from the perspective of infant–caregiver relationships and infant temperament. *Child Development, 56*, 1–14.

Sroufe, L. A., & Matas, L. (No date). *Continuity of adaptation in the second year: The relationship between quality of attachment and later competent functioning*. Unpublished manuscript, University of Minnesota.

Sroufe, L. A. & Rosenberg, D. (1982). *Coherence of individual adaptation in lower class infants and toddlers*. Paper presented to the International Conference on Infant Studies, Austin, TX.

Sroufe, L. A., & Waters, E. (1977). Attachment as an organizational construct. *Child Development, 48*, 1184–1199.

Sroufe, L. A., & Waters, E. (1982). Issues of temperament and attachment. *American Journal of Orthopsychiatry, 52*, 743–746.

Sroufe, L. A., Fox, N. E., & Pancake, V. R. (1983). Attachment and dependency in developmental perspective. *Child Development, 54*, 1615–1627.

Sroufe, L. A., Waters, E., & Matas, L. (1974). Contextual determinants of infant affective response. In M. Lewis & L. Rosenblum (Eds.), *The origins of fear*. New York: Wiley.

Stayton, D. J., & Ainsworth, M. D. S. (1973). Individual differences in infant responses to brief, everyday separations as related to other infant and maternal behaviors. *Developmental Psychology, 9*, 226–235.

Stayton, D., Hogan, R., & Ainsworth, M. D. S. (1971). Infant obedience and maternal behavior: The origins of socialization reconsidered. *Child Development, 42*, 1057–1069.

Stayton, D. J., Ainsworth, M. D. S., & Main, M. B. (1973). The development of separation behavior in the first year of life: Protest, following and greeting. *Developmental Psychology, 9*, 213–225.

Stearns, S. C. (1976). Life-history tactics: A review of the ideas. *Quarterly Review of Biology, 51*, 3–47.

Stearns, S. C. (1977). The evolution of life-history traits: A critique of the theory and a review of the data. *Annual Review of Ecology and Systematics, 8*, 145–171.

Stern, D. (1977). *The first relationship*. Cambridge, MA: Harvard University Press.

Stevenson, M. B., & Lamb, M. E. (1979). The effects of sociability and the caretaking environment on infant cognitive performance. *Child Development, 50*, 340–349.

Tajima, N. (1982–83). Infant's temperamental disposition, attachment, and self-recognition in the first 20 months of life. *Annual Report: Research and Clinical Center for Child Development*, Faculty of Education, Hokkaido University, Sapporo, Japan.

Thomas, A., & Chess, S. (1977). *Temperament and development*. New York: Brunner/Mazel.

Thompson, R. A. (1981). *Continuity and change in socioemotional development during the second year*. Unpublished doctoral dissertation, University of Michigan, Ann Arbor, MI.

Thompson, R. A., & Lamb, M. E. (August, 1982). *Temperamental influences on stranger sociability and the security of attachment*. Paper presented to the American Psychological Association, Washington, D. C.

Thompson, R. A., & Lamb, M. E. (1983a). Individual differences in dimensions of socioemotional development in infancy. In R. Plutchik & H. Kellerman (Eds.), *Emotion: Theory, research, and experience* (Vol. 2) *Emotions in early development*. New York: Academic Press.

Thompson, R. A., & Lamb, M. E. (1983b). Security of attachment and stranger sociability in infancy. *Developmental Psychology, 19*, 184–191.

Thompson, R. A., & Lamb, M. E. (1984a). Assessing qualitative dimensions of emotional responsiveness in infants: Separation reactions in the Strange Situation. *Infant Behavior and Development, 7*, 423–445.

Thompson, R. A., & Lamb, M. E. (1984b). Infants, mothers, families, and strangers. In M. Lewis (Ed.), *Beyond the dyad*. New York: Plenum.

Thompson, R. A., Lamb, M. E., & Estes, D. (1982). Stability of infant–mother attachment and its relationship to changing life circumstances in an unselected middle class sample. *Child Development, 53*, 144–148.

Thompson, R. A., Lamb, M. E., & Estes, D. (1983). Harmonizing discordant notes: A reply to Waters. *Child Development, 54*, 521–524.

Thompson, R. A., Cicchetti, D., Lamb, M. E., & Malkin, C. M. (1985). The emotional responses of Down Syndrome and normal infants in the Strange Situation: The organization of affective behavior in infants. *Developmental Psychology.*

Tinbergen, N. (1963). On aims and methods of ethology. *Zeitschrif Tierpsychologie, 20,* 410–433.

Tolan, W. J., & Tomasini, L. (1977). *Mothers of "secure" vs. "insecure" babies differ themselves nine months later.* Paper presented to the Society for Research in Child Development, New Orleans.

Tracy, R. L., & Ainsworth, M. D. S. (1981). Maternal affectionate behavior and infant–mother attachment patterns. *Child Development, 52,* 1341–1343.

Tracy, R. L, Farish, G. D., & Bretherton, I. (1980). *Exploration as related to infant–mother attachment in one-year-olds.* Paper presented to the International Conference on Infant Studies, New Haven, CT.

Tracy, R. L., Lamb, M. E., & Ainsworth, M. D. (1976). Infant approach behavior as related to attachment. *Child Development, 47,* 571–578.

Trivers, R. L. (1974). Parent–offspring conflict. *American Zoologist, 14,* 249–264.

Tronick, E. Z., Ricks, M., & Cohn, J. F. (1982). Maternal and infant affective exchange: Patterns of adaptation. In T. Field & A. Fogel (Eds.), *Emotion and early interaction.* Hillsdale, NJ: Lawrence Erlbaum Associates.

Tulkin, S. R. (1973). Social class differences in attachment behaviors of ten-month-old infants. *Child Development, 44,* 171–174.

van IJzendoorn, M. H., Goossens, F. A., Kroonenberg, P. M., & Tavecchio, L. W. C. (1984). *Dependent attachment: A characterization of B_4 children.* Paper presented to the International Conference on Infant Studies, New York.

van IJzendoorn, M. H., Tavecchio, L. W. G., Goossens, F. A., Vergeer, M. M., & Swaan, J. (1983). How B is B_4? Attachment and security of Dutch children in Ainsworth's Strange Situation and at home. *Psychological Reports, 52,* 683–691.

Vaughn, B. E., Crichton, L., & Egeland, B. (1982). Individual differences in qualities of caregiving during the first six months of life: Antecedents in maternal and infant behavior during the newborn period. *Infant Behavior and Development, 5,* 77–95.

Vaughn, B., Egeland, B., Sroufe, L. A., & Waters, E. (1979). Individual differences in infant–mother attachment at twelve and eighteen months: Stability and change in families under stress. *Child Development, 50,* 971–975.

Vaughn, B., Gove, F., & Egeland, B. (1980). The relationship between out-of-home care and the quality of infant–mother attachment in an economically disadvantaged sample. *Child Development, 51,* 1203–1214.

Vaughn, B., Taraldson, B., Crichton, L., & Egeland, B. (1980). Relationships between neonatal behavioral organization and infant behavor during the first year of life. *Infant Behavior and Development, 3,* 47–66.

Vaughn, B., Taraldson, B., Crichton, L., & Egeland, B. (1981). The assessment of infant temperament: A critique of the Carey Infant Temperament Questionnaire. *Infant Behavior and Development, 4,* 1–17.

Vogel, E. (1963). *Japan's middle class.* Berkeley: University of California Press.

Wackwitz, J. H., & Horn, J. L. (1971). On obtaining the best estimates of factor scores within an ideal simple structure. *Multivariate Behavioral Research, 6,* 389–408.

Waddington, C. H. (1957). *The strategy of the genes.* London: Allen and Unwin.

Ward, M. J., Malone, S. M., & DeAngelo, E. J. (1983). *Patterns of maternal behavior with first- and secondborn children: Evidence for consistency in family relations.* Paper presented at the Meetings of the Society for Research in Child Development, Detroit, MI.

Waters, E. (1977). *The stability of individual differences in infant–mother attachment.* Unpublished doctoral dissertation, University of Minnesota.

Waters, E. (1978). The reliability and stability of individual differences in infant–mother attachment. *Child Development, 49,* 483–494.

Waters, E. (1983). The stability of individual differences in infant attachment: Comments on the Thompson, Lamb, and Estes contribution. *Child Development, 54,* 516–520.

Waters, E., & Deane, D. (1982). Infant–mother attachment: Theories, models, recent data, and some tasks for comparative developmental analysis. In L. W. Hoffman, R. Gandelman, & H. R. Schiffman (Eds.), *Parenting: Its causes and consequences.* Hillsdale, NJ: Lawrence Erlbaum Associates.

Waters, E., Vaughn, B., & Egeland, B. (1980). Individual differences in infant–mother attachment relationships at age one: Antecedents in neonatal behavior in an urban, economically disadvantaged sample. *Child Development, 51,* 208–216.

Waters, E., Wippman, J., & Sroufe, L. A. (1979). Attachment, positive affect, and competence in the peer group: Two studies in construct validation. *Child Development, 50,* 821–829.

Weber, R. A., Levitt, M. J., & Clark, M. C. (1984). *Individual variation in attachment security and Strange Situation behavior: The role of maternal and infant temperament.* Paper presented at the International Conference on Infant Studies, New York, New York.

Wente, A. S., & Crockenberg, S. B. (1976). Transition to fatherhood: Lamaze preparation, adjustment difficulty, and the husband–wife relationship. *Family Coordinator, 28,* 351–357.

Williams, G. C. (1966). *Adaptation and natural selection.* Princeton: Princeton University Press.

Willemsen, E., Flaherty, D., Heaton, C., & Ritchey, G. (1974). Attachment behavior of one-year-olds as a function of mother vs. father, sex of child, session, and toys. *Genetic Psychology Monographs, 90,* 305–324.

Wold, H. (1970). Causal inferences from observation data: A review of ends and means. In M. C. Wittrock & D. E. Wiley (Eds.), *Evaluation of instruction: Issues and problems.* New York: Holt, Rinehart, & Winston.

Wold, H. (1982). Soft modeling: The basic design and some extensions. In K. Joreskog & H. Wold (Eds.), *Systems under indirect observation: Causality-structure-prediction.* Part II. New York: North-Holland Publishing Company.

Yarrow, L. J., & Goodwin, M. S. (1973). The immediate impact of separation: Reactions of infants to a change in mother figures. In L. J. Stone, H. T. Smith, & L. B. Murphy (Eds.), *The competent infant.* New York: Basic Books.

Author Index

N

Nakano, S., 164, 296
Nesselroade, J., 266, 280, 284, 296
Nesselroade, J. R., 91, 105, 294

O

Oleson, S. L., 76, 77, 284, 296
Otaki, M., 87, 183, 197, 288
Owen, M. T., 101, 102, 105, 124, 132, 296

P

Pancake, V. R., 145, 146, 148, 298
Palermo, M., 91, 105, 294
Parker, G. A., 48, 50, 274, 294, 296
Pasick, P. L., 91, 297
Pastor, D., 70, 71, 127, 288, 296
Pastor, D. L., 144, 145, 147, 165, 167, 296
Pattison, M., 161, 296
Pedersen, F. A., 105, 297
Pederson, D. R., 87, 105, 298
Pentz, T., 153, 297
Perrotta, M., 91, 201, 218, 290
Pettit, G. L., 77, 297
Pettit, G. S., 76, 77, 284
Pettit, M. G., 92, 289
Pine, F., 138, 246, 294
Pleck, J. H., 24, 52, 293, 297
Plunkett, J. W., 91, 297
Pribram, K. H., 13, 295

R

Rajecki, D. W., 22, 28, 60, 297
Reed, G. L., 24, 25, 297
Rheingold, H. L., 18, 287
Ricciuti, H. N., 227, 297
Richards, P., 87, 183, 197, 288
Ricks, M. H., 78, 90, 297, 300
Ritchey, G., 31, 301
Robertson, A., 127, 287
Robinson, J. G., 50, 287
Rode, S. S., 91, 297
Rogosa, D., 256, 297
Roloff, D. W., 91, 297
Rosen, K. S., 297
Rosenberg, D., 92, 127, 144, 288, 298
Rosenberg, S. E., 90, 297
Rosenthal, M. H., 19, 297

Rothbart, M. H., 77, 99, 105, 106, 297
Rousseau, J. J., 9, 10, 11, 297
Rovine, M., 73, 74, 75, 76, 82, 85, 87, 110, 113, 185, 206, 234, 285
Ruble, N., 91, 291
Rutter, M., 9, 10, 11, 24, 297

S

Sagi, A., 35, 41, 54, 56, 83, 84, 101, 102, 183, 188, 192, 193, 194, 195, 198, 207, 223, 293, 297, 298
Satoh, K., 5, 82, 108, 159, 164, 168, 188, 195, 196, 295
Schaffer, H. R., 3, 20, 21, 298
Schneider-Rosen, K., 85, 86, 129, 130, 137, 138, 168, 298
Schneirla, T. C., 298
Schultz, L. A., 85, 111, 161, 227, 229, 290, 293
Schwan, A., 111, 186, 187, 285, 290
Shoham, R., 35, 41, 54, 56, 83, 84, 101, 102, 183, 188, 192, 193, 195, 198, 207, 293, 298
Shuman, H. H., 91, 289
Smith, P. B., 87, 105, 298
Sheath, P., 212, 298
Sokol, R., 212, 298
Sorbom, D., 117, 236, 263, 264, 280, 292, 298
Sorce, J., 224, 232, 292
Spangler, G., 108, 185, 186, 187, 188, 197, 291
Spanier, G., 80, 298
Spence, M. J., 9, 298
Spiro, A., 91, 105, 294
Spitz, R. A., 21, 298
Sroufe, L. A., 5, 6, 14, 15, 17, 19, 25, 28, 35, 39, 40, 45, 56, 85, 91, 92, 94, 100, 123, 124, 126, 127, 128, 129, 131, 133, 136, 139, 140, 141, 142, 144, 145, 146, 147, 148, 149, 150, 155, 157, 158, 159, 160, 161, 165, 166, 167, 169, 170, 171, 172, 199, 284, 288, 289, 295, 297, 298, 300, 301
Stadtman, J., 63, 74, 295
Stayton, D. J., 5, 16, 18, 30, 36, 41, 60, 61, 94, 153, 182, 190, 203, 251, 284, 299
Stearns, S. C., 46, 47, 274, 299
Steinberg, L. D., 92, 285
Stenberg, C., 98, 137, 201, 223, 286
Stern, D., 232, 299
Stevenson, M. B., 163, 164, 193, 299
Stiefel, G. S., 91, 297
Suess, G., 108, 185, 186, 187, 188, 197, 291
Svejda, J., 224, 232, 292